MUSCLE CAR

CHRONICLE

BY THE EDITORS OF CONSUMER GUIDE® AUTOMOTIVE

Publications International, Ltd.

Very special thanks to:
Chris Martin, NHRA (National Hot Rod Association)

Thanks to:
Bud Davis and Gerald G. Kroninger, Sunoco; FCA North America; Ford Motor Company Archives; GM Media Archives; Holley, Inc.; Leslie Lovett, NHRA; Rich Molan and Hector Magana, Iskenderian Racing Cams; Roush Performance; Tom Shaw; Saleen; Judy Stahl, Stahl Headers, Inc.; Steeda; Geoff Stunkard

Technical Consultants
AMC: **Barbara Hillick;** Buick: **Terry Boyce; David W. Roman, Buick Motor Division;** Chevrolet: **Terry Boyce;** Chrysler/Dodge/Plymouth: **Jim Benjaminson;** Ford/Mercury: **Alex Gabbard;** Oldsmobile: **Helen J. Earley and James R. Walkinshaw, Oldsmobile History Center;** Pontiac: **Mike Grippo;** Studebaker: **Fred K. Fox**

PHOTO CREDITS
The editors would like to thank the following people for supplying the photography that made this book possible. They are listed below, along with the page number(s) of their photos:

Abey Studio: 128–129; **Orazio Aiello:** 135, 136, 231; **Auto Imagery, Inc.:** 315; **Greg Barrow:** 70, 83; **Scott Baxter:** 32–33, 198; **Ken Beebe/Kugler Studio:** 59, 91, 94–95, 110–111, 154, 155; **Kirk Bell:** 339; **Mark Bilek:** 328; **Joe Bohovic:** 123, 249, 251, 292–293; **Terry Boyce:** 48; **Scott Brandt:** 42; **Chan Bush:** 114; **David Chobat:** 241, 248; **Jeff Cohn:** 354, 356, 359; **Rick Cotta:** 329; **Leigh Dorrington:** 254; **Roland Flessner:** 317, 320; **Mitch Frumkin:** 107, 318, 323, 324, 328; **Chuck Giametta:** 327; **Thomas Glatch:** 16, 86, 87, 161, 183, 211, 218, 276; **Sam Griffith:** 24, 62–63, 72, 73, 80, 81, 150, 151, 176, 186, 202, 212, 213, 219, 224, 228, 229, 240, 245, 253, 320, 323, 325; **Jerry Heasley:** 47, 61, 106, 118, 135, 137, 164, 165, 202, 203, 204, 206, 212, 213, 230, 232, 318; **Brandon Hemphill:** 181; **Fergus Hernandes:** 12; **Alan Hewko/De Christopher's Studio:** 196; **Bill Hill:** 15; **Phil Hill:** 93; **S. Scott Hutchinson:** 37; **Bud Juneau:** 7, 9, 10, 11, 15, 17, 152, 153, 180, 185, 191, 203, 216, 217, 243, 245, 249, 277, 294; **Tim Kerwin:** 19; **Milton Gene Kieft:** 21, 98, 158, 179, 194, 195, 219, 310; **Dan Lyons:** 13, 19, 35, 94, 100, 101, 102, 256, 257, 312; **Vince Manocchi:** Cover, 10, 12, 16, 20, 21, 26, 56, 74, 148, 158, 197, 231, 248, 274, 312, 327, 330; **Jeff Medves:** 215; **Doug Mitchel:** 8, 11, 14, 15, 16, 17, 18, 20, 21, 22–23, 27, 29, 38, 44–45, 46, 52, 54–55, 66, 75, 76, 78, 79, 80, 81, 82, 84, 103, 104–105, 121, 124, 125, 129, 130, 140, 144, 145, 146, 152, 153, 161, 165, 169, 171, 174, 178, 199, 200, 201, 203, 205, 210, 212, 215, 218, 221, 222, 227, 228, 229, 238, 241, 244, 251, 253, 259, 260, 261, 263, 271, 273, 278, 288, 293, 299, 300, 302, 308–309, 318, 331, 354; **Mike Mueller:** 11, 15, 25, 49, 50, 51, 53, 63, 130–131, 132, 133, 156, 159, 162, 164, 165, 166, 170, 171, 190, 198, 204, 205, 207, 212, 213, 216, 225, 230, 242, 255, 259, 264, 280, 283, 295, 296; **Jay Peck:** 105; **Frank Peiler:** 113; **Photos by Morton:** 149; ***National Dragster* files:** 22–23, 45, 47, 48, 55, 59, 60, 61, 62, 64–65, 70, 71, 77, 78–79, 85, 89, 90, 92, 93, 94, 96, 97, 99, 100–101, 107, 109, 113, 114, 116, 118, 119, 122, 123, 124, 126–127, 134, 135, 142–143, 145, 146, 147, 149, 151, 152, 155, 156, 158, 163, 167, 173, 177, 186, 187, 188, 192, 196, 199, 200, 208, 214, 218, 244, 250, 261, 262, 264, 267, 272, 279, 281, 289, 291, 301, 303, 318, 319, 322, 324; **Rick Popely:** 327; **Tom Salter:** 243, 244; **William J. Schintz:** 269, 282; **Rick Simmons:** 108; **Mike Slade:** 194; **Jim Smart:** 38, 43, 70, 96, 109, 114, 134, 136, 193, 242, 267, 275; **Richard Spiegelman:** 99, 102, 114, 139, 196, 254; **Studio Image:** 237; **Gerald Sutphin:** 58, 68, 69;

Louis Weber, CEO
Publications International, Ltd.
8140 Lehigh Avenue
Morton Grove, IL 60053

ISBN: 978-1-68022-625-6

Manufactured in China.

8 7 6 5 4 3 2 1

Library of Congress Control Number: 2011925586

David Temple: 18, 112, 282; **Bob Tenney:** 68–69; **Rithea Tep:** 295; **Jim Thompson:** 240; **Bob Trevarrow:** 96; **Andre Van De Putte:** 213; **Rob Van Schaick:** 204, 209; **W. C. Waymack:** 121, 319; **Nicky Wright:** 12, 14, 16, 19, 20, 30, 31, 90, 115, 116, 141, 159, 160–161, 168, 190, 192, 193, 195, 204, 205, 207, 208–209, 211, 214, 217, 226, 233, 234–235, 236, 237, 238, 239, 247, 248, 251, 264, 266, 268, 270–271, 272, 286, 287, 306, 307, 311, 321

Owners:
Special thanks to the owners of the cars featured in this book for their enthusiastic cooperation. They are listed below, with the page number(s) on which their cars appear:

Cover: **June Cecil;** Page 7: **Cliff de Borba; Tony Capua;** 8: **Phil Kuhn; Briggs Cunningham; Philip Arneson; Bill Wagaman;** 9: **R. T. Brelsford; Doug Burnell;** 10: **John and Minnie Keys; Homer Jay Sanders Sr.; Richard Clements; Bob Hoffman;** 11: **Stanley and Phyllis Dumes; William D. Albright; Tim Wenzlowski;** 12: **Virgil and Dorothy Meyer; Gail and John Dalmolin; Rex and Golly Gilbert; Fredrick J. Roth; Jim Van Gondon;** 13: **Chuck Sarges; Richard Kalinowski;** 14: **Otto T. Rosenbusch; Tom Franks; Richard Bourbie;** 15: **J. Cain; F. Gaugh; T. Sheafer; Roger and Connie Graeber; Ken Block; Richard Bourbie; Bill Hill;** 16: **Don Simpkin; David M. Leslie; Bob Peiler; John Krempasky; Ken Regner;** 17: **Paul Oxley; Ken Perry; Bill Bodnarchuk; Paul Armstrong; George Berg;** 18: **Z. T. Parker; Dennis McNamara; Donald Bergman; Roger Fonk; G. Bappe;** 19: **Dr. William H. Lenharth; Stephen Capone; Tom Appeal, Studebaker National Museum;** 20: **George Berg; Charles Hilbert; Dean Ullman; Barry and Barb Bales;** 21: **Bob Moore; Mervin M. Afflerback; Richard Carpenter; Don and Barbara Finn;** 22–23: **Gary Thobe;** 24: **Kenneth J. Patt;** 26: **Larri Stumpf;** 27: **Glenn Moist;** 28: **Dick Tarnutzer, Dells Auto Museum, Lake Mills, Wisconsin;** 29: **Dave and Norma Wasielewski;** 30–31: **Barry and Barb Bales;** 32–33: **Jack Bratzianna;** 35: **William Korbel;** 37: **Paul Garlick;** 38: **Roger and Gerri Randolph;** 41: **George W. Rappeyea;** 42: **Robert and Karen Christanell;** 44: **Rusty Symmes;** 44–45: **Dan Mamsen;** 46: **Darryl McNabb;** 49: **Patt and J. R. Buxman;** 50–51: **Phil Fair;** 52: **Terry D. Davis;** 53: **K. and L. Coleman;** 54–55: **Alden Graber;** 56: **Bob Mosher;** 58: **Bob Burroughs;** 59: **Frank Spittle;** 62–63: **Michael and Patricia Kelso;** 63: **Henry Hart;** 66: **Rusty Symmes;** 68–69: **Amos Minter;** 68, 69: **Bob Burroughs;** 70: **Bill Blair;** 72–73: **Bill Jackson;** 74: **Barry Norman;** 76: **Guy Mabee;** 78–79: **Phil Hayenga;** 80–81: **Allen Gartzman;** 82: **Joe Zajac;** 83: **Bill Blair;** 84: **Rich Antonacci;** 86–87: **Sam Pierce;** 90: **Jim Donaldson;** 91: **Frank Spittle;** 94: **Dick Kainer;** 94–95: **Frank Spittle;** 98: **Dennis A. Urban;** 99: **Glenn Cole;** 100–101: **Don McLennan;** 102: **Ray and Lil Elias; Glen Cole;** 103: **Lynn Johnson;** 104–105: **Joe Kelly;** 105: **Fraser Dante, Ltd.;** 107: **Jerry Yonker;** 108: **Steve Shuman;** 110–111: **Frank Spittle;** 112: **Larry Barnett;** 113: **Frank Peiler;** 115–116: **Mike Guffey;** 121: **Kevin L. Fuller;** 123: **Walter Schenk;** 124–125: **William W. Kramer;** 128: **Alan N. Basile;** 129: **Alan N. Basile; Marvin Minarich;** 130–131: **Autoputer, Inc.;** 132–133: **Dennis M. Phipps;** 135: **Bob Macy; Ron C. Bealage;** 136: **Roger Brackett;** 139: **Glen Cole;** 140: **Richard Hanley;** 141: **Jerry and Carol Buczkowski;** 146: **James and Mary Engle;** 148: **Harry and Virginia DeMenge;** 149: **David B. Verdral;** 150–151: **Richard Witek;** 152: **Chris Terry; Dr. Randy & Freda Cooper; Jeff Hare; Joe Witczak;** 154–155: **Larry and Karen Miller;** 156: **Paul McGuire;** 157: **Ronald S. Mroz;** 158: **Bill Bush; Rich and Joan Young;** 159: **Mr. & Mrs. Richard D. Miller; Tom and Nancy Stump;** 160–161: **Bill Barnes;** 161: **Grady Hentz; Nathan Struder;** 162: **Tony and Suzanne George;** 164: **George N. Bowen;** 165: **George N. Bowen; Rich Neubauer; Tom and Katherine Stanley;** 166: **David L. Robb;** 167: **Jim LaBertew, RPM Motors;** 168: **Ross Arterbery;** 169: **John Vincent; Jeff and Trish Holmes;** 170: **Joe L. Saunders;** 171: **Joe L. Saunders; Jeff and Trish Holmes;** 174: **Jeffrey L. Hill;** 176: **James Lojewski;** 178: **Gerri Randolph;** 179: **Donald R. Crile;** 180: **Ramshead Auto Collection;** 181: **Northwest Auto Sales/Rick Robinson;** 186: **Dennis Guest;** 188: **Chris Pylar;** 189: **Chris Pylar;** 190: **Samuel Pampenella Jr.; Thomas S. Rapala;** 191: **James Karleskins;** 192: **Doug and Judy Badgley;** 193: **Doug and Judy Badgley; Dan Bohannon;** 194: **Mark Kuykendall; The Beechy Family;** 195: **Classic Car Center; The Beechy Family;** 196: **David Bartholomew;** 197: **Jim Lee;** 198: **Steve Maysonet;** 199: **Jon F. Havens; Bill Pearson; Torber Lozins; Felix Mozockie;** 200: **Gary Carlson;** 201: **Rodney Brumbaugh; Paul Gallo;** 202: **Dennis Reboletti; Dan Curry; Marion and Walter Gutowski;** 203: **Charley Lillard; Nick D'Amico; Sandy D'Amico; Dan Curry; Steven Knutsen;** 204: **Jerry Buczkowski; James E. Collins; Greg Grams, Volo Auto Museum;** 205: **Jay T. Nolan; James E. Collins; Jerry Buczkowski;** 207: **Joe L. Saunders; Robert Fraser; Steve Hinshaw;** 208–209: **Larry Bell;** 209: **Glen Quealy; Greg Grams, Volo Auto Museum;** 210: **Andre Peterson;** 211: **Al Fraser; Thom Moerman;** 212: **Tom Schulitter; Edwin Putz; Robert Kurtz;** 213: **Glenn Moist;** 214: **Gary Pahee; Chris Duwalt;** 215: **John Cook; William Peterson;** 216: **Jack Karleskind; Carl J. Beck;** 217: **Robert and Ann Klein; Scott Campbell;** 218: **Benchmark Classics/Justin Cole; Ray Dupis; George Weisser;** 219: **Robert Beechy; Rick Consiglio;** 222: **Bruce Rhoades; Greg White;** 224: **Craig P. Mentzer;** 225: **Craig P. Mentzer; Eugene Slocum; Dale Kumanchik;** 226: **Darryl A. Salisbury;** 227: **Richard P. Lambert;** 228: **Richard L. Burki; Jim and John Russell; Dan Parilli; Kent and Marsha Butterfield;** 229: **Dan Parilli;** 230: **Barry Waddell;** 231: **Dr. Mike Cruz; Michael J. Stoklasa;** 233: **Frank Kleptz;** 234–235: **Stephen Witmer;** 236: **Classic Car Centre;** 237: **Larry Bell; Joe Yanush;** 238: **Larry Bell; Greg and Rhonda Haynes; Jeff Knoll;** 239: **Greg and Rhonda Haynes; Walter P. Wise;** 240: **Bill Draper; Steve Engeman;** 241: **Jim Reilly; Bud Moore;** 242: **Steve Ames;** 243: **Classic Auto Showplace; Jack Karleskind;** 244: **Classic Auto Showplace; Dean Cardella; Fred and Kris Kuebler;** 245: **Dave Cobble II; Eric and Yoshio Nakayama;** 246: **Philip Lagerquist;** 247: **Rick Cain;** 248: **Jim Regnier; Richard Petty;** 249: **Wayne Hartye; Glen Stidger; David Arent; Richard Carpenter;** 251: **Joseph Ererle; Ronda Cunningham; Classic Car Centre;** 253: **Eric and Yoshio Nakayama; Russ Smith;** 254: **Peter N. Cambrola; Barb & Harm Van Der Veen;** 255: **Michael S. Gray;** 256–257: **Paul D. Pierce;** 259: **John R. Oehler; Allen Scherer;** 260–261: **David Ramally;** 263: **Odus West;** 264: **David Arent;** 265: **Yoshio and Eric Nakayama; Michael Piche;** 266–267: **Don and Karen Kerridge;** 268: **Thomas and Carol Podemski;** 269: **Dennis D. Rosenberry;** 270: **Dan Tessner;** 270–271: **Trevor Badgley;** 272: **Randy O'Daniel; Trevor Badgley;** 273: **Odus West;** 274: **Jay Dykes;** 275: **Danny and Steve Runyon;** 276: **Steven Jenear;** 277: **Ray Hermand; Eric and Yoshio Nakayama;** 278: **Mary Ann and Robert Moore;** 280: **Michael S. Gray;** 282: **Jim Turner; Lou Rehrig;** 283: **Rick Cybul;** 286: **Ron Edgerly;** 287: **Terry Swisher;** 288: **Jim McCann;** 291: **William Kroncke;** 292–293: **Ralph Millner;** 293: **Kevin Kloubec;** 294: **Gregg Gyurina;** 295: **Bill Schroeder; Ron Beal;** 296: **Fernando F. Alvare;** 299: **Jim Buhle; Randy Mucha;** 300: **Dennis W. Riely;** 302: **Charles M. Kerr;** 306: **James H. Carson;** 307: **James H. Carson; Doug Schlisser;** 308–309: **Larry Rowen;** 309: **Mark and Joni Walters;** 310: **David L. Hardgrove;** 311: **Thomas and Carol Podemski;** 312: **Harry DeMenge; Michael Rooney;** 318: **Bill Hoff; Mitch Undahl;** 319: **Melissa Polk;** 320: **Tony Kanzia;** 321: **Jerry Buczkowski**

CONTENTS

FOREWORD

To those who loved them—those who could recognize a muscle car with just a glance at a fender emblem—it was as if the streets in the Sixties and early Seventies were alive with muscle. Cars with roaring exhausts seemed to squeal away from nearly every stoplight.

In reality, the number of bona fide muscle cars was quite low when counted against the millions of automobiles Detroit was churning out.

For example, Pontiac's 1966 GTO holds the record for the highest one-year production of any genuine muscle car, with 96,946. Yet it accounted for barely 10 percent of Pontiac's sales for '66. In fact, Pontiac built 318,270 other Tempest and LeMans models alone that year. Even the most famous muscle-car engines were hardly more than footnotes to annual production tabulations. Chevrolet's storied 409-cid V-8 was installed in fewer than one percent of the cars in which it could be ordered throughout its run.

If the lore of muscle cars is out of proportion to their actual numbers, that merely underscores their impact. Indeed, these machines created an entire culture, with its own language and customs, heroes and pretenders. It is to those who loved these cars—and to those just discovering their magic—that *Muscle Car Chronicle* is dedicated.

By its narrowest definition, a muscle car is a rear-wheel-drive midsize two-door coupe or sedan with a powerful V-8. These types of cars usually have enough room underhood for huge V-8s and the generous exhaust systems they require. Midsize cars are also relatively lightweight, but distribute enough weight rearward to keep the back tires from spinning helplessly under hard acceleration.

Muscle Car Chronicle recognizes, however, that any worthwhile treatment of the subject must go beyond so confining a definition. What really counts is a car's use of high power to break away from the ordinary run of daily transportation. So here you'll find not only GTOs and GTXs, but Camaros and Chryslers, Shelby Cobras and Chevy IIs. Our story begins with the birth of the mass-produced high-compression V-8 in the 1949 Oldsmobile and Cadillac, and traces muscle's fascinating journey right up to today's supercharged Dodge Challenger and Charger SRT Hellcats.

While most muscle car fans look back fondly on the late Sixties and early Seventies, we find ourselves in the midst of a new muscle car era today, one with changing definitions for what a muscle car can be. Import-inspired "tuner" cars like the Ford Focus RS, muscular pickup trucks like the Ford F-150 Lightning, and even hopped up SUVs like the Jeep Grand Cherokee SRT have shown that muscle isn't limited to midsize cars.

Our mission is to celebrate all of these wonderful machines and to present them honestly. Unfortunately, sketchy record keeping by the manufacturers, midyear changes, and countless other variables make any reconstruction of the entire muscle history, especially those halcyon days of the Sixties, a difficult task.

To create *Muscle Car Chronicle*, we relied on data from the automakers, the National Hot Rod Association, and marque historians. We note the sources of the performance figures we quote. And we point out variances in those figures, which were not uncommon, given contemporary magazines' penchant for one-upmanship and the manufacturers' fondness for lacing the press test fleet with hopped-up ringers.

But while the details are important, the deeper satisfaction is in the color and personality of these powerful cars. Our picture-laden chronicle format is uniquely suited to conveying each car's individual character. So study or browse, read chronologically or jump in at your favorite year. Just be ready for the ride of a lifetime!

—The Editors of CONSUMER GUIDE®

1949-59

Postwar era begins with hot rodders racing 1930s roadsters with hopped-up V-8s • Organized drag racing emerges in late 1940s... National Hot Rod Association formed in 1951 • NASCAR created at Daytona Beach in 1947 • For '49, Oldsmobile stuffs 135-bhp overhead-valve V-8 into lightweight body, creating first postwar muscle machine • Step-down Hudson Hornet tears up stock-car tracks in early '50s • Chrysler launches 180-bhp "hemi" V-8 for '51 • Lincoln gets ohv V-8 for '52, wins *Carrera Panamericana* race • Ford and Mercury get ohv V-8 for '54, replacing famed flathead • First NHRA National Championship held in 1955 • '55 Chevrolet with 265-cid V-8 sets standard for burgeoning horsepower race • Chrysler introduces 300 coupe for '55, with 300-bhp hemi... hits one horsepower per cubic inch a year later • Fuel injection goes into Chevy for '57: 283 horses from 283 cid • Daytona International Speedway opens in 1958 • 100,000 fans attend '59 NHRA Championship at Detroit...quickest stock car's ET is just under 15 seconds; dragster hits 9.12

▲ The breakthrough overhead-valve V-8s in the '49 Cadillac and Oldsmobile were light, durable, and powerful. When Olds put its "Rocket" version into the lightweight 76-series body, it created the Rocket 88, forerunner of the factory "muscle car."

▲ Tom McCahill of *Mechanix Illustrated* marveled that the sizable '49 Cadillac "out-performs just about every car." With stick shift, a Caddy could hit 60 in 12.1 seconds. The 331-cid V-8 made 160 bhp at 3800 rpm on 7.5:1 compression. This was the first year for the Coupe de Ville pillarless hardtop coupe.

▲ With two-barrel carb and 7.25:1 compression, Oldsmobile's revolutionary "Rocket" V-8 developed 135 bhp at 3600 rpm. That was fine in this 3890-pound 98, on 125-inch wheelbase—but far livelier in a 119.5-inch 88, at 265 pounds less. Four-speed Hydra-Matic was standard. Holiday hardtop coupes were new, too.

▲A new one-piece windshield went on Cadillacs for 1950, and the 160-bhp 331-cid V-8 gave the heavy cruisers a surprising swiftness.

▲Luxury was paramount at Cadillac, but a Series 62 model, such as this Coupe de Ville, still could do 0-60 in 13 seconds and top 100 mph.

◀When sportsman Briggs S. Cunningham drove his highly modified Cadillac-powered special at the LeMans 24-hour endurance race in 1950, the French had an apt nickname for it: *Le Monstre*. A Cunningham-backed Caddy that looked far closer to stock took drivers Sam and Miles Collier to 10th place overall at an average 81.5 mph, with this bizarre creation finishing right behind.

▼Specs for the 303.7-cid Olds Rocket engine, "power sensation of the nation," were unchanged from 1949, at 135 bhp and 263 lbs/ft using 7.25:1 compression and a Rochester two-barrel carb. An "export kit" included a special cam, high-compression heads, heavy-duty wheels, and other goodies.

▲Oldsmobile touted the '50 Rocket 88's smooth ride as much as its "high-compression power" and optional "Whirlaway Hydra-Matic Drive."

▲An Oldsmobile 88 Deluxe club sedan weighed 3486 pounds, and its fastback body looked super with options. Cadet sunvisor added $27.

▲One of the fastest cars of its day, the Olds 88 ruled the NASCAR circuit. Two-door sedans lacked a hardtop's pizzazz, but 50,561 were built.

Prettiest Olds 88 for '50 was the Holiday hardtop; at 3510 pounds, it wasn't much heavier than a club coupe. Wheelbase of the 98 was down two inches, to 122; 88 remained 119.5. Tom McCahill's stick-shift 88 hit 60 mph in 12 seconds (13.4 with Hydra-Matic), a record for *Mechanix Illustrated.* A "Rocket 88 is as hot as a hornet's kiss," he said. *Motor Trend* kept a Hydra-Matic sedan in Low range and needed 12.22 seconds to get to 60 mph. Olds was NASCAR champ again, with 10 wins in 19 starts. It also won the Mexican *Carrera Panamericana* endurance road race. Finally, Joe Littlejohn set a two-way stock-class record of 100.28 mph on Daytona's sands.

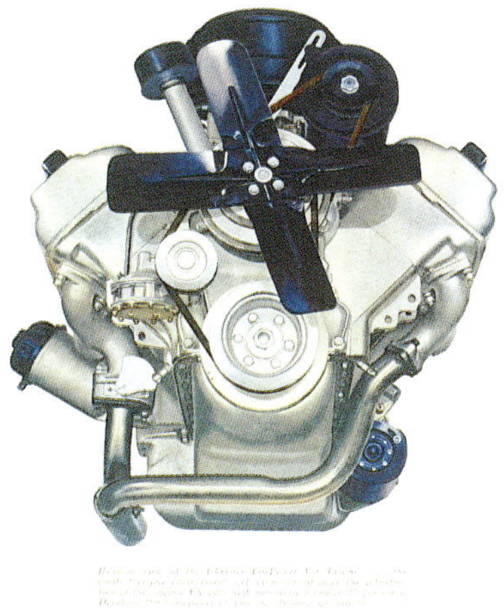

▲For '51, Chrysler put its new FirePower V-8 into the New Yorker and the smaller Saratoga.

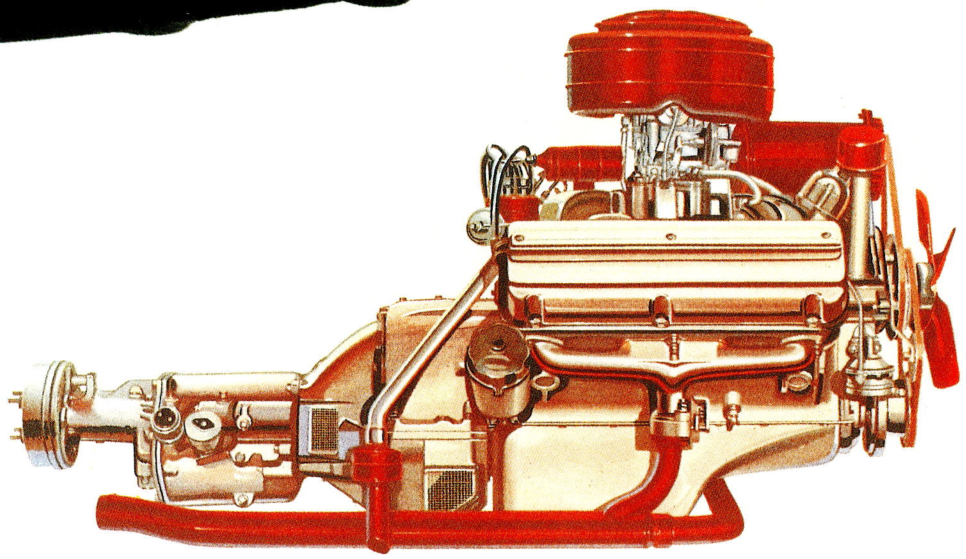

▲Chrysler's new V-8 not only had overhead valves, but hemispherical combustion chambers. The 331-cid "hemi" had 180 bhp at 4000 rpm via 7.5:1 compression. It helped raise Chrysler's luck in NASCAR.

▲For 1952, four Saratoga models carried the "hemi" and Fluid Torque Drive. A Saratoga could do 0-60 mph in 10 seconds.

▲A hot Hornet joined the "step-down" Hudson line for 1951 and ruled the stock-car tracks through '54 with its 308-cid L-head six.

▲ With its floor below the frame rails, Hudson had a low center of gravity for outstanding handling. The inline-six made 145 bhp at 3800 rpm on 7.2:1 compression with a two-barrel carb; Twin H-Power (dual carbs) made 170. In 35 starts, Hudson took 31 stock-car wins, 12 by Marshall Teague. Hornet for '52 included club coupe, hardtop, convertible, and this 3600-pound sedan, all on a 124-inch wheelbase.

▲ The '52 Lincoln Capri got a new 160-bhp 317.5-cid ohv V-8. Though topping two tons, hot-rod Lincolns grabbed the first five spots in the *Carrera Panamericana*. A ball-joint suspension helped handling.

▲ For '52, Oldsmobile's Super 88 got Quadri-Jet four-barrel carburetion and 160 bhp (versus 145 bhp in the regular 88). An "export kit" added a wild cam, tougher crank, and more.

▲ Cadillac's Eldorado convertible could be swift—once it got moving. The $7750 ragtop bowed for '53 with the usual 210-bhp 331-cid V-8. Touches included wire wheels, "Panoramic" wraparound windshield, cut-down doors, and metal tonneau. Just 532 were built.

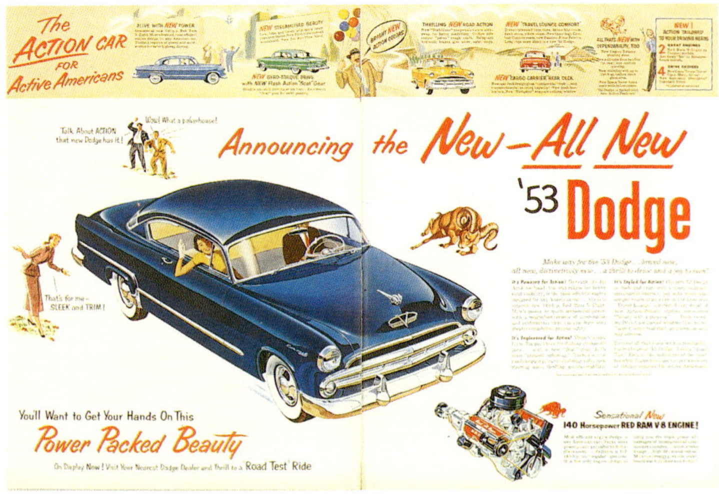

▲ Chrysler shrunk its "hemi" to 241-cid and gave its restyled '53 Dodge Coronet the first ohv V-8 in the moderately priced field. Transmission choices included three-speed, overdrive, Gyro-Matic, and new Gyro-Torque automatic. A Dodge set 196 AAA stock-car speed records.

◀ Dodge's Red Ram V-8 for '53 made 140 bhp at 4400 rpm using 7.0:1 compression, hydraulic lifters, and a Stromberg two-barrel carb. It ran on regular gas, and ads touted the "triple power advantages of hemispherical combustion chambers...short-stroke design [and] high-lift lateral valves." Moreover, the new Gyro-Torque Drive had a "'Scat' gear that's plain greased lightning." The "hemi" also had smooth manifolding, large and widely separated valves, and centrally located spark plugs. On the down side, it was costly to build. Danny Eames took one to 102.62 mph on a California dry lake.

▲ A Dodge Coronet convertible went for $2494 in 1953. Wheelbase was 114 inches on two-door Dodges, 119 on four-doors. Dodge promised a "magnificent reserve of acceleration" with the Red Ram V-8.

▲ At 3530 pounds on a 124-inch wheelbase, a '53 Hornet club coupe was no featherweight, but the 7-X engine helped it to 21 NASCAR wins. Stick-shifts worked through a fluid-cushioned clutch.

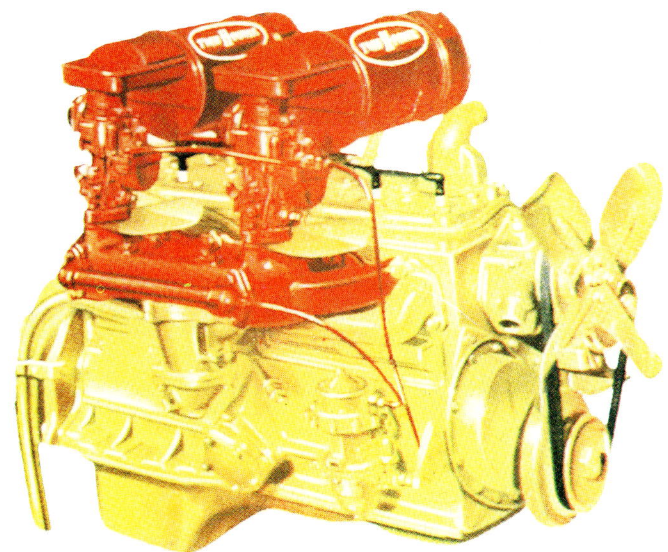

▲ A Hornet engine with Twin H-Power was easy to spot. Hudson made "severe usage" parts available to racers. The 7-X six featured a .020-inch overbore, special cam, and headers—for about 210 bhp.

▲ Olds still was losing to Hudson on stock-car tracks in 1953; the 165-bhp V-8 in the Super 88 (and bigger 98) wasn't enough. A new J-2 option added 8.5:1 heads, solid lifters, and full-race cam.

▲ New heads, four-barrel, and dual exhausts gave the '54 New Yorker's "hemi" 235 bhp. "Anything less is Yesterday's Car!" said ads. Chryslers averaged 118.18 mph in a 24-hour endurance run.

▲ Replacing the hallowed flathead for '54 was Ford's new 130-bhp ohv 239-cid, the hottest V-8 in the low-priced field. A 256-cid Police V-8 had 160 bhp. Ball joints replaced kingpins. Ford-O-Matic cost $184.

▲ A '54 Hudson Hornet Hollywood hardtop sold for $2988. Its 308-cid engine was the biggest L-head six at the time. It had 160 bhp with 7.5:1 compression and two-barrel carb. Twin H-Power added 10 bhp.

▲ Hornet ragtop sold for $3288. Hudson took 17 NASCAR wins in its last year of factory race support. On May 1, 1954, it merged with Nash to form American Motors. This was the step-down design's last year.

▲ The Hot One! Chevrolet triggered the horsepower race in 1955 with a magnificent new 265-cid V-8. It had 162 bhp with a two-barrel and 180 with the four-barrel, dual-exhaust "Power Pack." A V-8 Bel Air Sport Coupe cost $2166 and weighed 3165 pounds—less than a Ford or Plymouth hardtop. *Road & Track's* Power Pack Two-Ten with overdrive did 0-60 in 9.7 seconds and 17.4 at 77 mph in the quarter-mile.

▲ A '55 Bel Air convertible went for $2305. At midyear, Chevy advertised a special-order Power Kit to boost output to 195 bhp.

▲ Chevy's '55 V-8 weighed less than a six. Its thinwall castings, stud-mount rocker arms, and hollow pushrods could handle 5500 rpm.

▲ Luxury and performance combined in the 300-bhp, leather-lined Chrysler C-300 of '55. Just 1725 were built, priced at $4110.

▲ "America's Most Powerful Stock Car," crowed the ads. C-300s won 37 stock-car races and finished 1-2 at over 130 mph in Daytona's flying mile.

◀ Despite its two-ton heft, the C-300 plundered the nation's stock-car tracks. This is Tim Flock ripping through a turn at the original Daytona Beach track. Buck Baker was among the other legends to win with a C-300. A street-ready version could accelerate to 60 mph in 9 seconds and top out at 130 mph. A 300 set a class standing-start quarter-mile record at 76.84 mph. The godfather of the magazine road test, Tom McCahill, was a fan. He said the C-300 was "as solid as Grant's Tomb and 130 times as fast." He called it "a hardboiled, magnificent piece of semi-competition transportation."

▲ For the C-300, the 331-cid "hemi" made 300 bhp at 5200 rpm, versus 250 bhp in the New Yorker. It used solid lifters, 8.5:1 compression, a full-race cam, and twin four-barrel carbs.

▲ Built on New Yorker's 126-inch wheelbase, the C-300 had PowerFlite and a 150-mph speedometer. Wire wheels cost extra, but air conditioning, outside mirrors, and backup lights weren't factory-available.

▲ The new Fairlane topped the line of restyled '55 Fords and took some styling cues from the just-introduced Thunderbird. The Sunliner convertible went for $2324 with a V-8 and weighed 3382 pounds. Overdrive added $110; Ford-O-Matic, $178.

▲ Ford dropped the 239-cid ohv V-8 after one season, turning to a 272-cid enlargement with 162 bhp at 4400 rpm, or 182 with Power Pack.

▲ Pontiac was restyled for '55. This is the $2691 Star Chief convertible. Midyear brought a four-barrel Power Pack and 200 bhp.

▲ With stick shift, Pontiac's new "Strato Streak" 287.2-cid V-8 for 1955 had 173 bhp at 4400 rpm on a 7.4:1 compression. Hydra-Matic upped the ante to 180 bhp at 4600 rpm via an 8.0:1 squeeze.

The '56 Chevrolet

It looks high priced—but it's the new Chevrolet "Two-Ten" 4-Door Sedan.

For sooner and safer arrivals!

It's so nimble and quick on the road . . .

Of course, you don't have to have an urgent errand and a motorcycle escort to make use of Chevrolet's quick and nimble ways. Wherever you go, the going's sweeter and safer in a Chevy.

Power's part of the reason. Chevrolet's horsepower ranges up to 205. And these numbers add up to *action*—second-saving acceleration for safer passing . . . rapid-fire reflexes that help you avoid trouble before it happens!

True, lots of cars are high powered today, but the difference is in the way Chevrolet *handles* its power. It's rock-steady on the road . . . clings to curves like part of the pavement. That's *stability*—and it helps make Chevrolet one of the few great road cars!

Highway-test one, soon. Your Chevrolet dealer will be happy to arrange it. . . . Chevrolet Division of General Motors, Detroit 2, Mich.

THE HOT ONE'S EVEN HOTTER

▲ Cheaper and less bold than a Bel Air, a '56 Two-Ten was a threat with the right V-8 as Chevy brought performance to the people.

▲ A '56 Bel Air Sport Coupe went for $2275 with the 162-bhp, 265-cid V-8. Powerglides had 170. New options brought 205 bhp with a four-barrel, or 225 with dual quads and 9.25:1 compression.

▲ Complementing the 300B for '56 was DeSoto's Adventurer. It had a 320-bhp, 341-cid dual-quad V-8. Only 996 were built.

▲ Enlarging the "hemi" to 354 cid and adding a high-lift camshaft gave Chrysler's 300B 340 bhp—or 355 bhp with optional 10.0:1 compression.

▲ In addition to one horsepower per cubic inch, 300B buyers could now get air conditioning and a 6.17:1 (!) axle. Pushbutton three-speed TorqueFlite was standard, but manual was offered.

◀ Buick had switched from straight-eight to V-8 power in 1953. For '56, the 322-cid V-8 in the Super, Roadmaster, and Century yielded 255 bhp.

▶ Dodge got noticed in '56 not only for its new fins and tri-tone color schemes, but for a D-500 option that added 8.5:1 compression and Carter dual quads to the 315-cid V-8. It made 295 bhp and was offered on any model, including this Royal Lancer. Super Red Ram 315 continued with 230 bhp.

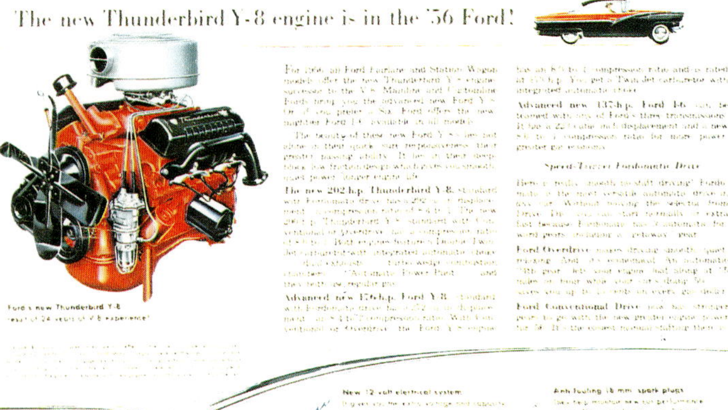

▲ Ford's new '56 Y-8 V-8 had 200 bhp, 202 with Fordomatic.

▲ At midyear, even the Customline two-door could get the 292-cid V-8.

▲ Mercury's '56 Montclair with Merc-O-Matic had a 225-bhp version of the "Safety-Surge" 312-cid V-8. A 260-bhp edition came later.

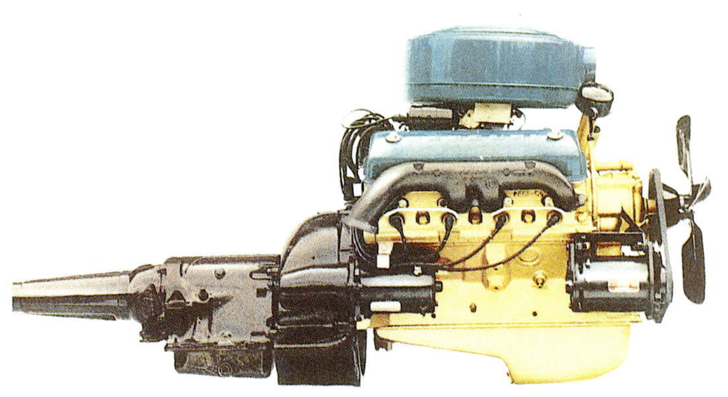

▲ *Auto Age* saw 0-60 mph in 12.2 seconds with a 225-bhp Montclair. Mercury won five NASCAR Grand National races in 1956.

▲ Packard's '56 Caribbean had motoring's largest V-8, at 374 cid.

▲ With 10.0:1 compression and dual quads, the 374 made 310 bhp.

▲ Leading the '56 Pontiac lineup was the Star Chief convertible. It had a 227-bhp version of the 316.6-cid V-8. Nearly all had Hydra-Matic.

▲ Stick-shift four-barrel 316.6s had 216 bhp, Hydra-Matics had 227. Special version got dual quads, 10.0:1 compression, and 285 bhp.

▲ Fury joined the '56 Plymouth line and got exclusive use of a 240-bhp, 303-cid, four-barrel V-8. Zero-60 mph took 9 seconds, the quarter, 16.5.

▲ With its 275-bhp, 352-cid, four-barrel Packard V-8, Studebaker's '56 Golden Hawk was good for 0-60 mph in 8.7 seconds. Other Hawks had Stude V-8s.

▲ Chevy's '57 was a future classic, but notable, too, was the newly enlarged 283-cid V-8, which had up to 270 bhp with dual quads.

▲ Hottest of the 283s was the fuel-injected version. With 10.5:1 compression and high-lift cam, it made a super-efficient 283 bhp.

▲ Chevy's 283-bhp "fuelie" had to use a three-speed manual. A 250-bhp version could have automatic.

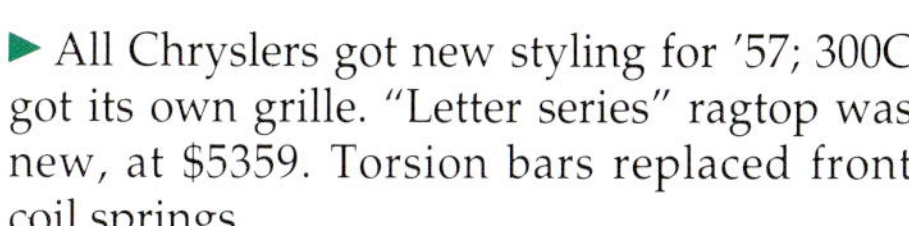

► All Chryslers got new styling for '57; 300C got its own grille. "Letter series" ragtop was new, at $5359. Torsion bars replaced front coil springs.

▲ Enlarged to 392 cid, the 300C's dual-quad hemi made 375 bhp on 9.25:1 compression, 390 on 10.0:1. Zero-60 mph took 8.4 seconds with TorqueFlite.

◄ DeSoto's stylish Adventurer hardtop (and new ragtop) got 345 bhp from a 345-cid V-8.

▲A '57 Ford Fairlane 500 Victoria hardtop with the 272-cid V-8 cost $2439; 292- or 312-cid "go" was optional. Ford outsold Chevy in '57.

▲Ford's '57 312-cid four-barrel "Thunderbird" V-8s had 245, 270, and 285 bhp; a Paxton supercharger gave 300 bhp, with 330 on tap for NASCAR racers.

▲Olds enlarged its 324-cid V-8 to 371 cubes for '57, biggest among GM cars. It had 277 bhp with a four-barrel in this Super 88.

▲Olds' three-deuce J-2 option made 300 bhp. Zero-60 mph took 9 seconds. Lee Petty hit 144.9 mph on Daytona sand with one, but NASCAR banned the J-2.

▲For 1957, the V-8 in the stunningly restyled Plymouth Fury grew to 318 cid and 290 bhp. *Motor Trend*'s stick-shift Fury hit 60 mph in 8.7 seconds.

▲Available in any '57 Plymouth, the new 318 had dual quads, high-lift cam, dual exhausts, and 9.25:1 compression. New TorqueFlite cost $220.

►The limited-edition Bonneville convertible joined Pontiac during the '57 season. It cost $5782 and only 630 were built, all with a fuel-injected V-8. The 370-cid mill delivered 310 bhp at 4800 rpm, 400 lbs/ft of torque at 3400, but had to haul 4285 pounds of Bonneville. A lighter Pontiac Chieftain with the 347-cid V-8 and Tri-Power could beat the Bonnie's 18-second quarter-mile time by 1.2 seconds. Pontiac issued three Tri-Power engines for '57, but two were for NASCAR.

▲ Rebel's V-8 had 255 horsepower at 4700 rpm, 9.5:1 compression, solid lifters, and a four-barrel. Only 1500 were built, priced at a hefty—for Rambler— $2786.

◀ Early muscle from Rambler! Squeezing the big Nash Ambassador's new 327-cid V-8 into a light Rambler body produced the '57 Rambler Rebel. Zero-60 times were close to 7 seconds—second only to a fuelie Corvette, according to *Motor Trend*.

▲ Studebaker gave its '57 Golden Hawk bigger tail feathers, and trimmed some weight by substituting its own V-8 for the Packard power of '57. Handling improved, and 0-60 still took about 9 seconds, the quarter, 17.3 seconds.

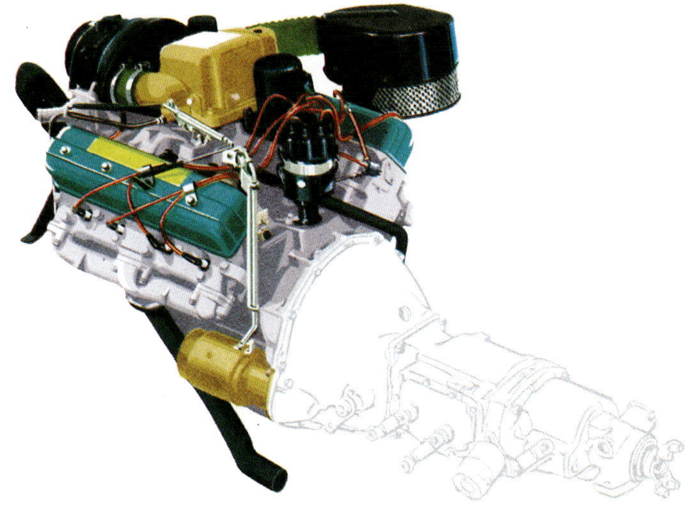

▲ In the Golden Hawk, Stude's 289-cid V-8 used a "Jet-Stream" supercharger to get 275 bhp at 4800 rpm and 333 lbs/ft of torque at 3200 rpm. An overdrive manual or Flight-O-Matic slushbox were offered.

▲ Overshadowed in later years by '57 models, the heavier '58 Chevy pleased buyers with its 2.5-inch longer wheelbase, smoother ride, and bigger size. Impala (shown) bowed as the new top-line hardtop and convertible.

▲ Big news under Chevy hoods for '58 was the 348-cid V-8 with up to 315 bhp from three deuces and 11.0:1 compression. A '57 283 fuelie was faster, but *Motor Trend*'s 348 still did 0-60 in 9.1 seconds and the quarter in 16.5.

▲ A jump to 10.0:1 compression gave the Chrysler 300D's hemi 380 bhp, up by 5, for '58. A few came with Bendix fuel injection.

▲ Ford engine options for '58 grew to include the new FE-series V-8, offered in 240- and 265-bhp 332-cid versions, and as a 300-bhp 352.

▲ Super 88 had chromey, barge-like styling—and the optional continental kit didn't help—but Olds advanced to fourth in sales for '58, partly on the strength of more potent 371-cid V-8s.

▲ The Rocket 371 made 305 bhp in the Super 88 and 312 in the 98, which rode a four-inch longer wheelbase.

▼ Bonneville became a separate Pontiac series for '58. The fancy convertible and hardtop used the Chieftain's 122-inch wheelbase (two less than Star Chief's). A Tri-Power ragtop paced the Indy 500.

▲ In Bonneville, Pontiac's 370-cid V-8 ranged from 255 bhp with a four-barrel to 300 with Tri-Power. About 200 Bonnevilles had Rochester fuel injection, available for $500 and good for 310 bhp.

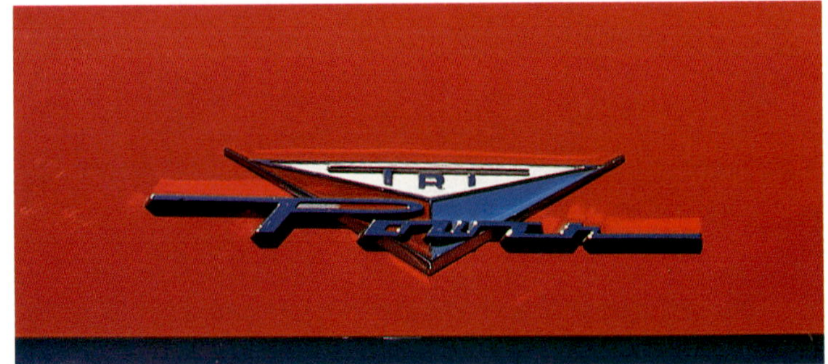

▲ Pontiac's $93.60 Tri-Power option used three two-barrel Rochesters, 10.5:1 compression, and a high-lift cam to get 300 bhp at 4600 rpm. Two NASCAR-certified V-8s arrived during the year, with 315/330 bhp.

▲"Batwing" fins and a "nostril" grille drew the eye to the '59 Chevy Impala, but buyers also savored an even dozen engine options.

▲Chevy's 348-cid V-8 now had 250 to 335 bhp, depending on carburetion and compression (up to 11.25:1). Four 283s were sold, at 170-290 bhp.

▲Engineer Robert M. Rodger with the dual-quad 413-cid wedge that replaced the hemi in Chrysler's '59 300E. Horsepower was still 380.

▲Late-1950s automotive styling themes reached a crescendo with the 1959 Custom Royal Lancer. D-500 power gave the Dodge some bite.

▲Dodge buyers got a 326-cid V-8, a 361 (295/305 bhp), or this 320-bhp D-500 383 (345 bhp with dual quads).

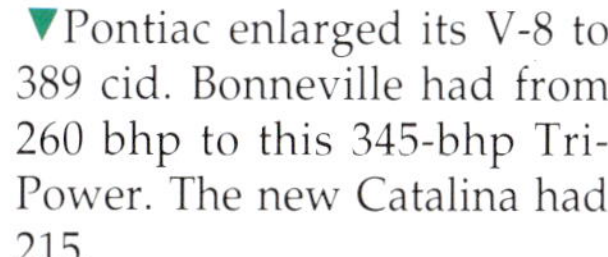

▼Pontiac enlarged its V-8 to 389 cid. Bonneville had from 260 bhp to this 345-bhp Tri-Power. The new Catalina had 215.

▲Chrysler built just 140 of its $5749 300E ragtops for '59. The new wedge V-8 was 100 lbs. lighter than the 392-cid hemi, and had 450 lbs./ft. of torque, up 15, so acceleration was even quicker.

▲Pontiac unveiled two trademarks for '59: a split grille and a "Wide-Track" chassis. Bonneville again topped the line, at $3257 for the Sport Coupe.

1960

Compact Chevrolet Corvair and Ford Falcon debut • Ram Induction launched on Chrysler 300F, yielding 375 or 400 bhp • Dodge and Plymouth get Ram Induction for their big V-8s • Lee A. Iacocca, appointed Ford Division's general manager, helps rekindle interest in performance • Smooth Ford Starliner appears, eager for NASCAR superspeedways • Ford announces triple two-barrel setup as dealer-installed option • Hurst-Campbell markets Dual-Pattern floor-shift conversion • Drag-oriented Pontiac with Tri-Power belts out 348 bhp • Pontiac develops racing chassis, offers Borg-Warner four-speed • Jim Wangers drags Pontiac to Super/Stock and stock eliminator wins at NHRA Nationals

1960 CHEVROLET HIGH-PERFORMANCE ENGINES

TYPE	CID	BORE × STROKE	BHP @ RPM	TORQUE @ RPM	FUEL SYSTEM	COMP. RATIO	AVAIL.
ohv V-8	283	3.88×3.00	230 @ 4800	300 @ 3000	1×4bbl.	9.5:1	full size
ohv V-8	348	4.13×3.25	250 @ 4400	355 @ 2800	1×4bbl.	9.5:1	full size
ohv V-8	348	4.13×3.25	305 @ 5600	350 @ 3600	1×4bbl.	11.0:1	full size
ohv V-8	348	4.13×3.35	320 @ 5600	358 @ 3600	1×4bbl.	11.25:1	full size
ohv V-8	348	4.13×3.35	280 @ 4800	355 @ 3200	3×2bbl.	9.5:1	full size
ohv V-8	348	4.13×3.35	335 @ 3600	362 @ 3600	3×2bbl.	11.25:1	full size

▼ The ultimate in big Chevy style and speed for '60 was an Impala Sport Coupe with the Special Super Turbo-Thrust 348. It made 335 bhp with Tri-Carb induction, solid lifters, and 11.25:1 compression. A four-speed manual gearbox also was available.

▲ Chevy's 348-cid V-8 had its moments. Here, Terry Prince in the Prince & Nicholson '60 Bel Air (left) launches on his way to the B/S title at the 1962 NHRA Winternationals. The two-door sedan turned 13.50s at 103 mph.

▲ Chevrolet toned down Impala's "batwing" tail for 1960. All full-size convertibles were Impalas.

▲ This was El Camino's last year as a full-size model. Chevy called it a "two-door sedan pickup."

▼ The Bel Air Sport Coupe debuted for '60 with Impala styling and available V-8 power starting at $2596, versus $2704 for the Impala Sport Coupe.

▶ Early Chrysler muscle was best expressed by a series of big, stylish two-door hardtops starting with the 1955 C-300 and its 300-bhp Hemi. By 1960, the "letter series" cars had progressed to the 300F. It continued the tradition of opulence and muscle, though front-end styling was now more similar to that of other Chryslers. Chrysler adopted unibody construction for '60, which weighed less than the former body-on-frame designs. At a princely $5411, the spirited 300 hardtop was "highly impractical—and definitely desirable," said *Car Life*. Pushbutton TorqueFlite automatic was standard, but a French-built Pont-a-Mousson four-speed manual transmission (as in Facel Vega) was optional for just this season, ending up in only seven 300Fs.

▲ Slipping into the four-place 300F was a snap, with automatic-swiveling front seats pointing the way. A full-length console was standard, along with a tachometer and an electro-luminescent instrument panel.

▼ Ram Induction was the big news under Chrysler 300F hoods. With long tubes, the 413-cid V-8 delivered 375 bhp. Optional short-ram tubes added 25 horses. A 375-bhp 300F could hit 60 mph in 7.1 seconds and do the quarter-mile in 16 flat. *Car Life* claimed a 0-60 time of 6.8 seconds—in a drizzle!

▲ Torsion-bar front suspension helped give the hot Chrysler its road-hugging ride. *Car Life* noted that body roll was "barely noticed," due partly to "extraordinary bucket seats." 300Fs took the top six spots in Daytona's flying mile, led by a record 144.927 mph with Gregg Ziegler behind the wheel.

▲ Chrysler began experimenting with ram induction in 1952, but didn't put it into production until 1960. It came standard on the 413-cid V-8 in the 300F, and was also available on 361- and 383-cid Dodge and Plymouth V-8s. Each four-barrel carb sat atop a small plenum chamber, and fed the cylinder bank on the opposite side via "outrigger" tubes. Said the 300F brochure: "Turn the key. The 'F' bursts into a throaty baritone. Heads turn, you tingle. A touch of the toe proves more. This car means what it says!"

1960 CHRYSLER HIGH-PERFORMANCE ENGINES

TYPE	CID	BORE × STROKE	BHP @ RPM	TORQUE @ RPM	FUEL SYSTEM	COMP. RATIO	AVAIL.
ohv V-8	413	4.19 × 3.75	375 @ 5000	495 @ 2800	2×4bbl.	10.0:1	1
ohv V-8	413	4.19 × 3.75	400 @ 5200	465 @ 3600	2×4bbl.	10.0:1	300F

1. New Yorker, 300F.

◀ Chrysler's Chief Engineer, R.M. Rodger, took a special interest in the "letter" cars, and encouraged owners to write with suggestions or criticism. Chrysler's ram induction recognized that pressure waves within the intake system could produce a "supercharging" effect. To yield peak power at mid-range speeds—when it's needed for highway acceleration—a 30-inch tube was optimum. One drawback: The ram effect occurs only in a rather narrow rpm range, so it had less impact as the engine revved.

▲ Sedate appearances can deceive, as in the case of this fawn/white Dodge Polara Suburban wagon with seating for nine. Under the hood dwells a 383-cid D-500 engine with ram induction, hooked to the usual TorqueFlite automatic. Luxury extras include swivel seat, rear air, and power locks. This restored wagon spent time in a junkyard.

▶ Fitted with cast aluminum ram induction, Dodge's 383 earned the D-500 badge and 330 bhp. With short-ram induction whipping up 340 bhp, a Dart Phoenix could storm to 60 mph in 8.5 seconds and turn 16.3 in the quarter. The larger Matador carried a 295-bhp 361 V-8, while full-size Polaras came only with 383s, either 325 or 330 bhp.

▲ Dart sedans, hardtops, and coupes had a 118-inch wheelbase, four inches shorter than the larger and heavier Matador and Polara. This Dart Phoenix hardtop coupe weighed 3605 pounds and listed for $2727 with V-8.

1960 DODGE HIGH-PERFORMANCE ENGINES

TYPE	CID	BORE × STROKE	BHP @ RPM	TORQUE @ RPM	FUEL SYSTEM	COMP. RATIO	AVAIL.
ohv V-8	361	4.13 × 3.38	295 @ 4600	390 @ 2400	1×4bbl.	10.0:1	Matador
ohv V-8	361	4.13 × 3.38	310 @ 4800	435 @ 2800	2×4bbl.	10.0:1	Pioneer, Phoenix
ohv V-8	383	4.25 × 3.75	330 @ 4800	465 @ 2800	2×4bbl.	10.0:1	1
ohv V-8	383	4.25 × 3.75	325 @ 4600	435 @ 2800	1×4bbl.	10.0:1	Pioneer, Polara
ohv V-8	383	4.25 × 3.75	330 @ 5200*	425 @ 3600	1×4bbl.	10.0:1	Pioneer, Phoenix

* 340 bhp with long-ram induction. 1. Pioneer, Phoenix, Matador, Polara.

◀ The Seneca was at the bottom of the Dart line, below the Pioneer and Phoenix. At 3530 pounds, the two-door Seneca sedan was the lightest Dodge available with a V-8 engine, though it was limited to the 230-bhp 318-cid unit. To get the 383, you had to move up to the Phoenix.

▶ Fords were restyled for '60. Wheelbase grew one inch, to 119, and overall length was up by nearly six. The Galaxie Starliner coupe had a slippery roofline tailored for NASCAR superspeedways.

▲ The 360-bhp "Interceptor 360" 352-cid V-8 was Ford's first performance engine since 1957. It had a Holly four-barrel on an aluminum intake manifold. Triple two-barrels became a midyear dealer option.

▲ Ford judged its Cruise-O-Matic automatic gearbox too weak for the Interceptor 360, so the engine initially was sold only with a Borg-Warner T-85 manual with three speeds or with overdrive (shown).

▼ A 360-bhp Ford Starliner averaged 142 mph at Daytona for 40 laps. Karol Miller drove one to a record 157.902 mph on the Bonneville flats. Ford's 15 wins topped the Grand National stock-car tour in 1960.

1960 FORD HIGH-PERFORMANCE ENGINES							
TYPE	CID	BORE × STROKE	BHP @ RPM	TORQUE @ RPM	FUEL SYSTEM	COMP. RATIO	AVAIL.
ohv V-8	352	4.00 × 3.50	300 @ 4600	381 @ 2800	1 × 4bbl.	9.6:1	full size
ohv V-8	352	4.30 × 3.70	360 @ 6000	380 @ 3400	1 × 4bbl.	10.6:1	full size

▲ Olds' "Regular Rocket" 371-cid V-8 (left) had up to 260 bhp; "Premium Rocket" 394 had 315.

▲ A Ninety-Eight convertible paced the Indy 500. It rode a 126.5-inch wheelbase and weighed 4349 pounds. Lighter and smaller were the Dynamic 88 and the Super 88. They had a 123-inch wheelbase. Oldsmobile's top performer was the Super 88 fitted with the optional 315-bhp, four-barrel 394-cid V-8.

1960 OLDSMOBILE HIGH-PERFORMANCE ENGINES							
TYPE	CID	BORE × STROKE	BHP @ RPM	TORQUE @ RPM	FUEL SYSTEM	COMP. RATIO	AVAIL.
ohv V-8	371	4.00 × 3.69	240 @ 4400	375 @ 2800	1 × 4bbl.	8.75:1	Dynamic 88
ohv V-8	371	4.13 × 3.69	325 @ 4600	435 @ 2800	1 × 4bbl.	9.75:1	Super 88
ohv V-8	394	4.13 × 3.69	315 @ 4600	435 @ 2800	1 × 4bbl.	9.75:1	Super 88,89

▶ Plymouth's most potent engine to date was the 383-cid V-8 with ram induction, here tagged "SonoRamic." Similar to the system installed on Chrysler 300F engines, its dual quads and long intake tubes produced up to 330 bhp. Plymouth was beginning to shake its staid, family-car image.

▶ Its longhorn, cross-ram manifolds packing a pair of big four-barrels, "SonoRamic" induction served as the opening salvo of Plymouth's performance makeover in the 1960s. With a single four-barrel, the 383 still made a respectable 310 bhp. The compact Valiant also debuted this year. A "Hyper-Pak" option for its 170-cid "slant six" borrowed the ram-induction principle and increased horsepower from 101 to 148 with a 10.0:1 compression.

1960 PLYMOUTH HIGH-PERFORMANCE ENGINES

TYPE	CID	BORE × STROKE	BHP @ RPM	TORQUE @ RPM	FUEL SYSTEM	COMP. RATIO	AVAIL.
ohv I-8	170	3.40 × 3.13	148 @ 5200	153 @ 4200	1 × 4bbl.	10.5:1	Valiant
ohv V-8	361	4.12 × 3.38	305 @ 4800	369 @ 3000	1 × 4bbl.	10.0:1	full size
ohv V-8	361	4.12 × 3.38	310 @ 4800	435 @ 2800	2 × 4bbl.	10.0:1	full size
ohv V-8	383	4.24 × 3.38	330 @ 4800	460 @ 2800	2 × 4bbl.	10.0:1	full size
ohv V-8	383	4.24 × .3.38	325 @ 4600	435 @ 2800	1 × 4bbl.	10.0:1	full size
ohv V-8	383	4.24 × 3.38	330 @ 5200	435 @ 3600	2 × 4bbl.	10.0:1	full size

▼ Plymouth went to unibody construction for 1960, but the styling was garish as tailfins had their last hurrah. This is the mid-line Belvedere hardtop.

▲ The Sport Fury was gone, but carrying on as Plymouth's cousin to the Dodge Dart was the 118-inch-wheelbase Fury, here in convertible form. At $2967, it was Plymouth's most expensive non-station wagon model. A 310-bhp Fury could manage 7.5 seconds to 60 mph, and 15.6 for the quarter-mile.

1960 PONTIAC HIGH-PERFORMANCE ENGINES							
TYPE	CID	BORE × STROKE	BHP @ RPM	TORQUE @ RPM	FUEL SYSTEM	COMP. RATIO	AVAIL.
ohv V-8	389	4.06 × 3.75	281 @ 4400	407 @ 2800	1 × 4bbl.	8.6:1	Bonneville
ohv V-8	389	4.06 × 3.75	283 @ 4400	413 @ 2800	1 × 2bbl.	10.25:1	1
ohv V-8	389	4.06 × 3.75	303 @ 4600	425 @ 2800	1 × 4bbl.	10.25:1	2
ohv V-8	389	4.06 × 3.75	318 @ 4600	430 @ 3200	3 × 2bbl.	10.75:1	3

1. Catalina, Ventura, Star Chief. 2. Bonneville, Bonneville Safari.
3. Catalina, Ventura, Star Chief, Bonneville

▶ Pontiac sales overtook Oldsmobile and Buick in 1959 and would continue to climb well into the decade. The '60s were basically facelifted '59s, though the Ventura trim level joined the line for this year only. Inside, the floor tunnel was lowered thanks to a redesigned Hydra-Matic transmission, and a removable "Sportable" transistor radio was optional.

▶ Pontiac temporarily dumped its split grille for a full-width design that helped to emphasize the wide-track theme. Wheelbase was 122 inches on Catalina and Ventura, 124 on Star Chief and Bonneville (shown). All used a 389-cid "Tempest" V-8. It came with a four-barrel on the Bonneville and made 281 horsepower with manual shift, 303 bhp with Hydra-Matic. Special four-barrel versions also came in 333-bhp tune, while Tri-Power setups yielded 318 or 348 bhp, with some sources listing up to 363 bhp.

▲ Only the $3530 Custom Safari wagon cost more than the $3476 Bonneville ragtop. Pontiac's other convertible was the $3078 Catalina. On Bonneville, leather upholstery with "Morrokide" accents was standard and fabric tops were available in six colors. The Bonneville drop top weighed 4030 pounds.

◀ While Pontiac ads sang the praises of security and even fuel economy, it was a different tune at racetracks. For example, Bobby Johns' '60 Catalina led to Daytona 500 at an average of nearly 160 mph until he spun out nine laps from the finish.

▲ At 3835 pounds, a Catalina two-door sedan was the lightest Poncho. On Labor Day at Detroit Dragway, Jim Wangers won NHRA top-stock eliminator in one. And a 333-bhp 389 street version was time at 7.8 seconds 0-60, and 16 seconds flat in the quarter-mile.

1961

Chevrolet turns to the 409—an engine soon to be immortalized in song as well as stats • Super Sport trim option debuts on all Chevrolet Impala models • Chrysler 300G offered in both convertible and hardtop form • Dodge and Plymouth start with 383-cid V-8s, later add 413 wedge • Dodge Lancer Hyper-Pak option wrings 196 bhp out of 225-cid six • Bore/stroke boost transforms Ford's 352-cid V-8 into a 390 • 401-bhp triple two-barrel Ford V-8 added during model year—deemed legal for drag racing • Ford offers its first four-speed • 375-bhp Ford Starliner exceeds 153 mph at Daytona • Sporty Falcon Futura appears with bucket seats but puny power • Oldsmobile adds "personal" Starfire convertible • Downsized bodies boost performance from Pontiac's hot 389s • Pontiac wins record 30 of 52 NASCAR Grand National stock-car starts • Compact Pontiac Tempest debuts

▲ Chevrolet full-size models got a big dose of sportiness in mid-1961 with the Super Sport option. Available on any Impala for $53.80, it included a host of styling and mechanical alterations. Inside was a Corvette-type grab-bar in front of the passenger, some special trim, and a 7000-rpm tachometer.

► The Super Sport package was ordered on just 453 '61 Impalas, most of them coupes, with a handful of convertibles getting the option. This striking example carries the full load of SS equipment, including sintered metallic brake linings. Also part of the package: special body trim, simulated knock-off spinner wheel covers, power steering/brakes, heavy-duty springs/shocks, and 8.00 × 14 whitewalls.

▲ Hottest 348-cid V-8 had 350-bhp with Tri-Power and solid lifters; the four-barrel gave 340 bhp. Both demanded manual shift, but the 305-bhp version could have Powerglide automatic. At mid-year, the 348 was bored and stroked to become the fabled "409," which had 360 bhp with a single four-barrel.

▲This year's Super Sport option was factory installed, but it's likely that some were built by dealers. The SS package was available only on Impalas with the 348 or 409, although the 348 could in fact be ordered on any full-size Chevy. That meant those triple carbs could imbue even a garden-variety Biscayne with enough firepower to surprise anyone who mistakenly thought you had to have SS icing to get 350-horse muscle.

▼ Big Chevys kept their 119-inch wheelbase for '61, but got shorter, narrower bodies. Top Impala was the Sport Coupe. This one has the SS option, T-10 four-speed, and 3.70:1 Positraction axle.

▲ Impala Sport Coupe started at $2704 with V-8, and weighed 3534 pounds. Like all big Chevys, it had new vent openings over the grille, but triple tailights identify Impalas from lesser models.

▲ Bel Air Sport Coupe shared Impala's graceful greenhouse, but was the mid-range model, with Biscayne the low-priced entry. Chevy's base V-8 was a 283, but fuel injection was no longer offered.

▲ Bel Air two-door sedans came only with the more conservative roofline and wraparound rear window. These sedans started at $2491 and were available with all engines except the Impala SS-only 409.

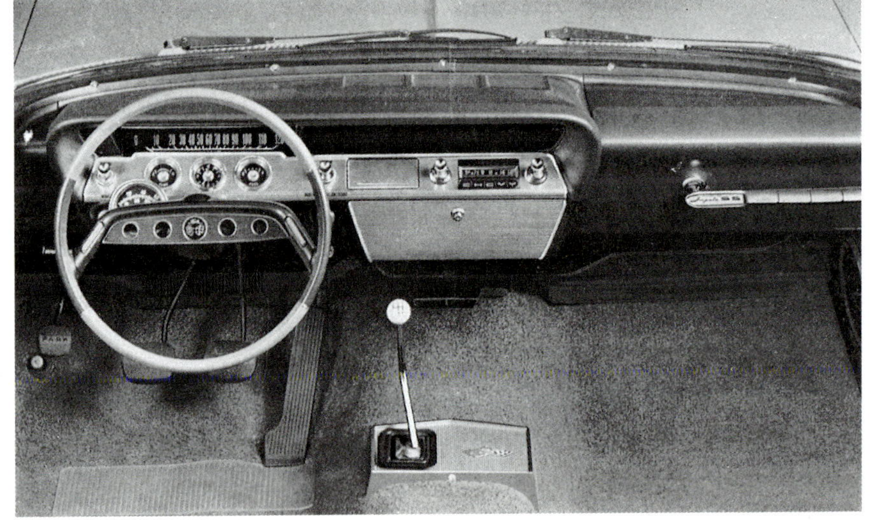

IT FEELS GOOD, LOOKS BETTER and GOES GREAT!

Take any one of Chevy's five '61 Impalas, add either the new 409-cubic-inch V8 or the 348-cubic-inch job and a four-speed floor-mounted stick, wrap the whole thing in special trim that sets it apart from any other car on the street, and man, you have an Impala Super Sport! Every detail of this new Chevrolet package is custom made for young men on the move. This is the kind of car the insiders mean when they say Chevy, the kind that can only be appreciated by a man who understands, wants, and won't settle for less than REAL driving excitement.

Here are the ingredients of the Impala Super Sport kit* • Special Super Sport trim, inside and out • Instrument Panel Pad • Special wheel covers • Power brakes and power steering • Choice of five power teams: 305 hp. with 4-speed Synchro-Mesh or heavy-duty Powerglide. 340 hp. with 4-speed only. 350 hp. with 4-speed only. 360 hp. with 4-speed only • Heavy-duty springs and shocks • Sintered metallic brake linings • 7,000-RPM Tach • 8.00 x 14 narrow band whitewalls • Chevrolet Division of General Motors, Detroit 2, Michigan.

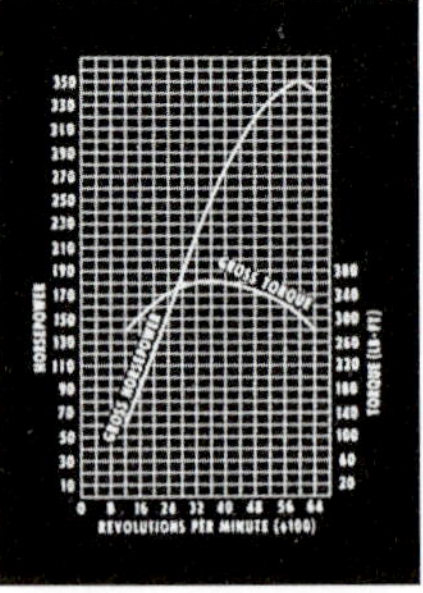

◀ Introduction of the SS kit coincided with the unveiling of the 409, and the tandem made for one of the coolest combinations on wheels. Only 142 409s were installed for '61, but they set the stage for the coming Super Sport mystique. Manufacturing problems kept initial production small, so most early 409s went to racers and road-testers. Belting out 360 bhp at 5800 rpm and a whopping 409 pounds/feet of torque, the hot V-8 could send an Impala to 60 mph in 7.8 seconds and through the quarter-mile in 15.8. Features included a dual-snorkel air cleaner, forged aluminum pistons, wild cam, solid lifters, Carter AFB carb, and 11.25:1 compression.

1961 CHEVROLET HIGH-PERFORMANCE ENGINES

TYPE	CID	BORE × STROKE	BHP @ RPM	TORQUE @ RPM	FUEL SYSTEM	COMP. RATIO	AVAIL.
ohv V-8	283	3.88 × 3.00	230 @ 4800	300 @ 3000	1×4bbl.	9.5:1	full size
ohv V-8	348	4.13 × 3.25	250 @ 4400	355 @ 2800	1×4bbl.	9.5:1	full size
ohv V-8	348	4.13 × 3.25	305 @ 5600	355 @ 3400	1×4bbl.	9.5:1	full size
ohv V-8	348	4.13 × 3.35	340 @ 5800	326 @ 3600	1×4bbl.	11.25:1	full size
ohv V-8	348	4.13 × 3.35	280 @ 4800	355 @ 3200	3×2bbl.	9.5:1	full size
ohv V-8	348	4.13 × 3.35	350 @ 6000	364 @ 3600	3×2bbl.	11.25:1	full size
ohv V-8	409	4.31 × 3.50	360 @ 5800	409 @ 3600	1×4bbl.	11.0:1	full size

▶ Canted quad headlamps led the way for this year's Chryslers, including the 300G. Again powered by the 375-bhp 413-cid V-8, the big sports-luxury coupe ran to 60 mph in 8.2 seconds and needed only 16.2 to finish the quarter-mile. An optional 400 bhp was again offered. Production of the 300 increased to 1617, 337 of them convertibles. Both body styles rode the New Yorker's 126-inch wheelbase.

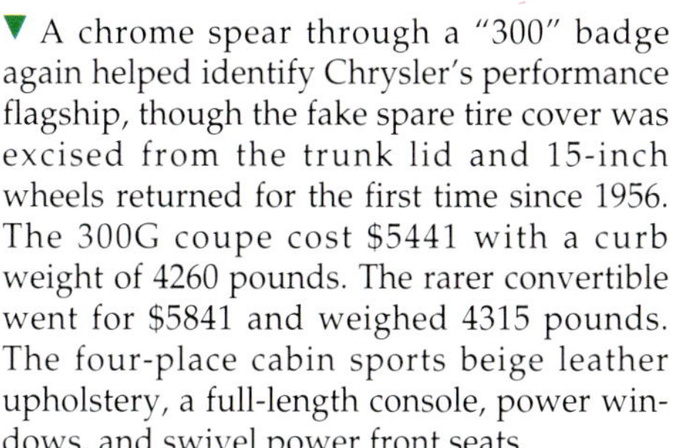

▼ A chrome spear through a "300" badge again helped identify Chrysler's performance flagship, though the fake spare tire cover was excised from the trunk lid and 15-inch wheels returned for the first time since 1956. The 300G coupe cost $5441 with a curb weight of 4260 pounds. The rarer convertible went for $5841 and weighed 4315 pounds. The four-place cabin sports beige leather upholstery, a full-length console, power windows, and swivel power front seats.

1961 CHRYSLER HIGH-PERFORMANCE ENGINES

TYPE	CID	BORE × STROKE	BHP @ RPM	TORQUE @ RPM	FUEL SYSTEM	COMP. RATIO	AVAIL.
ohv V-8	413	4.19 × 3.75	375 @ 5000	495 @ 2800	2 × 4bbl.	10.0:1	300G
ohv V-8	413	4.19 × 3.75	400 @ 5200	465 @ 3600	2 × 4bbl.	10.0:1	300G

▲ The hallowed "300" insignia stood for panache and power. A slightly modified 300G piloted by Gregg Ziegler rocketed through Daytona's flying mile at 143.027 mph. A stock version driven by Bud Faubel hit 90.7 mph in the standing mile.

▶ Dual quads and the signature long-ram induction tubing teamed 375 horses with a stout 495 pounds/feet of torque at just 2800 rpm. A three-speed manual with floor shift replaced the rare four-speed unit, though most buyers specified TorqueFlite automatic.

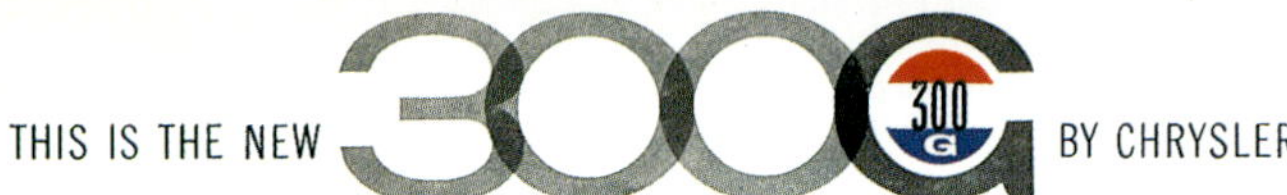

A car that heats up your blood. The 300-G . . . the 1961 version of Chrysler's championship breed of motorcars. A car that can take its well-proportioned heft and go record-breaking at Daytona Beach.* The rare American that's turned out one at a time; a few thousand times a year. You'll find this tiger powered by the latest in Chrysler's brilliantly engineered ram-injection V-8s. With a full 375 horsepower that you manage with incredible ease. Power brakes and steering help. But the real clue to the "G's" handling genius is its superbly balanced suspension. Conveniences are complete. Comfort is served in typical 300 style: four leather-lined, foam-padded bucket seats. This is a total machine. The one that can tour confidently with the best automobiles the world has to offer. The 300-G . . . a rare kind of car for a rare kind of man.

▲ Chrysler touted its 300G as a well-rounded car, able to "tour confidently with the best automobiles the world has to offer." Though, apparently, as "a rare kind of car for a rare kind of man," women drivers need not apply.

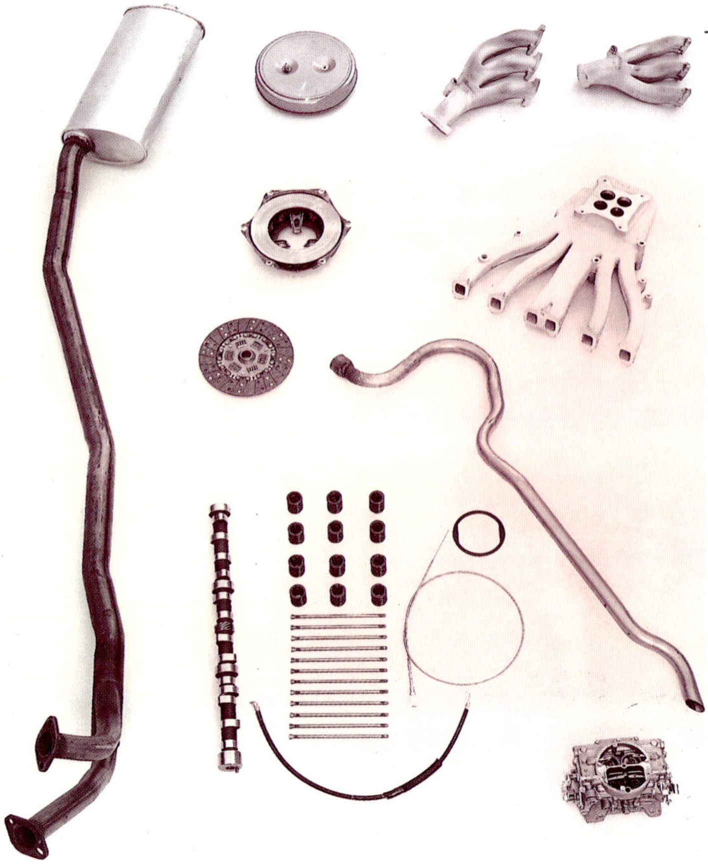

▲ Dodge offered this dealer-installed Hyper-Pak option for the venerable 225-cid "slant six" engine. An aggressive cam, four-barrel carb, long-ram manifold, and tuned headers helped boost horsepower from 145 to 196—nearly one bhp per cubic inch.

▲ Reverse-swept fins and a freshened nose gave the full-size Dodges a new look. Dart (above) road a 118-inch wheelbase and was the make's low-priced entry. Returning was the 325-bhp 383-cid D-500 V-8 option, available with dual-quad ram induction for 330 bhp, or 340 bhp with short-ram tubes. That gave the Dart roughly 10 pounds per horsepower, about the same as a 360-bhp/409 Impala.

▶ *Hot Rod* magazine ran a fully stock two-door Dart with Ram-equipped 383 and TorqueFlite through the quarter-mile in 15.25 seconds, hitting 89.59 mph. Later in the year, Dodges could be ordered with a 413-cid V-8 (right). Breathing through a single four-barrel carb, this Super D-500 engine yielded 350 horsepower. Optional Ram induction boosted it to 375 bhp.

▲ A stock D-500 383 powers this original Vermillion Red Dodge Polara convertible, with bright red deluxe interior. Three-speed TorqueFlite sends its 325 horses to a "Sure-Grip" 3.23:1 limited-slip axle. In addition to the D-500 package, options included power windows, brakes, steering and seats; "Auto Pilot"; "Safe-T-Matic" door locks; "Hi Way Hi-Fi" (a 16 2/3-rpm under-dash record player); "Aero wheel" squared-off steering wheel; bumper guards; spinner wheel covers; "Astrophonic" radio; "Mirromatic" rear-view mirror; and extended rocker-molding trim.

▲ Polara rode a 122-inch-wheelbase and was Dodge's flagship (the Matador model was dropped). Polaras nonetheless looked similar to Darts, and both could be fitted with the D-500 V-8s.

1961 DODGE HIGH-PERFORMANCE ENGINES

TYPE	CID	BORE × STROKE	BHP @ RPM	TORQUE @ RPM	FUEL SYSTEM	COMP. RATIO	AVAIL.
ohv V-8	383	4.25 × 3.75	325 @ 4600	425 @ 2800	1 × 4bbl.	10.0:1	Dart, Polara
ohv V-8	383	4.25 × 3.75	330 @ 4600	460 @ 2800	2 × 4bbl.	10.0:1	Dart, Polara
ohv V-8	383	4.25 × 3.75	340 @ 5000	440 @ 2800	2 × 4bbl.	10.0:1	Dart
ohv V-8	383	4.25 × 3.75	340 @ 5000	440 @ 2800	2 × 4bbl.	10.0:1	Dart
ohv V-8	383	4.25 × 3.75	330 @ 5200	425 @ 3600	1 × 4bbl.	10.0:1	Dart
ohv V-8	413	4.18 × 3.75	350 @ 4600	470 @ 2800	1 × 4bbl.	10.0:1	Dart
ohv V-8	413	4.18 × 3.75	375 @ 5000	465 @ 2800	2 × 4bbl.	10.0:1	Dart
ohv V-8	413	4.18 × 3.75	375 @ 5200	450 @ 2800	1 × 4bbl.	10.0:1	Dart

▲ With a single four-barrel carburetor instead of Ram Induction and with 10.0:1 compression, Dodge's basic 383-cid D-500 cranked out 325 bhp and 425 pounds/feet of torque. It was one of the era's most durable engines, but it didn't help Dodge sales, which slumped more than 25 percent. Dodge styling wasn't popular, competition increased, and sales were sluggish industry-wide. Still, 1961 marked the first time Dodge could take advantage of the 413 V-8, which previously had been installed only in big, heavy Chryslers. The 413 would quickly evolve into a series of Ramcharger powerhouses.

▲ Shorter by nearly four inches overall, and two inches narrower, big Fords sported a handsome facelift with round taillights and modest canted fins. Wheelbase was unchanged at 119 inches. This is the semi-fastback Starliner roof. A bore/stroke boost turned the FE-series 352-cid V-8 into a 390, ranking with Pontiac's 389. Two versions went on sale, at 300 and 375 bhp, plus the 330-bhp Police Special. All Ford V-8s adopted the "Thunderbird" designation.

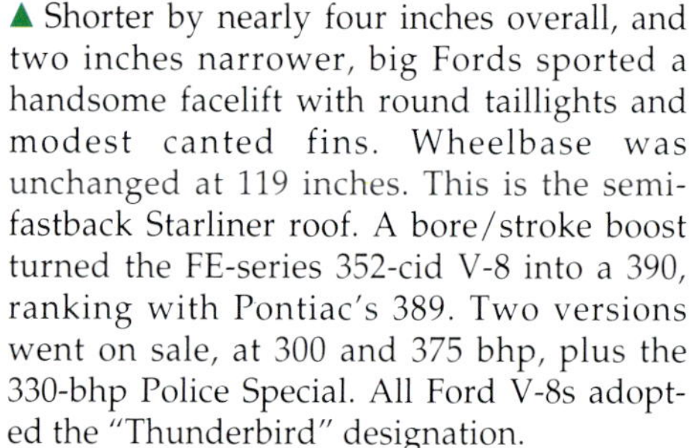

◀ Ford's big gun as the year opened was the "Thunderbird 390 Super," packing a 375-bhp wallop at 6000 rpm and 427 pounds/feet of torque at 3400. Power brakes and steering and air conditioning were unavailable with this engine. Described by *Hot Rod* as a "real charger," the 375-bhp V-8 had 10.6:1 compression, cast iron headers, and a Holley four-barrel. If that didn't satisfy, midyear brought triple Holley two-barrels and higher compression, good for 401 horses at 6000 rpm and 430 pounds/feet of twist. At NHRA Winternationals, Les Ritchey ran a tri-carb Ford to a 13.33-second ET at 105.50 mph.

▲ Full-size traditional-roof two-doors came in Custom 300, Fairlane, Fairlane 500, and Galaxie trim. Galaxie (shown) weighed 3537 pounds and cost $2538; the 390 four-barrel added $197.

▲ Two-tone upholstery added flash to a Sunliner ragtop; the available 390 V-8 could add dash, especially with Ford's first four-speed manual gearbox, a Borg-Warner T-10, added late in '61.

▲ Sunliner convertibles started at $2849, and found 44,614 customers. Less popular was the $2599 Starliner hardtop; with just 29,669 built, it would be dropped after this model year.

▲ Legendary stock-car racer Fred Lorenzen piloted Holman-Moody Fords to three Grand National wins in '61, driving both the ragtop and the Starliner. Ford took seven NASCAR victories that season.

▲ This Dynamic 88 Holiday hardtop coupe shows the crisp lines that freshened Oldsmobile's full-size roster. It started at $2956, weighed 3981 pounds, and was Olds' best-selling hardtop. The Super 88 line spawned a Starfire convertible at midyear. It was priced at $4647 and weighed 4330 pounds.

1961 OLDSMOBILE HIGH-PERFORMANCE ENGINES

TYPE	CID	BORE × STROKE	BHP @ RPM	TORQUE @ RPM	FUEL SYSTEM	COMP. RATIO	AVAIL.
ohv V-8	394	4.13 × 3.69	250 @ 4400	405 @ 2400	1 X 2bbl.	8.75:1	Super 88
ohv V-8	394	4.13 × 3.69	325 @ 4600	435 @ 2800	1 × 4bbl.	10.0:1	1
ohv V-8	394	4.13 × 3.69	330 @ 4600	440 @ 2800	1 × 4bbl.	10.25:1	Starfire

1. 88, Super 88, 98.

1961 FORD HIGH-PERFORMANCE ENGINES

TYPE	CID	BORE × STROKE	BHP @ RPM	TORQUE @ RPM	FUEL SYSTEM	COMP. RATIO	AVAIL.
ohv V-8	352	4.00 × 3.50	220 @ 4400	336 @ 2400	1 X 2bbl.	8.9:1	full size
ohv V-8	390	4.05 × 3.78	300 @ 4600	427 @ 2800	1 X 4bbl.	9.6:1	full size
ohv V-8	390	4.05 × 3.78	375 @ 6000	427 @ 3200	1 X 4bbl.	10.6:1	full size
ohv V-8	390	4.05 × 3.78	401 @ 6000	430 @ 3500	3 X 2bbl.	10.6:1	full size

▲ All big Oldsmobiles used 394-cid V-8s. Standard on the Dynamic 88 was a 250-bhp unit. Standard on the Super 88 and on the Ninety-Eight, and optional on the Dynamic 88, was a 325-bhp version. The Starfire boasted a special 330-bhp variant and about 7600 of the sporty convertibles were built. For '62, the Starfire model would become a separate series with both a ragtop and a hardtop. They were Oldsmobile's most expensive cars.

▶ "Fins vanish, fangs remain," was *Motor Life*'s take on Plymouth's reskinned Fury. A 330-bhp 383-cid Fury two-door hardtop turned a respectable 0-60-mph time of 7.4 seconds, with 15.1 in the quarter-mile. Even with the tamer 305-bhp "Golden Commando" 361-cid mill, a Fury could hit 60 in 9.3 seconds.

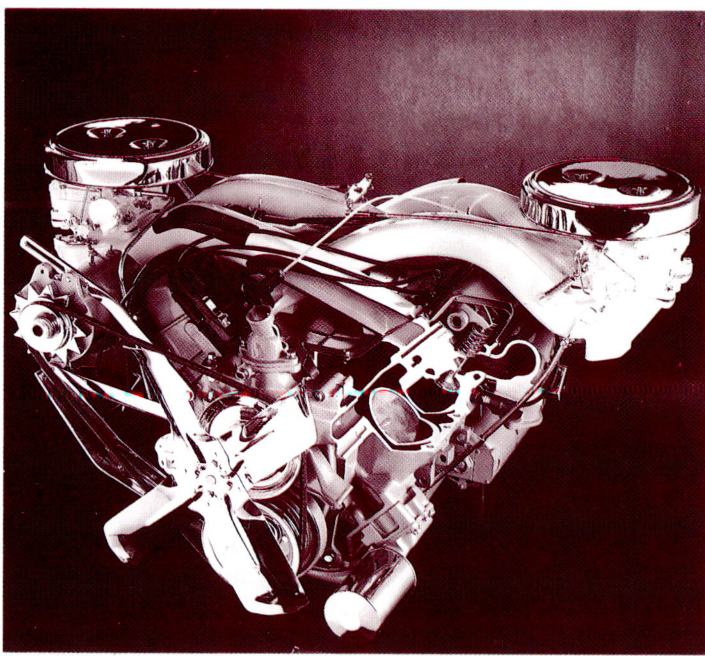

▲ The 383 had 325 bhp with a single four-barrel, 330 with long-tube ram induction, and 340 with a short-ram. But Ford now had 390 cid and Chevrolet added a 409, so Plymouth answered with the 350-bhp 413 at midyear.

1961 PLYMOUTH HIGH-PERFORMANCE ENGINES

TYPE	CID	BORE × STROKE	BHP @ RPM	TORQUE @ RPM	FUEL SYSTEM	COMP. RATIO	AVAIL.
ohv V-8	361	4.12 × 3.38	305 @ 4800	395 @ 3000	1 × 4bbl.	9.0:1	full size
ohv V-8	383	4.24 × 3.38	330 @ 4800	460 @ 2800	2 × 4bbl.	10.0:1	full size
ohv V-8	383	4.24 × 3.38	340 @ 5000	440 @ 2800	1 × 4bbl.	10.0:1	full size
ohv V-8	383	4.24 × 3.38	330 @ 5200	425 @ 3600	2 × 4bbl.	10.0:1	full size
ohv V-8	413	4.18 × 3.75	350 @ 4600	470 @ 2800	1 × 4bbl.	10.0:1	Fury
ohv V-8	413	4.18 × 3.75	375 @ 5000	465 @ 2800	2 × 4bbl.	10.0:1	Fury
ohv V-8	413	4.18 × 3.75	375 @ 5200	450 @ 2800	1 × 4bbl.	10.0:1	Fury

This Tri-Power Pontiac packs one horse for every 10½ pounds

Figure it out for yourself: a Catalina Sports Coupe at 3680 lbs., powered by the 348 H.P. Trophy V-8 = 1 H.P. per 10.57 lbs. Even most sports cars wish they could match it!

We trimmed off every bit of excess weight. There's less weight over-all and more of it is sprung between the wheels for a lot better balance.

Make no mistake: This is a big car—nearly 4000 pounds worth of solid road machinery, give or take a few depending on model and equipment. But the pay-off is how Pontiac moves its weight.

The 348 H.P. Trophy V-8 puts out one horse for every 10½ pounds. And other Pontiac V-8's (11 in all to choose from) have power-to-weight advantages that come close to matching it.

Stack Wide-Track up against all the others and you'll see no other car packs or pulls its weight so well. Test for yourself at your Pontiac dealer's.

PONTIAC MOTOR DIVISION OF GENERAL MOTORS CORPORATION

MOTOR TREND/APRIL 1961 87

▲ Pontiac returned to the split grille for '61, but it was on a revamped line of full-size models. Wheelbases shrunk, and restyled bodies lost four inches of length, two-and-a half inches of width, and one inch of height, yet taller roofs and lower floors actually made interiors larger. Ads like this helped enthusiasts zero in on one welcome effect of such downsizing: Performance. It touted the 389-cid, 348-bhp Tri-Power Trophy V-8 in a 3680-pound Catalina Sports Coupe and calculated that it was good for one horsepower per 10.5 pounds. "Even most sports cars wish they could match it!" bragged Pontiac.

▲ Ponchos were racetrack regulars in '62. Above, two '61s storm out of the hole at the NHRA Winternationals, where Lloyd Cox took Super Super/Stock Automatic with a 13-second ET at 107.78 mph. And on the NASCAR circuit, Pontiacs won a record 30 of 52 Grand National races, including Marvin Panch's Daytona 500 crown.

1961 PONTIAC HIGH-PERFORMANCE ENGINES

TYPE	CID	BORE × STROKE	BHP @ RPM	TORQUE @ RPM	FUEL SYSTEM	COMP. RATIO	AVAIL.
ohv V-8	389	4.06 × 3.75	235 @ 3600	402 @ 2000	1 × 4bbl.	8.6:1	1
ohv V-8	389	4.06 × 3.75	267 @ 4200	405 @ 2400	1 × 2bbl.	10.25:1	2
ohv V-8	389	4.06 × 3.75	283 @ 4400	413 @ 2800	1 × 2bbl.	10.25:1	3
ohv V-8	389	4.06 × 3.75	303 @ 4600	425 @ 2800	1 × 4bbl.	10.25:1	4
ohv V-8	389	4.06 × 3.75	287 @ 4400	416 @ 2400	1 × 4bbl.	10.25:1	2
ohv V-8	389	4.06 × 3.75	318 @ 4600	430 @ 3200	3 × 2bbl.	10.75:1	full size
ohv V-8	389	4.06 × 3.75	333 @ 4800	425 @ 2800	1 × 4bbl.	10.75:1	full size
ohv V-8	389	4.06 × 3.75	348 @ 4800	430 @ 3200	3 × 2bbl.	10.75:1	full size
ohv V-8	421	4.09 × 4.00	405 @ 5600	425 @ 4400	2 × 4bbl.	11.0:1	5

1. Bonneville. 2. Catalina, Ventura. 3. Star Chief. 4. Bonneville, Bonneville Safari. 5. Catalina cpe.

► Pontiac performance at the start of '61 meant the Tri-Power 389-cid V-8, which made up to 348 bhp from the factory, or 363 with a dealer-installed Super-Duty package. This Tri-Power 389 has aftermarket coil and plug wires, along with some non-stock chrome.

▼ Pontiac prepared a handful of lightweight drag Catalinas with aluminum front sheetmetal and drilled-out "Swiss-cheese" frames. This example also has the rare eight-lug aluminum wheels. Late in '61, Pontiac unleashed the Super Duty 421-cid V-8, rated at 405 bhp with dual quads.

▲ Teaming with ever-stronger engines was the weight-losing cutback in size. Bodies were trimmer on wheelbases that shrank from 123 inches to 119 on Catalina and Ventura (shown) and from 124 to 123 on Star Chief and Bonneville. This is a Sport Coupe.

▲ Bucket seats were part of Pontiac's new youthful image—an image fueling a sales upturn. Ventura models blended Bonneville luxury with Catalina svelteness.

▲ A Borg-Warner four-speed manual was now a production Pontiac item, having previously been a special-order factory option. Three-speed Hydra-Matic and beefed-up Super Hydra-Matic were the available automatics. Performance didn't have to be accompanied by austerity, as the interior of this well-equipped, air-conditioned Ventura demonstrates.

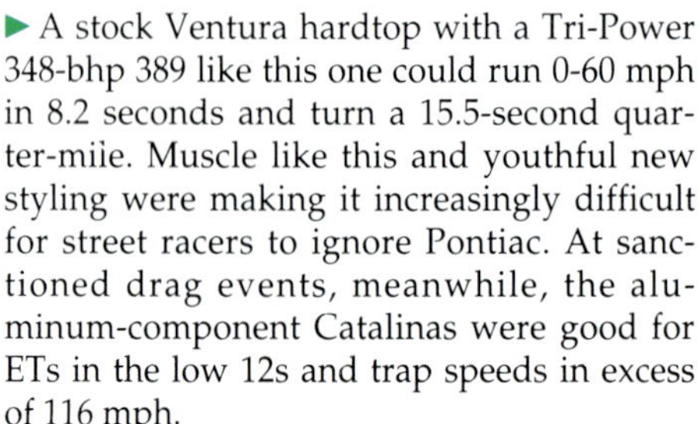

► A stock Ventura hardtop with a Tri-Power 348-bhp 389 like this one could run 0-60 mph in 8.2 seconds and turn a 15.5-second quarter-miie. Muscle like this and youthful new styling were making it increasingly difficult for street racers to ignore Pontiac. At sanctioned drag events, meanwhile, the aluminum-component Catalinas were good for ETs in the low 12s and trap speeds in excess of 116 mph.

1962

Performance gets the nod in this watershed year, as Big Three automakers pass the 400-cid mark • Beach Boys belt out their ode to Chevy's "real fine" 409, now able to crank out 409 bhp—the mystical 1 hp per cubic inch • New 327-cid V-8 replaces the venerable Chevrolet 348 mill • Chrysler markets low-bucks 300 as well as another "letter-series" • Downsized Dodges are treated to hopped-up Ram-Charger 413 engine—ready to terrorize dragstrips • Plymouth gets its own version of 413, known as Super/Stock • 406-cid V-8 lurks under Ford hoods—up to 405 horses on tap • Ford drops slippery Starliner; sells only square-cut models • Glamorous Ford 500XL hardtop and ragtop get midyear debut, a sales generator pioneered by Lee Iacocca • Mid-size Ford Fairlane bows, but muscular editions will come later • Oldsmobile introduces turbocharged F-85 Jetfire with fluid injection; performance fails to excite • Pontiacs earn 22 NASCAR victories out of 53 starts; Fireball Roberts wins Daytona 500 in one • Pontiac Grand Prix debuts

ac·cel′er·a′tor One who or that which accelerates; specif.: **a** On automobiles, a foot-operated throttle. **b** (*pron.* ak-sel′er-a′ter; *L.* ak-sel′er-a′tor) *Anat.* Any muscle or nerve that hastens a motion. **c** *Chem.* A substance that hastens a reaction. **d** *Physics.* Any device used to impart high speeds to charged particles. (Webster's New Collegiate Dictionary) CHEVROLET All the above is true, as far as it goes. What it doesn't say is that an Impala Super Sport has even more going for it than performance. It's a swinging car in every way. Bucket seats, special interior, distinctive exterior trim, all part of the Super Sport kit, optional at extra cost on Impala Sport Coupes and Convertibles, and it proclaims to the world that this machine doesn't take a back seat to anybody. To understand, you'll just have to try an Impala Super Sport, that is, step on that accelerator. You'll be impressed, or our name isn't

Chevrolet Division of General Motors, Detroit 2, Michigan. CHEVROLET IMPALA

MOTOR TREND/APRIL 1962 19

▲ Simple and understated, this ad went right to the heart of the matter. And greater availability of Chevy's 409-cid V-8 lent credence to the claim. In '61, only 142 cars got the 409. In '62, it went onto 15,019 Chevys.

1962 CHEVROLET HIGH-PERFORMANCE ENGINES

TYPE	CID	BORE × STROKE	BHP @ RPM	TORQUE @ RPM	FUEL SYSTEM	COMP. RATIO	AVAIL.
ohv V-8	327	4.00 × 3.25	250 @ 4400	350 @ 2800	1 × 4bbl.	10.5:1	full size
ohv V-8	327	4.00 × 3.25	300 @ 5000	360 @ 3200	1 × 4bbl.	10.5:1	full size
ohv V-8	409	4.31 × 3.50	380 @ 5800	420 @ 3200	1 × 4bbl.	11.0:1	full size
ohv V-8	409	4.31 × 3.50	409 @ 6000	420 @ 4000	2 × 4bbl.	11.0:1	full size

▲ Lighter in weight and $100 cheaper than an Impala, Chevrolet's Bel Air sport coupe was the "sleeper" choice among 409 buyers, many of whom ordered the optional 7000-rpm tach, which showed a 6200-rpm redline. The base single-quad 409 had 380 bhp. With twin Carter AFB four-barrels and a wild cam, the 409 developed a rated 409 horsepower at 6000 rpm, and 420 lbs/ft of torque at 4000, on 11:1 compression.

▲ Sing along: "She always turns in the fastest time. My four speed, dual quads, positraction 409. Giddy up, giddy up, giddy up 409...."

▲At the 1962 NHRA Winternationals, "Dyno Don" Nicholson won the Stock Eliminator title for the second straight year behind the wheel of a super-tuned 409.

▲Hayden Proffitt drove this four-speed Bel Air 409 to Stock Eliminator honors at the '62 U.S. Nationals. His winning ET was 12.83 seconds at 113.92 mph.

▲Asking for a 409 added $428 to the price of any full-size Chevrolet; $60 more bought this dual-quad edition. A four-speed cost $188 extra.

▲*Motor Trend* ran a Chevy hardtop with the 409-bhp 409 to 60 mph in 6.3 seconds and recorded a 14.9-second quarter-mile at 98 mph.

▼The Impala's formal hardtop roof mimicked a top-up convertible, but serious racers preferred the Bel Air's slantback profile. Black-wall tires and taxi-cab-grade hubcaps only enhanced the no-frills, no-nonsense image. The 409 was the first engine of the muscle age to acquire an identity all its own.

▲The only Impala two-doors for '62 were the convertible and this Sport Hardtop. Crossed flags above a 409 label identified the Impala as a machine to be reckoned with. And Super Sport versions were recognized by "spinner" wheelcovers, "SS" emblems, and anodized aluminum bodyside moldings.

▲On the Impala, bucket seats were a $102 option and were often ordered along with the Super Sport package. The SS package itself was a $54 option for Sport Coupes or convertibles and again included a center console and passenger grip bar. A tachometer was another factory option and mounted to the steering column.

▲Pick a 409 back in '62 and you had to take manual shift. Four-speed units were quickly becoming the racers' choice, although a three-speed gearbox was now available, too. After limited exposure in cars intended for sanctioned drag racing and for press-review, the Turbo-Fire 409 V-8 became a regular-production option for '62. Compared to the seldom-seen '61 edition, it had a stronger block and tougher cast alloy heads, plus revised pistons.

◀*Car and Driver* ran a 380-bhp 409 to 60 mph in 7.3 seconds and finished the quarter-mile in 14.9 at 94 mph. Late in the model year, Chevy built a limited run of lightweight 409 specials with aluminum front-end parts that shaved 130 pounds from the nose. Aluminum body panels could also be bought over the counter at Chevrolet dealerships.

▲ Attention-seekers couldn't ask for much more in '62 than an Impala SS 409 convertible. With a V-8, the ragtop started at $3026 and tipped the scales at 3560 pounds. Turbo-Fire 409s got the raves, but the Super Sport package actually was available with any Impala engine—even a puny six. Many buyers ordered the new 327-cid V-8, which replaced the 348. The 327 came in 250- or 300-bhp tune. It was more flexible than the 409 at low speeds, had excellent mid-range punch, and was more refined on the highway. And of course, it cost less and used less gas.

► "Dyno Don" Nicholson took this 409 Impala Sport Coupe to the B/FX class title at the '62 U.S. NHRA Nationals. Nicholson ran a 12.93-second quarter-mile at 113.63 mph. Bel Airs snared Super/Stock and stock eliminator honors at the Nationals, and a Bel Air was the S/S champ at the Winternationals. Meanwhile, in the stock-car-racing wars, the 409 powered Chevrolets to 14 NASCAR victories, most of them short-track events.

▲ The Chevy II compact bowed for '62, with four- and six-cylinder power. It wasn't long before hot rodders stuffed in 327s. Dick Rutherford ran this one with a fuel-injected 327 Corvette engine in A/FX (factory experimental) competition at the '62 Winternationals. Another 360-bhp conversion, by Bill Thomas, recorded a 0-60 mph time of 5.2 seconds.

▲ Chrysler's 300H coupe and ragtop again came with the 413 cid V-8, now at 380 bhp in standard tune. But "letter-series" fans hissed when Chryslers applied the 300 label—without the H—to a series that included a four-door hardtop and standard 383 cid V-8. The 300 cost $1700 less than the "H," and both could get the 413, so only 558 300Hs were ordered.

1962 CHRYSLER HIGH-PERFORMANCE ENGINES

TYPE	CID	BORE × STROKE	BHP @ RPM	TORQUE @ RPM	FUEL SYSTEM	COMP. RATIO	AVAIL.
ohv V-8	413	4.19 × 3.75	380@ 5200	450@ 3600	2 × 4bbl.	10.0:1	full size
ohv V-8	413	4.19 × 3.75	405@ 5400	373@ 3600	2 × 4bbl.	10.0:1	300H

◀ When "factory" street/strip goodies didn't pass muster, aftermarket firms were eager to fill the gap. Ed Iskenderian of Inglewood, California, earned a name for his roller cam kits. Young racers pored through each new "Isky" catalog, which featured tuning tips from the pros. And decals like this showed up on the back window of many a muscle car.

▲ Full-size Chryslers were becoming rare at the track, but Gary Nichols drove this one in the top-stack automatic class at the '62 Winternationals. A street 300H, with its 380 bhp, could hit 60 in 7.7 seconds and do the quarter in 16. The dual-quad 413 V-8 also was available in 405-bhp form.

▼ A chop in wheelbase from 118 inches to 116 and downsized sheetmetal shrunk the standard-size Dodge Polara (shown) and Dart to mid-size dimensions. Mainstream customers found this as controversial as the rather odd new styling. But racers liked the weight loss—and the revitalized 413-cid V-8.

▲ A watershed engine for Mopar—the Max Wedge 413. The 413-cid V-8 dated from 1959, but only this one was bred to go racing. It was rated at 410 bhp.

▲ Apart from tall floor shift and bucket seats, little inside this Polara's cabin suggests the thrills that await a tromp on the gas pedal.

▲ Chrysler chief designer Virgil Exner's styling was as flamboyant from the rear as the front. But this was the only view some got of a Max Wedge Polara.

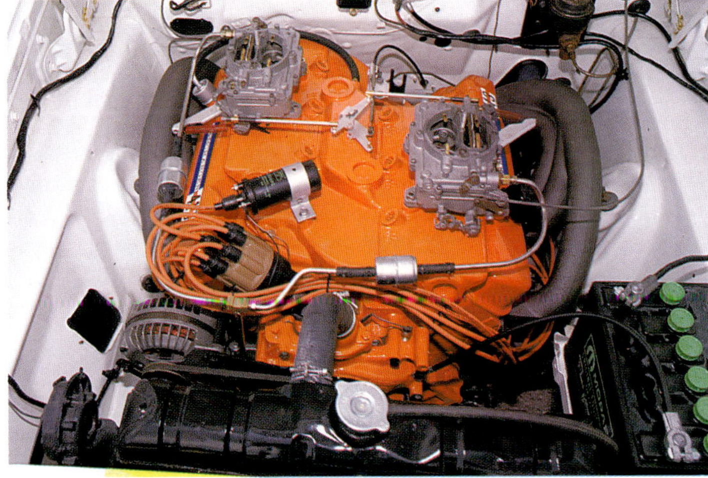

▲ Dodge tagged its hot 413 the Ram-Charger. It cost $374.40 more than a Dart with the 230-bhp 318-cid V-8. With dual 650cfm Carter four-barrels, solid lifters, aluminum pistons, and an 11.0:1 compression, the 413 cranked out 410 bhp. Special pistons gave 415 or 420 bhp (depending on the source).

▲ Dart was the cheapest "big" Dodge and was 200-pounds lighter than a Chevrolet Bel Air. A stock stripper Dart two-door sedan like this one with the 410-bhp 413 pulled only 8.4 pounds per horsepower, making possible its quick 5.8-second 0-60 mph time and 14.4-second quarter-mile ET.

▲ All 413s had wedge-shaped combustion chambers, but the Ram-Charger 413 was designed for "maximum" performance, hence, the unofficial "Max Wedge" title. Chrysler intended it for "sanctioned acceleration trials," not for the street; but more than a few Darts conducted "trials" away from the strip.

◀ Ram-Charger 413s set four NHRA class records in '62, including Dick Landy's 12.7-second ET with a three-speed manual, and Bill Golden's 12.5 with automatic. Ads claimed a Ram Dart "has about the best power-weight ratio ever offered on a production car."

▲ Bodyside "fins," "turbine" taillamps—love 'em or hate 'em. But there was no debate that this was, as its maker claimed, "The lean new breed of Dodge!" Wheelbase was a half-inch shorter than Ford's new intermediate Fairlane. "More live action because there's less dead weight," said Dodge.

▲ A three-speed manual floor-shift was standard, but this Dart has the optional TorqueFlite automatic. It was controlled by dashboard buttons, as on other Dodges, but was fortified for high-upshift abuse. A 3.91:1 axle was standard, but ratios from 2.93:1 to 4.89:1 could be ordered.

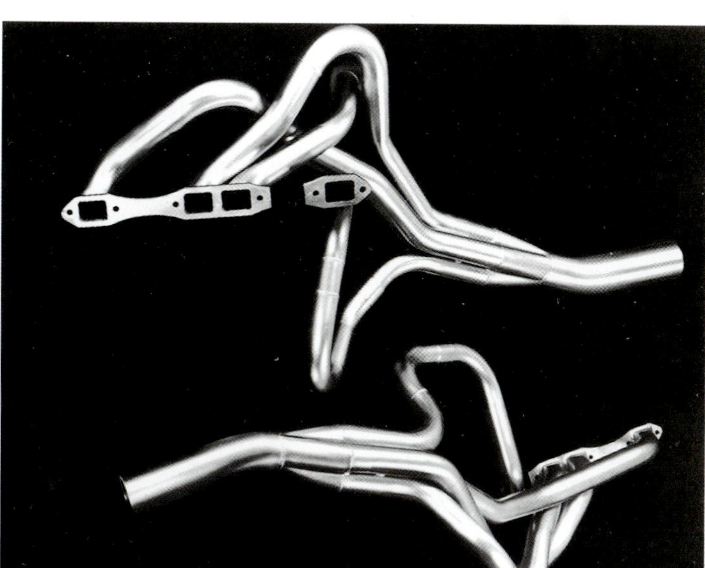

▲ Aftermarket exhaust headers such as these were a popular addition to further increase power. Evident are the extreme contortions necessary to keep tubing length equal for all eight cylinders and to fit the headers within the 413 Dodge's tight engine bay. The factory headers had a unique "ram's horn" shape to overcome space limitations.

1962 DODGE HIGH-PERFORMANCE ENGINES

TYPE	CID	BORE × STROKE	BHP @ RPM	TORQUE @ RPM	FUEL SYSTEM	COMP. RATIO	AVAIL.
ohv V-8	361	4.12 × 3.38	305 @ 4800	395 @ 3000	1×4bbl.	9.0:1	full size
ohv V-8	361	4.12 × 3.38	310 @ 5200	390 @ 3400	2×4bbl.	10.0:1	full size
ohv V-8	383	4.25 × 3.75	330 @ 4600	425 @ 2800	1×4bbl.	10.0:1	full size
ohv V-8	383	4.25 × 3.75	335 @ 5000	420 @ 3600	2×4bbl.	10.0:1	full size
ohv V-8	413	4.18 × 3.75	365 @ 4600	460 @ 2800	1×4bbl.	11.0:1	full size
ohv V-8	413	4.18 × 3.75	380 @ 5200	455 @ 3600	2×4bbl.	11.0:1	full size
ohv V-8	413	4.18 × 3.75	410 @ 5200	460 @ 4400	2×4bbl.	11.0:1	full size

▲ Ford answered Chevy's 409 and Chrysler's Max Wedge 413 with its first 400-plus-cid V-8. Delivered part-way through the '62 model year, it was basically a Ford 390-cid V-8 bored out to 406 cid. It had a .080-inch larger bore (now 4.13), but retained the 390's 3.78-inch stroke. Called the Thunderbird 406 High-Performance V-8, but available only in the new facelifted Galaxie, it signaled a fresh performance push for the blue-oval brigade.

1962 FORD HIGH-PERFORMANCE ENGINES

TYPE	CID	BORE × STROKE	BHP @ RPM	TORQUE @ RPM	FUEL SYSTEM	COMP. RATIO	AVAIL.
ohv V-8	390	4.05×3.78	300 @ 4600	427 @ 2800	1×4bbl.	9.6:1	full size
ohv V-8	406	4.13×3.78	385 @ 5800	440 @ 3800	1×4bbl.	11.4:1	full size
ohv V-8	406	4.13×3.78	405 @ 5800	448 @ 3500	3×2bbl.	11.4:1	full size

▲ Gold-colored "406" bird emblems on front fenders marked the hottest Fords; 390s used silver. The complete 406 package cost $379.70, and required not only the four-speed manual gearbox but either 6.70 or 7.10×15 tires (replacing the standard 14-inch rubber). Also included were heavy-duty shock absorbers and springs, fade-resistant drum brakes, a larger fuel line, heavier clutch, stabilizer bar, and high-capacity radiator.

▶ Breathing through a single Holley four barrel carb (shown), the 406 was rated at 385 bhp. As the Super High Performance Tri-Power, it wore three Holley two barrels and was rated at 405 horses and 448 pounds/feet of torque. Both versions had an 11.4:1 compression ratio, and cast-iron headers that fed into low-restriction dual exhausts. *Motor Trend* did 0-60 in 7.1 seconds with a 406 Galaxie sedan, lending weight to Ford's '62 sales theme: the "Lively" ones.

▲ Ford Division General Manager Lee Iacocca pioneered the concept of introducing new car models in the spring, instead of the more traditional fall product launch. In mid-'62 he unveiled the Galaxie 500XL Victoria hardtop coupe and 500XL Sunliner convertible. This Sunliner, with its optional stainless steel fender skirts, was among 13,108 XL convertibles built for '62.

▲ Ford's 406 has "something like Ferrari performance at a fifth of the price," said *Motor Trend*. This is the tri-carb 405-bhp edition.

▲ In addition to bucket seats and a console, Ford's 500XL could be ordered with a Borg-Warner four-speed manual and optional 8000-rpm tach.

▼ Galaxies wore round taillamps above semi-circular bumper cutouts. "Powered by one of the optional Thunderbird 406 High-Performance V-8s," said the sales brochure, a "Sunliner moves with a nimbleness and flight-like quality rivaled by only one other...the Thunderbird itself!"

SLEEPER!

To the old carnival guessing game of "Which shell is the pea under?" you can add another—"Which Galaxie is hiding the new six-barrel?"

You can get a very precise answer, it's true, when one of these sleepers suddenly goes "zzz-z-z-ZOW!" and vanishes. But that leaves you sitting foolishly in the middle of a lot of empty landscape.

Better to know beforehand. But how? You'd think 405 horsepower, header exhausts, six-barrel carbs, 406 cubic inches and 11.4 compression couldn't be hidden. But Ford's V-8 magicians have brewed up a real street machine—no wild 2000 r.p.m. idle, no dragster noises, no battle to fire it up. Girls drive these things down to the supermarket and never suspect they are a half-throttle away from escape velocity.

Of course, you do get a clue watching one straighten out a corner. They handle! Because this engine (and the 4-barrel version) come only as a package with Heavy Duty shocks, springs, driveshaft, U-joints, brakes—plus 15-inch wheels and nylon tires. That's what makes the tab of $379.70 so fantastic—and why there are so many Galaxie sleepers around to embarrass you. But why be dominated? Get your own 406 and you won't need to guess which Galaxie has the six-barrel.*

A PRODUCT OF Ford MOTOR COMPANY

*Manufacturer's suggested list price for extra equipment

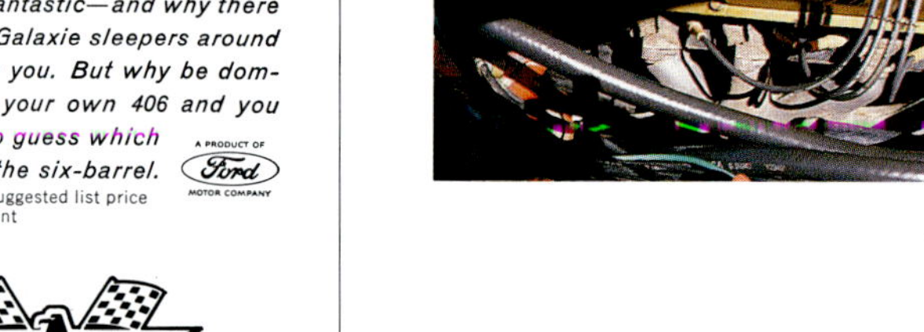

406

FORD V-8

MOTOR TREND/APRIL 1962 11

◀ Ford's copywriters played it both ways. The "six-barrel" 406-equipped Galaxie was actually a tame beast that bared its fangs only on demand. After all, Ford wanted to sell cars to "girls" and grandmas, too, not just dragstrip dudes. Sleepers they may have been, but 406 Galaxies still were too heavy to outgun the lighter 413 Dodges and Plymouths and the new Pontiacs. Ford did shave 164 pounds by offering aluminum bumpers and fiberglass body panels, but in quantities too small to rank as "production." So the NHRA put those cars into experimental classes, where the going was very tough.

▼ The oval air cleaner marks this 406 as the tri-carb sizzler. *Hot Rod* ran a 385-bhp version to 60 mph in 7.1 seconds, turning the quarter-mile in 15.3 at 93 mph. *Motor Trend* responded with a 6.5-second 0-60 time in a 405-bhp 406, but its quarter-mile was a 15.6 at 92. Early 406s were fragile, but heavier main webs and four-bolt caps remedied that as Ford's high-performance department, guided by NASCAR experience, began to get it in gear.

▼ All Galaxies wore a single wide bodyside molding, but lesser models lacked the XL's extra trim and bucket seats. Only the initiated knew at a glance that this plain-vanilla hardtop carried a 406—and in knockout-punch 405-bhp tune, to boot. Axle ratios as low as 4.11:1 could replace the standard 3.50:1 cog.

▲ Dick Heyler is pictured in his Cruise-O-Matic 406 Galaxie running in SS/SA at the '62 Winternationals. His sponsor, Ford dealer Ben Alexander, had costarred with Jack Webb in the '50s TV version of *Dragnet*.

▲ At 430 bhp in NASCAR tune, the 406 was still shy of the 465-bhp, 421-cid Pontiacs, and Ford stock-car wins, so important for publicity, were rare. NASCAR thwarted an effort to fit convertible Galaxies with aerodynamic "fastback" rooflines. So Ford enlarged the 406 to 483 cid and tested it for 500 miles on the Bonneville Salt Flats. It averaged 164 mph and saw 182 mph. But NASCAR never allowed the 483.

▲ Galaxies had nicely appointed interiors, and this one has the optional Ford air conditioning, as well as the extra-cost column-mounted tachometer kit. Since it's a 406, Ford's Borg-Warner T-10 four-speed (now a factory installation) was mandatory. Cruise-O-Matic three-speed automatic was okay with other engines.

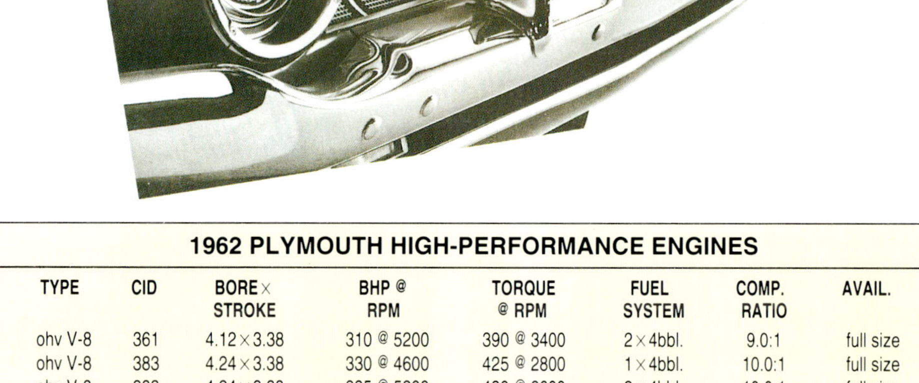

◄ Plymouth revived a name from 1959 for its new top-line '62s. Unlike lesser models, which came with a Slant Six, Sport Fury carried a standard 305-bhp 361 "Golden Commando" V-8, with options including a pair of 383s and the mighty 413. Interiors featured smart, two-tone vinyl buckets and center console. The coupe started at $2851, the convertible at $3082.

1962 PLYMOUTH HIGH-PERFORMANCE ENGINES

TYPE	CID	BORE × STROKE	BHP @ RPM	TORQUE @ RPM	FUEL SYSTEM	COMP. RATIO	AVAIL.
ohv V-8	361	4.12×3.38	310 @ 5200	390 @ 3400	2×4bbl.	9.0:1	full size
ohv V-8	383	4.24×3.38	330 @ 4600	425 @ 2800	1×4bbl.	10.0:1	full size
ohv V-8	383	4.24×3.38	335 @ 5200	420 @ 3600	2×4bbl.	10.0:1	full size
ohv V-8	413	4.18×3.75	365 @ 4600	460 @ 2800	1×4bbl.	11.0:1	Fury
ohv V-8	413	4.18×3.75	380 @ 5200	455 @ 3600	2×4bbl.	11.0:1	Sport Fury
ohv V-8	413	4.18×3.75	410 @ 5200	460 @ 5500	2×4bbl.	11.0:1	Sport Fury

▼ Full-size Plymouths were seven inches shorter this year, and up to 400 pounds lighter. Combine that with Mopar's newly fortified 400-bhp-plus 413-cid V-8, and Plymouth was now in the muscle big leagues. Plymouth called its version of this engine the Super Stock 413, and though relatively few were built, many of those that were went into bare-bones two-door sedans like this Belvedere. No stripes. No badges. Just thunder waiting to happen. It's a classic example of the unassuming look preferred by serious street racers. A 335-bhp 383-cid V-8 also was offered.

▼ Like Dodge, Plymouth downsized for '62, cutting the wheelbase of the Savoy, Belvedere, and Fury by two inches, to 116, and shedding pounds in the process. The Sport Fury coupe and convertible were midyear additions.

◀ Drag racing can be a family sport, as this 1962 portrait of a happy—and winning—Ohio clan proves. Only a few years earlier, Plymouth victories in such volume would have been unheard of. But Mopar was coming on strong, and 413 Plymouths were shattering NHRA Super Stock/Automatic records. Interestingly, Plymouth opened the '62 model year with the 305-bhp 361 V-8 as its top engine. Then, to remain competitive on the strip, it issued a batch of lightweight "Super/Stock" specials with the short-ram 413. Output was rated at 410 bhp, but really ran closer to 500 bhp. Super/Stock was the class in which they raced. At the time, the NHRA classified cars based on pounds per advertised horsepower. Chrysler's push-button TorqueFlite automatic was the hot choice behind the 413; the three-speed manual was actually slightly slower in the quarter and a four-speed wasn't offered.

▲ A lightweight Savoy two-door with the limited-production Super/Stock 413 V-8 made for a tough-to-beat combination on street or strip. At around 3200 pounds the Savoy weighed even less than its Dodge Dart cousin, and could be lightened further by being ordered without heater, radio, and sound deadening.

▶ Not an uncommon view to those who squared off against a Super/Stock 413 Savoy. Though they were available in the flashy Sport Fury, most of the beefed-up 410-bhp motors went into stripper two-doors aimed at the dragstrip. Owners took to calling these hot Dodge/Plymouth engines "Max Wedge," but Chrysler never used that designation.

▲ In a Savoy, both the grocery-getter and the go-getter shared the simplest of instruments and controls—though a tap on the gas would quickly make clear if there were a slant-six or a 413 beneath the hood. Racers rejoiced, but customers shunned this year's downsized models, and Plymouth sunk to No. 8 in sales.

▲ Plymouth's "RB-Block" 413 was known as the "Ram-Charger" over at Dodge. Both had a 4.19-inch bore and 3.75-inch stroke, with solid lifters and dual valve springs to halt valve float past 6000 rpm. Rods were magnafluxed, and short-ram intake manifolds carried twin 659cfm Carter AFB four-barrels. Cast-iron headers were routed upward to fit into the tight engine bay.

▲ Plymouth power and light weight paid off in a historic quarter-mile run by Tom Grove in July 1962. Grove drove his Super Stock Belvedere to an ET of 11.93 seconds at 118.57 mph. His was the first stock passenger automobile to beat 12 seconds in the quarter-mile. Here, Grove is behind the wheel of his "Melrose Missile II" at the '62 Winternationals.

▶ The extra gauges and the roll-cage members betray this '62 Fury as something special. It is in fact the Bonneville Salt Flats special in which Andy Granatelli hit 194 mph. And it's street legal! Power comes from a 413 bored to 480 cid, with twin McCulloch-Paxton superchargers feeding Carter dual quads, which were mounted on a modified Chrysler 300 intake manifold. A Hurst three-speed and 2.93:1 gears complete the drivetrain.

▼ Horsepower of the Fury's engine is uncertain, but it had to be substantial to push such an un-aerodynamic shape to more than 190 mph. Air intakes in place of headlamps, full-dish wheelcovers, and slight suspension modifications were the only other changes. At Riverside International Raceway, this car burned a 12.51 quarter-mile at 117.41 mph—not bad, considering the Bonneville gearing.

▶ At Pontiac, the push for performance had become relentless. After finishing 1-2-3 in the Daytona 500 in '61, and becoming one of the cars to beat on the drag strips and boulevards, it moved aggressively to develop and market speed equipment. The principal venue was the Catalina, which grew an inch in wheelbase, to 120, but was still three less than the bigger, heavier Star Chief and Bonneville. A minor restyle included a return to the popular split grille. Catalina was the only Pontiac eligible for the Super Duty engines: the 421-cid V-8, which again boasted 405 bhp, and the tough four-barrel 389-cid V-8, which was good for 385 bhp.

Pontiac Catalina

There's a good deal more to driving than a straight-line quarter-mile, and nobody knows that better than the performance-minded. Which is why Pontiac's Catalina shows up so often among you people.

One of the reasons for this popularity is the choice of engine/transmission teams. Standard equipment is a 215-hp Trophy V-8 hooked up to a three-speed stick, of course. But you can get a storming 405-horse engine and heavy-duty four-speed as extra-cost options. And other extra-cost options blanket the area in between, including automatics.

Wide-Track and Pontiac's own special handling precision come standard with the Catalina, naturally. So does a fat helping of pure luxury, without which you shouldn't allow yourself to be.

The great thing is that a new Catalina goes easy on your bankroll—this is Pontiac's lowest-priced full-sized series. Talk it over with your Pontiac dealer first chance you get. Plan to spend some time with him—you could use up a whole day just looking through that list of options, and a happier time you couldn't imagine.

(Oh, and if you'd like to check your Cat against the clocks, feel free. No fair making the Catalina do the pushing while the dragster has all the fun.) Pontiac Motor Division, General Motors Corporation.

MOTOR TREND/APRIL 1962 7

▼ Mickey Thompson, aboard the Royal Tempest Tiger, is on his way to eliminating Bill Lawton's Tasca Ford "Orbiter I" in the A/FX class at the '62 U.S. Nationals. Pontiac had chosen Ace Wilson's Royal Pontiac dealership in Royal Oak, Michigan, as ground zero for the distribution and promotion of its burgeoning catalog of speed equipment. Royal sold special Pontiac performance parts through the mail and over the counter. It also super-tuned Ponchos for the street and campaigned modified versions made all the hotter through the close cooperation of Pontiac engineers.

▶ At 16 years of age, Don Gay was probably the youngest Pontiac drag racer and was certainly among the fastest, with an A/S class time of 12.81 seconds at 111.52 mph in his 421 Catalina. Gay went on to fame as a Funny Car driver and dragstrip owner. Elsewhere, a "Royal Bobcat" Catalina hardtop with a 370-bhp 389 recorded a 6.5-second 0-60 mph run and a 14.5-second quarter-mile. And at the Detroit Dragway, Jim Wangers's Royal Bobcat Super Duty Catalina turned a 12.38-second quarter at 116.23 mph. Over in NASCAR, Pontiac took 22 checkered flags in 53 starts, including Fireball Roberts's victory in the Daytona 500. Joe Weatherly became the first Pontiac driver to win the Grand National driving title.

▲ This is one of a handful of lightweight '62 Catalinas that used aluminum for the hood, front bumpers, and front fenders. Aluminum fender liners and trunk lid, as well as aluminum intake and exhaust manifolds, also were offered. Weight shavings of 150 pounds or more were possible. Finally, a special dual-quad 421 was available at a breathtaking $2250—for the engine alone.

▲ Deadliest of the Super Duty 421s was a race-ready—but street-legal—version with four-bolt mains, forged rods and crank, solid lifters, and NASCAR heads. Two Carter 1000cfm AFB four-barrels rode a Mickey Thompson aluminum intake manifold. It was rated at 405 bhp, but real output was around 450.

1962 PONTIAC HIGH-PERFORMANCE ENGINES

TYPE	CID	BORE × STROKE	BHP @ RPM	TORQUE @ RPM	FUEL SYSTEM	COMP. RATIO	AVAIL.
ohv V-8	389	4.06 × 3.75	305 @ 4600	425 @ 2800	1 × 4bbl.	10.25:1	full size
ohv V-8	389	4.06 × 3.75	318 @ 4600	430 @ 3200	3 × 2bbl.	10.75:1	full size
ohv V-8	389	4.06 × 3.75	333 @ 4800	425 @ 2800	1 × 4bbl.	10.75:1	full size
ohv V-8	389	4.06 × 3.75	348 @ 4800	430 @ 3200	3 × 2bbl.	10.75:1	full size
ohv V-8	389	4.06 × 3.75	385 @ 5200	430 @ 3200	1 × 4bbl.	10.75:1	1
ohv V-8	421	4.09 × 4.00	405 @ 5600	425 @ 4400	2 × 4bbl.	11.0:1	2

1. Catalina Super Duty. 2. Catalina cpe.

▼ Semon E. "Bunkie" Knudsen, in his final season as Pontiac general manager, earned credit for sensible marketing of the Grand Prix "personal-luxury" coupe, which bowed mid-way through the '62 model year. Grand Prix followed the path of Ford's four-seat Thunderbird. Essentially, it was a Catalina hardtop with unique styling touches, bucket seats, and a console with tach and gauge package. No two-tone colors were used. Starting at $3835, the Grand Prix was a success.

▶ Grand Prix was available only with Pontiac's Trophy 389-cid V-8, but it was offered in a host of forms, from a 230-bhp two-barrel to the 348-bhp Tri-Power. A three-speed stick was standard, but most Grand Prixs carried the new "Roto" three-speed Hydra-Matic, which cost the same $231 as a four-speed manual floor-shift. Pontiac built 30,195 Grand Prixs in '62, and the division itself now ranked third in sales, up from a dismal ninth just six years earlier.

▼ Off the line at the '62 U.S. Nationals is Les Ritchey and the Ed Martin Ford against Ace Wilson's Royal Pontiac in SS/S eliminations. "Race on Sunday, Sell on Monday" had become more than wishful thinking. It was hard fact, and dealers knew that customers were paying attention to the publicity that came with competition. The link was perhaps strongest in stock-car racing, and here Pontiac was a real force. In winning Daytona, the Smokey Yunick-prepared Super Duty 421, running a single four-barrel as NASCAR required, pounded out some 440 bhp and qualified at 158.7 mph. A stock 421 Catalina averaged a record 113.2 mph in a 500-mile endurance test at Indianapolis.

▲ Pontiac hardtop coupes, including this Catalina, got a new convertible-inspired roofline. Though their impact was great, only about 200 Super Duty 421s actually were built, and there were even fewer Super Duty 389s.

▲ Clean lines and modest weight made the '62 Catalina hardtop a tempting machine, and there was little outward sign of whether it carried one of the many 389s or a gunslinger 421. Small hubcaps helped keep it mysterious.

▲ *Motor Trend* ran a dual-quad Super Duty 421 Catalina to 60 mph in a mere 5.4 seconds, blasting through the quarter-mile in just 13.9 at 107 mph. Those were superior numbers, given the poor traction afforded by tires of the day.

▲ The hottest Catalinas needed that big tach above the column to keep track of revs, especially when shifting a Borg-Warner/Hurst close-ratio four-speed. Otherwise, the interior was strictly stock Pontiac.

1963

Ford, GM, and Chrysler advertise 425 horsepower for hottest stock mills; experts know true figures are far higher • Displacement war escalates as Ford elbows its 406-cid V-8 to 427 cubic inches, and Mopar wedge grows from 413 to 426 cid . . . Chevrolet stands pat at 409 cid, except for rare 427-cid Z-11 • Race sanctioning bodies impose 427-cid limit • GM management orders all corporate-sponsored race activity halted • Chevy's lightweight Z-11 drag car arrives in small numbers for Super/Stock, with 427-cid-V-8 and 430 unfettered horses underhood • Ford debuts semi-fastback Galaxie 500 and 500XL hardtops at midyear • Special lightweight Catalinas save some 300 pounds, strike terror at dragstrips with Super Duty 421 V-8 • At NASCAR, Chevy's Impala 427 Mark IV qualifies fastest, but Fords end season with 23 victories, versus Plymouth's 19 (14 by Richard Petty) • Fords sweep first five spots in Daytona 500 • ETs of rail dragsters threaten 8-second mark, topping 180 mph . . . in stock classes, only a handful squeeze past 12 seconds

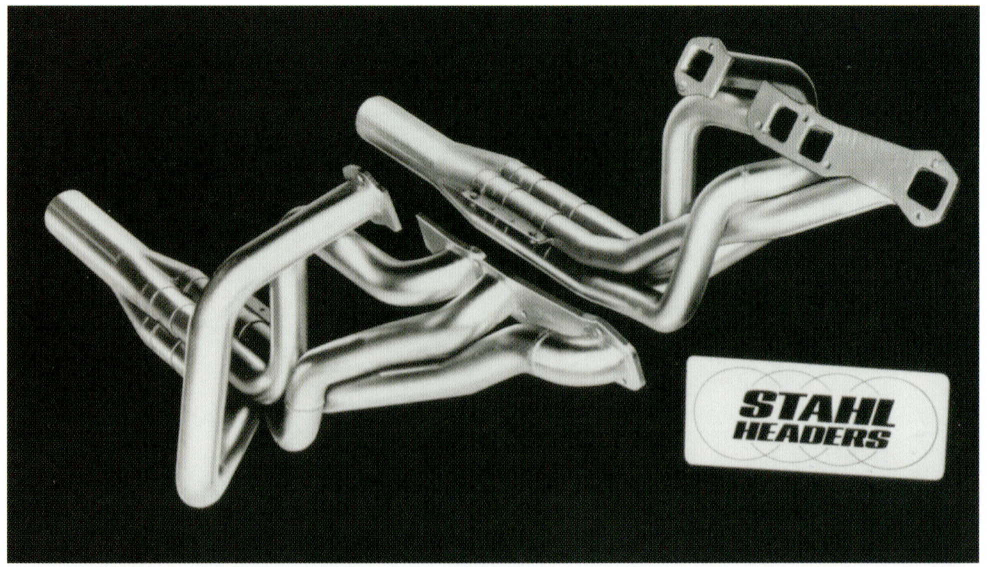

▲ Such goodies as Stahl exhaust headers helped send a stream of 409-equipped Chevrolets to the winner's circle. A record 16,902 of the 409s went to buyers, rated 340, 400, or a pavement-stomping 425 bhp.

1963 CHEVROLET HIGH-PERFORMANCE ENGINES

TYPE	CID	BORE × STROKE	BHP @ RPM	TORQUE @ RPM	FUEL SYSTEM	COMP. RATIO	AVAIL.
ohv V-8	327	4.00 × 3.25	250 @4400	350 @ 2800	1 × 4bbl.	10.5:1	full size
ohv V-8	327	4.00 × 3.25	300 @ 5000	360 @ 3200	1 × 4bbl.	10.5:1	full size
ohv V-8	409	4.31 × 3.50	340 @ 5000	420 @ 3200	1 × 4bbl.	10.0:1	full size
ohv V-8	409	4.31 × 3.50	400 @ 5800	425 @ 3600	1 × 4bbl.	11.0:1	full size
ohv V-8	409	4.31 × 3.50	425 @ 6000	425 @ 4200	2 × 4bbl.	11.0:1	full size
ohv V-8	427	4.41 × 3.50	430 @ 5800	430 @ 4000	2 × 4bbl.	13.5:1	Impala Sport Coupe

▲ Most teens merely swooned over factory-stock muscle, but some hit the strips themselves. Here, 18-year-old Butch Leal runs the Del Munson Stock Eliminator Chevy at the '63 Winternationals. Leal became one of the best-known players in NHRA Super Stock, A/FX, and Pro Stock. Over in NASCAR, Junior Johnson won two races in Chevrolets, helping give the automaker eight victories.

▼ Chevrolet unleashed a 427-cid version of the 409, called the Z-11. The limited production, dual-quad mill made 430 bhp at 6000 rpm, 425 pounds/feet of torque at 4200. Here, Ronnie Sox wheels the Friendly Chevrolet-backed "Mr. 427" in an A/FX showdown against Len Richter's Ford at the '63 U.S. Nationals.

▲ Chevrolet's bubble-roof '62 Bel Air hardtop (rear) was gone, leaving only the squared-off Impala. Deceptively ordinary, this '63 Impala contains the Z-11 drag package. About 100 were built for Super/Stock, typically with an aluminum hood, front fenders and bumpers, to cut 180 pounds. The 427-cid engine matched the new NASCAR and NHRA displacement limits.

▲ Intended for competition only, Z-11s like this one were sold only to factory-approved buyers. On the street, Chevy's 340-bhp version of the 409, with hydraulic lifters and lower compression (10:1 instead of 11:1), proved more practical. *Car Life* smoked one to 60 mph in 6.6 seconds with Powerglide, while *Motor Trend* managed a 15.9-second quarter-mile.

◄ A display featuring Sunoco's "Magic 8" custom-blending dial was used to help educate sales reps at a meeting in Atlantic City. As compression ratios rose in the early 1960s, higher-octane gasoline became mandatory.

"When the 'Orange Monster' strikes," ads warned, "records topple!" The monster was Chrysler's new Ram Charger 426-cid wedge, basically a bored 413, but with internal hop-ups and more power. Dodge ads claimed the Ram Charger would "burn rubber as long as you let it." (Below right): Herman Mozer's Super Stock Automatic dropped teammate Jim Thornton for Top Stock Eliminator at the '63 NHRA Nationals, then jailed "Lawman" Al Eckstrand with a 12.22 at 116.73 mph.

THE DEPENDABLES FROM DODGE!

A WOLF...

IN STREET CLOTHING

Stock car racing is the ultimate measure of a car's capabilities. And the '63 Dodge has been doing very well, thank you. Fact is, it's chewing up competition on tracks all over the country. We aren't the least bit surprised. Racing takes raw power and Dodge has it. Racing takes control. Dodge has that, too. Experts call its torsion-bar suspension the best in the business. Racing demands toughness. Dodge's unitized body is welded, one piece. Tough, tight. As rattle-free as can be. What's best is this: All the things that make Dodge such a wolf on the tracks make it a model of deportment for your everyday driving. Performance? You've got it—with a wide choice of prize-winning V8 power. You've got a lot more going for you, too. Maneuverability, money-saving dependability and something extra nice—a low price. Dodge is on the move, all right. And we urge you to sample some of its high adventure soon. See your Dodge Dealer. He's got The Dependables in a size to suit you. Compact Dart. Standard-size Dodge. Big 880. Pick a size, pick a price, pick a Dodge.

HOT 1963 DODGE

DODGE DIVISION CHRYSLER MOTORS CORPORATION | '63 DODGE: A FULL LINE OF CARS IN THE LOW-PRICE FIELD. THREE SERIES: 24 MODELS. HARDTOPS, SEDANS, CONVERTS, WAGONS.

Jim Thornton and Herman Mozer (979) coming off the line in S/SA class.

Some days you win

Mozer and Al Eckstrand in final run for Top Stock Eliminator title.

Some days you lose

The fortunes on the straight and narrow warpath change as quickly as the gears in the go-box! Today you tear 'em up. Tomorrow is another day. Your machine has got to be mean . . . you've got to be good . . . and you've got to come out of the hole with more togetherness than Amos and Andy! That's the drama of the drag strip, man and machine.

That's why more than 100,000 buffs bulged the track at Indy for the NHRA's big showdown—the world championships.

And what a showdown! On Saturday, Jim Thornton in a '63 Dodge downed his Ramcharger teammate, Herman Mozer, on his way to royalty in the Super Stock Automatic Class. Next day, running for the meet's most coveted honor—Top Stock Eliminator—Mozer turned the tables and gave Thornton the thumb. But the event was far from over. Mozer still had to face the present "Mr. Eliminator," Al Eckstrand in Lawman, another specially equipped '63 Dodge. And another winner is defeated. Mozer edged him by 1/100th of a second with an e.t. of 12.22.

Some days you win. Some days you lose. That's what keeps the quarter-mile jaunt so interesting. But have you noticed? When a Dodge loses these days . . . it's to another Dodge.

DODGE DIVISION CHRYSLER MOTORS CORPORATION

▲ Sagging '62 sales taught Dodge its lesson. Styling for '63 was toned down, and the wheelbase of its standard-size cars grew by three inches, to 119. They were called 330, 440, and Polara (shown).

◄ The 426 had 415 bhp on 11.0:1 compression; or 425 bhp on 13.5:1. Stage II and Stage III versions followed during the year, with larger-bore Carter carbs. Valve lift and duration grew, tightest compression dropped to 12.5:1, and recast heads were installed.

1963 DODGE HIGH-PERFORMANCE ENGINES							
TYPE	CID	BORE × STROKE	BHP @ RPM	TORQUE @ RPM	FUEL SYSTEM	COMP. RATIO	AVAIL.
ohv V-8	383	4.25 × 3.75	325 @ 5200	420 @ 3600	2×4bbl.	11.0:1	full size
ohv V-8	426	4.25 × 3.75	370 @ 4600	460 @ 2800	1×4bbl.	11.0:1	full size
ohv V-8	426	4.25 × 3.75	375 @ 4600	465 @ 2800	1×4bbl.	13.5:1	full size
ohv V-8	426	4.25 × 3.75	415 @ 5600	470 @ 4400	2×4bbl.	11.0:1	full size
ohv V-8	426	4.25 × 3.75	425 @ 5600	480 @ 4400	2×4bbl.	13.5:1	full size

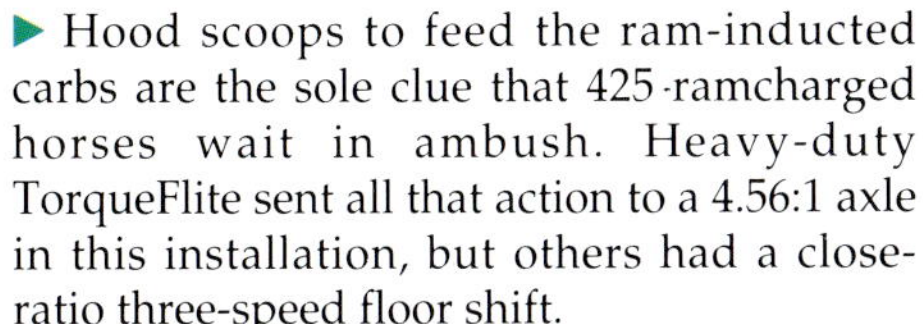

▲ "Strictly business" was the rule when a customer ordered a Stage II or III Ramcharger V-8 in a basic Dodge 330 two-door. This factory-built 3200-pound lightweight racer wears an aluminum front end and deletes the radio and heater.

► Hood scoops to feed the ram-inducted carbs are the sole clue that 425-ramcharged horses wait in ambush. Heavy-duty TorqueFlite sent all that action to a 4.56:1 axle in this installation, but others had a close-ratio three-speed floor shift.

▲ The colorful "Candymatic" Dodge drag car was a national Top Stock Eliminator. Its name combined the candy-stripe theme with the idea of an automatic transmission, in this case controlled by Hurst's new shifter.

▲ Stock-car racing, declared a Dodge ad, proved "the ultimate measure of a car's capability." Perhaps, but many savored the straight-line thrill of cars like "Candymatic" at the strip, and of their own Dodges on the street.

▶ Detroit lawyer Elton A. "Al" Eckstrand's "Ramchargers" Polara was top Stock Eliminator at the '63 NHRA Winternationals in Pomona, California. His ET was 12.44 seconds at 115.08 mph. This car used a Hurst Dual Gate shifter. This popular aftermarket piece combined the set-and-forget convenience of a regular automatic with an adjacent "gate" into which the shift lever could be moved and then slammed manually through rapid 1-2-3 upshifts.

▼ This is how the "Ramchargers" drag car looked in its original livery, before adopting the "Candymatic" name and awning-stripe paint scheme. Though professionally tuned, its engine was basically the same as that available to anyone through the factory. Brochures warned that the 426 Ramcharger warmed up slowly (having no heat applied to the manifold) and was "not a street machine." Rather, it was "designed to be run in supervised, sanctioned drag-strip competition by those qualified....Yet, it is stock in every sense of the word."

▲ Ford came on strong in NASCAR for '63, with "Tiny" Lund winning the Daytona 500 in a Galaxie. In drag racing, however, the competition weighed about 3200 pounds, some 300 less than a Galaxie. Ford fought back with a series of 50 lightweight Galaxies with fiberglass front body panels and aluminum front bumpers that slashed about 174 pounds. These 3425-pound race-only Fords ran 12.07-second ETs at 118 mph, but still weren't fast enough to win any NHRA national titles. This is Dick Brannan giving it his best in one of the '63 lightweights.

◀ Shelby's AC Cobra sports car was bred for twisty-course road racing, but in Dragonsnake form, it was ready to take on the quarter-mile. Dragonsnakes were made available for 1963 and were sold with 23 options designed specifically for drag racing. Their Ford HiPo 289-cid V-8 was available in four stages of tune: 271, 300, 325, and 380 bhp. Dragonsnake prices ranged from $6795 to $8995.

▲ Based on the British AC Ace roadster, the Shelby Cobra was the product of Ford V-8 power and the imagination of a race-car driver and builder from Texas, Carroll Shelby. They were expensive, exclusive, and fast.

▲ The Cobra sports car was in a way a classic example of the muscle car philosophy: scads of horsepower in the lightest car to be found. Earliest examples used Ford's 260-cid, then the 289, and finally the mighty 427.

◄ Full-size Fords entered '63 with carried over '62 powertrains. But the 406-cid V-8 was soon replaced by a new 427, which ostensibly was the 390/406 FE-series bored by .010 inch. The 427 got significant improvements over the 406, including a forged steel crankshaft, cross-bolted main-bearing caps, forged aluminum pistons, and an aluminum intake manifold. Though called a 427, actual displacement was 425 cubic inches. The lightweight valvetrain could withstand 7000 rpm. An oval air cleaner held an exposed filter element between aluminum upper and lower sections. The strongest 427 used a pair of 652-cfm Holley four barrels for an advertised 425 bhp at 6000 rpm and 480 pounds/feet of torque at 3700. With a single 780-cfm Holley, the engine had 410 bhp at 5600, and 476 pound/feet of torque. Both versions ran 11.5:1 compression. Chrome valve covers were included.

▲ Ordering a 427 for $405.70 ($56 more for twin-carb) brought a tougher suspension, rear axle, and brakes; heavy-duty driveshaft and U-joints; and 15-inch wheels. A four-speed manual was mandatory.

1963 FORD HIGH-PERFORMANCE ENGINES

TYPE	CID	BORE × STROKE	BHP @ RPM	TORQUE @ RPM	FUEL SYSTEM	COMP. RATIO	AVAIL.
ohv V-8	260	3.80 × 2.87	260 @ 5800	281 @ 3300	1 × 4bbl.	10.5:1	Cobra
ohv V-8	289	4.00 × 2.87	271 @ 6000	312 @ 3400	1 × 4bbl.	10.5:1	full size, Cobra
ohv V-8	390	4.05 × 3.78	330 @ 5000	427 @ 3200	1 × 4bbl.	9.6:1	full size (police)
ohv V-8	390	4.05 × 3.78	340 @ 3200	430 @ 3200	3 × 2bbl.	10.5:1	full size
ohv V-8	406	4.13 × 3.78	385 @ 5800	440 @ 3800	1 × 4bbl.	11.4:1	full size
ohv V-8	406	4.13 × 3.78	405 @ 5800	448 @ 3500	3 × 2bbl.	11.4:1	full size
ohv V-8	427	4.23 × 3.78	425 @ 6000	480 @ 3700	2 × 4bbl.	11.5:1	full size (race)

▲ In February 1963, Ford introduced slanted rear rooflines for the "1963 ½" Galaxie 500 (shown) and 500XL series. Called the Sports Hardtop, the semi-fastback was two inches lower than the equivalent notchback and allowed a great aerodynamic advantage on NASCAR superspeedways.

▲ A precursor to the 1964 Fairlane Thunderbolt was this '63 run by Rhode Island Ford dealer Bob Tasca. With the factory's help, Tasca squeezed a 427 into the intermediate and unveiled it on Labor Day Weekend at the NHRA Nationals in Indianapolis. Running in factory experimental, it turned a 12.21 at 118.42, but still got beat by a Z-11 Chevy. Production Fairlanes were offered with a 271-bhp version of the 289 V-8. With a four-barrel and 11.0:1 compression, it was Ford's first performance engine in a mid-size.

▶ Camshaft profiles could easily spell the difference between winning and losing—at the strip or on the street. Iskenderian, one of the best-known aftermarket firms, rode to the rescue with its line of mild to moderate to wild racing cams. If the stock bumpstick just wouldn't do, an "Isky" cam could increase valve duration and lift for better breathing and more power.

▲ Both the 427-cid V-8 and the Galaxie fastback-style roofline debuted in mid-'63. The hot new engine and aerodynamic roof were an inspired duo in stock-car racing and carried the blue oval to the 1963 NASCAR championship.

▲ All full-size Fords got fresh sheetmetal for '63, and after midyear were known as the "Super Torque" Galaxies. Engine choices started with a 260-cid V-8, soon replaced by the 289; but pedal-down Ford fans could reach all the way to the carryover 406, or the new 427. This Rangoon Red 500XL drop top represents big Ford style and muscle at its most stylish. It has the 406-cid V-8 with Tri-Power carburetion.

◀ Fast fun in the sun. This Galaxie 500XL convertible has the $188 optional Borg-Warner four-speed manual transmission, with a big 8000-rpm Rotunda tachometer above the steering column to help the driver get the most out of that stout 406. Lesser V-8s were offered with automatic, either the $212 Cruise-O-Matic three-speed or the $190 Ford-O-Matic two-speed. This ragtop has the rare $94 Ford AM/FM radio, but not the $102 power windows.

▶ While the new 427 grabbed the headlines at midseason, Ford's familiar 406-cid V-8 carried the ball early in the year. When equipped with the three-deuce setup, as is this one, it again delivered an attention-getting 405 bhp. The four-barrel 406 made 385 bhp. Incidently, the tri-carb hardware was shipped from the factory in the car's trunk, to be installed by the dealer's service department. Dealers could also install a nasty set of exhaust cutouts, for $55, though Ford urged buyers not to use them on the street. By spring 1963, Ford advertisements no longer mentioned either 406. One more performance-packed engine had faded into history, giving way to a brash newcomer.

1963 MERCURY HIGH-PERFORMANCE ENGINES

TYPE	CID	BORE × STROKE	BHP @ RPM	TORQUE @ RPM	FUEL SYSTEM	COMP. RATIO	AVAIL.
ohv V-8	427	4.23 × 3.78	410 @ 5600	476 @ 3400	1 × 4bbl.	11.5:1	full size
ohv V-8	430	4.30 × 3.70	320 @ 4600	465 @ 2600	1 × 4bbl.	10.1:1	full size

◀ Mercury's counterpart to the 1962½ Galaxie Sport Hardtop was the Marauder, a new nameplate that eschewed the reverse-slant "Breezeway" roof of other big Mercs. Engine choices began with a 250-bhp V-8, but stretched to the dual-quad, solid-lifter 427. Pioneer auto writer Tom McCahill said the big 427 Marauder "has more hair on its chest than a middle-aged yak."

1963 OLDSMOBILE HIGH-PERFORMANCE ENGINES

TYPE	CID	BORE × STROKE	BHP @ RPM	TORQUE @ RPM	FUEL SYSTEM	COMP. RATIO	AVAIL.
ohv V-8	215	3.50 × 2.80	215 @ 4600	300 @ 3200	1 × 1bbl.*	10.25:1	Jetfire
ohv V-8	394	4.13 × 3.69	330 @ 4800	440 @ 2800	1 × 4bbl.	10.25:1	S-88, 98
ohv V-8	394	4.13 × 3.69	345 @ 4800	440 @ 3200	1 × 4bbl.	10.5:1	Starfire

*Turbocharged.

▲ There's "nothing like it on the road today," claimed Olds. The Jetfire used a four-barrel carb, but also injected a mixture of distilled water and methyl alcohol into the fuel/air charge. This kept the combustion chamber cool enough to prevent knock under the 10.25:1 compression.

◀ Oldsmobile took a different high-performance tack: turbocharging. Its F-85 Jetfire, unveiled in spring 1962 and carried over for '63 (left), turbocharged a 215-cid aluminum V-8 for 215 bhp, 60 more than the non-turbo version. Fitted with buckets and console, Olds said the $3049 hardtop aimed at "the man who thrives on high adventure." But most testers were disappointed with the Jetfire's 8-10-second 0-60s and near 19-second quarter-miles.

▲ Plymouth's full-size line lost some of its eccentric styling for '63 and gained the 426 Super Stock wedge as a new high-performance engine. It made 415 or 425 bhp, depending on tune, and would turn this and other similarly plain Belvederes into a real pavement rippers.

▲ Little inside suggested the thrills awaiting a stab at the accelerator. The floor-mounted shift lever for the three-speed 'box may have been a clue, however. Four-speed transmissions hadn't yet arrived on Chrysler products.

▲ Plymouth's Super Stock 426 breathed through twin Carter AFB four-barrels offset atop a cross-ram manifold. Exhaust was handled by the ram's-horn headers. The 415 bhp was from 11:1 compression, the 425 bhp from 13.5:1.

◀ Tom Grove, of Union City, California, was one of the West Coast's quickest Mopar drag racers. Here, Grove's "Melrose Missile III" Plymouth takes on Bill Hanyon's Fury at the '63 NHRA Winternationals. "Street" versions of this car were available through any dealer. At the Pomona dragstrip, *Hot Rod* took a 426 Super Stock Plymouth with automatic and 4.56:1 axle to a 12.69-second ET at 112 mph. The magazine explained that the 13.5:1-compression 426 "is strictly a ¼-mile sprinter and not designed for street driving. Plymouth recommends that full throttle bursts be limited to 15 seconds and then only if the gasoline used is 102 octane or better." Even the 11:1 Super Stock was "a thoroughbred designed for the track, not a workhorse for pulling a plow." Mopar 426 Wedge engines set eight NHRA records in 1963.

▲ Any win is a good win, and Plymouth's were not confined to the dragstrips in '63. The Chrysler division came on strong in oval racing, especially on the shorter tracks. Here, A.J. Foyt steers one between turns. Plymouth took the USAC Manufacturers' Trophy, while Richard Petty was at the wheel in 14 of Plymouth's 19 NASCAR wins, a total second only to Ford's 23 victories.

1963 PLYMOUTH HIGH-PERFORMANCE ENGINES

TYPE	CID	BORE × STROKE	BHP @ RPM	TORQUE @ RPM	FUEL SYSTEM	COMP. RATIO	AVAIL.
ohv V-8	383	4.24 × 3.38	330 @ 4600	425 @ 2800	1 × 4bbl.	10.0:1	full size
ohv V-8	426	4.25 × 3.75	370 @ 4600	460 @ 2800	1 × 4bbl.	11.0:1	full size
ohv V-8	426	4.25 × 3.75	375 @ 4600	465 @ 2800	1 × 4bbl.	13.5:1	full size
ohv V-8	426	4.25 × 3.75	415 @ 5600	470 @ 4400	2 × 4bbl.	11.0:1	full size
ohv V-8	426	4.25 × 3.75	425 @ 5600	480 @ 4400	2 × 4bbl.	13.5:1	full size

▼ "Golden Commando" was the tag Plymouth gave to its 383-cid V-8, a consistent performer that in 330-bhp form could take a Sport Fury hardtop to 60 mph in 7.2 seconds and to a 15.9-second quarter-mile. Hamilton Motors of Detroit sponsored a series of drag Plymouths under the "Golden Commando" banner, including this 426 wedge Super Stock Automatic car. Drivers such as Al Eckstrand, Bill Shirey, Forest Pitcock, and John Dallafior put in seat time with these potent Plymouths.

1963 PLYMOUTH LINEUP

Fury Convertible—Dark Metallic Blue

Fury 2-Door Hardtop—Ruby

Sport Fury Convertible—Ebony

Sport Fury 2-Door Hardtop—Coppertone

Fury 4-Door Hardtop—Metallic Green

Fury 4-Door Sedan—Light Beige

Fury 4-Door Station Wagon—Light Blue

Belvedere 4-Door Sedan—Medium Metallic Blue

Belvedere 2-Door Sedan—Metallic Brown

Belvedere 4-Door Station Wagon—Ebony

Belvedere 2-Door Hardtop—Medium Beige

Savoy 4-Door Sedan—Light Green

Savoy 2-Door Sedan—Ruby

Savoy 4-Door Station Wagon—Metallic Brown

▲ Despite the polished brightwork, the 426 in Vanke's Plymouth was not pretty to competitors. These mills held a host of super-tough internal components.

▲▼ Arlen Vanke ran one of the quickest—and cleanest—Plymouths in the NHRA wars. Cars with the basics of his two-door 426-cid Savoy were offered to the public. They were among 105 lightweight Plymouths that saved 150 pounds through the use of front fenders and a scooped hood made of aluminum, and by deleting most every convenience item. At midyear came the Stage III 426, a more radical wedge with larger primary bores for its twin Carter AFBs, a higher-lift (.520-inch) camshaft, and larger-chamber heads.

▼ Tom Grove's "Melrose Missile IV" was a 12.37-second Super/Stock threat, but that still wasn't enough to beat Dave Strickler's lightning-fast "Old Reliable" Chevy for NHRA's U.S. Nationals Top Stock title in '63.

▲ Though the 426-cid Super Stock engine wasn't recommended for street use, it was nevertheless available on uplevel Plymouths. Witness this striking Sport Fury ragtop with its 425 bhp and TorqueFlite automatic.

▲ Bright and sassy, this Super Stock Sport Fury is a very pretty sleeper. Note the automatic transmission's pushbutton gear selection aligned vertically to the left of the steering wheel.

▲ Few believed the conservative figures, but Super Stock 426 engines were rated at 415 bhp with 11:1 compression, or 425 with 13.5:1. "Getup and go Plymouth!" was one slogan this year. And how!

▲ Full-size Pontiacs got new sheetmetal from the beltline down and adopted the stacked headlamps that would become their trademark for the next several years. All big Ponchos could get the 421-cid V-8. It was offered in 353-bhp form with a four-barrel, or as the 421 HO (High Output) in 370-bhp guise with a Tri-Power setup. This particular Catalina, however, has the rare 405-bhp Super Duty 421, which was intended for the dragstrip. Note the desirable eight-lug wheels.

▼ With the Super Duty 421 underhood, this was Pontiac's seat of power for '63. The clean Catalina goes with a rugged four-speed manual hooked to a 4.30:1 Positraction rear axle. The factory tachometer and vacuum gauges were new options for '63 (a tilt steering wheel also was new). Bucket seats are tritone white/burgundy/wine. An AM/FM radio completes the picture.

▲ *Motor Trend* ran a four-speed dual-quad Super Duty Catalina to a 0-60 run of 5.4 seconds and a quarter-mile of 13.9 seconds at 107 mph—on street tires. Even the "ordinary" 370-bhp Tri-Power 421 could turn ETs in the mid-14s.

◀ Only 88 Super Duty engines were built for '63. Most went into Catalinas. They came in three levels of tune, each with less torque—but more horsepower and a higher rev capability—than a regular 421. Pontiac's Special Equipment catalog warned that Super Dutys were "designed only for all-out performance enthusiasts."

1963 PONTIAC HIGH-PERFORMANCE ENGINES

TYPE	CID	BORE × STROKE	BHP @ RPM	TORQUE @ RPM	FUEL SYSTEM	COMP. RATIO	AVAIL.
ohv V-8	389	4.06 × 3.75	313 @ 4600	430 @ 3200	3×2bbl.	10.25:1	full size
ohv V-8	421	4.09 × 3.75	353 @ 5000	455 @ 3400	1×4bbl.	10.75:1	full size
ohv V-8	421	4.09 × 3.75	370 @ 5200	460 @ 3800	3×2bbl.	10.75:1	full size
ohv V-8	421	4.09 × 4.00	390 @ 5800	425 @ 3600	1×4bbl.	12.0:1	1
ohv V-8	421	4.09 × 4.00	405 @ 5600	425 @ 4400	2×4bbl.	12.0:1	1
ohv V-8	421	4.09 × 4.00	410 @ 5600	435 @ 4400	2×4bbl.	13.0:1	1

1. Catalina cpe.

◀ Here's one Pontiac Catalina that wasn't intended for Sunday drives—unless those journeys were taken in 1320-foot bites. Ultra-light bucket seats, T-handle shifter, oversized tachometer, radio-delete, auxiliary gauges, and, of course, the racing helmet, attest to its mission as a quarter-mile warrior.

▶ In place of the back seat, this fierce Catalina sports a set of support braces to help maintain solidity in case of mishap. The fire extinguisher could come in mighty handy, too. All-synchro four-speeds were the racers' choice on the strip, but conventional Catalinas might have a three-speed manual gearbox or Super Hydra-Matic.

▲ Riding a 120-inch wheelbase, the comparatively lightweight Catalina was the sensible choice to carry Super Duty power. Still, a stock hardtop tipped the scales at 3725 pounds, so every bit of weight-cutting helped when performance was at stake. Special Catalinas built for dragging saved 300 pounds through use of aluminum bumpers and bucket seats, bell housing, front-end sheetmetal, and axle centers. Frames were lightened, batteries moved to the trunk, and insulation and sound deadening omitted.

◀ Most ferocious of the Super Duty 421 V-8s was this dual-quad trooper. It ran a 13.0:1 compression, good for 410 bhp at 5600 rpm and a walloping 435 pounds/feet of torque at 4400. At 12.0:1 compression were the single-carb Super Duty, with 390 bhp at 5800 rpm, and the other dual-quad, with 405 bhp at 5600. Both of those "lesser" Super Duty V-8s delivered 425 pounds/feet of torque.

▲As it turned out, Pontiac Motor Division wasn't quite as "passionate" about racing as this Catalina's nomenclature suggests. Early in 1963, GM ordered a halt to factory participation in racing and a de-emphasis on high performance. Pontiac did drop out of direct involvement in racing, but the 421 engine remained available, and in fact was offered in all the full-size models for the first time in '63. This drag car's "Swiss Cheese" license tag refers to its frame, portions of which were drilled through with holes at the factory to reduce weight.

▲"Here's What The Other '63s Wished They Looked Like," promised Pontiac ads. Well, perhaps not exactly like this particular Catalina, which sacrificed some of its beauty for a two-fisted drag-strip wallop. This Catalina drag car boasts 405 horsepower, but as usual, actual output was anybody's guess. Catalina and Grand Prix rode a 120-inch wheelbase, three inches shorter than the Bonneville and Star Chief.

▲ The lightest, cheapest two-door Catalina with a High Output Tri-Power 421 HO and four-speed could turn mid-14s right out of the box. The 421 HOs were available with three- or four-speed manual or Super Hydra-Matic automatic. Pontiac recommended a 3.42:1 axle as a good acceleration/cruising compromise, though dealer-installed ratios up to 4.44:1 were available. This Marlin Aqua Sports Sedan spent four years of its early life racing in A/Stock; it has less than 6000 miles on the odometer.

◀ The tri-carb 421 HO had 370 bhp at 5300 rpm, and 460 lbs/ft of torque at 3800 with three Rochester two-barrels and 10.75:1 compression. The four-bolt block had a forged crank and hydraulic lifters. It cost $404 to $445 more than a 389-cid, depending on the combination of equipment.

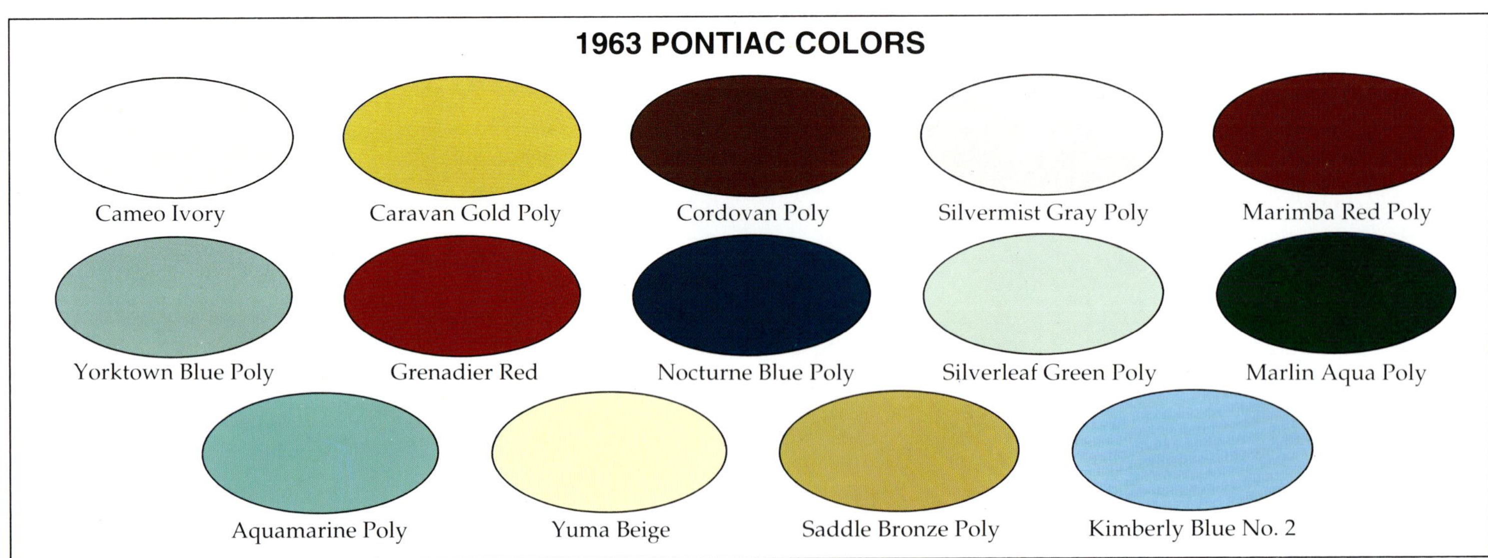

We designed two new cars—and built a lot of our record-setting Avanti into them. Added the supercharged Avanti R2 engine.

...And took them to the Flats for final evaluation and endurance tests. The results surprised even us: R2 Super Lark—132 mph! R2 Super Hawk—140 mph! With 2 up. Under bad weather and surface conditions—even snow. USAC timed the bit, official.

That kind of performance told us these cars were ready to join the Studebaker line. R2 Super Lark and R2 Super Hawk are now available on special order at your Studebaker dealer's.

The package of pow and pizzazz: R-2 blown mill, 4-speed box, Avanti wheels inside 6.50-15's. Anti-sway rod forward; trac rods, rear. HD springs and shocks at both ends. Our disc binders. Belts. (Now installed on **all** cars from Studebaker, by the way.) Sundry little signs on each car to tell the peasantry you've got an extreme automobile. When parked. Under way, they'll know without sign language. Warning: The color choice is limited. But you have your own spray gun, don't you?

▲ A hero to Pontiac partisans in 1963—and for years afterward—was "Akron Arlen" Vanke. His A/FX "Tin Indian III" is shown at the NHRA Winternationals. A fellow Pontiac driver, Bill Shrewesberry, took A/FX honors at the '63 Winternationals with a torrid 12.04-second ET at 116.27 mph. Big Ponchos were out-digging plenty of rivals, but the high-performance focus would soon be shifting to mid-size cars—a shift for which Pontiac itself could take credit. In a hint of what was to come, 11 Super Duty V-8s were installed in compact Tempests.

◀ Studebaker soon would fade from the American scene, but its R2 supercharged editions were quick at the Bonneville Salt Flats: 132 mph for the sedate Super Lark, 140 for the sleek Super Hawk. Meanwhile, an R3 Studebaker Avanti did a record 168.15 mph for the flying kilometer. Occasionally, a tame-looking R2 Lark would blow away a scoffing rival at the dragstrip, but as on the street, it was too little, too late.

1963 STUDEBAKER HIGH-PERFORMANCE ENGINES

TYPE	CID	BORE × STROKE	BHP @ RPM	TORQUE @ RPM	FUEL SYSTEM	COMP. RATIO	AVAIL.
ohv V-8	289	3.56 × 3.63	240 @ 4800	305 @ 3200	1 × 4bbl.	10.25:1	1
ohv V-8	289	3.56 × 3.63	290 @ 5200	330 @ 3600	1 × 4bbl.	9.0:1*	1

* Supercharged. 1. Hawk, Lark, Avanti.

1964

425 horsepower remains top advertised industry figure; displacement race also stands pat • Crafty Pontiac launches legendary GTO as Tempest LeMans option with 389-cid V-8 • Mustang unveiled as 1964½ model • Mid-size Chevelle debuts with available 283-cid V-8, but soon a trio of 327s deliver up to 365 bhp...Malibu hardtop and ragtop offered with Super Sport package • Hemi V-8 returns to Dodge/Plymouth ranks after five-year absence; leads Chrysler to 26 NASCAR victories—but Ford wins 30 • Tamer "Street Wedge" debuts under Dodge/Plymouth hoods • Ford tries to legalize SOHC (overhead-cam) 427 for oval tracks; NASCAR nixes the notion • Race-ready Thunderbolt Fairlane sends Ford back to the winner's circle at dragstrips with ETs in the 11s • A/FX (Factory Experimental) compact Ford Falcons and Mercury Comets hit dragstrips with 427-cid engines • Richard Petty wins his first Daytona 500 in a Hemi Plymouth • At Tucson Dragway, a Dodge "Charger" sets S/FX mph quarter-mile record of 135.55 mph

▲ Full-size Chevrolets adopted a larger, more formal look as the mid-size Chevelle targeted the burgeoning youth market. This Meadow Green Biscayne two-door sedan carries the hottest 409 V-8, again rated at 425 horsepower and hooked up to a Muncie four-speed and 3.70:1 Positraction differential. The 409 also came in 340-and 400-bhp configurations, but quarter-mile rivals were tougher than ever. The 409's days were numbered.

▲ Chevrolet's full-size Super Sport became a distinct Impala series, not an option package. Offered as a hardtop or convertible, a new AM/FM radio was offered, while a walnut-grained steering wheel added class.

▲ A total of 185,325 SS Impalas went to customers in '64, typically loaded with luxury rather than strict stand-on-the-pedal power. Only the tamest 340-bhp 409 could be ordered with air conditioning.

▲ Open the early-muscle dictionary to "sleeper" and this may be what you'll see: Budget-model Biscayne body; blackwall tires; taxi-cab hub caps. Open the throttle on this car, however, and you'll surely have to hang on as 425 pounds/feet of torque turn those skinny bias-plies into gummy smoke generators. Still, times were changing, and production of the 409 fell 48 percent, to 8864 installations for '64.

▲ A big tachometer and a dash without a radio is one way to spot a muscle-car interior. Another is the M20 four-speed gearbox. The close-ratio M21 could have a 4.11:1 or 4.56:1 axle with Positraction.

▲ Full-size Chevrolets were fading from the performance scene, but the 409 maintained the sales catalog's promise that it would be "especially saucy in highway passing situations." The sizzling 427 Z-11 option was killed.

▲ Street racers learned the signs. A burbly exhaust note and a lumpy idle would be the first clues, and the crossed-flags 409 insignia would confirm it: One of these 425-bhp heavyweights was not to be taken casually.

1964 CHEVROLET HIGH-PERFORMANCE ENGINES

TYPE	CID	BORE × STROKE	BHP @ RPM	TORQUE @ RPM	FUEL SYSTEM	COMP. RATIO	AVAIL.
ohv V-8	283	3.88 × 3.00	220 @ 4800	295 @ 3200	1 × 4bbl.	9.25:1	Chevelle
ohv V-8	327	4.00 × 3.25	250 @ 4400	350 @ 2800	1 × 4bbl.	10.5:1	full size, Chevelle
ohv V-8	327	4.00 × 3.25	300 @ 5000	360 @ 3200	1 × 4bbl.	10.5:1	full size, Chevelle
ohv V-8	327	4.00 × 3.25	365 @ 6200	350 @ 4400	1 × 4bbl.	11.0:1	Chevelle
ohv V-8	409	4.31 × 3.50	340 @ 5000	420 @ 3200	1 × 4bbl.	10.0:1	full size
ohv V-8	409	4.31 × 3.50	400 @ 5800	425 @ 3600	1 × 4bbl.	11.0:1	full size
ohv V-8	409	4.31 × 3.50	425 @ 6000	425 @ 4200	2 × 4bbl.	11.0:1	full size

▲ The engine bay of Chrysler's letter-series cars still was an eye-opener with the ram-inducted twin-quad setup that added 30 bhp to the standard 360-bhp 413-cid V-8. And an optional four-speed manual replaced a three-speed. But while 3647 300Ks were sold for '64—compared to just 400 300Js for '63—Chrysler's proud letter-series model was not the hot rod its forbearers had been.

▶ A drop in power and deletion of such standard items as leather upholstery reduced letter-series prices and increased sales to record levels. The hardtop listed for $4056. The convertible returned after a one-year absence. It started at $4522, and 625 were sold. Still, few two-ton 300Js went to dragstrips, as performance buyers turned elsewhere. This was the last of the "true" letter-series 300s.

1964 CHRYSLER HIGH-PERFORMANCE ENGINES

TYPE	CID	BORE × STROKE	BHP @ RPM	TORQUE @ RPM	FUEL SYSTEM	COMP. RATIO	AVAIL.
ohv V-8	383	4.25 × 3.38	305 @ 4600	410 @ 2400	1 × 2bbl.	10.0:1	full size
ohv V-8	413	4.19 × 3.75	340 @ 4600	470 @ 2800	1 × 4bbl.	10.0:1	full size
ohv V-8	413	4.19 × 3.75	360 @ 4800	470 @ 3200	1 × 4bbl.	10.0:1	300K
ohv V-8	413	4.19 × 3.75	390 @ 4800	485 @ 3600	2 × 4bbl.	10.0:1	300K

▲ Backed by Hodges Dodges, the "Original Ramchargers" Candymatic Mopar invariably hung on into the late rounds at major NHRA events. That's what it's doing at the Pomona Winternationals against a Ford Thunderbolt. The Dodge 330 two-door sedan carried Chrysler's 426-cid Super Stock wedge V-8.

▲ One of the best-known Chrysler Corporation racers on the West Coast was "Dandy Dick" Landy, seen here in full flight at the '64 Winternationals.

This is a Top Stock Eliminator. What did he eliminate? And why.

Dave Strickler in his '64 Dodge Ramcharger, Top Stock Eliminator in the 1964 AHRA Phoenix Dragstrip Championships.

On a straightaway track, from a standing start, he beat another car to the finish line one quarter of a mile away. He continued to beat (and eliminate) one car after another in his class. Until only he was left.

Dragstrip racing—America's newest million-fan sport—operates under clearly defined, rigidly enforced rules. It is a supreme challenge in acceleration.

It was not surprising that a competition equipped Dodge won. It would be highly unusual if a Top Stock Eliminator was not a Dodge or Plymouth. Dragstrip competition, stock car races, and road rallies continue to confirm the excellence of Chrysler Corporation engineering, developed through years of extensive research and testing in the laboratory and on the proving grounds.

Want to eliminate all other cars? Test drive a '64 from Chrysler Corporation.

Plymouth • Dodge • Chrysler • Imperial

Visit Chrysler Corporation's "Autofare" at the N. Y. World's Fair

▲ Dodge not only informed readers that Dave Strickler won Top Stock Eliminator in the AHRA's Phoenix Dragstrip Championship, it told them what that meant. Some Super Stock Dodges used aluminum doors, front fenders, and hood.

▲ Roger Lindamood's "Color Me Gone" Dodge turned an 11.31 at 127.84 mph at the NHRA Nationals and beat Jim Thornton and the Ramchargers for Top Stock.

▲ An altered wheelbase gave Dave Strickler's "Dodge Boys" coupe better weight distribution, helping him take A/FX honors at the '64 NHRA Nationals.

Dick Landy
"Landy's Dodge"

Bill Flynn
"Yankee Peddler"

Mary Ann Foss
"Go-Hummer"

Bill Golden
"Little Red Wagon"

Bob Harrop
"Flying Carpet"

Roger Lindamood
"Color Me Gone"

Sam Kennedy
"Hemi-Charger"

Shirley Shahan
"Drag-On-Lady"

▲ Men dominated this gallery of early Mopar drivers, but an increasing number of women were able to match reflexes and skill with the best of them to the delight of drag-strip crowds.

▲ George Hurst developed and marketed high-performance shifters, and promoted them vigorously. Here he is in a Polara convertible—complete with Miss Golden Shifter—at the '64 Winternationals. Hurst awarded a Polara hardtop to the team of Sox and Martin, who won Super Stock in a '64 Mercury Comet.

▲ For '64, big Dodges got a smoother front end, as seen on this Polara 500 convertible, while two-door hardtops got a new reverse-taper rear roof pillar. Returning for its last season was the raucous 426-cid wedge with 425 bhp and 13.5:1 compression. An easier-to-manage 365-bhp "Street Wedge" variant with 10.3:1 compression, milder cam, and single four-barrel without ram induction was also made available.

▶ The new 426 Street Wedge had a chrome air cleaner and valve covers, but not the upswept headers. Brochures warned that sale of the dual-quad 426 wedge was "limited to recognized and qualified competition participants only." But they had a cautionary note about the new wedge, too. "Quite frankly," Dodge said, "it is recommended for the performance specialist only."

1964 DODGE HIGH-PERFORMANCE ENGINES

TYPE	CID	BORE × STROKE	BHP @ RPM	TORQUE @ RPM	FUEL SYSTEM	COMP. RATIO	AVAIL.
ohv V-8	383	4.25 × 3.75	330 @ 4600	425 @ 2800	1 × 4bbl.	10.0:1	full size
ohv V-8	426	4.25 × 3.75	365 @ 4800	470 @ 3200	1 × 4bbl.	10.3:1	full size
ohv V-8	426*	4.25 × 3.75	415 @ 5600	470 @ 4400	2 × 4bbl.	11.0:1	full size
ohv V-8	426	4.25 × 3.75	425 @ 5600	480 @ 4400	2 × 4bbl.	12.5:1	full size
ohv V-8	426*	4.25 × 3.75	425 @ 6000	480 @ 4600	2 × 4bbl.	12.5:1	full size

* Hemi.

▲ King Kong returns! Chrysler revived its mighty Hemi V-8 for '64, unveiling it at Daytona in February 1964, where it promptly swept the first three places in NASCAR's biggest race. The 426-cid monster still was a few years away from street duty, but did find a home beneath the hood of a few special drag-prepped 330/440/Polara Dodges. This 330 two-door is one of those factory-built race cars.

▲ Called the Maximum Performance Package, Dodge's drag-ready Hemi setup used lightweight Dodge van bucket seats and eliminated the rear seat, radio, heater, and carpeting.

▲ Though it resembled the hemi-head Mopars of the 1950s, this one was based on the RB wedge. Dodge claimed 425 bhp at 6000 rpm with 12.5:1 compression, and 415 bhp with an 11.0:1 squeeze. Actual outputs were closer to 570 bhp.

▲ The Maximum Performance Package moved the battery to the trunk and used aluminum for the hood, front fenders, doors, and some minor body panels.

▲ Spotter's guide: The hood scoop on Ramcharger 426 wedges had two distinct openings. The 426 Hemis could be identified by their single large opening.

▲ Hemis used the new heavy-duty-side-loading Chrysler four-speed manual or the three-speed TorqueFlite, which was in its last year with pushbuttons.

▲ The Hemi's large, half-arc combustion chambers allowed fuel to burn quicker and more completely with reduced risk of dangerous knocking. Breathing and heat dissipation at high rpm also were outstanding, though the complex valve network with dual rocker shafts helped push manufacturing cost high.

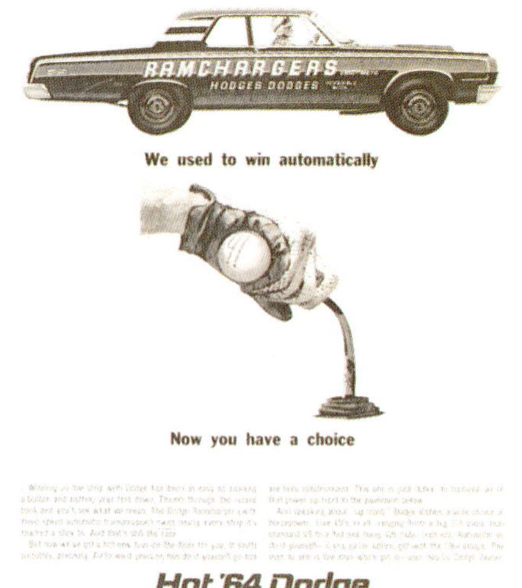

▲ After setting a slew of quarter-mile records with automatic, Dodge announced its new four-speed.

▲ NASCAR versions of the Hemi used a single Holley four-barrel atop a dual-plane high-rise intake manifold. Drag Hemis used a ram-tuned aluminum induction system with Carter dual quads. These heavily modified "Dodge Chargers," however, had superchargers.

▲ The S/FX Chargers had 850-900 bhp. At 135.33 mph in the quarter, no stock-body car was faster.

▲ Trophies by the truckload: Hemis powered Jim Thornton (above) among others to NHRA titles, while in NASCAR, Richard Petty drove one to his first Daytona 500 win.

▲ Ford showed a fresh face for '64, but still found itself fighting an uphill battle in drag racing. Nonetheless, the blue-oval boys were promoting the sportiness of their full-size cars, even claiming that their three-speed's new synchronized first-gear "may wean you away from automatics yet."

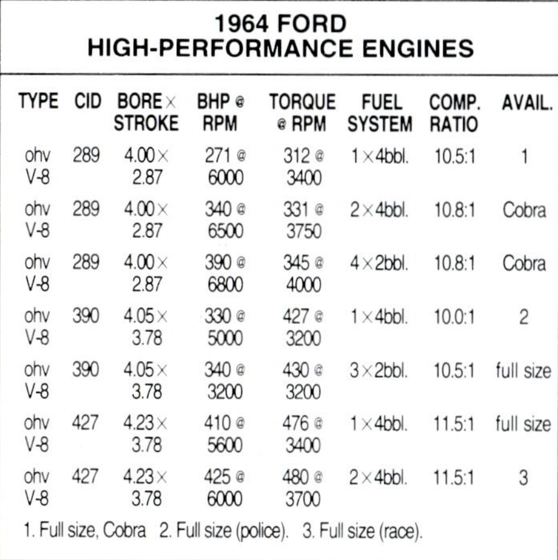

1964 FORD HIGH-PERFORMANCE ENGINES

TYPE	CID	BORE × STROKE	BHP @ RPM	TORQUE @ RPM	FUEL SYSTEM	COMP. RATIO	AVAIL.
ohv V-8	289	4.00 × 2.87	271 @ 6000	312 @ 3400	1 × 4bbl.	10.5:1	1
ohv V-8	289	4.00 × 2.87	340 @ 6500	331 @ 3750	2 × 4bbl.	10.8:1	Cobra
ohv V-8	289	4.00 × 2.87	390 @ 6800	345 @ 4000	4 × 2bbl.	10.8:1	Cobra
ohv V-8	390	4.05 × 3.78	330 @ 5000	427 @ 3200	1 × 4bbl.	10.0:1	2
ohv V-8	390	4.05 × 3.78	340 @ 3200	430 @ 3200	3 × 2bbl.	10.5:1	full size
ohv V-8	427	4.23 × 3.78	410 @ 5600	476 @ 3400	1 × 4bbl.	11.5:1	full size
ohv V-8	427	4.23 × 3.78	425 @ 6000	480 @ 3700	2 × 4bbl.	11.5:1	3

1. Full size, Cobra 2. Full size (police). 3. Full size (race).

▲ Ford was tops in NASCAR, taking 30 Grand National wins to 13 for Dodge, 12 for Plymouth. Ned Jarrett got 15 of them in his No. 11 Galaxie. When NASCAR disallowed its overhead-cam proposal, Ford adopted a high-rev kit that, despite the 410 rating, gave the 427 stock-car motor 550 bhp at 7000 rpm.

▲ Ford's poor power-to-weight ratio was usually its Achilles' heel in quarter-mile competition. But a hot 300-bhp-plus HiPo 289 in a featherweight AC Cobra body was one place things evened out. Here, Ed Hedrick's "Fuchsia" Dragonsnake does battle with a '62 Pontiac Catalina. This sub-12-second Cobra held the NHRA A, B, and C/Sports national records in 1963 and '64.

▲Billy Cox's A/SA lightweight 427 Galaxie puts the power down at the '64 Winternationals.

▲Even with the hottest 427s, big Fords were seldom a match for lighter Mopars and Pontiacs at the drags.

▲The few Galaxie Lightweights had a fiberglass nose with bubble hood to clear the new manifold.

▲The Thunderbird 427 Super High Performance big-block was again rated at 425 bhp with dual quads below its pretty, elongated air cleaner. The single-quad version again made 410 bhp. *Motor Trend* ran a 425-bhp 427 with a 4.11:1 axle to 60 mph in 7.4, seconds, and needed 15.4 for the quarter. Not great, but as the Ford ads said, with 480 pounds/feet "those SuperTorque Ford engines climb hills like a homesick Swiss yodeler." Ford's purpose-built drag-racing 427 used a high-rise manifold that lifted the air cleaner above the stock hood line, requiring a teardrop-shape bubble hood that later became a popular street-warrior accessory.

▲New lower-body sculpturing gave Ford's sleek Galaxie 500XL a fresh base for its semi-fastback roofline. Wheelbase was unchanged at 119 inches. About 265,000 Galaxie hardtops were sold, but not too many carried either of the 427 engines. The 300-bhp 390-cid four-barrel or even the 250-bhp 352 four-barrel were more popular to buyers with sporting inclinations.

▲Other factory stockers sold to pro drivers were stripped for dragstrip action, but few were starker than a Ford Fairlane Thunderbolt. A trunk-mounted 95-pound bus battery was one of dozens of modifications to the mid-size. With fiberglass doors, front body panels, and bumpers, and Plexiglass windows, a T-Bolt weighed just over the NHRA's 3205-pound minimum.

▲Nonessentials were taboo: sunvisors, outside mirrors, sound deadener, armrests—even the jack and lug wrench. The back seat stayed, but lightweight front buckets were borrowed from Ford's Econoline light trucks. A Ford Rotunda brand tach sat atop the dash, and an oil pressure gauge was mounted below.

▲Stuffing the high-riser 427 into a Fairlane was a battle requiring considerable modification of the front suspension. Then the eight equal-length exhaust headers had to be routed through the suspension components. Two trannies were offered: a Hurst-shifted T-10 four-speed with 4.44:1 axle, or PCA-F automatic with 4.58:1. Huge traction bars and asymmetrical rear springs helped get the power to the pavement. "Officially" rated 425 bhp at 6000 rpm, the engine actually produced at least 500 bhp.

▲With the strong 427 burdened by too much weight in the Galaxie, the solution was obvious: Put the mill in a lighter car. Tempting as the mid-size Fairlane was, its engine bay just couldn't hold a big-block. Or could it? The job wasn't easy, but with help from Dearborn Steel Tubing, a contract car builder, Ford concocted a handful of race-ready and street-legal, if not exactly streetable, Thunderbolts.

▲ Georgia racer Phil Bonner at the wheel of a Thunderbolt strains to catch Al Eckstrand's "Lawman" Plymouth in the first round of eliminations at the '64 Winternationals. T-Bolts fared well in Super/Stock class. Gas Ronda turned an 11.60 at 124.38 mph at the Winternationals, helping Ford win the Manufacturer's Cup.

▼ Butch Leal dropped his "California Flash" moniker for "Mr. 427" in 1964, and the name fit as he piloted his T-Bolt to the S/S title at the NHRA Nationals in Indianapolis. His ET was 11.76 seconds at 122.78 mph. Here, Leal gets the drop on the Dana Brothers Dodge at the '64 Winternationals.

▲ Ford sold one lucky group of racers T-Bolts for $1, but the usual price was $3900 ($100 more for automatic), double the cost of a regular Fairlane. Few non-racers took the plunge. *Hot Rod* warned that the brutal machine was "not suitable for driving to and from the strip, let alone on the street."

▲ Ford planned to build just 50 Thunderbolts as A/FX cars, but constructed 127, enough to qualify for Super/Stock, where they were very hot. The thick hose visible here is one of the flexible ducts that fed the carbs through screened ram-air intakes installed in place of the inner headlamps.

▲ Mercury's Comet was basically a stretched Falcon, but Ford extended the corporate Total Performance push to include an A/FX Comet version of the Thunderbolt. Here they are in action at the '64 Winternationals.

▲ Ronnie Sox's 427 Comet hardtop turned an 11.49 at 123.45 mph to beat Nicholson's wagon for the A/FX prize at the '64 Winternationals.

▲ The lightweight 427 Comet was built as a wagon as well as a hardtop. It hauled. Don Nicholson's "Marauder" wagon turned ETs of around 11.5 at 121 mph at the NHRA's '64 Winternationals.

▲ When veteran fuel dragster racer Jack Chrisman installed a supercharged, nitro-burning, 427-cid Mercury wedge into the Sachs and Sons Comet for exhibition use, he initiated what would become one of drag racing's biggest classes. These were eventually termed "funny cars" after Chrysler's 1965 altered-wheelbase effort. Chrisman's ability to run mid-10s at tire-blazing speeds would thrill crowds that year and lead a revolution toward ultra-radical stockers in the next year.

1964 MERCURY HIGH-PERFORMANCE ENGINES

TYPE	CID	BORE × STROKE	BHP @ RPM	TORQUE @ RPM	FUEL SYSTEM	COMP. RATIO	AVAIL.
ohv V-8	390	4.05 × 3.78	330 @ 5000	427 @ 3200	1 × 4bbl.	10.0:1	full size
ohv V-8	427	4.23 × 3.78	410 @ 5600	476 @ 3400	1 × 4bbl.	11.5:1	full size
ohv V-8	427	4.23 × 3.78	425 @ 6000	480 @ 3700	2 × 4bbl.	11.5:1	full size (race)
ohv V-8	430	4.30 × 3.70	320 @ 4600	465 @ 2600	1 × 4bbl.	10.1:1	full size

▲ Oldsmobile could claim the first "muscle car" with its Rocket 88 of 1949. But it didn't return to the formula until mid-1964. That's when it massaged its Police Apprehender Pursuit package into the 4-4-2 option for its new F-85/Cutlass series, which had moved from a compact to mid-sized. The 4-4-2 package was optional in any F-85 or Cutlass except the wagon, though it was poorly promoted and only 2999 buyers ordered it.

◀ In its first season, 4-4-2 stood for four-barrel carb, four-speed manual transmission, and dual exhausts. The $136 package included a 330-cid V-8, beefed-up suspension with rear stabilizer, and Red-Line tires.

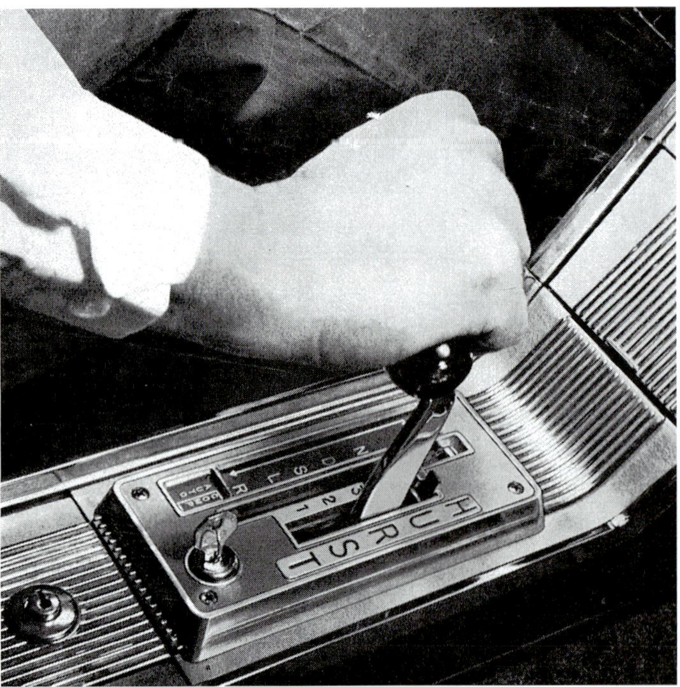

Hurst *Dual Gate*

complete control for beefed-up "hydros"

Now complete instructions for beefing "hydro" transmissions are included in every Dual Gate kit. Leading transmission experts tell you how to convert your "hydro" to a neck-snapping screamer. It's a job you can easily do yourself for peanuts. And you really control that power with a Dual Gate. You thrill to jet-fast getaways . . . enjoy dragstrip performance with the Competition Gate. The other gate? A mild-mannered automatic setup that's just for "her." For 2-car performance on a 1-car budget, get a Hurst Dual Gate from your speed shop today. And if you are thinking new car . . . the Dual Gate is designed for many fine 64s, like Pontiac and Olds, as standard equipment.

HURST

HURST PERFORMANCE PRODUCTS, INC., GLENSIDE, PA.

▲ The 4-4-2's V-8 made 310 bhp, 20 more than the regular four-barrel, thanks to a higher-lift cam, heavy-duty bearings, and dual-snorkel air cleaner. It turned 0-60 times of 7.5 seconds and 15.5 quarter-miles.

1964 OLDSMOBILE HIGH-PERFORMANCE ENGINES

TYPE	CID	BORE × STROKE	BHP @ RPM	TORQUE @ RPM	FUEL SYSTEM	COMP. RATIO	AVAIL.
ohv V-8	330	3.94 × 3.39	290 @ 4800	355 @ 2800	1×4bbl.	10.25:1	1
ohv V-8	394	4.13 × 3.69	330 @ 4600	440 @ 2800	1×4bbl.	10.25:1	2
ohv V-8	394	4.13 × 3.69	345 @ 4800	440 @ 3200	1×4bbl.	10.5:1	3

1. F-85, Cutlass 442, Jetfire. 2. 88, S-88, 98. 3. S-88, 98, Starfire, Jetstar I.

▲ Big Plymouths got a cleaner nose and handsome V-shaped rear-roof pillars. The 426-cid V-8 was back, but a new Street Wedge version made things easier for Plymouth drivers on the road. Reintroduction of the killer Hemi, meanwhile, made things much tougher for Plymouth rivals on the track.

▼ Bill Shirey in "Golden Commando #4" and Bill Hanyon aboard the Milne Brothers Plymouth charge the Pomona strip at the '64 Winternationals. These wedges ran mid-11s at 115-118 mph. In NASCAR, Plymouth Hemis swept the Daytona 500 1-2-3.

1964 PLYMOUTH HIGH-PERFORMANCE ENGINES

TYPE	CID	BORE × STROKE	BHP @ RPM	TORQUE @ RPM	FUEL SYSTEM	COMP. RATIO	AVAIL.
ohv V-8	383	4.24 × 3.38	330 @ 4600	425 @ 2800	1 × 4bbl.	10.0:1	full size
ohv V-8	426	4.25 × 3.75	365 @ 4800	470 @ 3200	1 × 4bbl.	10.3:1	full size
ohv V-8	426	4.25 × 3.75	415 @ 5600	470 @ 4400	2 × 4bbl.	11.0:1	full size
ohv V-8	426	4.25 × 3.75	425 @ 5600	480 @ 4400	2 × 4bbl.	12.5:1	full size
ohv V-8	426*	4.25 × 3.75	415 @ 6000	470 @ 4600	2 × 4bbl.	11.0:1	full size
ohv V-8	426*	4.25 × 3.75	425 @ 6000	480 @ 4600	2 × 4bbl.	12.5:1	full size

* Hemi.

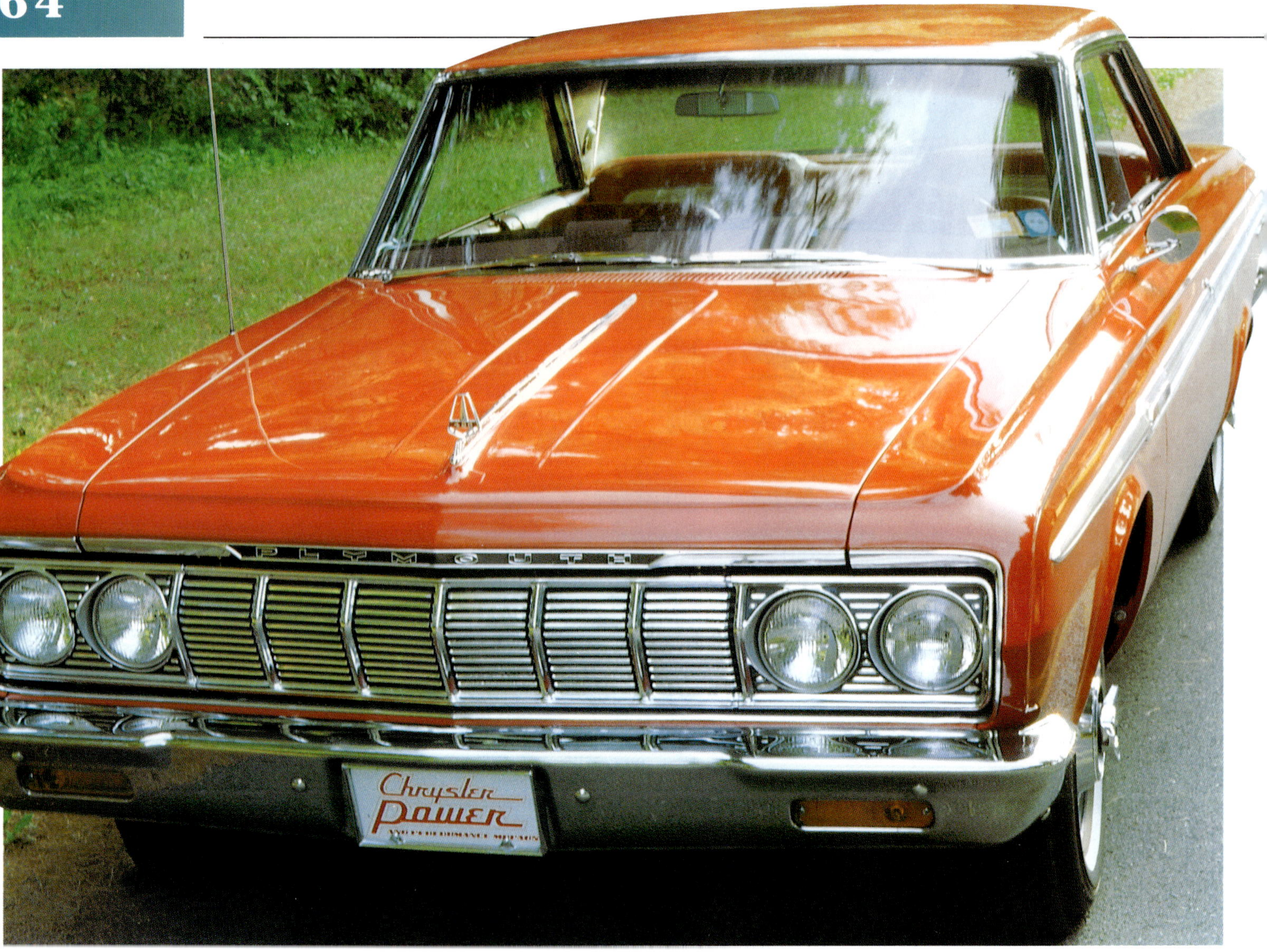
PLYMOUTH
Chrysler Power

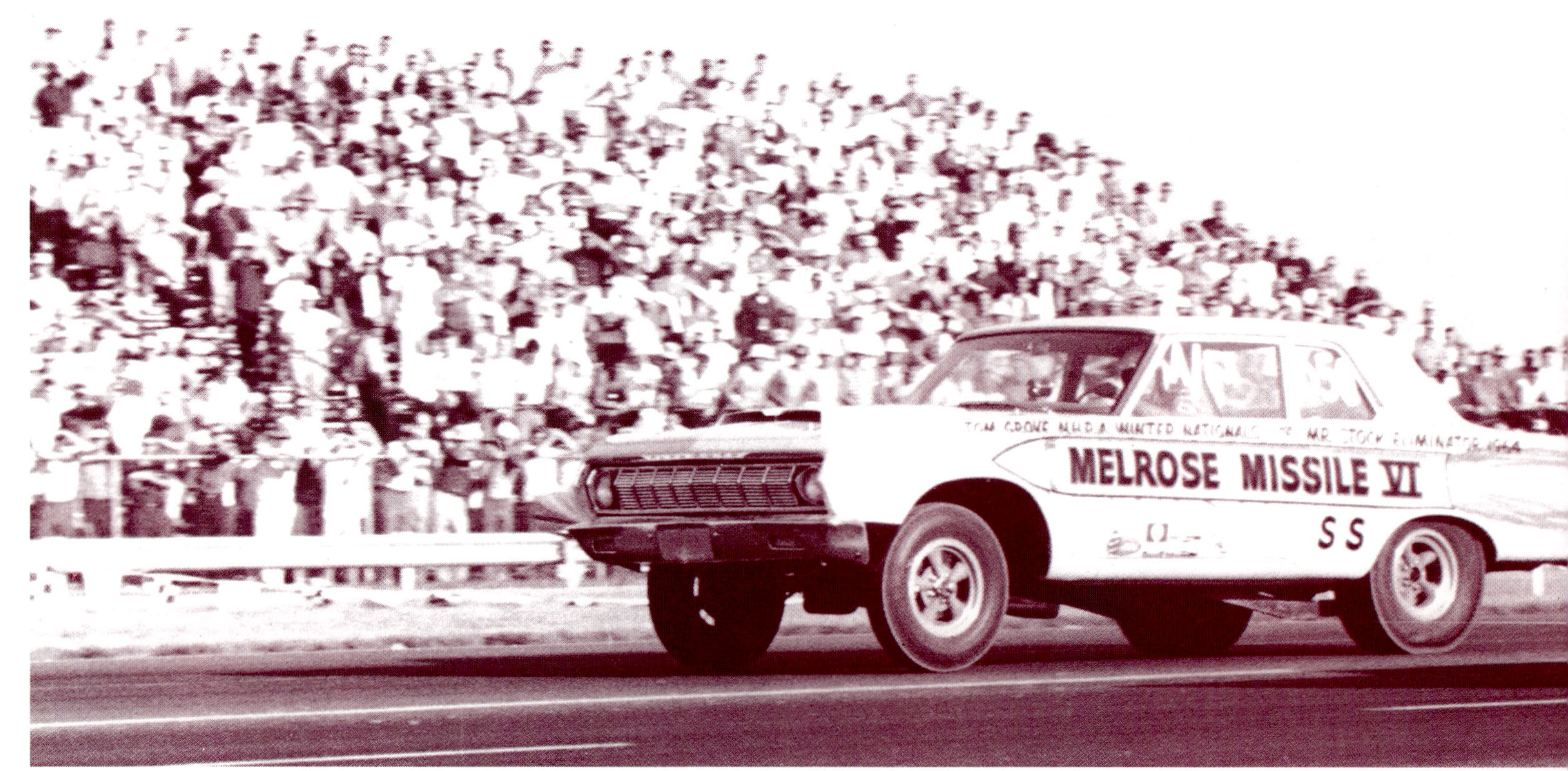

MELROSE MISSILE VI
SS

◀ The 425-bhp 426 Stage III still topped the wedge tower of power, but the owner of this Sport Fury ordered the new 365-bhp Street Wedge, which Plymouth billed as the Commando 426. It was more streetable, but still tough. *Motor Trend* saw 0-60 mph in 6.3 seconds and ran the quarter in 15.2 at 95.5 mph with the Street Wedge and a 3.91:1 axle.

▶ Whether tucked under the hood of this Plymouth Sport Fury or a subtler Belvedere or Savoy, the new hydraulic-lifter Street Wedge whipped up 365 bhp at 4800 rpm and 470 lbs/ft of torque at 3200. The engine was treated to high-performance valve springs, pistons and cam, plus a dual-point distributor, unsilenced air cleaner, dual exhaust, and heavy-duty clutch.

◀ Unlike the wilder wedges, the street version had a provision to heat the intake manifold for cold startups, and its 10.3:1 compression would suit ordinary fuel. A single four-barrel replaced dual quads and a conventional exhaust manifold supplanted the tuff ram's-head headers.

▶ Bucket seats and a console again graced the Sport Fury, but the driver faced a fresh dashboard with four gauges in a brushed-metal panel. And a four-speed manual gearbox could now be ordered. Handling got a boost as rear track width grew 2.5 inches.

▼ It's a clash of altered-wheelbase A/FX Mopars at the '64 Nationals. Jim Thornton's Ramchargers Dodge clocked an 11.32 ET, but it wasn't enough to beat the searing 11.04 at 127.47 turned in by Tom Grove in his Melrose Missile VI Plymouth.

▲ Norman Thatcher drove this stock-bodied '64 Sport Fury to 205.55 mph in the flying mile at the Bonneville Salt Flats. He became the first person to top 200 mph in a supercharged production sedan. Thatcher was a 67-year-old grandfather at the time.

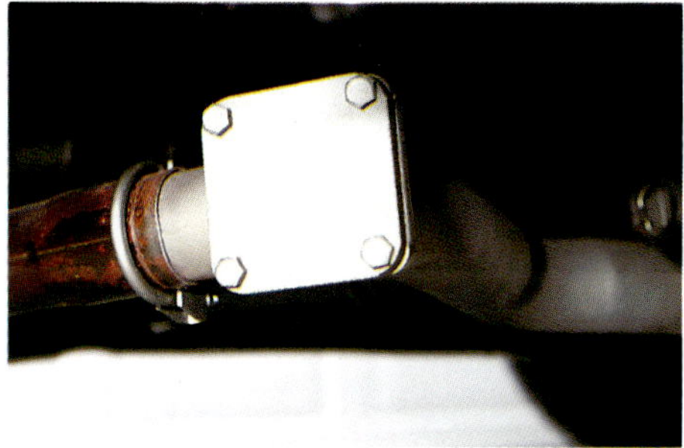

▲ Mopar's high performance big-blocks came with header cut-outs that were simple to remove for the strip or serious street action.

▲ Still available was the potent 415-bhp Super Stock III wedge with dual quads and upswept headers.

▼ Cars with the 415-bhp wedge got a stock hood sans scoop, though sharp aftermarket wheels were common.

▲ This is it. The 1964 Pontiac Tempest GTO was the first modern mass-production automobile to put big-cube power in a mid-size body—the formula that defined the true muscle car. Pontiac circumvented a GM rule prohibiting intermediates from having V-8s over 330 cid by making its 389-cid V-8 part of an option package for the new Tempest, a ploy that didn't require corporate approval. The name *Gran Turismo Omologato* was borrowed from the Ferrari 250 GTO. It stands for a production grand touring machine homologated, or sanctioned, to race.

◀ A Hurst-stirred Muncie four-speed sends 348 bhp at 4800 rpm from this GTO's Tri-Power 389 to a 3.55:1 Positraction rear axle. With a single four-barrel, output was 325 bhp. Both versions ran on 10.75:1 compression and developed 428 lbs/ft of torque. GTOs came in pillared sport coupe, hardtop coupe, and convertible form. All had bucket seats and a simulated engine-turned instrument surround. A three-speed floor shift was standard, two-speed automatic optional.

◀ Credit for the GTO concept generally goes to Pontiac ad exec Jim Wangers, himself a racer, though some cite engineers John DeLorean and Bill Collins. Regardless, it was a grand slam. Pontiac hoped to sell a modest 5000 '64 GTOs; final production was 32,450.

▶ Affectionately tagged the Goat, the GTO was the first factory hot rod with its own identity. It developed a cult following and influenced other makers to create similar machines.

1964 PONTIAC HIGH-PERFORMANCE ENGINES							
TYPE	CID	BORE × STROKE	BHP @ RPM	TORQUE @ RPM	FUEL SYSTEM	COMP. RATIO	AVAIL.
ohv V-8	389	4.06×3.75	325@4800	428@3200	1×4bbl.	10.75:1	Tempest GTO
ohv V-8	389	4.06×3.75	348@4800	428@3600	3×2bbl.	10.75:1	Tempest GTO
ohv V-8	421	4.09×3.75	320@4400	455@2800	1×4bbl.	10.5:1	full size
ohv V-8	421	4.09×4.00	350@4600	454@3200	3×2bbl.	10.75:1	full size
ohv V-8	421	4.09×3.75	370@5200	460@3800	3×2bbl.	10.75:1	full size

▲ Only 6644 GTO convertibles were built for '64, including this Marimba Red ragtop. The 389-cid engine was just one part of the GTO package. An extra-tough suspension used a thicker ($^{15}/_{16}$-inch) front sway bar, heavy-duty Delco shocks, and stiffer springs. Red-line high-speed 7.50 × 14 tires rode 6JK wide-rim wheels.

◄ For the GTO, the 389 got high-output heads from the 421 V-8, a high-lift cam, and a Carter AFB four-barrel. Tri-Power setups like this used three Rochester two-barrels and were ordered on 8245 '64 Goats. Axle ratios from 3.08:1 to 3.90:1 were offered. The GTO package added $296 to the price of a LeMans. The pillared coupe cost $2852, the hardtop $2963, and the convertible $3081.

▲ Finned drum brakes were standard on GTOs, but a $75 "roadability group" added sintered metallic linings, a heavy-duty radiator, and Safe-T-Track differential. Twin hood scoops looked good, but weren't functional.

◄ *Road & Track*'s four-barrel GTO with a 3.23:1 axle did 0-60 in 6.9 seconds and the quarter in 15.0 at 91.5 mph. With Tri-Power, *R&T*'s numbers were 5.7 seconds 0-60 and 14.1 at 104.2 in the quarter.

▲ Buyers could tailor GTOs to taste. Extras included transistorized ignition, a Rally wood steering wheel, and in-dash tachometer. Dealers could install side-exit exhaust splitters.

▲ Part of the GTO's magic was that it was first to integrate all the best performance cues in a single package. It had style, and muscle to back it up. *Motor Trend* turned a 15.8 ET at 93 mph with a four-barrel four-speed.

Get in, turn on, leave abruptly.

This is where you aim a Catalina *2+2* from. Bucket seats, nylon-blend carpeting, custom steering wheel, the whole bit, all color-coordinated, in either sports coupe or convertible form.

The standard 389-cubic inch engine puts out 283 bhp when coupled to a 4-speed box*, 267 bhp with 3-speed Hydra-Matic*. (The *2+2* comes only with one of these two transmissions.) Both shifters are mounted in the standard console.

Much automobile.

If you want to make even more automobile of it, there's nothing to stop you from huddling with a Pontiac salesman and a list of performance options and doing wild things with an order form.

*Optional at extra cost

the 2+2 makers—Pontiac

PONTIAC MOTOR DIVISION • GENERAL MOTORS CORPORATION

▲ Though overshadowed by the new mid-size GTO, Pontiac's Catalina had something new this year: a 2+2 option package with bucket seats, console, and special interior. It was available for $291 on hardtops and convertibles.

▼ The pillared coupe was the lightest and cheapest GTO; 7384 were made. Pontiac was out of "factory" racing, but had a high profile on the street.

▲ Like other full-size models, Catalinas wore slightly more rounded bodies for '64. The 2+2 package was ordered on 7998 of them. A lowly 389-cid two-barrel was standard, but an ad explained that customers could do "wild things with an order form" if extra performance was a priority.

▲ The 2+2 option was Pontiac's first performance package on a full-size model. "Considering the range of options and accessories we've got, no two 2+2s need be alike," said one Pontiac ad.

▲ Optional 2+2 engines included this 330-bhp Tri-Power 389, as well as three 421s, up to the 370-bhp Tri-Power 421, which was capable of 7.2-seconds 0-60 mph and a 16.1-second quarter-mile. The Super Duty engines were gone.

▲ A Studebaker Daytona convertible with the rare R2 supercharged V-8 races at the '64 Winternationals. Only 703 of these Studes were built.

▲ One of the winningest teams on Southern California 'strips was Gordon Williams and his '63 R1 unsupercharged 289-cid, 240-bhp Studebaker Lark.

1965

Top horsepower rating remains 425...Ford's 427-cid is the largest engine • Sanctioned drag racing more popular than ever, now has five major national events...action on the street also picks up • Chevy's hallowed 409 departs, but is replaced by future-great 396 • Buick joins muscle-car melee, stuffing 400-cid V-8 into mid-size Skylark to create Gran Sport • Olds improves 4-4-2 option • Chevelle turns up heat with rare 375-bhp SS 396 Z-16 • Nova available with 327-cid • Mustang enters first full season, adds 2+2...fiery Shelby GT-350 bows • Mopar escalates factory-backed drag wars with radical altered wheelbase intermediates • Ford counter-punches with overhead cam 427 Mustangs • GTO sales more than double • Chrysler retires letter-series cars...turns attention to mid-size muscle • Wild wheelie exhibitions by the Little Red Wagon and Hemi Under Glass thrill drag crowds • Don Garlits goes 206.88 mph and Art Malone turns a 7.56-second ET • NASCAR disallows Mopar Hemi; Chrysler returns when Hemi is reinstated...too late: Fords rule NASCAR with 48 wins.

▲ When GM raised the engine limit for mid-size cars to 400 cid, Buick renamed its 401-cid V-8 the "400" and jammed it into the Skylark. The resultant midyear Gran Sport was Buick's first modern muscle car. Its 325 bhp was less than that of the GTO or 4-4-2, but it had more torque. All Grand Sports got a reinforced convertible frame, dual exhausts, huskier suspension, and bucket seats.

▲ Gran Sports cost about $460 more than Skylarks, which were already among GM's pricier intermediates. Pillared coupes, hardtops, and ragtops were offered. *Motor Trend* got 0-60 mph in 7.8 seconds, the quarter in 16.6 at 86 mph.

1965 BUICK HIGH-PERFORMANCE ENGINES

TYPE	CID	BORE × STROKE	BHP @ RPM	TORQUE @ RPM	FUEL SYSTEM	COMP. RATIO	AVAIL.
ohv V-8	300	3.75 × 3.40	250 @ 4800	335 @ 3000	1 × 4bbl.	10.25:1	Special, Skylark
ohv V-8	401	4.19 × 3.64	325 @ 4400	445 @ 2800	1 × 4bbl.	10.25:1	1
ohv V-8	425	4.31 × 3.64	340 @ 4400	465 @ 2800	1 × 4bbl.	10.25:1	Wildcat, Electra 225
ohv V-8	425	4.31 × 3.64	360 @ 4400	465 @ 2800	1 × 4bbl.	10.25:1	Wildcat, Electra 225

1. Skylark, Gran Sport, Wildcat, Electra 225

▲ Dick Harrell's 427 Retribution Chevy II (far lane) goes against Tom "Mongoose" McEwen's rear-engined Hemi Cuda at Lions Drag Strip in early 1965. The '65 season was start of the "funny car" movement, with gutted, altered-wheelbase street cars thrilling crowds across the nation. Chevy was officially out of competition, but was well-represented by independent racers.

1965 CHEVROLET HIGH-PERFORMANCE ENGINES

TYPE	CID	BORE × STROKE	BHP @ RPM	TORQUE @ RPM	FUEL SYSTEM	COMP. RATIO	AVAIL.
ohv V-8	327	4.00 × 3.25	300 @ 5000	360 @ 3200	1 × 4bbl.	10.5:1	1
ohv V-8	327	4.00 × 3.25	350 @ 5800	360 @ 3600	1 × 4bbl.	11.0:1	Chevelle
ohv V-8	396	4.09 × 3.76	325 @ 4800	410 @ 3200	1 × 4bbl.	10.25:1	full size
ohv V-8	396	4.09 × 3.76	425 @ 6400	415 @ 4000	1 × 4bbl.	11.0:1	full size
ohv V-8	396	4.09 × 3.76	375 @ 5600	420 @ 3600	1 × 4bbl.	11.0:1	2
ohv V-8	409	4.31 × 3.50	340 @ 5000	420 @ 3200	1 × 4bbl.	10.0:1	full size
ohv V-8	409	4.31 × 3.50	400 @ 5800	425 @ 3600	1 × 4bbl.	11.0:1	full size

1. Full size, Chevelle, Chevy II. 2. Chevelle SS 396.

◀ Chevy had offered a 220-bhp four-barrel 283 in its compact '64 Nova. For '65, the bowtie boys dropped in the 327-cid small-block. The four-barrel 327 had either 250 or 300 bhp. Its most stylish application was the Nova Super Sport (shown), which came only as a $2433 hardtop. The 327 could also be ordered in a no-frills Chevy II two-door sedan. Powerglide and a Muncie four-speed were optional along with Positraction, tach, and sintered metallic brake linings.

Chevy's mid-size Chevelle was making the best of its 327-cid V-8s, but it couldn't match the big-block GTO and 4-4-2. That changed at midyear with the Z-16, a 375-bhp 396-cid avenger. It was fitted to just 201 Malibu SS models, which got special trim, heavy-duty suspension, and a 160-mph speedometer. It added $1501.05 to the $2647 base Malibu SS hardtop.

The Z-16 Turbo-Jet 396 was basically a hydraulic-lifter version of the 375-bhp 396 offered in the 'Vette. The Malibu's had a Holley four-barrel and 11.0:1 compression. A Muncie four-speed was mandatory, with axle ratios of up to 4.56:1 available. Mid-14-second quarters at around 100 mph were no sweat.

The '65 Chevelle also could have the 300-bhp 327. At midyear, regular and Super Sport Malibus were available with the L79 327, a 350-bhp screamer that essentially was a hydraulic-lifter version of the solid-lifter 365-bhp 327 in the Corvette. Automatic wasn't offered, but with a four-speed, Positraction, and standard 3.31:1 gear, an L79 Malibu could easily turn high 14s.

Malibu SS models with the Z-16 got a fortified convertible-type frame, strengthened front suspension, front and rear anti-roll bars, bigger brakes, and faster power steering. Still, handling was poor with nearly 58 percent of the weight on the front tires. Tamer SS models were far more common, and Super Sport output set a record: 101,577 out of 326,977 Chevelles.

▶ GT trim sharpened Dodge's milquetoast Dart. The hardtop and convertible compacts rode a 111-inch wheelbase. The GT was available for '64 with a two-barrel 273 V-8 at a modest 180 bhp. For '65, it had a 235-bhp version of the 273 twisting a standard three-speed gearbox, optional four-speed, or TorqueFlite. The basic 3.23:1 axle could be replaced by a 2.93:1 or 3.55:1 cog. *Car and Driver* managed 8.2 seconds to 60 mph and a 16.9-second quarter at 87 mph with a GT hardtop. For serious dragstrip work, Fibercraft made Darts with fiberglass body panels, slashing some 400 pounds.

▲ Dart GT touches included full-length racing stripes and rocker-panel vents. Real Cragar mags were a Dart GT option this year.

▲ On the surface, the GT was a dressed-for-success Dart 270 with bucket seats, extra chrome, and a stylized badge.

▶ Dart GT's free-revving, short-stroke, hydraulic-lifter 273 used a Carter AFB four-barrel and 10.5:1 compression. The engine cost only $99.40 extra. The GT hardtop started at $2372; ragtop, $2591. A four-speed may have been the choice of stoplight strokers, but *Car and Driver* said TorqueFlite was "one automatic transmission that can actually be shifted," giving it "overwhelming superiority over manual units in super stock drag racing."

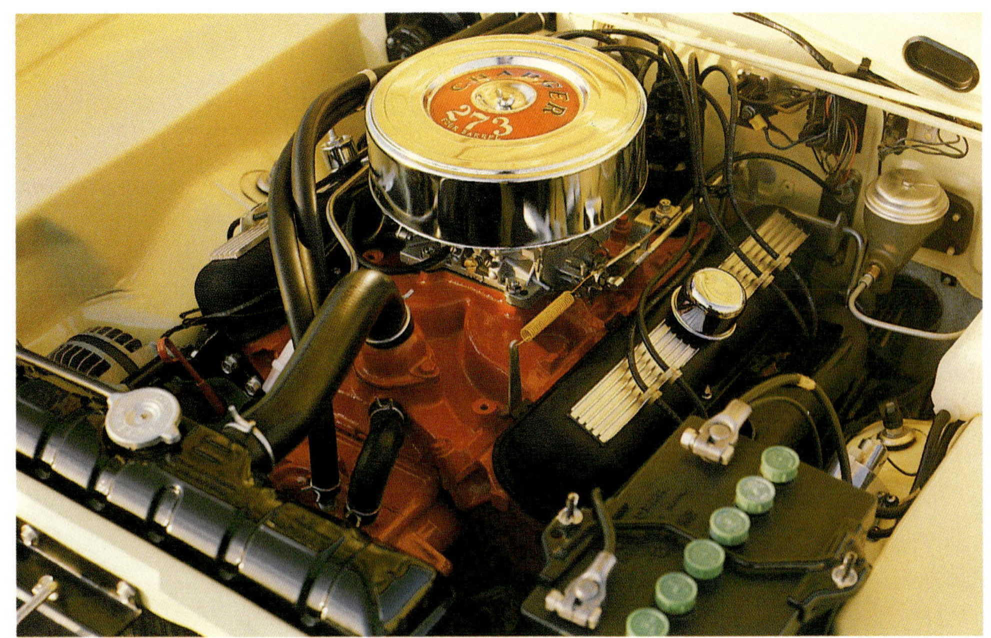

▲Bill "Maverick" Golden's "Little Red Wagon" had a fuel-injected 426 Hemi mounted amidships in a lightened Dodge A-100 pickup. It could turn 10.55-second ETs at 127 mph, but its claim to fame was crowd-pleasing wheelstands that it could sustain for the full quarter mile.

▲Performance was focusing on mid-size models, and at Dodge that meant the new 117-inch wheelbase Coronet. A hot street setup was Mopar's 426 RB-Wedge "civilized" to 10.3:1 compression and 365 bhp.

▲The 426 Street Wedge package added $513.60 to a $2674 Coronet 500 hardtop. *Motor Trend* saw 60 mph in 7.7 seconds and a 15.7 ET at 89 mph. Four-speed or TorqueFlite (shown) were offered.

▲ Factory-built drag Super/Stock Hemi Coronets for '65 had to use all-metal bodies but got two inches trimmed from the stock 117-inch wheelbase.

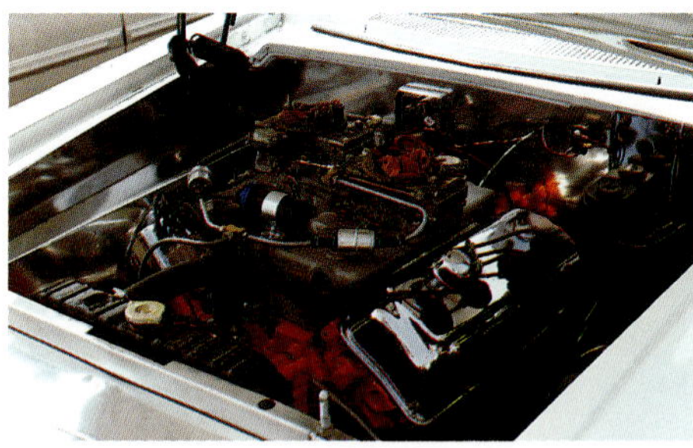

▲ Drag-race Hemis had dual quads on a ram-tuned magnesium manifold with new aluminum heads. Rating was 425 bhp; actual output was over 550 bhp.

▲ NASCAR said the Hemi wasn't a production engine and banned it in early '65. But it thrived under the NHRA's multi-class rules.

▲ The exciting "Bounty Hunters" Coronet was among the Mopars that fell between the nearly stock class and the profoundly altered factory-racer categories.

▲ Ed Knezevich piloted the "Mister Ed" Coronet. Dodges took plenty of Super/Stock wins, including NHRA Nationals. Bob Harrop topped SS/A class.

▲ This "funny" Hemi-Charger Coronet, lined up against a '56 Pontiac, advertises its achievements: a 10.45-second ET and 138.46 mph trap speed.

▲ This stock-wheelbase Dick Landy Dodge replica may have fit into NHRA's A/FX division. Landy's real car (see pg 116) was far more radical and was never legal for A/FX.

▲ Street Dodges wouldn't have the Hemi until '66, but drag racers took full advantage of the engine's superior ability to breath at high rpm.

▲ Tangled tubing tips off twin turbochargers. One of "Bud" Faubel's 426 Dodges used two water-cooled AiResearch turbos and fuel injection.

▲ Super/Stock Automatic tag is misleading; the turbo Honker was primarily an unlimited-class racer. Said *Hot Rod* of one Bud run: "... about 400 feet out of the chute there was an audible increase in the engine revs, almost to 'scream' pitch, tire smoke appeared [generous amounts of it] and there was some evidence of skating as if the increased power, as a result of the 'chargers kicking in, was trying to cut loose."

▲ "Candymatic" meant automatic transmission. Dodge dropped its pushbuttons for '65, and race engineers modified the column-mount shifter to a P-R-N-1-2-D sequence so drivers could upshift from Neutral simply by pulling the lever down as speed increased.

▲ Responding to the popularity of ultra-stock bracket exhibitions in '65, factory-backed racers ventured beyond the frontiers of Super/Stock, to where altered wheelbases, fuel injection, and few restrictions on weight lurked. The Hodges Dodges Coronet was there, waiting.

▲ Chrysler revamped a Hilborn fuel-injection system to suit its Hemis and shipped the modifications to its corps of factory-supported altered-wheelbase racers. The 14-inch velocity stacks gave a ram effect, helping the basic race 426 engine to over 600 bhp on gasoline.

▲ The Yankee Peddler did battle in the "Run-What-Ya-Brung" match races, where mid-9-second ETs ruled. Note the relocated fuel tank. Running nitromethane, these cars had an estimated 700 bhp. The Peddler was among the '65 Chrysler altered-wheelbase factory-supported cars.

▲ "Bud" Faubel was among the Mopar-backed drivers to get one of six Coronets with the wheels moved forward—the rears by 15 inches, the fronts by 10—to relocate weight for unlimited-class wars.

▲ The fiberglass hood, front bumper, front fenders and doors, instrument panel and deck lid totaled only 80 pounds. Lighter Dart spindles and brakes saved another 50 pounds for factory racers.

1965 DODGE HIGH-PERFORMANCE ENGINES

TYPE	CID	BORE × STROKE	BHP @ RPM	TORQUE @ RPM	FUEL SYSTEM	COMP. RATIO	AVAIL.
ohv V-8	273	3.63 × 3.31	235 @ 5200	280 @ 4000	1 × 4bbl.	10.5:1	Dart
ohv V-8	383	4.25 × 3.75	330 @ 4600	425 @ 2800	1 × 4bbl.	10.0:1	Coronet
ohv V-8	383	4.25 × 3.75	340 @ 4600	470 @ 2800	1 × 4bbl.	10.1:1	full size
ohv V-8	426	4.25 × 3.75	365 @ 4800	470 @ 3200	1 × 4bbl.	10.3:1	1
ohv V-8	426*	4.25 × 3.75	425 @ 6000	480 @ 4600	2 × 4bbl.	12.5:1	Coronet

* Hemi. 1. Coronet, full size.

▲ Chrysler's run of altered-wheelbase '65 intermediates bridged the gap between door-slammers and future full-blown funny cars. "Dandy" Dick Landy's, like the others, had a wheelbase of about 110 inches and weighed around 2700 pounds. Canvas straps helped hold hood at 140 mph.

▲ NHRA banned these Mopars, so they ran in AHRA and match-race competition. Relocated axles and trunk-mounted battery helped achieve a 44/56 percent weight distribution for good dig off the line.

▲ Landy suits up for work in his Coronet "funny" car. The burly Californian liked push-button shift controls and re-engineered them into this car. *Hot Rod* called his "the most controversial stocker ever built [and] the quickest and the fastest in the land."

▲ Landy's Dodge started '65 with a dual-quad Hemi, good for 10.2s at 138 mph. Fuel-injection added in the spring got ETs into the mid-9s and made this the first stock-body racer to exceed 140 mph in the quarter. Chicago's "Mr. Norm," meanwhile, ran a blown version to an 8.63.

▲ Ford's big cars shed 100 pounds, but gained new styling and a NASCAR-inspired front-suspension so strong that stock-car racers of all makes used it through the 1970s. The new nine-inch differential also became a legend. This Galaxie 500XL convertible went for $3498.

▲ Midyear brought a new 427-cid block with more efficient lubrication. The "side-oiler" 427 had dual Holley quads and 11.1:1 compression, but kept the 425-bhp rating. A rare Galaxie option, it helped Ford to its best NASCAR year with 48 wins in 55 events. This is Dan Gurney at the wheel.

▲ A 300-bhp 390 V-8 added $137.60 to the $3233 price of this Galaxie 500XL hardtop. The 330-bhp "Interceptor" 390 cost $225.30. And the 425-bhp 427 was advertised as "competitively priced." A 427 hardtop could do 14.93-second quarter-miles at 101.69 mph. Not bad for a heavyweight. Ford ads called the 427 Galaxie "The Velvet Brute."

▲ Few '65 Galaxies drag raced, so '64s like this one battled the 1965 rivals. Dearborn stayed performance focused, however, and during the year unleashed an astonishing 427-cid side-oiler that had hemispherical combustion chambers and single overhead cams. It was rated at 616-bhp with a single four barrel, or 654 with dual quads. Neither version was available factory installed in any Ford, so NASCAR said it wasn't a true production engine, and banned it accordingly. But the SOHC 427 went on to become a major force in drag racing.

▲ Carroll Shelby followed his AC Cobra with a super-Mustang, the GT-350. A 306-bhp HiPo 289 GT-350 listed for $4547. About 30 of the 562 GT-350s were racing GT-350Rs with a 360 bhp 289 and $6950 price. Most were road racers, but a few, like this one, hit the strips.

▲ Street Falcons had at most a 200-bhp 289. But this A/FX version with fiberglass fenders and doors had a 427 High-Riser. It was built for drag racer Dick Brannan and turned 11-second ETs.

1965 FORD HIGH-PERFORMANCE ENGINES

TYPE	CID	BORE × STROKE	BHP @ RPM	TORQUE @ RPM	FUEL SYSTEM	COMP. RATIO	AVAIL.
ohv V-8	289	4.00×2.87	271 @ 6000	312 @ 3400	1×4bbl.	10.5:1	1
ohv V-8	289	4.00×2.87	340 @ 6500	331 @ 3750	2×4bbl.	10.8:1	Cobra
ohv V-8	289	4.00×2.87	306 @ 6800	329 @ 4000	1×4bbl.	10.0:1	2
ohv V-8	289	4.00×2.87	390 @ 6600	345 @ 4000	4×2bbl.	10.8:1	3
ohv V-8	390	4.05×3.78	330 @ 5000	427 @ 3200	1×4bbl.	10.0:1	full size
ohv V-8	427	4.23×3.78	425 @ 6000	480 @ 3700	2×4bbl.	11.2:1	4
sohc V-8	427	4.23×3.78	616 @ 7000	696 @ 4400	1×4bbl.	12.0:1	race
sohc V-8	427	4.23×3.78	654 @ 7000	739 @ 4400	2×4bbl.	12.0:1	race

1. full size, Mustang. 2. Shelby GT-350. 3. Cobra (race). 4. full size (race).

▲ The 289 AC Cobra, shown here, was joined at midyear by a 427 model. It looked quite similar to the 289 version, but shared little with it. The 427 had more than 500 horsepower and could turn sub-13-second ETs.

▲ High-compression V-8s demanded super-premium gasoline. Sunoco and other brands offered a broad selection of blends, and stickers touting fuel were added to other decals on both street and strip cars.

If you see this on the window

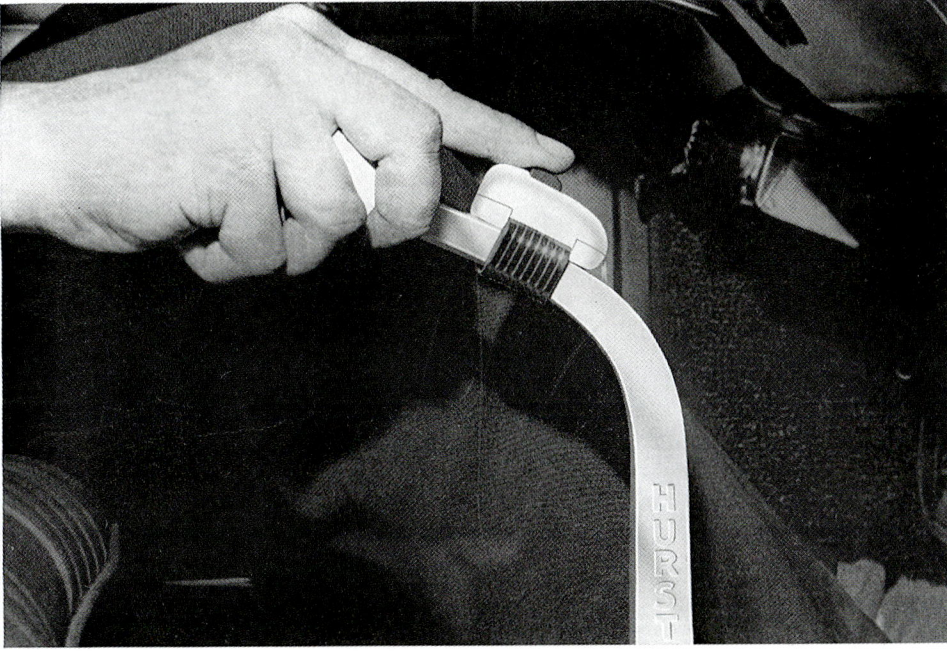

and this on the stick, you're about to get beat.

The name of the game is "How not to get hole shot." And the way to assure it is with Hurst's new line-holding LINE/LOC system.

Line/Loc is an electrically operated control that hooks into the brake system—front and/or rear, but ideally just into the front system. The switch mounts on your shifter with an off-on warning light on the dash.

When you come to the line you brake, press down the Line/Loc switch, hold it, get off the brake pedal and onto the accelerator and work your R.P.M. up to where you want it. There's no chance of creeping because the front brakes hold you precisely on the line as long as you hold down the switch. Now watch the lights flash down the tree and when it's time to go, lift your finger off the switch and you're *gone*—out of the hole on the split part of a second, with hardly a chance of a false start. Naturally the Line/Loc, like all Hurst products, has been tested unmercifully. And proved in action, too, by people like Gas Ronda, Ronnie Sox and Don Nicholson.

Stop by your local speed shop for details. Or write direct to Hurst Performance Products, Glenside, Pennsylvania 19038.

HURST

◀ Hurst Performance Products had been marketing slick aftermarket transmission linkages to rodders for years and by the mid-'60s they were also part of "factory" performance packages. Hurst helpers let automatic transmissions be shifted manually in hard acceleration. For manuals, its Line/Loc allowed the driver to rest at the starting line without holding down the brake pedal. An electric switch on the shifter activated the brakes while the driver revved to the engine's sweet spot without creeping. As the start-up tree flashed its last filament, the driver released the switch to catapult out of the hole.

▼ One of history's most popular and influential cars, Mustang bowed in April 1964 with a six or a 260-cid (later 289-cid) V-8. The solid-lifter 271-bhp HiPo came in June, and 2+2 fastbacks were added in fall, 1965. Even the HiPo was little threat to true muscle cars: *Sports Car Graphic* ran one with a 4.11:1 gear to 60 mph in 7.5 seconds and turned a middling 15.7 at 89 mph in the quarter. Mustangs had more success at the strip, especially in A/FX classes, where larger engines could be used. Les Ritchey ran one of the most powerful, with Weber carbs on a SOHC 427. He was '65 NHRA Nationals A/FX champ, burning Indianapolis with a 10.67 ET.

▲ Bill Lawton took Factory Stock Eliminator and A/FX honors at the '65 NHRA Winternationals. His best ET was 10.92 at 128.20 mph. Lawton's was part of a small fleet of factory-prepped and supported A/FX Mustangs modified to run the SOHC 427. They had a fiberglass front clip with bubble hood and 'glass doors. Most used dual quads.

▶ Paul Norris cuts loose in the Stark-Hickey Ford A/FX Mustang at the '65 U.S. Nationals; this car was also driven by Dick Brannan. Street Mustangs had the 210-bhp 289 two barrel or the 271-bhp HiPo ($334.60). A $1232.30 Cobra kit added four Webers for 343 bhp. A four-speed added $188, automatic trans $189.60, special camshaft $75.10, and heavy-duty distributor $49.80.

▶ The mean A/FX Mustangs shut down a fleet of Mopars and Mercury Comets at a classic Winternationals brawl in Pomona. Gas Ronda, Bill Lawton, Len Richter, and Phil Bonner were among the Ford drivers. Richter turned 10.91 in the early rounds, but twisted an axle and sat out the final, which went to Lawton. These Mustangs had highly modified front suspensions to clear the 427. Narrowed rear axles allowed 10-inch slicks. Unlike the '64 Fairlane Thunderbolts, the A/FX Mustangs were race-only and not sold to the public.

▲ Mercury's Comet Cyclone could be special-ordered with the HiPo 289. On the strip, it was another host to the SOHC 427. A/FX Comets were driven by some big names, including Arnie "The Farmer" Beswick and Hayden Proffitt. "Dyno" Don Nicholson ran one to a 10.60 at 131.72. Ed Schartman was a Super Stock Eliminator with 10.70-10.80 ETs. And Doug Nash's B/FX 289 Comets ran in the 11.30s. Finally, Jack Chrisman, in the Sachs & Son blown "funny" Comet, turned a 10.13 at a startling 156.25 mph in B/Fuel.

1965 MERCURY HIGH-PERFORMANCE ENGINES

TYPE	CID	BORE × STROKE	BHP @ RPM	TORQUE @ RPM	FUEL SYSTEM	COMP. RATIO	AVAIL.
ohv V-8	289	4.00 × 2.87	271 @ 6000	312 @ 3400	1 × 4bbl.	10.5:1	Comet
ohv V-8	390	4.05 × 3.78	330 @ 5000	427 @ 3200	1 × 4bbl.	10.0:1	full size
ohv V-8	427	4.23 × 3.78	425 @ 6000	480 @ 3700	2 × 4bbl.	11.5:1	full size
ohv V-8	430	4.30 × 3.70	320 @ 4600	465 @ 2600	1 × 4bbl.	10.1:1	full size

◀ After a season of 330-cid propulsion, Oldsmobile's 4-4-2 coupe moved up to 400 cubes. So 4-4-2 now meant 400 cid, four-barrel, and dual exhausts. On a 10.25:1 squeeze, the V-8 got 345 bhp and 440 lbs/ft of torque (up 85). *Car Life* did 0-60 in 7.8 seconds, the quarter-mile in 15.5 at 84 mph.

1965 OLDSMOBILE HIGH-PERFORMANCE ENGINES

TYPE	CID	BORE × STROKE	BHP @ RPM	TORQUE @ RPM	FUEL SYSTEM	COMP. RATIO	AVAIL.
ohv V-8	400	4.00 × 3.98	345@ 4800	440@ 3200	1 × 4bbl.	10.25:1	1
ohv V-8	425	4.12 × 3.98	360@ 4800	470@ 2800	1 × 4bbl.	10.25:1	98, 88
ohv V-8	425	4.12 × 3.98	370@ 4800	470@ 3200	2 × 4bbl.	10.5:1	2

1. Cutlass 4-4-2, F-85 2. Starfire, Jetstar I, 88, 98.

▲ Chrysler didn't forget Plymouth when it came to purpose-built "unlimited" cars. This particular '65 "Melrose Missile" Belvedere, being launched by Tom Grove, was one of a few assembled without an altered wheelbase, however. It was therefore legal in the NHRA's A/FX class, where it ran a dual-quad 426 Hemi. It had an acid-dipped steel unibody with fiberglass hood, fenders, doors, and bumper. Drag competition was growing more complex each year, with a bewildering proliferation of NHRA classes and categories; four were added for '65, for a total of 75. Stockers alone split into 27 classes, depending on pounds per horsepower.

◀ Junior muscle cars were increasingly popular, and Plymouth had one for '65. Based on the compact Valiant, the bubble-back Barracuda bowed as a 1964½ model and by '65 was the best-selling Plymouth. The '65 Formula S package brought a 235-bhp 273-cid "Commando" V-8, plus heavy-duty springs/shocks and sway bar, fatter Goodyear Blue Streak tires on 14-inch rims, and a 6000-rpm tach. *Car and Driver* did 0-60 in 9.1 seconds, the quarter in 17.5 at 88.5 mph with a 3.23:1 gear. *Hot Rod* turned a 16.43 at 89. Some Barracudas ran in sports-car rallies.

▶ In the Formula S, the 273 featured a hotter cam, Carter four-barrel, and 10.5:1 compression with hydraulic lifters. A three-speed was standard; four-speed or TorqueFlite was optional. Front disc brakes could be dealer-installed. With its "throaty, quick-tempo exhaust," a Formula S "was indeed a force to be reckoned with," claimed *Hot Rod*.

▼ NASCAR "outlawed" Chrysler's Hemi for the first half of the '65 season, so Richard Petty stuffed one into a Super/Stock Barracuda and headed for the strip. "43 Jr." managed a 10.46 ET in an AHRA event. When NASCAR reinstated the Hemi, Petty returned to win four NASCAR races in Plymouths.

▲ Plymouth moved the Sport Fury onto a 119-inch wheelbase and toward luxury for '65. Taking its place as the top sporty model was the Satellite (shown), built on a 116-inch wheelbase.

▶ While 426 Wedges made the thunder, far more Satellite buyers opted for the more-sedate but still-strong 383-cid Commando V-8. The reliable four-barrel mill's 330 bhp and surplus of usable torque made it an excellent street choice.

◀ "Drag-On-Lady" Shirley Shahan, a 27-year-old California clerical worker, took up drag racing while dating her husband-to-be, racer H.L. Shahan. She set a National S/SA record of 127.30 mph and turned an 11.21-second ET in her stock-wheelbase Hemi Belvedere.

▲ Of 25,201 '65 Satellites, just 1860 were convertibles. The ragtop cost $2869, $220 more than the hardtop coupe.

◀ Satellite came standard with bucket seats, center storage console, and custom wheel covers with spinner hubs. This one has the optional console-mounted tachometer and TorqueFlite automatic. Manuals of three- and four-speeds also were available. V-8s of 273-, 318-, and 361-cid were offered. The 383 came in 270- and 330-bhp tune, and the 426 Street Wedge made 365. Late in the year, a few Satellites and Belvederes were built with the 426 race Hemi, rated at 425 bhp.

1965 PLYMOUTH HIGH-PERFORMANCE ENGINES

TYPE	CID	BORE × STROKE	BHP @ RPM	TORQUE @ RPM	FUEL SYSTEM	COMP. RATIO	AVAIL.
ohv V-8	273	3.63 × 3.31	235@ 5200	280 @ 4000	1 × 4bbl.	10.5:1	Dart
ohv V-8	383	4.24 × 3.38	330 @ 4600	425 @ 2800	1 × 4bbl.	10.0:1	Satellite, Fury
ohv V-8	426	4.25 × 3.75	365 @ 4800	470 @ 3200	1 × 4bbl.	10.3:1	Satellite, Sport Fury
ohv V-8	426*	4.25 × 3.75	425 @ 6000	480 @ 4600	2 × 4bbl.	12.5:1	Satellite

*Hemi

▶ Ronnie Sox and Buddy Martin came over from Mercury in '65 for a long and successful career racing Chrysler products. This is Sox in the Super Stock "Paper Tiger" Hemi Belvedere.

▲ Chrysler built six altered-wheelbase Plymouths as companions to the six altered-wheelbase Dodges. One went to the Golden Commandos, the Plymouth-supported race team that was the counterpart to the Dodge-sponsored Ramchargers.

▼Al Eckstrand, a corporate lawyer, pilots the Commandos' fuel injected Hemi. These cars turned low-9s at more than 140 mph. This one is actually a hardtop; sedan door frames were used to hold in the Plexiglas windows, which didn't roll down. At the Pomona Winternationals, Bill "Grumpy" Jenkins was Top Stock Eliminator in the more-conventional Hemi-powered "Black Arrow" Plymouth with an 11.39 ET at 126.05.

▲ The '65 Hemi was lightened with aluminum heads and intake manifold. These motors were hand assembled by selected Chrysler technicians, who stamped their names on the finished engine. A total of 380 Dodge/Plymouth race Hemis were built this year. Meanwhile, the 426 Wedge would be dropped after '65, to evolve later into the 440.

▲ After running with a stock wheelbase in the NHRA's A/FX class, (see page 122), the Melrose Missle was reconstructed with an altered wheelbase for work in match races. Note the packed drag chute: stock-bodied cars were getting fast enough to need them after the run.

▲ Pontiac redesigned its big cars for '65. Wheelbase was up one inch on Catalina and Grand Prix, to 121, and new sheetmetal made them look even larger. The 2+2 Catalina option package continued, with new louvers on the front fenders and "2+2" tags on the rears. Some 11,521 were sold.

▼ The 421-cid V-8 was now standard on the 2+2. Three were available. A Carter four-barrel yielded 338 bhp. Next up: a Tri-Power with 356. Top dog was the 421 HO with Tri-Power, higher-lift cam, and long-branch headers for 376 ponies. A three-speed with Hurst shifter and Safe-T-Track diff were standard; four-speed and Turbo Hydra-Matic were options.

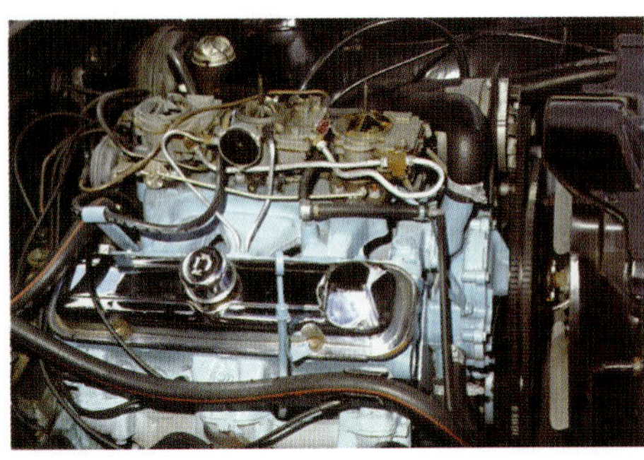

▲ Priced at a modest $244, the 2+2 option could be ordered for Catalina convertibles as well as hardtops. Bucket seats and tachometer were part of the package, and 5316 had a floor-shifted manual gearbox. Transistorized ignition, extra-stiff springs, alloy wheels and 17.5:1 power steering finished the package.

◀ A good 2+2 with the base 338-bhp 421 could turn a 7.4-second 0-60 and a 15.8 quarter; with 376 bhp, 7.2 and 15.5 were possible. *Car and Driver* later admitted its recorded 3.9-second 0-60 time was "rather preposterous," but its 2+2 had been supertuned by the Bobcat boys from Royal Pontiac in Michigan.

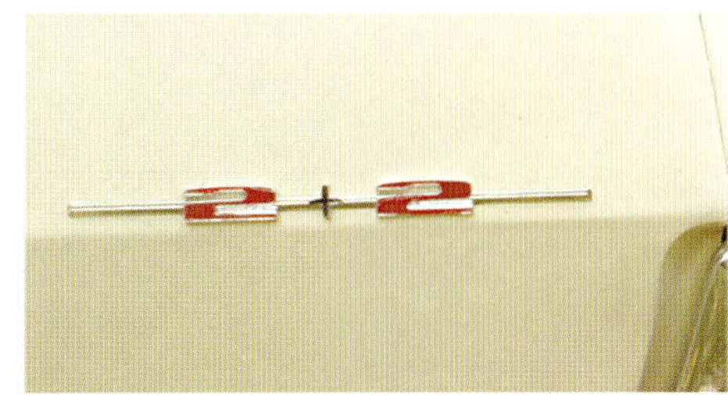

▲ Pontiac described the 2+2 as "A flying machine for people who can't stand heights."

▲ GTOs got a reskin with stacked headlamps for '65. This one is famous as the Goat given away in a contest to name the number of times "tiger" was heard in the song "GeeTO Tiger."

▲ A Wisconsin 19-year-old won the Hurst-sponsored contest and the GTO, which was stock except for special gold paint and Hurst wheels. GTO production more than doubled, to 75,352, for '65.

▲ GTO kept its 389, but the base version gained 10 bhp, to 335, and the Tri-Power (shown) added 12, to 360, thanks to a revised induction system and improved camshaft profile.

▲ GTO was again a $290 Tempest option. The hood scoop still was just for show, but about 200 cars were fitted by dealers with an optional "Ram Air" setup that made the scoop functional.

▲ No supercar cabin was cooler in '65. Newly available were an AM/FM radio and a Rally Cluster with an 8000-rpm tach. The standard Hurst-shifted three-speed could be replaced by a heavy-duty three-speed, close- or wide-ratio Hurst-shifted Muncie four-speed, or two-speed automatic. Six axle ratios were offered, from 3.08:1 to 4.33:1.

▲ *Car Life* reported that its Tri-Power with a 4.11:1 gear did 0-60 in 5.8 seconds, the quarter in 14.5 at 100 mph. A 335-bhp convertible could do 0-60 in 7.2. Aluminum front brake drums were new options.

1965 PONTIAC HIGH-PERFORMANCE ENGINES

TYPE	CID	BORE × STROKE	BHP @ RPM	TORQUE @ RPM	FUEL SYSTEM	COMP. RATIO	AVAIL.
ohv V-8	326	3.72 × 3.75	285@ 5000	359 @ 3200	1 × 4bbl.	10.5:1	1
ohv V-8	389	4.06 × 3.75	333 @ 5000	429 @ 3200	1 × 4bbl.	10.5:1	full size
ohv V-8	389	4.06 × 3.75	335 @ 5000	431 @ 3200	1 × 4bbl.	10.75:1	GTO
ohv V-8	389	4.06 × 3.75	338 @ 4800	433 @ 3600	1 × 4bbl.	10.75:1	full size
ohv V-8	389	4.06 × 3.75	360 @ 5200	424 @ 3600	3 × 2bbl.	10.75:1	GTO
ohv V-8	421	4.09 × 3.75	338 @ 3600	459 @ 2800	1 × 4bbl.	10.5:1	full size
ohv V-8	421	4.09 × 4.00	356 @ 4600	459 @ 3200	3 × 2bbl.	10.75:1	full size
ohv V-8	421	4.09 × 3.75	376 @ 5000	461 @ 3600	3 × 2bbl.	10.75:1	full size

1. Tempest, LeMans

1966

Horsepower race stands pat with Chrysler Hemis and Ford side-oiler 427 atop the heap at 425 bhp…Ford's "7-Liter" 428 is the biggest stock block • Mopar unleashes the Street Hemi in Plymouth Satellite and in Dodge's Coronet and striking new Charger fastback • Chevrolet Nova is a giant killer with its newly available 350-bhp 327 • All Chevelle Super Sports become SS 396s after 396 is made standard • Big Chevys add 427-cid V-8 option • Ford builds 57 Fairlane drag specials with 427 V-8…but too few to make an impact on the street • Hertz puts a handful of Shelby GT-350 Mustangs into its rental fleet • Mercury launches Comet Cyclone GT…paces Indy 500 and comes on strong in NASCAR • Olds issues rare W-30 drag option for 4-4-2 • Pontiac elevates the GTO to a series of its own, still with 389-cid V-8 • Emergence of the true funny car led by the flip-top Comets of Don Nicholson and Ed Schartman…these cars point the way to some of the wildest wheeled vehicles ever • Gas Ronda's SOHC 427 Mustang is the first unblown, full-bodied car to run a sub-8-second ET • Rail dragsters dip into 7.30s

▲ Fresh sheetmetal gave Buick's Skylark Gran Sport a new look. Rear-facing hood scoops were non-functional. Little changed beneath the skin, though there was a 340-bhp upgrade from the 325-bhp V-8.

▲ New roofline with sail-panel rear pillars looked sharp, but GS option accounted for only 13,816 of 106,217 Skylarks built for '66. The pillared coupe cost $2956; the Sport Coupe, $3019 (shown); and the convertible, $3167.

◀ GS emblems were on blacked-out grille and rear fenders. Dual exhausts and heavy-duty suspension were standard. Options included metallic brake linings and a rear stabilizer bar.

1966 BUICK HIGH-PERFORMANCE ENGINES

TYPE	CID	BORE × STROKE	BHP @ RPM	TORQUE @ RPM	FUEL SYSTEM	COMP. RATIO	AVAIL.
ohv V-8	340	3.75 × 3.85	260 @ 4200	365 @ 2800	1 × 4bbl.	10.25:1	1
ohv V-8	401	4.19 × 3.64	325 @ 4400	445 @ 2800	1 × 4bbl.	10.25:1	2
ohv V-8	425	4.31 × 3.64	340 @ 4400	465 @ 2800	1 × 4bbl.	10.25:1	3

1. Skylark, Sportwagon, LeSabre. 2. Skylark Gran Sport, Wildcat, Electra 225. 3. Riviera, Wildcat, Electra 225.

◀ The GS leaned toward luxury, but was no slouch. *Car and Driver*'s 340-bhp GS with the 3.36:1 axle went to 60 mph in 6.8 seconds and turned a 14.92 quarter-mile at 95 mph. *Motor Trend* managed 7.6 seconds to 60 and 15.47 at 90.54 mph on the strip.

▲ With the base engine and automatic in its Buick GS, *Car Life* needed 7.4 seconds to reach 60 mph, and 15.3 for the quarter. Hardtops sold best. Only 1835 pillared coupes and 2047 convertibles were built.

▲ Half-a-dozen axle ratios, from 2.78:1 to 4.30:1, could kick a Gran Sport off the line. The performance cogs, at $42 extra, incorporated a Positive Traction axle. Fender vents, like hood scoops, were fake.

◀ In standard form, Buick's 401-cid "Wildcat 445" four-barrel V-8 was rated at 325 bhp, but a 340-bhp version also was available. A three-speed manual came with either; a four-speed added $184, and Super Turbine automatic cost $205. Power steering ($95), power brakes ($42), and chrome-plated wheels ($73) were other options, while the heater/defroster could be deleted for a $71 credit. Buick promised that its lively GS "would rattle your faith in the established order of sporting machinery."

▲ Bill "Grumpy" Jenkins storms off the line at the '66 Winternationals in defense of his Mr. Stock Eliminator title earned in the previous year's event. This 327 Chevy II ran a 12.09 at 118.42. Jenkins was a Pennsylvanian who became a Chevy hero, but oddly enough, won his '65 Winternationals crown in a Plymouth.

▲ Nova got new skin and a 275-bhp, 327-cid V-8 to replace the 250- and 300-bhp variants. It turned ETs in the low 16s. Big news was availability of the 350-bhp L79 327 first seen in '65 Chevelles. It got a Nova into the low 15s at 93 mph, to the surprise of bigger supercars. Super Sport package added $159.

▶ All Malibu Super Sports got the 396-cid V-8 for '66, thus earning the SS 396 designation. The base Turbo-Jet had 325 bhp with a Holley four-barrel. The 360-bhp L34 upgrade used a four-bolt-main block and bigger four-barrel. Both had 10.25:1 compression. About 100 cars had a solid-lifter L78, basically an upgrade of the '65 Z-16. It had 375 bhp, 11.0:1 compression, and an 800cfm Holley. A three-speed was standard; four-speed and Powerglide were available.

▲ The departure from stock was nearly complete. Racers were now using fiberglass body shells over tube-frame chassis instead of the factory-altered production platforms of just a year earlier. Bobby Wood's supercharged "Palomino II" Chevelle was an example of a real "funny car." The best were turning mid-8s at around 160 mph. Masks protected drivers from nitro-fuel fumes.

◀ Like the NASCAR-bred 427-cid V-8 from which it was derived, the 396 in the Chevelle SS had "porcupine," or canted-valve, heads for improved airflow. *Car and Driver*'s L34 with a 3.65:1 axle turned a very serious 14.66 at 99.8 mph, with an estimated 0-60 time of 6 seconds flat. The SS hardtop listed for $2776, the ragtop for $2984. Wheels on this car are from a later model year.

▲ Chevy rebored its 396 V-8 at midyear, restoring it to 427-cid size. In street tune, the Mark IV big-block had 390 bhp; a "special performance" solid-lifter version with a four-bolt main block gave 425. The 427 was offered only in the Corvette and in the full-size models. This Impala ragtop has Super Sport mag-type wheelcovers.

▲ Mid-size muscle was hot, and SS Impala sales fell sharply for '66. But a plain Biscayne with the rare 425-bhp 427 was still a street threat, and a B/S Biscayne was NHRA Winternationals Junior Stock champ. Both 427s could have a three-speed, the M21 close-ratio four-speed, or the new-but-noisy M22 "Rock Crusher." Turbo Hydra-Matic came only with the 390-bhp version.

1966 CHEVROLET HIGH-PERFORMANCE ENGINES

TYPE	CID	BORE × STROKE	BHP @ RPM	TORQUE @ RPM	FUEL SYSTEM	COMP. RATIO	AVAIL.
ohv V-8	283	3.88×3.00	220 @ 4800	295 @ 3200	1×4bbl.	9.25:1	1
ohv V-8	327	4.00×3.25	275 @ 4800	355 @ 3200	1×4bbl.	10.25:1	1
ohv V-8	327	4.00×3.25	350 @ 5800	360 @ 3600	1×4bbl.	11.0:1	Chevy II
ohv V-8	396	4.09×3.76	325 @ 4800	410 @ 3200	1×4bbl.	10.25:1	Chevelle, full size
ohv V-8	396	4.09×3.76	360 @ 5200	420 @ 3600	1×4bbl.	10.25:1	2
ohv V-8	396	4.09×3.76	375 @ 5600	415 @ 3600	1×4bbl.	11.0:1	2
ohv V-8	427	4.25×3.76	390 @ 5200	460 @ 3600	1×4bbl.	10.25:1	full size
ohv V-8	427	4.25×3.76	425 @ 5600	460 @ 4000	1×4bbl.	11.0:1	full size

1. Chevelle, Chevy II, full size. 2. Chevelle SS 396 and El Camino.

▲ This was the year of the Street Hemi. At Dodge, the new detuned version of the '65 race Hemi went in the Coronet and the new Charger. The 425-bhp 426 added $1000 to a $2705 Coronet 500 hardtop. It was big-league quick. *Car and Driver*'s did 0-60 mph in 5.3 seconds and the quarter in 13.8 at 104 mph. *Motor Trend* called its acceleration "absolutely shattering."

▲ Chicago's Dodge dealers took the reasonable course and based their Coronet drag car on the pillared coupe, which at 3215 pounds was the lightest body style available with the hot Hemi. Dodge built 250,842 Coronets and 37,344 Chargers for '66, but the Street Hemi was ordered in fewer than 1000 of them.

1966 DODGE HIGH-PERFORMANCE ENGINES

TYPE	CID	BORE × STROKE	BHP @ RPM	TORQUE @ RPM	FUEL SYSTEM	COMP. RATIO	AVAIL.
ohv V-8	273	3.63 × 3.31	235 @ 5200	280 @ 4000	1 × 4bbl.	10.5:1	Dart GT
ohv V-8	361	4.12 × 3.88	265 @ 4400	380 @ 2400	1 × 4bbl.	9.0:1	Coronet
ohv V-8	383	4.25 × 3.75	270 @ 4400	390 @ 2800	1 × 4bbl.	9.2:1	full size
ohv V-8	383	4.25 × 3.75	325 @ 4800	425 @ 2800	1 × 4bbl.	10.0:1	Coronet, full size
ohv V-8	426*	4.25 × 3.75	425 @ 5000	490 @ 4000	2 × 4bbl.	10.25:1**	Charger
ohv V-8	440	4.32 × 3.75	350 @ 4400	480 @ 2800	1 × 4bbl.	10.1:1	full size

* Hemi. ** Std. comp. ratio: 10.2:1

▲ A couple of good 'ol Mopar NASCAR boys, Cotton Owens and David Pearson, backed the "Cotton Picker," a match-race drag car that ran just for the '66 season. It had a fiberglass Dart wagon body and a rear-mounted race Hemi.

▶ Actual horsepower was near 500, but Dodge advertised its Street Hemi at 425 bhp on a 10.25:1 compression. A detuned version of the 12.5:1-squeeze race Hemi, the solid-lifter 426-cid V-8 had a milder camshaft for smoother low-rpm running and a heat chamber so it could warm up properly. Coronets and Chargers ordered with the Hemi got stiffer springs and bigger (11-inch) brakes. Front discs were optional. And instead of the usual five-year/50,000-mile coverage, Hemi buyers got a year and 12,000. Chrysler warned that even that would be voided if the car was "subjected to any extreme operation [i.e., drag racing]."

▶ Roger Lindamood's popular "Color Me Gone" Charger had a nitro-burning, fuel-injected Hemi and ran 8.50s at 160-170 mph. Despite the highly altered wheelbase and use of fiberglass body panels, this car retained the near-stock driving position.

▲ Charger bowed for '66 on the Coronet's 117-inch platform, but added a fastback roofline, hidden headlamps, and full-width taillights.

▲ "Beauty and the beast" was how Dodge described a Charger with the 426. "The Hemi was never in better shape," it crowed.

▲ Given a good launch, a Hemi Charger would rocket to 60 mph in about 5.3 seconds and devour the quarter-mile in around 13.8 at 104 mph. Its inline dual Carter four-barrels sat atop an aluminum intake manifold.

▲ A Street Hemi added $877.55 to Charger's $3122 base price and included heavy-duty suspension, four-ply nylon Blue Streak tires, and 11-inch brakes. But it was still too wild for most buyers. Of 37,344 Chargers built for '66, only 468 had the Hemi.

◀ Charger cost $417 more than a Coronet 500 hardtop, and part of the deal was a state-of-the-art '60s interior. It had lots of chrome, four bucket seats, available center consoles front and rear, and full instrumentation that included a 150-mph speedometer and 6000-rpm tach. A 318-cid V-8 with three-on-the-tree was standard. Chargers with the 361- or 383-cid V-8, or the Hemi, got the four-speed manual or TorqueFlite automatic programmed for full-throttle shifts at 5500 rpm. *Hot Rod* ran the 325-bhp 383 to a 16.28-second ET at 85 mph.

▲ This is no garden-variety Charger, but one of 85 delivered with a NASCAR-replica package that included a rear lip spoiler. The tires were stock, but they were mounted on deep-offset steel wheels that were the same as those on the race cars.

▲ NASCAR replicas had a stock Street Hemi, but added a special cowl-induction air cleaner, Mallory ignition, and an extra NASCAR-style motor mount.

▲ Hemis powered Dodge to the '66 NASCAR manufacturer's title. This is David Pearson, who won the driver's championship with 15 wins.

▲ Charger's rear buckets folded to create a cargo bay four feet wide and seven-and-a-half-feet long.

▲ "The hot new leader of the Dodge Rebellion....looks like a pampered thoroughbred, comes on like Genghis Khan," Dodge said of its '66 Charger.

▲ Ford's Thunderbolt drag car had set the stage for the emergence of a streetable 427-cid V-8 in the reskinned '66 Fairlane. The limited-edition package was available in specially built two-door hardtops and sedans.

▲ Fairlane's side-oiler 427 had 410 bhp with a single four-barrel, 425 with dual quads (shown). Both had 11.1:1 compression and solid lifters. Fitting the 427 required bigger front springs and relocated shock towers. Also included: A four-speed 'box, handling package, and front disc brakes. Interior was stock except for 9000-rpm tachometer.

▲ The 427 Fairlane's lift-off fiberglass hood was held by four NASCAR tie-down pins and had a functional air scoop. A production run of at least 50 was needed to qualify the car for the NHRA's A/S Super Stock class, and Ford is believed to have built just 57. Box-stock, they'd turn 14.5-second quarter miles at 100 mph. But most went to professional drag teams, where they were supertuned and not really road-worthy. Thus, Ford street racers were denied a potent weapon against the big-block GM and Mopar intermediates.

1966 FORD HIGH-PERFORMANCE ENGINES

TYPE	CID	BORE × STROKE	BHP @ RPM	TORQUE @ RPM	FUEL SYSTEM	COMP. RATIO	AVAIL.
ohv V-8	289	4.00×2.87	271 @ 6000	312 @ 3400	1×4bbl.	10.5:1	1
ohv V-8	289	4.00×2.87	340 @ 6500	331 @ 3750	2×4bbl.	10.8:1	Cobra
ohv V-8	289	4.00×2.87	306 @ 6800	329 @ 4000	1×4bbl.	10.0:1	Shelby GT-350
ohv V-8	289	4.00×2.87	390 @ 6600	345 @ 4000	4×2bbl.	10.8:1	Cobra
ohv V-8	390	4.05×3.78	335 @ 4800	427 @ 3200	1×4bbl.	11.0:1	Fairlane
ohv V-8	427	4.23×3.78	410 @ 5600	476 @ 3400	1×4bbl.	11.1:1	Fairlane, full size
ohv V-8	427	4.23×3.78	425 @ 6000	480 @ 3700	2×4bbl.	11.1:1	Fairlane, full size
sohc V-8	427	4.23×3.78	616 @ 7000	515 @ 3800	2×4bbl.	12.0:1	race
ohv V-8	428	4.13×3.98	360 @ 5400	459 @ 3200	1×4bbl.	10.5:1	full-size

*Hemi.

1. Falcon, Fairlane, Mustang.

▲ Street Mustangs were taking it on the chin with their 289-cid small blocks, but with the single-overhead-cam 427, highly modified examples were dragstrip terrors. Hubert Platt's turned 8.50s at 161 mph.

▶ The "Cammer" 427 Mustangs were a step beyond A/FX, competing head-to-head with Mopar and Mercury "ultra-stock" cars. This is Bill Lawton's at the '66 AHRA Winter-nationals.

▶ Gas Ronda's 427 Mustang was the first unblown, full-bodied car to break into the 8-second range. He did it in '66 at Bakersfield, California, beating Tom "Mongoose" McEwen's Hemi Barracuda in a match race. Ronda's historic run was an 8.96 at 155 mph. Here, he's battling a Sox and Martin 'Cuda at the '66 NHRA Winter-nationals in Pomona.

▲The 427 Fairlane initially ran in A/Stock against the Street Hemis. The Ford was down some 50 bhp to the Mopars, but it weighed about 200 pounds less, so the better ones held their own. The Lafayette Ford-sponsored ride driven by Bob Spears was a regional Stock Eliminator champ in '65 and '66. *Hot Rod* tried a showroom-fresh 427 Fairlane, complete with full wheelcovers and whitewall tires. "Even with the shift not working as slick as we like, it's almost like child's play to make a good run," wrote *Hot Rod*. "Bring the revs up to about a grand....Let the clutch out. Easy on the gas until you're underway and then pin the pedal to the mat. Ahhhhh! All those eight butterflies are flapping open and the sleek Fairlane body is twisting its way to the right, fighting the torque. The tach touches six grand and—wham!—second gear. The body rocks back momentarily before you catch your breath...then through third and fourth...all the way through the lights and beyond. No sweat."

▲All Fairlanes but the GT could get the 427. All were white hardtops with GT-level suspensions and de-baffled stock mufflers.

▲Big Fords could have a dual-quad "7-Liter" 425-bhp 427, though they were not often winners on street or strip. An exception was Mike Schmitt's Galaxie. Its 11.85 at 119.6 won the '66 NHRA Winternationals Street class.

▼The NHRA didn't quite know what to make of these nitromethane, or "fuel," burning cars, so for a time it classified them as C/FD, for "fuel dragster." Holman and Moody built the chassis for Ronda's car, which located the engine about 18 inches behind the stock placement. Race weight was around 2100 pounds.

▲ The funny car as we know it debuted in January 1966. It was Don Nicholson's Eliminator I Comet, the first full "flip-top" body on a chromemoly tube-frame. This also was the first sub-8-second funny car, running a 7.94 on September 14 at Martin, Michigan.

▲ "Dyno" Don Nicholson took his nickname from the "Dyno-tuned" prep work of his early mounts.

◄ A classic example of the link between success on the track and sales promotion was this Mercury ad from the July '66 issue of *Hot Rod*. It touted the drag-pack option for the street Comet's 390-cid V-8, noting that "it puts you into C/Stock with a vengeance." Nicholson's fiberglass flip-top Eliminator I, on the other hand, used an injected SOHC 427 with 900 bhp in an 1800-pound car. Ed Shartman's similar funny Comet was the only other racer at Nicholson's level during the '66 season. Both were running 7.80s at 175 mph; other "funny cars" were in the 8.30s.

▲ Jack Chrisman's blown and injected Comet was set up for top speed and hit 188 mph before being destroyed by an engine fire.

▲ With a 335-bhp 390, a good Comet Cyclone GT could turn a 15.2 at 92 mph, but the going was tough on the street against Mopars.

1966 MERCURY HIGH-PERFORMANCE ENGINES							
TYPE	CID	BORE × STROKE	BHP @ RPM	TORQUE @ RPM	FUEL SYSTEM	COMP. RATIO	AVAIL.
ohv V-8	390	4.05 × 3.78	335 @ 4800	427 @ 3200	1 × 4bbl.	11.0:1	Cyclone GT
ohv V-8	410	4.05 × 3.78	330 @ 4600	444 @ 2800	1 × 4bbl.	10.5:1	full size
ohv V-8	428	4.13 × 3.98	360 @ 5400	459 @ 3200	1 × 4bbl.	10.5:1	S-55, full size

▼ New sheetmetal and a slightly wider track distinguished the '66 Olds 4-4-2. Still an option, the 4-4-2 package added only $185 to the price of an F-85, $151 to a Cutlass. 4-4-2s gained their own grille and taillamps and a fake front-fender scoop this year. A trifling compression hike brought five extra horses to the standard 400-cid V-8. Olds built 21,997 4-4-2s for '66; this is one of about 2750 convertibles.

▶ Comet graduated to the Fairlane platform for '66, in hardtop and convertible form. The $2700 base version had a 289. The $2891 GT had the 390. A four-speed was optional at $183; the Sport Shift three-speed automatic cost $184.

▶ Super Stock 4-4-2s could benefit from the new W-30 option, a drag-racing package available through dealers. It added fiberglass inner fenders, trunk-mounted battery, cold-air induction, and radical cam. Only 54 were built.

▲ Base 4-4-2 V-8 four-barrel (shown) had 350 bhp, but a new triple-two-barrel option ($114) bumped output to 360. *Motor Trend*'s tri-carb four-speed hit 60 mph in 7.2 seconds and did the quarter in 15.2 at 96.6 mph.

▲ Best-selling 4-4-2 was the Holiday hardtop, going to 10,053 customers. Not many ordered the extra-cost factory tachometer. Bucket seats with console were an option, too.

▲ The rare W-30 forced-air option slashed 0-60 times to 6.3 seconds and quarter-mile ETs to 14.8 at 97 mph. True to the Oldsmobile ethic, however, most 4-4-2s had a softer nature. *Car Life* called even the tri-carb model a "Civilized Supercar....[that] lacks, or perhaps one should say masks, the brutal nature which is apparent in some of the others."

▲ Bold insignia identified the sportiest Olds. *Car Life* lauded the 4-4-2's road manners, saying it had a softer ride, yet better handling and steering control than the Chevelle SS and GTO, GM's two other A-body intermediates. Part of the credit went to the rear anti-roll bar standard on the 4-4-2 (Chevelle got one for '66, also). Estimated fuel economy with the tri-power was 10-13 mph.

1966 OLDSMOBILE HIGH-PERFORMANCE ENGINES

TYPE	CID	BORE × STROKE	BHP @ RPM	TORQUE @ RPM	FUEL SYSTEM	COMP. RATIO	AVAIL.
ohv V-8	330	3.94×3.38	320 @ 3600	360 @ 3600	1×4bbl.	10.25:1	1
ohv V-8	400	4.00×3.98	350 @ 3600	440 @ 3600	1×4bbl.	10.5:1	4-4-2
ohv V-8	425	4.12×3.98	300 @ 4400	430 @ 2400	1×2bbl.	9.0:1	2
ohv V-8	425	4.12×3.98	365 @ 4800	470 @ 3200	1×4bbl.	10.25:1	3
ohv V-8	425	4.12×3.98	375 @ 4800	470 @ 3200	1×4bbl.	10.5:1	4
ohv V-8	425	4.12×3.98	385 @ 4800	480 @ 3200	1×4bbl.	10.5:1	Toronado

1. Cutlass, Jetstar 88, F-85, Vista Cruiser. 2. Delta 88, Dynamic 88. 3. 98, Delta 88, Dynamic 88. 4. Starfire, 98, Delta 88.

▲ Billows of smoke from *all four wheels* erased most doubt that this twin-engine four-wheel-drive 4-4-2 was, as Hurst Performance Products billed it, "drag racing's wildest exhibition vehicle." Its supercharged 425-cid Toronado V-8s burned a nitro-alcohol blend.

◄ "Gentleman Joe" Schubeck launches the Hairy Olds. The car had two Hurst shifters, double instrumentation, and dual fuel throttles. Eleven-inch racing slicks rode all four corners. Its trap speeds were around 170 mph.

▲ A/S class champ Jere Stahl accepts the trophy for his performance at the NHRA Nationals.

▲ Jere Stahl, of Stahl exhaust-header fame, on his way to Top Stock Eliminator at the '66 U.S. Nationals at Indy. Stahl's Hemi-powered '66 Plymouth Belvedere turned a best ET of 11.73 at 119.68 mph.

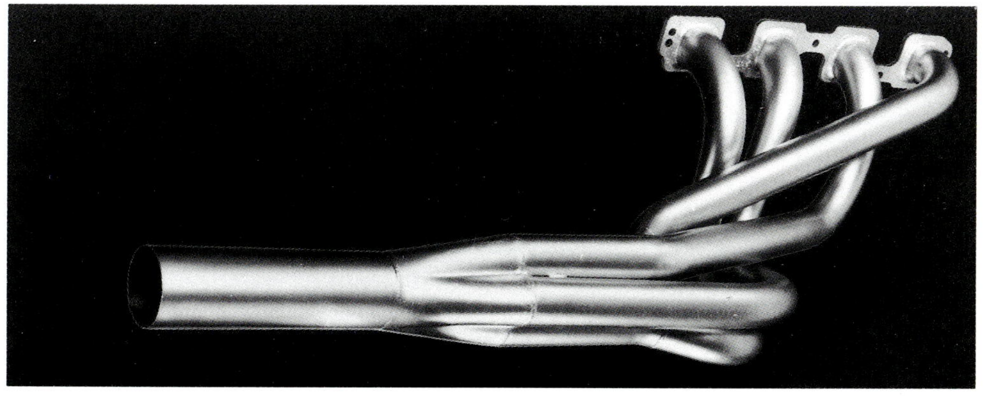

◄ Stahl Engineering of York, Pennsylvania, was one of the best-known fabricators of specialty exhaust systems in the 1960s. Pictured here is a set of "Total Tuned" four-into-one Stahl headers for Mopar's Street Hemi. Jere Stahl was one of many dragstrip aces who blended engineering expertise, an aftermarket company connection, and skill behind the wheel. A competitor was Los Angeles-based Doug's Headers, which advertised "individualized headers for all V-8s," including a Street Hemi system priced at $150.

▲ Like its Dodge Coronet cousin, the Plymouth Satellite could get a Street Hemi this year. It added $907.60 to the $2695 price of a hardtop.

▲ *Car and Driver* said the Satellite Hemi had "the best combination of brute performance and tractable street manners we've ever driven."

▶ The Street Hemi had cast-iron instead of aluminum heads and an aluminum intake manifold instead of a ram-type magnesium unit. Compression slipped from 12.5:1 to 10.25:1. Alloy heads and a wilder cam were factory options, however. A Sure-Grip axle was mandatory with both the four-speed and TorqueFlite. A tachometer added another $48.35.

▲ *Car and Driver*'s Hemi Plymouth hit 60 mph in 5.3 seconds and turned an ET of 13.8 at 104 mph. *Car Life* took 7.1 seconds to 60, with an ET of 14.5 at 95 mph. Front discs were unavailable, but police-grade 11-inch drums landed the Satellite.

1966 PLYMOUTH HIGH-PERFORMANCE ENGINES

TYPE	CID	BORE × STROKE	BHP @ RPM	TORQUE @ RPM	FUEL SYSTEM	COMP. RATIO	AVAIL.
ohv V-8	273	3.63 × 3.31	235 @ 5200	280 @ 4000	1 × 4bbl.	10.5:1	1
ohv V-8	361	4.12 × 3.88	265 @ 4400	380 @ 2400	1 × 4bbl.	9.0:1	Belvedere
ohv V-8	383	4.24 × 3.38	270 @ 4400	390 @ 2800	1 × 4bbl.	9.2:1	Belvedere
ohv V-8	383	4.24 × 3.38	325 @ 4800	425 @ 2800	1 × 4bbl.	10.0:1	2
ohv V-8	426*	4.25 × 3.75	425 @ 5000	490 @ 4000	2 × 4bbl.	10.25:1	Satellite
ohv V-8	440	4.32 × 3.75	365 @ 4600	480 @ 3200	1 × 4bbl.	10.1:1	Sport Fury

* Hemi.
1. Valiant, Barracuda. 2. Satellite, Fury, VIP

▲ *Car Life*'s Hemi Satellite listed for a hefty $4360, with options. The editors praised its balance of power and civility, but reported that brisk cornering brought copious body lean and tire howl, the power steering was without road feel, and early rear-brake lock induced skidding. Normal fuel economy was estimated at 10-13 mpg, but would be less during acceleration runs, when the TorqueFlite automatically shifted to second at 4900 rpm and to third at 5200. "Wide-open throttle from rest induces noisy, unproductive wheelspin and a great amount of tire smoke," *Car Life* noted.

◀ Ken Heinemann blasts off in the "Brand X Eliminator" Belvedere at Bristol, Tennessee. Heinemann's Hemi was a consistent 12-second, 120-mph car, but was shut down by Shirley Shahan in her "Drag-On-Lady" Plymouth with an 11.26 at 126.7 for A-Stock/Automatic honors at the '66 Winternationals. The Hemi invited hyperbolae. Here's how *Hot Rod* began its preview: "Pow! For '66, Plymouth will offer 426 inches of 'street hemi,' a fire-breathing, dual-four-throat version of the hottest stocker in drag strip hollow."

▲ Adding a "Formula S" package to the bucket-seat Barracuda brought an upgraded suspension, blue-streak tires, and 150-mph speedometer.

▲ Front-disc brakes were a new $82 option on the '66 Barracuda. The 273-cid V-8 with a four-barrel had 235-bhp and 8-second 0-60 ability.

▼ With Sox at the wheel, the Sox and Martin '65 Plymouth was the first nonsupercharged, stock-bodied car to run below 10-seconds. The following season, they turned 8.40s at 165 with their nitro-burning A/XS (Experimental Stock) '66 Hemi Barracuda, built around a stock body. But the duo was unable to compete with Mercury's new flip-top Comets. After this season, Sox and Martin focused on stock classes, where their success translated into a longtime partnership with Plymouth and a thriving high-performance parts business of their own.

▶ North Carolinians Buddy Martin (left) and Ronnie Sox formed the Sox & Martin racing venture in 1962 and won their first NHRA title with a '64 Comet. They switched to Plymouth for '65, and in '67 began to concentrate on the stock classes. They became one of the muscle era's winningest teams and were priceless promoters of Plymouth performance.

▲ Pontiac signaled its continued interest in the big-muscle market by making the 2+2 a separate model for '66. It was still based on the Catalina, which, along with the Grand Prix, lost two inches of body length while keeping the 121-inch wheelbase.

▼ Production of the 2+2 dropped by nearly half for '66, to 6383, as enthusiasts focused on mid-size muscle. The big Ponchos, however, were unmatched at blending luxury with performance. The convertible started at $3602; the hardtop coupe at $3298.

▲ Buckets and console were 2+2 standards, but a tach and auxillary gauges cost extra. All came with a Hurst-shifted three-speed floor shift, but a four-speed or Turbo Hydra-Matic were optional. Pontiac told buyers to ask for the "GTO/2+2 performance catalog—and go-go-go."

▲ Only the full-size Pontiacs could get the 421-cid V-8, and only on the 2+2 was it standard. The base four-barrel had 338 bhp; optional Tri-Power 421s like this one had 356 or 376 bhp. Axle ratios from 3.08 to 4.11 were available, as was the aluminum wheel/hub combo.

▲ Private teams bore the brunt of converting GM cars for the radically modified classes. One that did was Gay Pontiac of Texas. Here's teenager Don Gay in the altered-wheelbase 421 "Infinity" GTO. The blown fuelie had a steel center body section and fiberglass front and rear clips. At the Winternationals, the rose-colored Goat "funny car" turned a 9.40 at 151.77 mph.

▲ The GTO was still Tempest-based, but became a series all its own for '66. Hood scoops looked hot, but were functional only when optional Ram Air induction was installed. Checking that item gave the Tri-Power 389 the benefit of cold-air entry, even though output was the same 360 bhp as the "ordinary" tri-carb mill. The GTO's plastic grille was an industry first. This blue hardtop wears the rare red plastic inner fender liners. Axle ratios spanned 3.08:1 to 4.33:1.

▶ GTO's four-barrel 389 again made 335 bhp. Tri-Power (shown) cost $112.51 extra. *Car and Driver*'s Tri-Power with a 3.55:1 gear took 6.5 seconds to 60 mph and turned the quarter in a quick 14.05 at 105 mph. *Car Life*'s four-speed four-barrel with the 3.08 axle and air conditioning needed 6.8 seconds to 60 and 15.4 at 92 for the quarter. It averaged 12.4 mpg. This was the factory Tri-Power's last season; at midyear, GM banned all multi-carb packages.

▲ Twin '66 GTOs joust for C/S honors at the NHRA Nationals: Ace Wilson's Royal (foreground), versus the "Tin Tiger." Royal Pontiac, a Michigan dealer, turned out savagely modified "Royal Bobcat" GTOs.

▲ Standard GTO gear included a three-speed column shift, heavy-duty springs/shocks, and front stabilizer bar. A wood-trimmed dash was standard, but a gauge cluster with tach cost extra.

▲ Voluptuous new Coke-bottle contours and continued strong performance resulted in sales of 96,946 GTOs, the highest-ever one-year production total for a true muscle car. Styling highlights included the recessed backlight and cool fluted taillamps.

▲ This is one of 12,798 GTO ragtops built for '66. It cost $3082 and weighed 3555 pounds. The $2847 hardtop weighed 3465; 73,785 were built. The $2783 pillared coupe weighed 3445 pounds, and 10,363 were built.

▲ *Car Life* said the lightly loaded rear wheels of its nose-heavy GTO "skitter and skip on anything but the driest pavement." Braking power was poor, but the shifter was sweet, the motor willing, and assembly quality high.

▲ With its standard bucket seats and dashboard covered in genuine wood veneer, the GTO set the standard for sporty interiors.

1966 PONTIAC HIGH-PERFORMANCE ENGINES

TYPE	CID	BORE × STROKE	BHP @ RPM	TORQUE @ RPM	FUEL SYSTEM	COMP. RATIO	AVAIL.
ohv V-8	326	3.72 × 3.75	285@ 5000	359@ 3200	1 × 4bbl.	10.5:1	1
ohv V-8	389	4.06 × 3.75	290@ 4600	418@ 2400	1 × 4bbl.	10.5:1	full size
ohv V-8	389	4.06 × 3.75	325@ 4800	429@ 2800	1 × 4bbl.	10.5:1	2
ohv V-8	389	4.06 × 3.75	333@ 5000	429@ 3200	1 × 4bbl.	10.75:1	2
ohv V-8	389	4.06 × 3.75	335@ 5000	431@ 3200	1 × 4bbl.	10.75:1	GTO
ohv V-8	389	4.06 × 3.75	360@ 5200	424@ 3600	3 × 2bbl.	10.75:1	GTO
ohv V-8	421	4.09 × 3.75	338@ 4600	459@ 2800	1 × 4bbl.	10.5:1	full size
ohv V-8	421	4.09 × 4.00	356@ 4600	459@ 3200	3 × 2bbl.	10.75:1	full size
ohv V-8	421	4.09 × 3.75	376@ 5000	461@ 3600	3 × 2bbl.	10.75:1	full size

1. Tempest, LeMans 2. Grand Prix, full size

1967

Corvette has top advertised horsepower, 435 ... Hemi is right behind at 425... Mopar's 440-cid V-8 is biggest muscle engine • Several General Motors models actually lose horsepower after GM dictates that only Corvette can have more than one bhp per 10 pounds of car weight • Camaro launched as rival to Ford's Mustang ... SS 396 and Z-28 versions show Chevy is serious about this • Pontiac goes ponycar with Firebird and available 400-cid V-8 • Ford answers with second-generation Mustang with available 390-cid V-8...Shelby GT-500 gets 428-cid V-8 • 427-equipped Camaros modified by Don Yenko are quickest Chevys on the street • Inspired by GTO, Chrysler intermediates finally get some sporting individuality with debut of Dodge Coronet R/T and Plymouth GTX...440 Magnum or 426 Hemi are underhood • Mopar plays big-block catch-up, squeezing 383 V-8 into Dart and Barracuda • Super Stockers break into the 10-second range • Chuck Kurzawa's "Ramchargers" rail dragster turns a 6.76 at 223.88 mph—quickest ET to date

▲ Buick renamed its Gran Sport the GS400 to denote its new 400-cid V-8, which replaced the old 401-cid design. Transmission choices included a three-speed, Muncie four-speed, or Super Turbine automatic.

▲ Buick said GS400 was the "epitome" of the big, fast, American sporting car. Sales stayed around 14,000: 2140 convertibles, 10,659 hardtops, 1014 pillared coupes. All had red- or white-stripe F70 × 14 Wide-Oval tires.

▶ Hot fun in the summertime was just a turn of the key away in a GS400 ragtop. This one has the optional Strato buckets, $184 four-speed manual, and tachometer. A 3.36:1 final drive was standard with the four-speed, but ratios up to 4.30:1 were available on special order. With a list price of $3167, the convertible was the most expensive GS.

1967 BUICK HIGH-PERFORMANCE ENGINES

TYPE	CID	BORE × STROKE	BHP @ RPM	TORQUE @ RPM	FUEL SYSTEM	COMP. RATIO	AVAIL.
ohv V-8	340	3.75 × 3.85	260 @ 4200	365 @ 2800	1 × 4bbl.	10.25:1	1
ohv V-8	400	4.04 × 3.90	340 @ 5000	440 @ 3200	1 × 4bbl.	10.25:1	GS400
ohv V-8	430	4.19 × 3.90	360 @ 5000	475 @ 3200	1 × 4bbl.	10.25:1	2

1. GS340, Special Skylark, Sportwagon, LeSabre. 2. Riviera, Wildcat, Electra 225.

▲ Buick broadened the GS's appeal with the new GS340. All were hardtops with a 260-bhp, 340-cid four-barrel and three-speed or automatic. All had white or silver paint with a red side stripe and fake hood scoops.

▲ The GS340 listed for just $2845. Only 3692 were built, but other junior muscle cars would follow.

▲ "Your father never told you there'd be Buicks like this," said the ads. Hood scoops on the GS400 now faced forward, but still weren't functional. The ragtop started at $3167, the hardtop at $3019, the coupe at $2956. Bucket seats and a Positive Traction limited-slip axle were options.

▲ The GS400 helped shake up Buick's staid image, but never had the following of the Chevy SS or GTO.

▲ The new 400 had a futuristic plastic air cleaner. Like its 401-cid predecessor, it had a 10.25:1 compression, hydraulic lifters, and made the same 340 bhp as the top 401. But the smoother, more-modern V-8 could rev higher and was easier to keep in tune.

▲ Zero-60 claims varied widely for the GS400. *Car and Driver* said it took 6 seconds with automatic, 6.6 with a four-speed. *Car Life* said its 6-second run beat the 6.1 of a Ram Air GTO. More realistic times were 7.8 to 60 and around 15.9 in the quarter.

▲ Bill Jenkins was the '67 NHRA Super Stock Eliminator. "Grumpy's" 427 Camaro ran 11.55 seconds at 115.97 mph at Indy.

▲ The Z-28 was torrid right out of the box. Ben Wenzel's was B/Stock champ at the '67 Nationals with a 12.33 ET at 113.92 mph.

▲ SS Camaros got 350- or 396-cid V-8s, but Z-28s had this solid-lifter 302, rated at 290 bhp.

▲ Chevy's counterpunch to the Mustang in SCCA Trans Am battle was the Z-28. To make the SCCA's 305-cid limit, its 302 was a 327 with the 283's forged crankshaft. It had big-port heads from the Corvette L-69, a hot cam, and a Holley quad on an aluminum manifold. The peaky 302 was lethargic below 3000 rpm, a gun above.

▼ The Z-28 option added $400 to Camaro's $2466 base price; mandatory Muncie four-speed and power front discs brought the total near $3150. Only 602 were built. *Car and Driver*'s did 14.9 at 97 mph in the quarter.

▲ Chevy created the SS 427 Impala for '67, but the 385-bhp big-block could still be ordered in plainer Impalas like this base hardtop.

▲ Any full-size Chevy could be ordered with the 427, though most big-car bow tie enthusiasts were content with the 396's 325 bhp.

▲ For '67, the 427 officially came only in 385-bhp tune, but the 425-bhp L72 was still available. The four-speed's 3.73:1 was the hottest axle.

▲ On SS Impalas, bucket seats, console, and full instrumentation were moved to the options list. SS models could be ordered with any engine.

▲ "For the man who'd buy a sports car if it had this much room," was how Chevy promoted the new SS 427 Impala. It came with stiffer springs and shocks, a front stabilizer bar, and 8.24×14 red-stripe tires. *Car Life*'s 427 Impala hit 60 in 8.4 seconds and turned a 15.75 at 86.5 in the quarter.

1967 CHEVROLET HIGH-PERFORMANCE ENGINES

TYPE	CID	BORE × STROKE	BHP @ RPM	TORQUE @ RPM	FUEL SYSTEM	COMP. RATIO	AVAIL.
ohv V-8	302	4.00×3.00	290 @ 5800	290 @ 4200	1×4bbl.	11.0:1	Camaro Z-28
ohv V-8	327	4.00×3.25	275 @ 4800	335 @ 3200	1×4bbl.	10.0:1	1
ohv V-8	327	4.00×3.25	325 @ 5600	355 @ 3600	1×4bbl.	11.0:1	2
ohv V-8	350	4.00×3.48	295 @ 4800	380 @ 3200	1×4bbl.	10.25:1	3
ohv V-8	396	4.09×3.76	325 @ 4800	410 @ 3200	1×4bbl.	10.25:1	4
ohv V-8	396	4.09×3.76	350 @ 5200	415 @ 3400	1×4bbl.	10.25:1	5
ohv V-8	396	4.09×3.76	375 @ 5600	420 @ 3600	1×4bbl.	11.0:1	5
ohv V-8	427	4.25×3.76	385 @ 5200	460 @ 3400	1×4bbl.	10.25:1	full size
ohv V-8	427	4.25×3.76	425 @ 5600	460 @ 2000	1×4bbl.	11.0:1	full size

1. full size, Chevelle, Chevy II, Camaro. 2. Chevelle, Chevy II. 3. Camaro SS 350. 4. full size, Camaro SS, Chevelle SS 396. 5. Camaro SS 396, Chevelle SS 396.

▲ Mildly facelifted Chevelle SS 396 kept the prior year's non-functional hood blisters. Underhood changes also were modest. At $2825 for the coupe and $3033 for the ragtop, the Super Sports cost about $285 more than comparable Malibu models.

▶ A 325-bhp version of the 396 was standard in the Chevelle SS, while the $105 L34 upgrade (shown) dropped from 360 bhp to 350 because of GM's new edict against any car but Corvette having more than one bhp per 10 pounds of car weight.

▼ Ordering the new $121 power front-disc brake option brought Rally-style 14-inch slotted wheels to replace the usual small hubcaps or SS covers. Three-speed Turbo Hydra-Matic joined two-speed Powerglide as an option in place of the three- or four-speed sticks.

▲ "If you have a taste for action, here's the satisfier," Chevy said of the 396. A heavy-duty suspension and F70×14 red- or white-stripe tires were part of the package. Options included Strato bucket seats and a tach.

▲ This is the 325-bhp 396. The 375-bhp L-78 was also available. *Motor Trend*'s L-78 four-speed coupe turned a 14.9 ET at 96.5 mph.

▲ Nova Super Sport fans mourned the passing of the 350-bhp 327 V-8, though a few of those L79 mills probably were installed on special order. That left the capable-but-ho-hum 275-horse 327 as the top V-8. Other changes to Chevy's compact were minimal. With Camaro's arrival, output of the Nova SS skidded to 10,100 out of 106,000 Chevy IIs built.

▲ About 8200 of the Nova SS hardtops got the 327 V-8. They started at $2590, $103 more than a six-cylinder version. Mainly an appearance package, the Nova SS did include bucket seats.

▲ Even though the 350-bhp 327 was no longer officially available in the Nova SS, this hardtop's license suggests that it's one of the rare few. Transmissions were the same as in '66, but axle ratios got a shuffling.

▶ Coronet changed little for '67, but Dodge did add the R/T—for "Road and Track"—as the new muscle model. Standard were fake hood vents, a Charger-inspired grille with exposed headlamps, and the biggest displacement V-8 of the day, Mopar's 440. The Hemi was the only engine option. Only 628 R/T ragtops were built for '67.

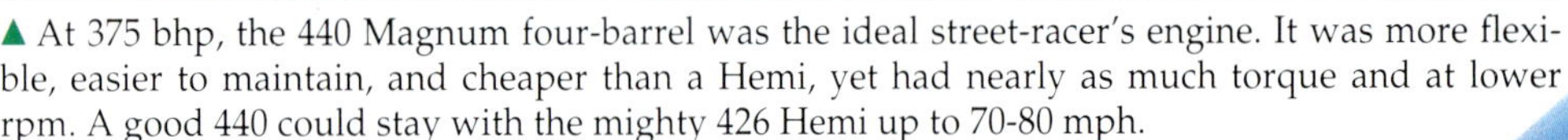

▲ At 375 bhp, the 440 Magnum four-barrel was the ideal street-racer's engine. It was more flexible, easier to maintain, and cheaper than a Hemi, yet had nearly as much torque and at lower rpm. A good 440 could stay with the mighty 426 Hemi up to 70-80 mph.

▲ The 440 was limited to full-size cars before the Magnum was fitted to the R/T. A four-speed was standard; TorqueFlite and $111 front disc brakes were optional. All R/Ts got a Sure-Grip diff and beefed suspension.

▲▼ A 440 R/T automatic like the one above turned a 15.4 quarter at 94 mph for *Motor Trend*, while *Hot Rod*'s TorqueFlite 440 did the quarter in 14.91 at 93.16. Just 283 of the 10,181 Coronet R/Ts built for '67 got the $907.50 Hemi option (below). *Motor Trend*'s Hemi automatic turned a lukewarm 15.0 at 96 mph. Dodge ads warned that a Coronet R/T was "not for the timid."

▼ At $3199 for the hardtop and $3438 for the convertible, the 440 R/T was, according to *Super Stock* magazine, "one of the best all-around performance packages being offered."

▲ Charger got only minor alterations for '67. Big news was availability of the 440 Magnum engine. Sales, however, dropped by more than half, to 15,788. A vinyl roof, in white or black, was a new option.

▲ A rear lip spoiler was added for '67. Charger's shape should have been a boon on NASCAR superspeedways, but the car never was a major NASCAR force. Don White drove his '67 Charger to the championship in USAC, where shorter tracks prevailed.

▲ Charger's center console became an option and no longer extended to the rear seat. Standard was a front center cushion with fold-down armrest, permitting seating for five instead of four. Both the four-speed and TorqueFlite came with Sure-Grip. Extinguisher was not stock.

1967 DODGE HIGH-PERFORMANCE ENGINES

TYPE	CID	BORE × STROKE	BHP @ RPM	TORQUE @ RPM	FUEL SYSTEM	COMP. RATIO	AVAIL.
ohv V-8	383	4.25 × 3.75	280 @ 4200	400 @ 2400	1 × 4bbl.	10.0:1	Dart GT
ohv V-8	383	4.25 × 3.75	325 @ 4800	425 @ 2800	1 × 4bbl.	10.0:1	1
ohv V-8	440	4.32 × 3.75	350 @ 4400	480 @ 2800	1 × 4bbl.	10.1:1	full size
ohv V-8	440	4.32 × 3.75	375 @ 4600	480 @ 3200	1 × 4bbl.	10.1:1	2
ohv V-8	426*	4.25 × 3.75	425 @ 5000	480 @ 4000	2 × 4bbl.	10.25:1	3

* Hemi.
1. Coronet, Charger, full size. 2. Coronet R/T, Charger, full size. 3. Coronet, Charger.

◀ Just 118 '67 Chargers got the Hemi, again conservatively rated at 425 bhp. *Car Life* ran one to 60 in 6.4 seconds, and to an ET of 14.16 at 96.15 mph on the standard 3.23:1 axle. With the 375-bhp 440, most testers saw 0-60 times of around 8.0 and ETs of around 15.0.

▲ Tom "The Mongoose" McEwen (center) drove Ford's SOHC 427 exhibition racer on its one and only run, an 8.28 at 171 mph at the '67 Winternationals in Pomona.

▲ The 427 Fairlanes were back, including one driven by NASCAR veteran Lee Roy Yarbrough (top left). The Paul Harvey rig was among the best, running in the low 10.9s at 127 mph, but competition was tougher than ever, and the Fairlanes didn't win a single national championship.

▶ NHRA switched the 427 Fairlanes among several classes during the '66 season, forcing them to run against all manner of purpose-built machinery, including the sub-9-second "ultra-stock" SOHC Mustangs. By '67, the rules anchored Fairlanes like this one in the Super Stock/B category, where Mopars were giving everyone a rough time.

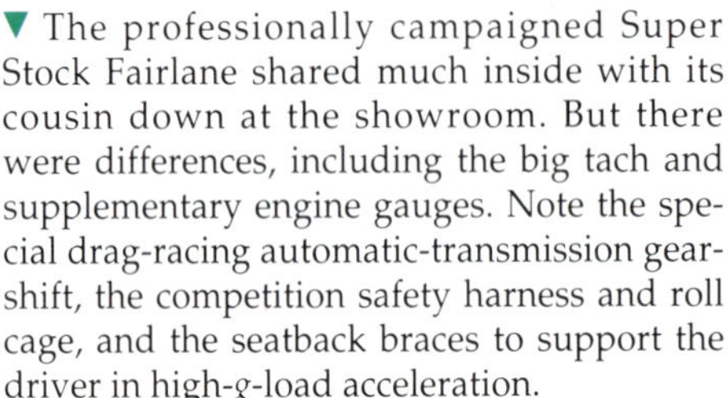

▼ The professionally campaigned Super Stock Fairlane shared much inside with its cousin down at the showroom. But there were differences, including the big tach and supplementary engine gauges. Note the special drag-racing automatic-transmission gearshift, the competition safety harness and roll cage, and the seatback braces to support the driver in high-*g*-load acceleration.

▲ The 427 became a Fairlane regular-production option for '67. The solid-lifter mill had 410 bhp with a single four-barrel or 425 with dual quads. Super-tuned drag versions like this one could expect over 500 bhp. The big impact was in NASCAR, where 427 Fairlanes ran non-stock tunnel-port heads and Galaxie front suspensions. Mario Andretti won the Daytona 500 in one. It was one of 10 Ford victories, but again, Plymouth dominated.

◀ This quarter-miler's frame was modified by Holman and Moody of Charlotte, North Carolina, which also built Fairlane's NASCAR underpinnings. Its fuel tank was shortened to make way for the Ford nine-inch differential with 5.67:1 gearing. A ladder-bar rear suspension works with the massive slicks to put a tornado's worth of torque on the pavement.

▲ The stock steel hood was available this year on 427 Fairlanes; the cop-baiting fiberglass version with the air scoop was made optional.

▲ Even though the 427 engine was now a regular production option, fewer than 200 are thought to have been ordered. Chrome valve covers were standard.

▲ Only a base, 500, or 500XL Fairlane could get a 427 engine. GTs stuck with two- and four-barrel 390 V-8s, the latter down by 15 bhp, to 320.

▲ Fairlane 500XL blended pleasant accommodations with decent go: *Motor Trend*'s 390 GTA (for Automatic) did the quarter in 16.2 at 89 mph and got between 10.8 and 12.5 mpg. XL hardtops started at $2724; convertibles at $2950. GT models added another $115 and came with front disc brakes.

▲ Big Fords had given up most performance pretensions; Blue Oval boosters had turned to Fairlanes and Mustangs for drag duty. Fresh sheetmetal gave the '67s a rounded profile, as seen on this XL convertible. Engine choices ranged from a 200-bhp 289 V-8 to 427- and 428-cid big-blocks.

▲ The biggest engine in the Ford stable was the "7-Litre" 428, a quiet long-stroke V-8 with the low-rpm power needed to move full-size cars. It was rated at 345 bhp, and had 462 pounds/feet of torque at just 2800 rpm with a single four-barrel carburetor. The hotter 427 was available for its final year, and racers could still buy the SOHC 427 over the counter. But the bloom was off big-car muscle.

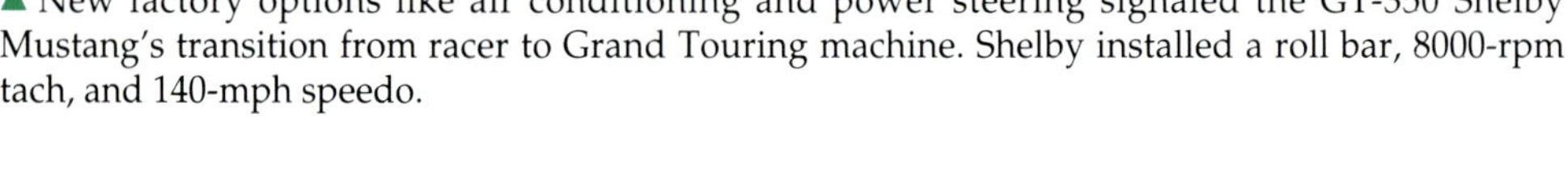
▲ New factory options like air conditioning and power steering signaled the GT-350 Shelby Mustang's transition from racer to Grand Touring machine. Shelby installed a roll bar, 8000-rpm tach, and 140-mph speedo.

▲ GT-350s again used the 306-bhp solid-lifter 289 with a 715cfm Holley and aluminum high-rise manifold. Headers were no longer standard.

▲ Shelby Mustangs broke into big-blocks for '67 with introduction of the GT-500. It used Ford's 428-cid "Police Interceptor" V-8 rated at 360 bhp.

▲ *Motor Trend*'s GT-500 did 0-60 in 6.2 seconds and the quarter in 14.52 at 101.35 mph on 3.50:1 gears. The standard heavy-duty suspension was similar to the '67 Mustang GT/GTA's, though adjustable Gabriel shocks replaced the previous Shelby's Konis. Tires grew to E70×15. Wheel options were these Kelsey-Hayes MagStars or cast-aluminum Shelby 10-spokes.

1967 FORD HIGH-PERFORMANCE ENGINES

TYPE	CID	BORE × STROKE	BHP @ RPM	TORQUE @ RPM	FUEL SYSTEM	COMP. RATIO	AVAIL.
ohv V-8	289	4.00×2.87	271 @ 6000	312 @ 3400	1×4bbl.	10.5:1	Mustang
ohv V-8	289	4.00×2.87	306 @ 6800	329 @ 4000	1×4bbl.	10.0:1	1
ohv V-8	390	4.05×3.78	320 @ 4800	427 @ 3200	1×4bbl.	10.5:1	2
ohv V-8	427	4.23×3.78	410 @ 5600	476 @ 3400	1×4bbl.	11.0:1	Fairlane, full
ohv V-8	427	4.23×3.78	425 @ 6000	480 @ 3700	1×4bbl.	11.0:1	3
ohv V-8	428	4.13×3.98	345 @ 4600	462 @ 2800	1×4bbl.	10.5:1	full size
ohv V-8	428	4.13×3.98	360 @ 5400	459 @ 3200	1×4bbl.	10.5:1	4
sohc V-8	427	4.23×3.78	616 @ 7000	515 @ 3800	2×4bbl.	12.0:1	race

1. Shelby GT-350. 2. Mustang, Fairlane 3. Fairlane, full size 4. Shelby GT-350, full size.

◀ The 428 had an aluminum "427" medium-riser manifold with twin 600cfm Holleys, an oval alloy air cleaner, and aluminum valve covers. A Toploader four-speed or C-6 automatic mated with axles ranging from 3.50:1 to 4.11:1. A few GT-500s got the 427-cid medium-riser V-8.

◀ Fairlane's Mercury cousin, the Comet, wasn't officially offered with the 427 engine, though 50 or so were built. The top official choice was the 320-bhp, 390-cid four-barrel Cyclone GT. The hardtop listed for $3034, the convertible for $3294. Both came with the twin-scoop fiberglass hood and front disc brakes. This car has aftermarket mags instead of the standard wheelcovers, which looked like chrome wheels.

▲ Mercury dressed the '67 Cyclone in checkered-flag badges and body-side stripes, but still didn't ignite much sales interest. Just 3797 were built; Pontiac, by contrast, assembled nearly 82,000 GTOs. Arrival of the new Cougar helped divert what interest there was in Mercury sportiness.

▲ The exhibition-racer, fiberglass-shell, tube-frame dragsters had been called funny cars for several seasons, but it wasn't until '67 that the NHRA established an official Funny Car class. Jack Chrisman switched to an enclosed body for his '66 Cyclone and went to work.

▲ Chrisman's flip-top GT-1 Funny Car used a Cyclone-replica fiberglass body, but about the only thing the same as on the production car was the wheelbase, which retained the stock 116-inch span. His SOHC 427 used a supercharger, which made it a better top-speed machine than non-blown rivals. Chrisman usually lagged behind for the first 300-400 feet, however, until the boost was up; then he surged forward as if an afterburner had kicked in. A competitor had to have a good lead by then to stay ahead of the GT-1's 180-mph-plus charge. What performance image Mercury had in the mid-'60s was nurtured by its Cyclone-bodied Funny Cars.

1967 MERCURY HIGH-PERFORMANCE ENGINES

TYPE	CID	BORE × STROKE	BHP @ RPM	TORQUE @ RPM	FUEL SYSTEM	COMP. RATIO	AVAIL.
ohv V-8	390	4.05 × 3.78	320 @ 4800	427 @ 3200	1 × 4bbl.	10.5:1	Cyclone
ohv V-8	427	4.23 × 3.78	410 @ 5600	476 @ 3400	1 × 4bbl.	11.0:1	Comet
ohv V-8	427	4.23 × 3.38	425 @ 6000	480 @ 3700	1 × 4bbl.	11.0:1	Comet

▲ Don Nicholson's Eliminator II was among the most successful Funny Cars. He scored 135 NHRA victories in a 10-month span, for a 90.6 winning percentage. Near-stock driver's position is thought to have been a bow to the Mercury public-relations effort.

▲ Nicholson poses with the injected SOHC 427, which made more than 900 bhp. Dyno Don blasted the Eliminator II to a record 7.6-second ET, while Jack Chrisman drove it to 184.42 mph at Riverside. *Drag Racing* magazine named it "Performance Car of the Year."

▲ "Sedate it ain't," was Oldsmobile's tag line for the '67 4-4-2. Priced at $184.31, the performance package now included functional hood louvers and made available such options as transistorized ignition and front disc brakes.

▲ The 4-4-2's 400-cid four-barrel was again rated at 350 bhp. The tri-power option died, but the W-30 setup with its air-induction and radical camshaft was back. *Car and Driver* hit 60 in 7.5 seconds and ran the quarter in 15.8 at 91 mph with a regular 350-bhp version. *Hot Rod*'s W-30 turned a 13.9 with the four-speed, 14.5 with automatic.

1967 OLDSMOBILE HIGH-PERFORMANCE ENGINES

TYPE	CID	BORE × STROKE	BHP @ RPM	TORQUE @ RPM	FUEL SYSTEM	COMP. RATIO	AVAIL.
ohv V-8	330	3.94 × 3.39	310 @ 5200	340 @ 3600	1 × 4bbl.	9.0:1	1
ohv V-8	330	3.94 × 3.39	320 @ 5200	360 @ 3600	1 × 4bbl.	10.25:1	1
ohv V-8	400	4.00 × 3.98	300 @ 4600	425 @ 2600	1 × 2bbl.	10.5:1	Supreme
ohv V-8	400	4.00 × 3.98	350 @ 5000	440 @ 3600	1 × 4bbl.	10.5:1	2

1. Supreme, Cutlas, F-85, Vista Cruiser. 2. 4-4-2, Supreme.

▲ Plymouth finally took an encompassing approach to mid-size performance, creating an executive-class hot rod for '67 with the Belvedere GTX. It used the Super Commando 440 or 426 Street Hemi.

▲ This badge added $546 to the $3178 GTX coupe or $3418 convertible. Of course, you got a legendary 425-bhp engine in the bargain.

▲ Hemi engines were specially built at Chrysler's Marine/Industrial Division plant. Quality was extremely high, and they ran with surprising smoothness. *Car and Driver*'s Hemi GTX shot to 60 in 4.8 seconds and ran the quarter in 13.5 at 105 mph. "They don't call it King Kong for nothing," said one Plymouth advertisement.

▲ Plymouth built 12,500 GTXs for '67. Of the 720 ordered with the Hemi, 407 had the TorqueFlite and 313 had the four-speed.

▲ A 150-mph speedometer and bucket seats were standard on the GTX; a console floor shift was optional with the automatic.

▲ This special-order A/Stock Belvedere drag car carried a blueprinted and ultra-tuned Street Hemi. All sound insulation was deleted, lightweight van seats were used, and the battery was moved to the trunk. With street tires, these cars were reportedly legal for road use. At the NHRA Springnationals, "The Boss" Plymouth Hemi GTX campaigned by Sox & Martin in Super Stock turned an 11.34-second ET at 123.45 mph with Ronnie Sox at the wheel. The Plymouth public-relations machine was in high gear, and fans were encouraged to attend Sox & Martin Supercar Clinics held at dragstrips prior to the actual runs.

▲ The big hood scoop on the A/Stock Belvedere fed the Street Hemi's dual quads. Actual horsepower may have been as high as 550. NASCAR versions used a single four-barrel and powered Richard Petty to the most remarkable one-year record in stock-car-racing history. Petty started 48 Grand National races in his "Petty Blue" No. 43 GTX and won 27 of them. Plymouth took 31 checkered flags in all to dominate the series.

1967 PLYMOUTH HIGH-PERFORMANCE ENGINES

TYPE	CID	BORE × STROKE	BHP @ RPM	TORQUE @ RPM	FUEL SYSTEM	COMP. RATIO	AVAIL.
ohv V-8	383	4.24×3.38	280 @ 4200	400 @ 2400	1×4bbl.	10.0:1	Barracuda
ohv V-8	383	4.24×3.38	325 @ 4800	425 @ 2800	1×4bbl.	10.0:1	Satellite, Fury
ohv V-8	426*	4.25×3.75	425 @ 5000	490 @ 4000	2×4bbl.	10.25:1	GTX
ohv V-8	440	4.32×3.75	350 @ 4400	480 @ 2800	1×4bbl.	10.1:1	Sport Fury
ohv V-8	440	4.32×3.75	375 @ 4600	480 @ 3200	1×4bbl.	10.1:1	GTX, Fury VIP

* Hemi.

▲ Plymouth built about 55 of these drag Belvederes, while Dodge built roughly the same number of similar race-only Coronets. The two are known today as RO/WO-series cars. This one has nonperiod wheels.

▲ Stripes and (non-functioning) scoops erased any notion of the GTX as a sleeper. TorqueFlite with modified upshift points was standard; a four-speed was optional. Heavy-duty suspension and upgraded 11-inch drum brakes were standard; front discs were optional.

◀ The 440 retained the 10.1:1 compression it had in the full-size models, but for Super Commando duty got a revised camshaft, free-flowing exhaust system, and an unsilenced air cleaner. It made 375 bhp, 25 more than the other 440s. *Car Life*'s automatic with 3.23:1 gears did 0-60 in 6.6 seconds, the quarter in 15.2 at 97, and averaged 12.3 mpg.

▲ Plymouth officially listed the 325-bhp, 383-cid four-barrel as the top Satellite engine, but as this photo shows, some evidently were powered by the 426 Hemi. The 440 was not available.

▲ Satellite shared the GTX's interior, but got a satin-silver Aluma-Plate lower-body finish. The hardtop cost $2747. The convertible, which this year gained a glass backlight, cost $2986.

▲ Plymouth's 383 V-8 was one of the era's most durable engines, doing duty in a variety of models and holding its own when tuned for performance applications, as is this four-barrel variant.

▲ Barracuda gained two inches of wheelbase, to 108, and two inches in engine bay width—enough to hold the 383. The four-barrel mill was optional on the top-of-the-line Formula S fastback. At 280 bhp, it was good for mid-15-second ETs at 92 mph, but left no room in the nose-heavy car for a power steering pump.

▲ Mopar versus Pontiac was a classic mid-'60s tussle. Here, Dick Landy's '67 Coronet R/T hardtop gets the drop on a '67 GTO in B/SA class action. A Royal "Bobcat" modified GTO with Ram Air turned a 13.09-second ET at 106.5 mph in the hands of *Motor Trend*, hitting 60 in just 4.9 seconds. *Hot Rod*'s automatic Bobcat turned a 13.89.

▲ GTO was back, stylish as ever, but the 389 had been bored to become the newly standard 400-cid V-8. Three versions were offered, all with 10.75:1 compression. In base trim, the 400 had 335 bhp via a Quadrajet carb; the High Output had a long-duration cam, improved exhaust manifolds, and 360 bhp at 5100 rpm. Ram Air with a functional hood scoop rated the same 360 horses, but at 5400 rpm. Ram Air cost $76.89 and came only with a 4.33:1 axle.

1967 PONTIAC HIGH-PERFORMANCE ENGINES

TYPE	CID	BORE × STROKE	BHP @ RPM	TORQUE @ RPM	FUEL SYSTEM	COMP. RATIO	AVAIL.
ohv V-8	326	3.72 × 3.75	285@5000	359@3200	1 × 4bbl.	10.5:1	1
ohv V-8	400	4.12 × 3.75	290@4600	428@2500	1 × 4bbl.	10.5:1	Catalina, full size
ohv V-8	400	4.12 × 3.75	325@4800	410@3400	1 × 4bbl.	10.75:1	Firebird Formula 400
ohv V-8	400	4.12 × 3.75	325@5200	410@3600	1 × 4bbl.	10.75:1	Firebird Formula 400
ohv V-8	400	4.12 × 3.75	325@4800	445@2900	1 × 4bbl.	10.5:1	Bonneville, full size
ohv V-8	400	4.12 × 3.75	333@5000	445@3000	1 × 4bbl.	10.5:1	Bonneville, full size
ohv V-8	400	4.12 × 3.75	335@5000	441@3400	1 × 4bbl.	10.75:1	GTO
ohv V-8	400	4.12 × 3.75	350@5000	440@3200	1 × 4bbl.	10.5:1	Grand Prix
ohv V-8	400	4.12 × 3.75	360@5100	438@3600	1 × 4bbl.	10.75:1	GTO
ohv V-8	400	4.12 × 3.75	360@5400	438@3800	1 × 4bbl.	10.75:1	GTO
ohv V-8	428	4.12 × 4.00	360@4600	472@3200	1 × 4bbl.	10.5:1	full size
ohv V-8	428	4.12 × 4.00	376@5100	462@3200	1 × 4bbl.	10.75:1	full size

1. Tempest, LeMans, Firebird H.O.

▲ This Goat's slightly elevated stance was a typical modification, though its tires are not of the period. Cross-hatch grille and "lid-less" taillamps help identify the '67s. Power front discs were a $105 option.

▲ A three-speed manual was standard; a Muncie four-speed a $184 option. A Hurst Dual Gate shifter was a factory-order item with the $226 Turbo Hydra-Matic. Eight axle choices ranged from 2.78:1 to 4.33:1.

▼ Competition ate into GTO sales. Production slipped to 81,722, (including 9517 convertibles), but nearly half had stick shift. The pillared Sports Coupe started at $2871, the hardtop $2935, and the ragtop $3165.

▲ *Motor Trend* tried two Ram Air Goats, both with Royal "Bobcat Kits," open headers, 3.90:1 gears, Hurst linkages, and 8.50×14 M&H Super Stock rear tires. The four-speed's best ET was 13.09 at 106.5; the Turbo Hydra-Matic's was 13.36 at 105. With stock tires, the ETs were slower by .75 to 1.12 seconds. The cars averaged 13.5 mpg highway, 11.5 around town.

▲ Firebird alighted a few months after the comparable Camaro. Choices ranged from a base hardtop with an OHC six-cylinder, to 326-cid V-8s, to the 325-bhp Firebird 400 (Ram Air $616 extra). *Hot Rod* turned a 15.4 at 92 with a regular 400 ragtop. It had automatic, 3.08:1 gears, and a test weight of 3855 pounds.

▼ Pontiac's big 2+2 returned with a new base engine: a 428-cid four-barrel with 360 bhp. A high-output edition had 376 bhp. The 2+2 reverted to a $400 Catalina option, however, and sales were so low that it was dropped after this year. It went out with bucket seats, floor-shifted three-speed, dual exhaust, and heavy-duty suspension. Gauges and a hood-mounted tach could be ordered, too.

1968

Plymouth debuts the Road Runner ... its blend of fun, power, and affordability is widely influential • American Motors saddles up for the ponycar wars with the Javelin and its two-seat AMX derivative • General Motors redesigns its intermediates on shorter wheelbases; all get rounded new bodies and stay aggressive toward performance • Chevy IIs can get big-block 396 with 375 bhp • Dodge groups its hot cars under the "Scat Pack" umbrella ... highlight is the dramatically restyled Charger • Coronet Super Bee answers Road Runner • Special Hemi Darts and Barracudas go dragging • Ford reaches the upper-echelon of production-car power with the new 428 Cobra Jet V-8 ... it goes first into a troop of Mustangs that quickly dominate their NHRA Super Stock classes with ETs in the 11s • Hurst/Olds 4-4-2 gets a 455-cid Toronado V-8 • Bill "Grumpy" Jenkins' 427 Camaro breaks into the 9-second range • Top Fuel car hits 6.87 at 230.76 • Cale Yarborough and Lee Roy Yarbrough finish Daytona 500 1-2 in new Mercury fastbacks...Ford gets 20 NASCAR wins

▲ Hardly known for high performance, AMC scored with the AMX. Based on the new Javelin fastback, the AMX was shorter by a foot and had just two seats. Its 97-inch wheelbase was one inch less than Corvette's, and its $3245 base price with the standard 225-bhp 290-cid V-8 was $1100 below that of a 'Vette.

▲ AMX's had balanced handling, as well as good straight-line kick. A 280-bhp, 343-cid V-8 could replace the 290, but most buyers opted for the 315-bhp 390. A Borg-Warner four-speed was standard; three-speed automatic optional. A "Go" package added power front discs, E70×14 tires, Twin-Grip limited slip, and racing stripes.

▲ Derived from the 343, AMX's 390 V-8 has the same 10.2:1 compression, but a stronger block, forged rods and crank, and bigger bearings. All AMX mills used a single four-barrel. Factory-order axles ranged from 2.87:1 to 3.54:1; dealers could install 4.10:1 or 5.00:1 gearing.

◀ Pete's Patriot was the first significant AMC drag car. It was a Street Eliminator champion and is shown here with Loren Downing at the wheel at the '68 NHRA U.S. Nationals. As for the customer AMXs, *Car and Driver* said the four-speed's shift linkage was "an abomination...a long, wobbly business with lots of play in every direction," yet its 390 still took just 6.6 seconds to 60 mph and turned a 14.8 ET at 95 mph. The editors said the AMX couldn't match a Corvette's road manners, but that it "will get you down the road and around the corners in admirable fashion." Just 6275 '68 AMXs were built.

1968 AMC HIGH-PERFORMANCE ENGINES							
TYPE	CID	BORE × STROKE	BHP @ RPM	TORQUE @ RPM	FUEL SYSTEM	COMP. RATIO	AVAIL.
ohv V-8	343	4.08 × 3.28	280 @ 4800	365 @ 3000	1 × 4bbl.	10.2:1	1
ohv V-8	390	4.17 × 3.57	315 @ 4600	425 @ 3200	1 × 4bbl.	10.2:1	1

1. Javelin, AMX, Ambassador Rebel

▼ General Motors redesigned its intermediates on a shorter 112-inch wheelbase for '68, and that spelled big styling changes for the Chevrolet Chevelle, Olds 4-4-2, Pontiac GTO, and Buick's Gran Sport. The Buick shed its sedan proportions for the fashionable long-hood, short-deck look. Replacing the GS340 as the junior partner to the 400-cid GS400 was the GS350 hardtop. It had a 280-bhp four-barrel 350-cid V-8.

◀ Most GS Buicks were hardtops or convertibles, though some dealers stocked a pillared coupe known as the California GS; it came with the 350-cid engine. Transmission choices continued from '67, along with the Positraction option. Prices were up only $100 from '67, and GS production nearly doubled, to a record 21,514, with 8317 of them GS350s.

▲ Despite a wheelbase that was shorter by three inches and a body that was briefer by four, the new GS400 hardtop weighed 3514 pounds; the convertible, 3547. Both were slightly heavier than before, so acceleration was no better.

▶ Once again, the GS400's 400-cid V-8 had 340 bhp. Strong on mid-range torque, it performed without the peakiness that was typical of most high-performance V-8s of the day. A chrome air cleaner went over the Rochester four-barrel.

1968 BUICK HIGH-PERFORMANCE ENGINES

TYPE	CID	BORE × STROKE	BHP @ RPM	TORQUE @ RPM	FUEL SYSTEM	COMP. RATIO	AVAIL.
ohv V-8	340	3.80 × 3.85	280 @ 4600	375 @ 3200	1 × 4bbl.	10.25:1	1
ohv V-8	400	4.04 × 3.90	340 @ 5000	440 @ 3200	1 × 4bbl.	10.25:1	GS400, Sportwagon
ohv V-8	430	4.19 × 3.90	360 @ 5000	475 @ 3200	1 × 4bbl.	10.25:1	2

1. GS340, California GS, Special, Skylark, Sportwagon, LeSabre. 2. Wildcat, Electra 225, Riviera.

▲ Though a good GS400's mid-15-second ETs were no quicker than in '67, the shorter wheelbase, widened 59-inch front track, heavy-duty springs and shocks, and stabilizer bar gave it better handling and a less-floaty ride. In the Buick tradition, these were solid, stylish cars, and they blended power with poise in a mix that appealed to the more mature driving enthusiast. Base price of the GS350 was $2926; the GS400 started at $3127 for the hardtop and $3271 for the convertible.

◀ Camaro's $400 Z-28 package was little changed, though now it had fender emblems. Chevy made heavier-duty four-speeds available, and four-wheel disc brakes were a midyear "service option." When ordered with the Rally Sport package (note RS grille badge), any Camaro got hidden headlamps.

▲ Camaro was coming on strong at the strip, as well as on road courses. In the Trans Am sedan series, Chevy finally accomplished what it had set out to do with the Z-28. Mark Donohue's dark blue No. 6 Sunoco Camaro won 10 of the 11 races in the series to capture the championship in the over-two-liter class.

▲ Z-28's solid-lifter 302 was again rated at 290 bhp with the standard 800cfm Holley four-barrel. Newly available was a special manifold with twin 600cfm Holley quads at $500, plus dealer installation. *Hi Performance Cars* magazine tried a dual-quad Z-28 and turned the quarter in 13.75 at 107 mph. Though omitted from sales brochures for the second year running, Chevy did advertise the Z-28 as "closest thing to a Corvette yet," and production jumped to 7198.

1968 CHEVROLET HIGH-PERFORMANCE ENGINES

TYPE	CID	BORE × STROKE	BHP @ RPM	TORQUE @ RPM	FUEL SYSTEM	COMP. RATIO	AVAIL.
ohv V-8	302	4.00 × 3.00	290 @ 5800	290 @ 4200	1 × 4bbl.	11.0:1	Camaro Z-28
ohv V-8	327	4.00 × 3.25	275 @ 4800	355 @ 3200	1 × 4bbl.	10.0:1	1
ohv V-8	327	4.00 × 3.25	325 @ 5600	355 @ 3600	1 × 4bbl.	11.0:1	Chevelle
ohv V-8	350	4.00 × 3.48	295 @ 4800	380 @ 3200	1 × 4bbl.	10.25:1	2
ohv V-8	396	4.09 × 3.76	325 @ 4800	410 @ 3200	1 × 4bbl.	10.25:1	3
ohv V-8	396	4.09 × 3.76	350 @ 5200	415 @ 3400	1 × 4bbl.	10.25:1	4
ohv V-8	396	4.09 × 3.76	375 @ 5600	420 @ 3600	1 × 4bbl.	11.0:1	4
ohv V-8	396*	4.09 × 3.76	375 @ 5600	420 @ 3600	1 × 4bbl.	11.0:1	5
ohv V-8	427	4.25 × 3.76	385 @ 5200	460 @ 3400	1 × 4bbl.	10.25:1	full size
ohv V-8	427	4.25 × 3.76	425 @ 5600	460 @ 2000	1 × 4bbl.	11.0:1	full size

* RPO L89, aluminum heads, available 12/67.
1. full size, Chevelle, Chevy II, Camaro. 2. Camaro SS 350, Chevy II SS 350. 3. full size, Camaro SS 396, Chevelle SS 396. 4. Camaro SS, Chevelle SS 396, Chevy II SS 396. 5. Chevelle SS 396, Camaro SS 396.

▶ Camaros lost their wing windows with the advent of the flow-through Astro-Ventilation system. Side marker lights also identified a '68. Of 235,147 Camaros built for this year, 27,844 got the SS package.

▲ Performance models, such as this SS 396, gained five-leaf rear spring and staggered shocks to minimize axle tramp. SS models also got a blacked-out tail panel and gained front disc brakes as standard.

▲ Turbo Hydra-Matic Camaros gained a stirrup-shaped shifter, and the optional rev counter and clock could be combined into a single gauge Chevy tabbed the "Tick-Tock Tach."

▶ The SS Camaro's four-barrel V-8s again began with a 295-bhp, 350-cid unit. The 396-cid big-block (shown) gained a 350-bhp edition to go along with the carryover 325- and 375-bhp versions. About 270 of the 396 engines received special-order aluminum cylinder heads, but their 375-bhp rating was unchanged.

▲ For '68, SS 396 models also got their own hood with dual banks of four non-functional ports. A distinctive band around the nose helped SS Camaros stand out.

▲ Downsized and restyled, the 1968 Super Sport Chevelle began the best-selling four-year run of any big-block intermediate. Now a distinct series, the SS 396 was muscle for the common man.

◀ SS 396 Chevelles got a black-out grille and rear panel and light-colored cars got a dark lower body treatment. The double-dome hood was carried over, and F70×14 tires were made standard. Front disc brakes were a $100 option.

▲ SS 396 hardtops started at $2899; Chevy built 60,499 of them. Ragtops began at $3102; 2286 were built. As in previous years, the El Camino pickup could also be ordered with a 396.

▶ A 325-bhp 396 (shown here) was standard. The 350-bhp L-34 cost $105. Top dog was the solid-lifter 375-bhp L-78. Just 4751 were ordered.

▲ *Motor Trend*'s 3922-pound base-engine SS 396 coupe with automatic and A/C turned a 15.8 at 90 mph. Its rough-running L-34 was slower, but *MT* said a few "performance preparations" would get a good L-34 stick into the high 13s.

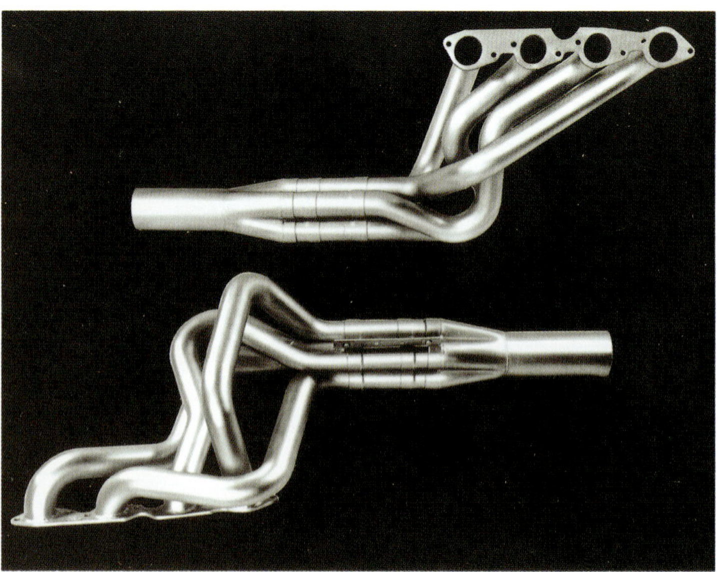

▲ As usual, the aftermarket delivered an alluring selection of high-performance components for big-block Chevelles. These Stahl exhaust headers fit 1968-72 models. Hooker, Doug's, and Jardine were other header brand names.

▲ Charter members of Dodge's "Scat Pack" performance team for '68 were (from top) the Dart GTS, Coronet R/T, and Charger R/T. Audiences of the hit film *Bullitt* thrilled as the new 440 Magnum-equipped Charger R/T tore about hilly San Francisco in a classic duel with Steve McQueen's 390 Mustang. Would McQueen have caught a Hemi?

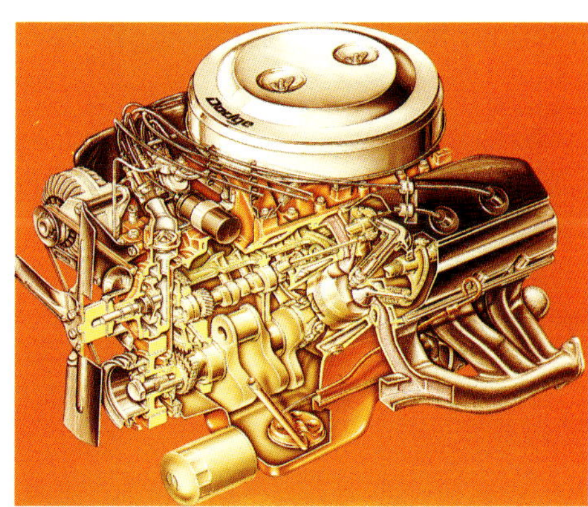

▲ The 426 Hemi still was rated at 425 bhp. At Dodge, it added $605 to the Coronet R/T and Charger R/T, and nearly $1000 to the new Coronet Super Bee. Air conditioning was unavailable with the Hemi.

1968 DODGE HIGH-PERFORMANCE ENGINES

TYPE	CID	BORE × STROKE	BHP @ RPM	TORQUE @ RPM	FUEL SYSTEM	COMP. RATIO	AVAIL.
ohv V-8	340	4.04 × 3.31	275 @ 5000	340 @ 3200	1 × 4bbl.	10.5:1	Dart GT
ohv V-8	383	4.25 × 3.75	300 @ 4400	400 @ 2400	1x4bbl.	9.2:1	Dart GT
ohv V-8	383	4.25 × 3.75	290 @ 4400	390 @ 2800	1 × 4bbl.	9.2:1	1
ohv V-8	383	4.25 × 3.75	330 @ 5000	425 @ 3200	1 × 4bbl.	10.0:1	1
ohv V-8	383	4.25 × 3.75	335 @ 5200	425 @ 3400	1 × 4bbl.	10.0:1	Dart 383 GTS
ohv V-8	426*	4.25 × 3.75	425 @ 5000	490 @ 4000	2 × 4bbl.	10.25:1	2
ohv V-8	440	4.32 × 3.75	350 @ 4400	480 @ 2800	1 × 4bbl.	10.1:1	full size
ohv V-8	440	4.32 × 3.75	375 @ 4600	480 @ 3200	1 × 4bbl.	10.1:1	2

* Hemi.
1. Coronet, Charger, full size. 2. Coronet R/T, Charger R/T.

▲ Super Bee, a midyear offshoot of the Coronet, was Dodge's response to Plymouth's Road Runner. A "stripper" performance car, its $3037 base price included a 335-bhp, 383-cid V-8, four-speed with Hurst Competition-Plus shifter, heavy-duty suspension, and Charger instrumentation. Pillared coupe was the only Super Bee body for '68.

▶ Tongue-in-cheek icons and wild graphics were part of late-'60s culture, and Dodge was right there with the "Scat Pack" bumblebee. Dodge promoted its hot models as "The cars with the bumblebee stripes."

▲ Standard in the Coronet R/T and Charger R/T was Mopar's fine 375-bhp, 440-cid Magnum four-barrel. It was a smooth runner with root-rousing torque.

▲ Coronet R/T wrapped new sheetmetal around its carryover platform. The convertible cost $3630; the coupe, $3530.

▲ R/T instrumentation was stock Coronet unless the optional round-gauge Rallye cluster was ordered. *Car Life*'s Coronet R/T ragtop hit 60 in 6.6 seconds and did the quarter in 14.69 at 97.4 mph.

▶ The 440 in *Motor Trend*'s Coronet R/T hardtop would "wind easily to 6000 rpm," but *MT* got its best times by manually shifting the TorqueFlite at 5300 rpm. With 3.54:1 gears, the car took 6.9 seconds to 60 mph and turned 15.1 at 95 mph in the quarter. Massive wheelspin was a problem, and the R/T averaged only 11 mpg around town, but *MT* said the optional $73 front disc brakes did their job. The standard heavy-duty suspension gave the nose-heavy car adequate handling, but the $95 optional power steering was numb. Assembly quality was high. Only 230 Coronet R/T buyers picked the Hemi over the Magnum.

▲ "Dandy" Dick Landy gave the new Charger some of its most successful exposure. His Hemi was set up for the AHRA's new Super Stock category, a forerunner of the NHRA's Pro Stock class. His 426 used the stock Carter dual AFB four-barrels, but added an eight-quart deep-sump oil pan, Isky cam, and 30-inch Doug's headers. A Hurst Competition Plus shifter worked the four-speed to a stock Sure-Grip with a 4.88:1 final drive.

▲ The second-generation Charger was one of the '60's handsomest muscle cars, aptly described by *Car and Driver* as "all guts and purpose." At $3480, the R/T included the 440 Magnum, heavy duty brakes, R/T handling package, and F70 × 14 Red Streak or white sidewall tires. The bumblebee stripes could be deleted from the order form. Divided front-bench "bucket" seats were standard, but a tach was a $49 option.

◀ Just 475 '68 Charger R/Ts were ordered with the 426 Hemi, and only 211 of those had the four-speed. With TorqueFlite and standard 3.23:1 gears, *Car and Driver*'s Hemi Charger got to 60 mph in 6.0 seconds and turned a killer 13.5 at 105 in the quarter. For most buyers, the standard 440 Magnum was enough. It gained a high-flow unsilenced air cleaner for '68, and *Motor Trend* said it breathed much better. Manually shifting the TorqueFlite, *MT* got its 440 Charger to 60 mph in 6.5 seconds and through the quarter in 14.85 at 95.5 mph.

▲ Landy's 3650-pound Hemi Charger turned a 10.86 at 127 mph. Cragar wheels and 10.50 × 15 Goodyear slicks got the power down. Dick's brother Mike ran a 3550-pound Super Stock 440 Coronet R/T to an ET of 11.99 at 118.

▲ A full-width hidden-headlamp grille, flying-buttress rear roof, and race-inspired fender-top gas cap were Charger trademarks and helped increase production sixfold over 1967, to 96,100. "...You wouldn't change a line of it if you could," boasted Dodge.

▲ The Dart GTS got Mopar's fine 340- or 383-cid V-8s, but about 48 were fitted with a 440 Magnum by Hurst-Campbell Inc., of Michigan.

▲ The 440 Darts were sold by "Mr. Norm's" Grand Spaulding Dodge in Chicago, which also stuffed some Hemis into the lightweight compacts.

▲ Shirley Shahan's Hemi Dart wasn't one of her more successful "Drag-On-Lady" rides, but its high-10- low-11-second capability gave this big-block 'Cuda a run for its Winternationals money. On the street, a GTS with the 275-bhp 340 was as quick as one with the optional 383; the big-block's extra weight in the nose hurt traction off the line, offsetting its 60 more bhp.

▶ The GTS came with a Rallye Suspension, buckets, tail stripes, fake hood vents, and E70 × 14 tires. The 340 hardtop cost $3163, the convertible, $3383. *Car and Driver*'s 340 GTS turned a 14.4 at 99 mph with a 3.91:1 rear axle.

▲ Fairlane retained its previous chassis, but gained new styling, including a fastback body that gave Ford's intermediates an edge on NASCAR ovals. The 427-powered Fords took 20 checkered flags, and David Pearson won the driver's title in a Holman-Moody fastback. The 427 also powered Fairlane drag cars, including Hubert Platt's Super Stock/F Automatic runner, here in action at the '68 NHRA U.S. Nationals. This was an 11.9-12.0-second car.

◀ Ford's new fastback came in Fairlane 500 form and as the new Torino and Torino GT (shown). The 390-bhp 427 was phased out during the model year, and for a time, the 335-bhp, 390-cid four-barrel was top dog. *Motor Trend* left the Cruise-O-Matic in D and ran its 390 GT to an ET of 15.1 at 91 mph. Phased in during '68 was the new 335-bhp, 428-cid Cobra Jet, which made its biggest impact in Mustangs.

1968 FORD HIGH-PERFORMANCE ENGINES

TYPE	CID	BORE × STROKE	BHP @ RPM	TORQUE @ RPM	FUEL SYSTEM	COMP. RATIO	AVAIL.
ohv V-8	390	4.05×3.78	265 @ 4400	390 @ 2600	1×2bbl.	9.5:1	Fairlane, Torino
ohv V-8	390	4.05×3.78	280 @ 4400	403 @ 2600	1×2bbl.	10.5:1	Mustang
ohv V-8	390	4.05×3.78	315 @ 4600	427 @ 4800	1×4bbl.	10.5:1	1
ohv V-8	390	4.05×3.78	335 @ 4800	427 @ 3200	1×4bbl.	10.5:1	Fairlane
ohv V-8	427*	4.23×3.78	390 @ 5600	460 @ 3200	1×4bbl.	10.9:1	2
ohv V-8	428	4.13×3.98	335 @ 5400	440 @ 3400	1×4bbl.	10.6:1	3
ohv V-8	428	4.13×3.98	360 @ 5400	460 @ 3200	1×4bbl.	10.5:1	3

* Discontinued at midyear.
1. Fairlane, Torino, Falcon, Thunderbird. 2. Fairlane, Torino, Mustang. 3. Fairlane, Mustang, Shelby.

▲ For '68, Mustang's 289-cid V-8 was replaced by a new 302. To better compete with Chevy's Z-28 on the track, Ford for '69 built the Boss 302, rated at 290 bhp. It included a solid-lifter cam, larger-valve heads, aluminum intake manifold, and a Holley 780-cfm four barrel.

▲ Some '68 Mustang literature mentioned an optional 427, but none were built. Ford instead offered the 428 Cobra Jet, beginning in April, 1968. The first 50 were white, light-weight fastbacks (above and opposite top), built to meet the NHRA's production minimum. After the initial run, 428 CJs were available in any body style. Factory backed 428 CJs dominated the '68 Winternationals.

▶ The 428 Cobra Jet was based on the staid 428 big-car motor, but had larger-valve heads and a version of the Police Interceptor intake manifold. Strip versions used a wilder cam than the street engine, with solid lifters and even bigger valves. Both ran a 735-cfm Holley four barrel and were rated by the factory at 335 bhp; the more realistic figure was closer to 410 bhp.

▲ The first 20 Super Stock 428 CJ Mustangs built by Ford for racing shifted weight to the rear and deleted radio and heater. Holman & Moody built two others, and all eliminated sound deadener.

▲ SS/E at the '68 Winternationals was an all-Cobra Jet final as Al Joniec shut down Hubert Platt with an ET of 11.49 at 120.6 mph. Joniec then snared SS Eliminator with a 12.5 at 97.9 mph on the Pomona track.

◀ The 428 CJ was offered to the public in 2+2s with the GT package and added $393—$526 for the Ram Air version. The latter was good for ETs in the mid-13-second range at 100-105 mph. The Equa-Loc diff ($79) and the Competition Handling Package ($62) were wise options.

▲ Blown SOHC 427 Mustangs continued hot in the flip-top Funny Car ranks. Bill Lawton's was named "Mystery 7" for the ET range it inhabited.

▲ A handful of Shelby Mustang ragtops had been built to order, but for '68, it was "official." Convertible production: 404 GT-350s, 402 GT-500s, and 318 GT-500KRs. Each was about one-third of fastback production.

▲ At midyear, the GT-500's 360-bhp 428 Police Interceptor was replaced by a Cobra Jet with medium-riser heads and a 735cfm Holley. With that, the GT-500KR (King of the Road) tag was adopted. Horsepower was closer to 400 than the rated 335. A GT-500KR convertible cost a princely $4594.

Carroll Shelby has gone and done it!

Convertible types, rejoice! He's built Shelby COBRA GT performance, handling, style and safety into a Mustang *convertible* complete with the best-looking roll bar in the business. If you don't flip your lid over this, you just don't flip (unless his Mustang-based Cobra GT 2 + 2 fastback gets to you). ☐ Both styles are available in GT 350 or GT 500 versions. The GT 350 boasts 302 cubic inches of Ford V-8 performance with an optional Cobra supercharger for added zip. The GT 500 really delivers with your choice of two great V-8's . . . 428 cubic inches are standard. A new 427 engine is the ultimate performance option. ☐ All the Le Mans-winning handling and safety features are better than ever for 1968. They're wrapped up in a fresh new luxury package. And the Mustang base means an exciting price. ☐ Any questions? Your Shelby Cobra dealer has some great answers!

Shelby COBRA GT 350/500

▲ Shelby ragtops got a roll bar, and all '68s gained '65 Thunderbird sequential taillights. Production of Shelby Mustangs moved from California to Michigan, where Ford had more control over them. It was a turning point, and Shelbys began to lose their individuality.

▲ *Hot Rod*'s four-speed GT-500KR fastback turned the quarter in 14.01 at 102.73. For '68, the Shelby Mustangs got a new fiberglass fascia and redesigned hood with air scoops at the leading edge.

▲ This GTE version of Mercury's Cougar has the 390-bhp 427 offered during early '68. All were automatics. *Car Life*'s did the quarter in 15.1 at 93.6 mph, but the 3.50:1 gears lacked a limited-slip, so the launch was hampered by tire spin.

▲ "The entire world will come to recognize this engine—the 428 Cobra Jet—at the pop of a hood," declared *Motor Trend*. The 428 CJ came to Mercury in mid '68, where it was offered in high-performance Cougars and mid-size Cyclones. It had the same 335-bhp rating as at Ford. *Car Life*'s 428 CJ Cyclone automatic ran a 14.4 at 99.4 mph. Its 3.91:1 gears had the 428 turning 5300 rpm through the traps, 300 rpm short of maximum engine speed, "and the strong powerplant was still pulling hard at these lofty speeds," wrote the editors.

1968 MERCURY HIGH-PERFORMANCE ENGINES

TYPE	CID	BORE × STROKE	BHP @ RPM	TORQUE @ RPM	FUEL SYSTEM	COMP. RATIO	AVAIL.
ohv V-8	390	4.05×3.78	265@4400	390@2600	1×2bbl.	9.5:1	Cyclone
ohv V-8	390	4.05×3.78	280@4400	403@2600	1×2bbl.	10.5:1	1
ohv V-8	390	4.05×3.78	325@4800	427@3200	1×4bbl.	10.5:1	2
ohv V-8	390	4.05×3.78	335@4800	427@3200	1×4bbl.	10.5:1	3
ohv V-8	427*	4.23×3.78	390@5600	460@3200	1×4bbl.	10.9:1	4
ohv V-8	428	4.13×3.98	335@5400	440@3400	1×4bbl.	10.6:1	5

* Dicontinued at midyear.

1. Cougar, Montego. 2. Cougar GT, XR7, Cyclone, Montego. 3. Montego, Cyclone. 4. Cougar GTE, Cyclone. 5. Montego, Cyclone, Cougar.

▲Mercury continued with Don Nicholson's 1000-bhp blown SOHC '68 Cougar funny car. After a spate of fires and supercharger explosions, Nicholson turned to AHRA Super Stock and NHRA Pro Stock.

▲A new Montego nameplate graced Mercury's intermediates, with the 428 CJ Cyclone GT atop the line. *Motor Trend*'s turned a 13.8 at 101.6 with 4.11:1 gears, automatic, and the Traction-Lok differential.

◀NHRA's handicapping system allowed cars of very different specification to race each other. Here, the '48 Ford Anglia of Rob Riffle takes on a very special '68 Cougar driven by Darrell Droke. The old ultralight British Fords were popular choices for installation of American V-8 muscle. The "Top Cat" Cougar, meanwhile, used a 289-cid V-8 with Gurney/Westlake heads. It was a sort of factory secret weapon and was in fact streetable, though never built for production. It ran in the high-10s and low-11s at around 120 mph.

▲Olds intermediates got new styling for '68 and the 4-4-2's 400-cid V-8 gained a new under-bumper Force-Air induction system good for 360 bhp. The blueprinted W-30 version could turn 13.3s at 103 mph. The most radical '68 4-4-2, however, was the Hurst/Olds. This is one of only 515 built. All had a 455-cid Toronado V-8 with a radical cam, recurved distributor, Rochester Quadrajet, and Force-Air induction for 390 bhp.

1968 OLDSMOBILE HIGH-PERFORMANCE ENGINES							
TYPE	CID	BORE × STROKE	BHP @ RPM	TORQUE @ RPM	FUEL SYSTEM	COMP. RATIO	AVAIL.
ohv V-8	400	3.87×4.25	290 @ 4600	425 @ 2400	1×2bbl.	9.0:1	4-4-2
ohv V-8	400	3.87×4.25	325 @ 4800	440 @ 3200	1×4bbl.	10.5:1	4-4-2
ohv V-8	400	3.87×4.25	350 @ 4800	440 @ 3200	1×4bbl.	10.5:1	4-4-2
ohv V-8	400	3.87×4.25	360 @ 5400	440 @ 3600	1×4bbl.	10.5:1	4-4-2
ohv V-8	455	4.13×4.25	390 @ 5000	500 @ 4200	1×4bbl.	10.25:1	Hurst/Olds

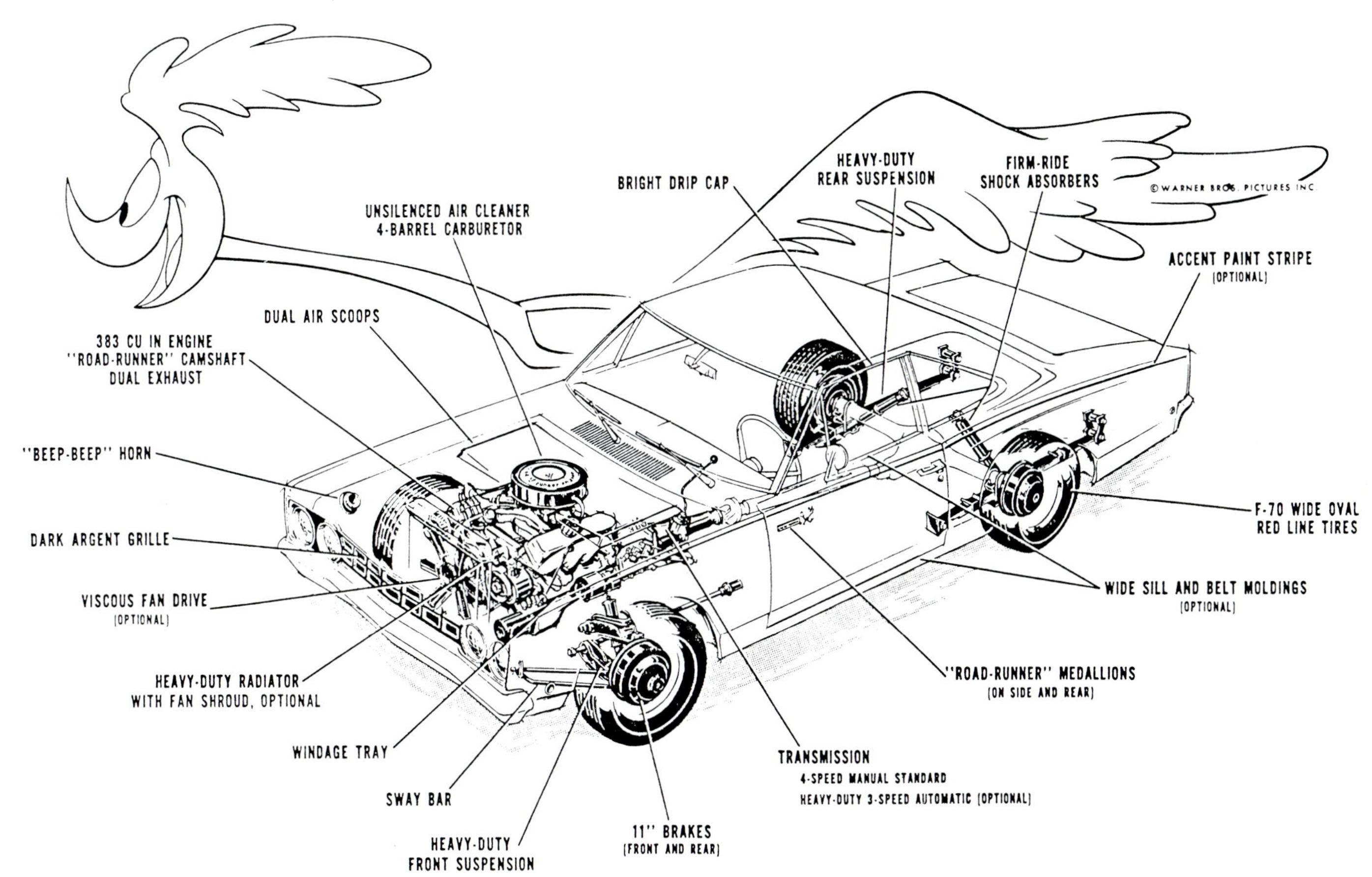

▲ One of muscle's most influential cars: the '68 Plymouth Road Runner. It was a $2986 factory hot rod in plain Belvedere skin.

▲ The base V-8 was a 335-bhp 383 four-barrel with heads from the 440. The 425-bhp 426 Hemi (shown) was the sole option, at $714.

▲ Plymouth's Sox & Martin team quickly put a Hemi Road Runner into drag duty. Street versions were turning mid-13s at 105 mph. A $139 SureGrip axle with 3.54:1 cogs was a mandatory Hemi option.

▲ Street 'Runners had F70×14 rubber; F70×15 on the Hemi. *Motor Trend*'s 383 automatic with 3.55:1 SureGrip turned 15.0 at 93 mph. Coupes, hardtops, and convertibles were offered, all with a "beep-beep" horn.

▲ Except for safety equipment and extra gauges, Ronnie Sox's work station wasn't much different from the low-bucks bench-seat cabin of the standard Road Runner, including the available "pistol grip" shift lever.

▲ Road Runner was a hit, with 44,599 built the first year. But just 1019 had the Hemi. This is Sox and Martin's mill, which includes Edelbrock's NASCAR-designed "Rat Roaster" intake manifold. A later owner has added other performance parts.

▼ GTX continued atop the line of restyled mid-size Plymouths. Like Road Runner, it used the Belvedere/Satellite platform, but again came standard with the 375-bhp, 440-cid four-barrel. GTX sales rose to 18,940 this year.

▲ The GTX ragtop started at $3590; the hardtop at $3355. Just 1026 convertibles were built. *Car Life*'s Hemi convertible with automatic and 3.23:1 gears turned a 14.0 ET at 96.5.

1968 PLYMOUTH HIGH-PERFORMANCE ENGINES

TYPE	CID	BORE × STROKE	BHP @ RPM	TORQUE @ RPM	FUEL SYSTEM	COMP. RATIO	AVAIL.
ohv V-8	340	4.04×3.31	275 @ 5000	340 @ 3200	1×4bbl.	10.5:1	Barracuda
ohv V-8	383	4.25×3.38	290 @ 4400	390 @ 2800	1×2bbl.	9.2:1	1
ohv V-8	383	4.25×3.38	300 @ 4400	400 @ 2400	1×4bbl.	10.0:1	2
ohv V-8	383	4.25×3.38	330 @ 5200	425 @ 3200	1×4bbl.	10.0:1	1
ohv V-8	383	4.25×3.38	335 @ 5200	425 @ 3400	1×4bbl.	10.0:1	3
ohv V-8	426*	4.25×3.75	425 @ 5000	490 @ 4000	2×4bbl.	10.25:1	GTX
ohv V-8	440	4.32×3.75	350 @ 4400	480 @ 2800	1×4bbl.	10.1:1	Sport Fury
ohv V-8	440	4.32×3.75	375 @ 4600	480 @ 3200	1×4bbl.	10.1:1	4

*Hemi.
1. Satellite, Fury. 2. Barracuda, Fury. 3. Road Runner. 4. GTX, Fury VIP.

▲ Just 450 GTXs got the optional Hemi in '68. With the less-costly and easier-to-maintain 440, a hardtop automatic with 3.23:1 gears turned a 14.6-second ET 95.6 mph for *Car Life*.

▲ GTX used the well-appointed Satellite interior, with bucket seats and console. The TorqueFlite automatic was standard with either engine; a four-speed manual was a no-cost option and included the 3:54:1 SureGrip.

▲ Don Grotheer's Hemi Barracuda turned high-9s at around 135 mph to set NHRA national SS/B and SS/BA speed and ET records.

▲ Plymouth contracted with Hurst Performance for a limited run of '68 Hemi Barracudas for sale to factory-approved drag racers.

▲ Arlen Vanke's SS/B Hemi 'Cuda (foreground) caught and beat "Grumpy" Jenkins's 427 SS/C Camaro to win Super Stock Eliminator at the '68 NHRA Nationals. Vanke's winning run was a 10.64 at 118.11 mph.

▲ NHRA founder Wally Parks bestows the hardware on Vanke for his performance at the '68 NHRA Nationals in Indianapolis.

▲ The Sox & Martin Hemi Barracuda took the SS/D class at the '68 Springnationals with an ET of 11.20 at 106.5. Their immaculate red-white-and-blue Mopars were a valuable tool for promoting Chrysler performance.

▲ Hot street Barracudas got this frisky 275-bhp 340 four-barrel or the 383, now with 300 bhp.

◀ Pontiac's redesigned GTO retained its Tiger's temper. The 400-cid V-8 was again the only engine for '68, but power was up. *Motor Trend* smoked a 360-bhp Ram-Air version to a 14.45-second ET at 98.2 mph. Its base 350-bhp model turned a 15.1 at 95 mph.

▲ Hidden headlamps were a GTO option, but most buyers chose them. The optional hood-mounted tach looked boss, but wasn't that practical in poor weather. The new Endura energy-absorbing bumper that formed the nose was an industry first—though a chrome bumper was available. GTO's weight was up, but a three-inch wheelbase cut and G77×14 tires helped improve handling. Of the 87,684 GTOs built for 1968, 9980 were convertibles.

1968 PONTIAC HIGH-PERFORMANCE ENGINES

TYPE	CID	BORE × STROKE	BHP @ RPM	TORQUE @ RPM	FUEL SYSTEM	COMP. RATIO	AVAIL.
ohv V-8	350	3.88 × 3.75	320 @ 5100	380 @ 3200	1 × 4bbl.	10.5:1	Tempest, Firebird HO
ohv V-8	400	4.12 × 3.75	330 @ 4800	430 @ 3300	1 × 4bbl.	10.75:1	Firebird 400
ohv V-8	400	4.12 × 3.75	335 @ 5000	430 @ 3400	1 × 4bbl.	10.75:1	Firebird 400
ohv V-8	400	4.12 × 3.75	340 @ 4800	445 @ 2900	1 × 4bbl.	10.5:1	full size
ohv V-8	400	4.12 × 3.75	350 @ 5000	445 @ 3000	1 × 4bbl.	10.5:1	Grand Prix
ohv V-8	400	4.12 × 3.75	350 @ 5000	445 @ 3000	1 × 4bbl.	10.75:1	GTO
ohv V-8	400*	4.12 × 3.75	360 @ 5100	445 @ 3600	1 × 4bbl.	10.75:1	GTO
ohv V-8	428	4.12 × 4.00	375 @ 4800	472 @ 3200	1 × 4bbl.	10.5:1	full size
ohv V-8	428	4.12 × 4.00	390 @ 5200	462 @ 3400	1 × 4bbl.	10.75:1	full size

*Ram Air, Ram Air II 366 bhp.

▲ For $3101, GTO hardtop buyers got 350 bhp, 15 more than in '67. A two-barrel, 265-bhp economy version cost no more. The H.O. 400 had 360 bhp, same as the Ram-Air 400, but the Ram Air had open hood scoops and higher rpm capability. A Hurst-shifted three-speed, a Muncie M21 close-ratio four-speed, or M40 Turbo Hydra-Matic were offered.

▲ Strong acceleration, good road manners and braking, fine instrumentation: "Our complaints are minor. Our praise is high," said *Motor Trend*. "Pontiac has improved on their GTO—which took some doing."

▲ Compared to the base 400, the H.O. (shown) got a different series four-barrel and, with manual transmission, a hotter cam. Ram Air cost $342 extra, came only with 4.33:1 gears, and not with air conditioning.

▲ The second-generation Goat's curvaceous styling was a triumph and its bucket-seat interior was a study in the art. Front disc brakes remained optional at $63. At midyear, Ram Air II replaced the initial Ram Air. It retained the 360-bhp rating, but gained new heads, forged pistons, and other hop-ups.

▲ The 2+2 survived in spirit in such cars as this Ventura, special-ordered with eight-lug wheels, four-speed, and 375-bhp, 428-cid V-8.

▲ Firebirds did their share of drag-strip duty, but weren't as successful as Camaro and Mustang. This "Tiger" is at the NHRA Nationals.

▼ Like its Camaro cousin, Firebird lost its vent windows for '68, but changed little otherwise. The 400 V-8 added five horses to both base and Ram Air versions (now 330 and 335 bhp).

▲ The optional hood-mounted tach looked neat, but was hard to read in rain or snow or when driving with the bright sun at your back.

▲ The 326 was bored to 350 cid as the new base Firebird V-8. It had 265 bhp, 320 with the $181 four-barrel. Rear suspension on the 400 models gained multi-leaf springs and staggered shocks to combat wheel hop. Ram Air versions kept their functional hood scoops and high-output cam. A four-speed Ram Air ragtop with 3.90:1 gears turned a 15.0 at 110 for *Sports Car Graphic*.

▲ Firebird fancied itself a grand touring machine, not merely a pony car, but it nonetheless shared its dash and interior appointments with Camaro.

1969

Muscle nears its peak, with special-edition supercars from all manufacturers • AMC and Hurst create SC/Rambler compact, capable of ETs near 14 seconds • Buick GS 400 bulks up with Stage 1 and 2 engine options • COPO (Central Office Production Order) Camaros and Chevelles unleashed with 427-cid V-8s • Impala SS 427 is last gasp for full-size Chevy muscle • Dodge issues wild street versions of the aero Charger 500 and winged Charger Daytona to qualify them for NASCAR • 440 Six Pack debuts in Dodge Super Bee and Plymouth Road Runner • 'Cuda option for Barracuda can get 383 and 440 V-8s • Ford issues 428 CJ Cobra Fairlanes, plus droop-nosed NASCAR Torino Talladega and Mercury Cyclone Spoiler • Mustangs add limited-edition Boss 302 and Boss 429 • Pontiac GTO "Judge" bows with Ram-Air V-8... Firebird Trans Am arrives at midyear • Quickest Super Stock time at World Finals is 10.23 by Ronnie Sox in '68 'Cuda • Mark Donohue's 170-mph Camaro Z-28 wins second Trans Am crown • Richard Petty moves to Ford, wins 10 NASCAR races

▲ This June 1968 archival shot suggests that American Motors considered producing a 1969 "Rebel Machine." It did introduce such a car, but as a 1970. The production car had stripes and a big hood scoop, not this Machine's menacing dark hues, flat hood, and fab "gear" fender logo. Some AMC aficionados say versions of a '69 Machine did in fact show up outside AMC.

▲ Rambler's compact sedan could get a 290 V-8 from the factory, but this '67 American, shown running at the '69 NHRA Winternationals, has been modified to hold AMC's 390. Tipping the scales at around 2600 pounds, the junior Rambler was a good starting point for modified production.

▲ This '69 Javelin, sponsored by a Southern California dealership, ran mid- to low-11s in Super Stock/Automatic. AMC never had a well-financed drag team and it supported independents in an effort to gain exposure its meager advertising budget couldn't.

1969 AMC HIGH-PERFORMANCE ENGINES

TYPE	CID	BORE × STROKE	BHP @ RPM	TORQUE @ RPM	FUEL SYSTEM	COMP. RATIO	AVAIL.
ohv V-8	343	4.08 × 3.28	235 @ 4400	345 @ 2600	1 × 2bbl.	9.0:1	Rebel, Ambassador
ohv V-8	343	4.08 × 3.28	280 @ 4800	365 @ 3000	1 × 4bbl.	10.2:1	1
ohv V-8	390	4.17 × 3.57	315 @ 4600	425 @ 3200	1 × 4bbl.	10.2:1	1

1. AMX, Javelin, Rebel, Ambassador.

▲ AMC consulted the muscle-car bible, put its biggest engine into a compact body, and got help from Hurst Performance Research to create the Rogue-based Hurst SC/Rambler. It bowed in mid-1969 and sold for that year only. About two-thirds of the 1512 built had this wild paint scheme.

► AMC promised that the 3160-pound SC/Rambler would turn 14 3-second ETs. Some road testers bested that by a tenth or two, and at 100 mph. A $61 AM radio was the sole option on the $2998 hardtop.

▲ Tongue-in-cheek graphics gave the low-down on the SC/Rambler's fiberglass ram-air hood scoop. *Car and Driver* likened the car to a "tri-colored nickelodeon." *Road Test* called it a "drag strip eliminator at a penny pinching price."

◄ SC/Rambler borrowed a 315-bhp 390 V-8 from the AMX and gave it ram-air induction. A Borg-Warner four-speed with T-handle Hurst shifter helped send the power to a Twin-Grip diff with 3.54:1 gears. E70 × 14 tires, front-disc brakes, and a Sun 8000-rpm tach were also standard.

▲ Good news for the '69 AMX was replacement of AMC's balky shift linkage with a Hurst setup. Also new: a 140-mph speedometer and optional leather upholstery. Production reached 8293 for the year.

▲ AMX's optional 390 (shown) didn't change. But AMC built 52 drag-intended Super Stock AMXs with twin Holley carbs, 12.3:1 heads, and more. AMC said 340 bhp; the NHRA said 420. Best ET: 10.73 at 128.

▲ Buick's GS 400 gained functional hood scoops for '69, but big news was the new Stage 1 and Stage 2 engine options. Both added to the standard 400-cid V-8 a high-lift cam, special Quadrajet carb, and larger exhausts. They earned a 3.64:1 axle with four-speed, 3.42:1 with automatic, both with limited-slip. This is a Stage 1 ragtop with tires from a later period.

▲The standard 400 four-barrel was rated at 340 bhp at 5000 rpm. Various sources list the Stage 1 version at 345 or 350 bhp at 5800 rpm. A Stage 2 camshaft was listed in Buick parts books, and some experts say that approximately 10-15 sets of Stage 2 heads were cast in 1969-70. But the special heads apparently went to insiders and racers, not the public.

1969 BUICK HIGH-PERFORMANCE ENGINES

TYPE	CID	BORE × STROKE	BHP @ RPM	TORQUE @ RPM	FUEL SYSTEM	COMP. RATIO	AVAIL.
ohv V-8	340	3.80 × 3.85	280 @ 4600	375 @ 3200	1 × 4bbl.	10.25:1	1
ohv V-8	400	4.04 × 3.90	340 @ 5000*	440 @ 3200	1 × 4bbl.	10.25:1	2
ohv V-8	430	4.19 × 3.90	360 @ 5000	475 @ 3200	1 × 4bbl.	10.25:1	3

* 350 bhp with Stage 1 pkg, 360 bhp with Stage 2.
1. GS 350, LeSabre, Special Deluxe, Skylark. 2. GS 400, Sportwagon, LeSabre. 3. Riviera, Electra, Wildcat.

▲ Front disc brakes and a heavy-duty Rallye suspension were GS options. Ordering buckets added a console for the Turbo Hydra-Matic shifter. Base price of the GS 400 ragtop was $3325.

▲ GS production rose by nearly 6000, to 2454 GS 400 convertibles, 10,743 GS 400 coupes, 8317 GS 350 coupes, and 4831 California GS coupes. The latter two used a 200-bhp four-barrel 350.

▲ New sheetmetal gave Camaro an angular look, but engine choices didn't change. SS offerings included the 375-bhp 396 at $316 and an aluminum-head 396 for $711. The optional Muncie M21 four-speed gained Hurst linkage, and with 3.73:1 gears, a 396 turned high-14s.

▲ Four-wheel discs were a new Z-28 option at $500, but most went into race models. Tires grew to E70×15s. The Z-28 package was offered only on coupes and tacked $458 onto the $2726 base. RS option added hidden headlamps. Low-15-second ETs were common.

▲ Z-28's solid-lifter 302 was again underrated at 290 bhp. It gained four-bolt main-bearing caps during the year, while a rear-facing scoop was newly available. Axles ranged from 3.07:1 to 4.10:1.

▲ A '69 Camaro paced the Indy 500, but unlike in '67, Chevy issued a Pace Car Replica. Most of the 3675 built had a 300-bhp 350 V-8; about 100 had the 396. All were white with "hugger" orange stripes. The SS package included F70×14 tires, Rally wheels, and power front discs.

▲ Convertibles also got Pace Car trim. A rear lip spoiler was now an SS option. So was the "Super Scoop" force-air induction hood that drew on the high-pressure area at the windshield base. A union strike lengthened the '69 model year, helping boost Camaro output to 243,085.

▲Chevy built 69 drag-ready ZL-1 Camaros with aluminum-block 430-bhp 427s and sold them though selected dealers for $7300. Another variety of COPO (Central Office Production Order) Camaro was the Yenko/SC (shown). Don Yenko, a performance-oriented Pennsylvania dealer, added unique graphics to his 427 Camaros. This LeMans Blue coupe is one of 201 he built. The 427 Camaros turned high-12s/low-13s at over 110 mph.

▲Yenko got Chevy to factory equip Camaros with the L72 iron-block 427; Chevy rated them at 425 bhp, Yenko said 450. Also included on the SC was a close-ratio four-speed and a 140-mph speedometer.

▲The Chevelle SS 396 became a $348 Malibu option for '69, but that didn't dim sales, which hit a record 86,307. *Car and Driver*'s 325-bhp coupe with the $222 auto trans and $42 optional 3.55:1 limited-slip did 0-60 mph in 5.8 seconds and ran the quarter in 14.4 at 97.35 mph.

▲SS 396 Chevelles again had 396-cid V-8s in three different horsepower ratings: 325 (shown), 350, or 375 bhp. About 500 cars with the 425-bhp L-72 427 went to buyers with connections via the COPO ordering process.

▲The SS 396 option was offered on the Sport Coupe, convertible, and the Chevelle 300 pillared coupe. It included the 396 engine, power front discs, and seven-inch sport wheels. *Car and Driver* said its SS 396 coupe was remarkably refined. It praised the heavy-duty suspension, but deemed the brakes "barely acceptable." The editors recommended spending $253 for the 375-bhp engine.

▲▼ This SS 396 four-speed ragtop has the optional $175 buckets and center console. Head restraints cost $17, and a tach and extra gauges added $95. Note the sport steering wheel and eight-track tape player.

▶ The Impala SS was in its final year and went out in style with the 427-cid V-8 as standard (above right). Horsepower was up by five, to 390. The $422 SS package for coupes and convertibles included G70 tires on 15-inch wheels, black-accented grille, and SS badges. Three- and four-speed manuals and the Turbo Hydra-Matic were available. About 10 percent of the 2455 SS Impalas built for '69 were ragtops. Exhaust headers on this one are non-stock.

▲ Once again, Don Yenko had his own idea of power for the Chevy Nova. He built approximately 37 427 Novas, featuring the same 425-bhp L72 big block used in 1967-69 Yenko Camaros. Also included were stripes and Yenko logos on the headrests.

▲ Those who couldn't find $5000-plus for a Yenko 427 Nova could turn to a fine selection of showroom SS Novas. Chevy built 17,654 of them, most with the base 300-bhp 350. Chevy also offered SS 396 Novas and built 1947 in 350-bhp tune and 5262 in 375-bhp form. *Hot Rod*'s 375-bhp 396 four-speed with 3.55:1 gears turned a 13.87 at 105.14 mph.

▲ To build his 427 Novas, Yenko first ordered cars with the 396-cid/375-bhp big block. Then his shop swapped that engine for the L72 427. "The car was a beast, almost lethal," writer Jerry Heasley quoted Don Yenko as saying.

1969 CHEVROLET HIGH-PERFORMANCE ENGINES

TYPE	CID	BORE × STROKE	BHP @ RPM	TORQUE @ RPM	FUEL SYSTEM	COMP. RATIO	AVAIL.
ohv V-8	302	4.00×3.00	290 @ 5800	290 @ 4800	1×4bbl.	11.0:1	Camaro Z-28
ohv V-8	350	4.00×3.48	300 @ 4800	380 @ 3200	1×4bbl.	10.25:1	1
ohv V-8	396	4.09×3.76	325 @ 4800	410 @ 3200	1×4bbl.	10.25:1	2
ohv V-8	396	4.09×3.76	350 @ 5200	415 @ 3400	1×4bbl.	10.25:1	2
ohv V-8	396	4.09×3.76	375 @ 5600	420 @ 3600	1×4bbl.	11.0:1	2
ohv V-8	**396***	**4.09×3.76**	**375 @ 5600**	**420 @ 3600**	**1×4bbl.**	**11.0:1**	**Camaro, Chevelle**
ohv V-8	427	4.25×3.76	335 @ 4800	460 @ 3200	1×4bbl.	10.25:1	full size
ohv V-8	427	4.25×3.76	390 @ 5400	460 @ 3600	1×4bbl.	10.25:1	full size
ohv V-8	427	4.25×3.76	425 @ 5600	460 @ 4000	1×4bbl.	11.0:1	Camaro, full size
ohv V-8	**427****	**4.25×3.76**	**430 @ 5600**	**460 @ 4000**	**1×4bbl.**	**12.5:1**	**Camaro**

***L-89 engine, aluminum heads. **ZL-1 engine, aluminum block and heads.**
1. Chevelle, Nova, Camaro, full size. 2. Camaro, Chevelle, Nova.

▲ The Hemi Dodge Darts built in '68 were still dominant race cars in '69. Actual fabrication was done by Hurst.

▲ Hemi Darts came with lightweight fiberglass body parts, stripped-down interiors, 4.88 rear gear, and a cross-ram equipped high-compression engine. They were for strip use only and had no warranty.

▲ Dodge made 600 440 Darts in '69. By that time, some '68 Hemi Darts, such as this one, had been modified enough to compete in NHRA's A/MP (Modified Production) class.

▼ This Dart GTS has the optional 335-bhp 383 Magnum in place of the standard 340 four-barrel. A four-speed and 3.91:1 Sure-Grip top it off.

▲ The hardtop GTS started at $3226, the ragtop at $3419. But the "Bumblebee" stripe could also adorn the new Dart Swinger 340 hardtop, which had GTS performance but cost $390 less.

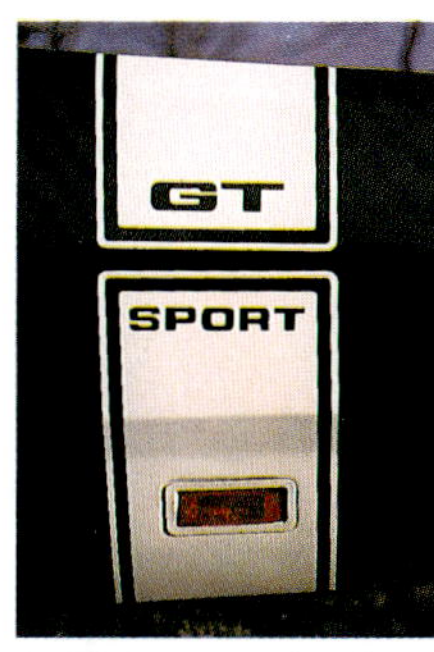

▲ This was the last year for the GTS, but the Swinger 340 continued.

▲ A 383 like this in a Dart seemed like a good idea, but too much weight and resulting tire spin meant that without suspension modification, it was unlikely to beat the mid-14 ETs of a good 340.

▲ Dodge built 6700 GTS Darts and an unspecified number of Swinger 340s for '69. All got heavy-duty suspension.

▲ Rated at 275 bhp, Mopar's 340 may have had 325 or more. To *Car Life*, it was "as cleverly engineered as the 426 Hemi, just not so fussy." *Car and Driver* called its 340 Dart GTS (four-speed, 3.91:1 gears, 14.4 ET at 99 mph) "a giant killer."

▲ What might a Charger R/T roadster be like? Dodge answered with this exercise for the '69 auto-show circuit. The two-seater had a cut-down windshield, special rear-deck cowls, body-colored bumpers, and non-glare hood panels. Finally, trunk and door handles were deleted.

▲ Experimentation went on outside Dodge, as well. Western Liquid Gas Association and Impco Carburetion sponsored this Hemi Charger 500 modified to run on propane. It turned 11-second ETs at 121 mph.

▲ "You in a heepa trouble, boy," Sheriff Joe Higgins advises Buddy Baker. Higgins was a fictional Dodge pitchman; Baker was a genuine NASCAR star.

▲ Keith Black, renowned builder of Mopar performance engines, put his talent into this promotional Charger Daytona.

▲ Precursor to the winged Daytona was the Charger 500. Dodge built street versions (52 with a Hemi, 340 with the 440) to qualify it for NASCAR. *Car Life*'s Hemi turned a 13.68 at 104.8 mph. This 440 is one of 106 with a four-speed. The 500 wasn't as fast as the new aero Fords and Mercurys on superspeedways.

▲ Charger 500 used a flush-fitted Coronet grille with exposed headlamps and a flush-mounted back window to cut turbulence on the superspeedways.

▲ King Kong returned unchanged and underrated at 425 bhp. Dodge built 20,057 Charger R/Ts for 1969. The majority had the fine 375-bhp four-barrel 440 Magnum. Just 232 were ordered with the 426 Hemi, which was again the only R/T engine option.

▲ Daytonas and Charger 500s got the raves, but most customers were happy with the mainstream models—albeit Hemis like this one were rare. Changes for '69 were few: The grille got a louvered divider; elongated taillamps replaced four round ones; and the bucket seats were revised.

▼ When the Charger 500 fell short of expectations, Dodge went all out with the 1969½ Charger Daytona. It was built for NASCAR superspeedways, but street versions looked just as wild. Standard was the 375-bhp 440 Magnum; 70 of the 503 built held a Hemi at $648 above the $3993 base. "You may not like it, but you'll never forget it," said *Road Test*.

▲The Super Bee coupe was joined by a hardtop for '69, and at midyear, the 440 "Six Pack" joined the standard 383 and optional Hemi.

▲Of 27,800 Super Bees built for '69, 1907 had the $463 triple-deuce option and 259 got the Hemi. The coupe started at $3076, the hardtop at $3138.

▲The Six Pack's 1375cfm of triple Holley carburetion was fed by a huge scoop on the pinned-down fiberglass hood. Output was 390 bhp. To the 440 four-barrel, the Six Pack mill added Hemi valve springs, a revised camshaft, magnafluxed rods, and dual-point distributor. Standard was a four-speed and Dana 9¾-inch Sure-Grip axle with 4.10:1 gears. Sinister black-painted wheels with chrome lugs also were standard. *Car Life*'s four-speed turned a 13.8 at 104 mph.

1969 DODGE HIGH-PERFORMANCE ENGINES

TYPE	CID	BORE × STROKE	BHP @ RPM	TORQUE @ RPM	FUEL SYSTEM	COMP. RATIO	AVAIL.
ohv V-8	340	4.04×3.31	275 @ 5000	340 @ 3200	1×4bbl.	10.5:1	1
ohv V-8	383	4.25×3.75	290 @ 4400	390 @ 2800	1×2bbl.	9.2:1	Coronet, full size
ohv V-8	383	4.25×3.75	330 @ 5200	410 @ 3600	1×4bbl.	10.0:1	Dart GTS
ohv V-8	383	4.25×3.75	330 @ 5000	425 @ 3200	1×4bbl.	10.0:1	Charger, full size
ohv V-8	383	4.25×3.75	335 @ 5000	425 @ 3200	1×4bbl.	10.0:1	Coronet Super Bee
ohv V-8	426*	4.25×3.75	425 @ 5000	490 @ 4000	2×4bbl.	10.25:1	2
ohv V-8	440	4.32×3.75	350 @ 4400	480 @ 2800	1×4bbl.	10.1:1	full size
ohv V-8	440	4.32×3.75	375 @ 4600	480 @ 3200	1×4bbl.	10.1:1	Charger, full size
ohv V-8	440	4.32×3.75	390 @ 4700	490 @ 3200	3×2bbl.	10.5:1	Super Bee

*Hemi.
1. Dart Swinger 340, Dart GTS. 2. Coronet, Charger, Super Bee.

▲Coronet R/T returned for '69 with a revised grille and taillamps, but few other alterations. The 375-bhp 440 Magnum continued as standard; the 425-bhp 426 Hemi was again optional.

▲A Performance Axle Package for the Coronet R/T put 3.55:1 gearing into a Sure-Grip diff and was augmented by Hemi handling components. The Track-Pak option offered a 3.54:1 Dana and four-speed.

▲*Car and Driver* was delighted when its 383 Super Bee automatic with the $102 3.55:1 limited-slip option turned an ET of 14.04 at 99.55 mph. Then it discovered that the distributor and large-diameter exhaust were non-stock. It estimated a true production example would run a still-laudable 14.2-second quarter-mile at 98.4 mph.

▲Newly optional for 383 Super Bees and 440 Coronet R/Ts and standard on Hemi R/Ts was a Ramcharger fresh-air induction package with a two-scoop hood. Available axle ratios were as long as 4.10:1.

▲At $88.55 extra, styled wheels dressed up the Super Bee. Power front discs added $93. *Car and Driver* praised the Super Bee's "exceptionally well-coordinated feel" and the completeness of its instrument panel, which was borrowed from the Charger.

▲ Ford jumped on the budget-muscle bandwagon with the '69 Fairlane Cobra. It was a dressed-down Torino with plain bench seats, fleet-grade hubcaps, and the 428 Cobra Jet engine. This notchback has optional wheels. The SportsRoof fastback was the other Cobra body style.

▲ At under $3200 with standard four-speed, ads touted the Fairlane Cobra as "Bargain day at the muscle works." Early models carried a multi-colored decal of a stylized snake, fangs bared and tires trailing flames. This metal Cobra emblem replaced it on cars made later in the model year.

▲ Cobra's standard 428 CJ breathed through a 735cfm Holley four-barrel and exhaled via new cast-iron headers. Intake and exhaust ports were bigger than in '68, and peak horsepower arrived at 5200 rpm instead of 5400. Ram Air (shown) was a $133 option, but didn't change the 335-bhp rating. C-6 SelectShift Cruise-O-Matic was optional. Axles ranged from 3.25:1 to 4.30:1.

▲ Ram-Air Cobras with automatic and 3.50:1 limited-slip turned a 14.04 at 100.61 mph for *Car and Driver*, and a 14.5 at 100 for *Motor Trend*. A four-speed/3.50:1 ran a 14.9 at 95.2 for *Car Life*. *Car and Driver* said Ram Air cut the ET by .2 seconds and added 1.4 mph.

▲ Ram Air was dubbed CJ-R and brought a hood scoop with a vacuum flap that opened at full throttle. It required purchase of a tach, buckets, and wide-ovals. A competition suspension with staggered rear shocks, F70 × 14s on six-inch rims, and hood pins were Cobra standards.

▲ Ford countered the Charger 500 with a droop-snoot Torino and had to offer street versions to qualify the design for NASCAR racing. The modified SportsRoof was named for the Talladega speedway.

▲ NASCAR required that 500 Torino Talladegas be built; Ford made 754, including prototypes. Each had the 335-bhp 428 CJ, C-6 Cruise-O-Matic, 3.25:1 Traction-Lok, and Competition Handling Suspension.

▼ Torino GT returned in SportsRoof, hardtop, and convertible. A hood scoop was new, but functioned only with the 428 CJ-R option.

▲ Standard in Torino GT was a 302-cid V-8, but most buyers went with a 351 or optional 390 four-barrel, and a few for the 428 CJ (shown). Ford ads warned that a 428 CJ-R was "not for the timid soul."

▲ Snake decal identifies this promotional shot as one of an early Cobra. The 428s in both SportsRoofs and Talladegas were successful in stock-car racing, winning the Daytona 500 and the NASCAR crown.

1969 FORD HIGH-PERFORMANCE ENGINES

TYPE	CID	BORE × STROKE	BHP @ RPM	TORQUE @ RPM	FUEL SYSTEM	COMP. RATIO	AVAIL.
ohv V-8*	302	4.00 × 3.00	290 @ 5800	290 @ 4300	1 × 4bbl.	10.5:1	Mustang
ohv V-8	351	4.00 × 3.50	290 @ 4800	380 @ 3400	1 × 4bbl.	11.0:1	1
ohv V-8	390	4.05 × 3.78	320 @ 4600	427 @ 3200	1 × 4bbl.	10.5:1	1
ohv V-8**	428	4.13 × 3.98	335 @ 5200	440 @ 3400	1 × 4bbl.	10.6:1	1
ohv V-8	429	4.36 × 3.59	360 @ 4600	480 @ 2800	1 × 4bbl.	10.5:1	full size
ohv V-8*	429	4.36 × 3.59	375 @ 5200	450 @ 3400	1 × 4bbl.	10.5:1	Mustang

* BOSS ** Cobra Jet.

1. Fairlane, Torino, Mustang, Shelby.

▲ Ford's Camaro Z-28 fighter was the Boss 302. It had a handling suspension, F60×15 tires, quicker steering, and a modified 302-cid four-barrel rated at 290 bhp. With 3.91:1 gears, it turned ETs of 14.8 at 96 mph. It cost $3588, and 1934 were built for '69.

▲ In the late '60s, Ford's racing support ranged from Le Mans sports-racers, to Indy open-wheel cars, to Daytona stockers, to the nation's dragstrips. Here's Hubert Platt's factory-supported 11-second Super Stock Mustang at the NHRA Winternationals.

▲ Mach 1 debuted for '69 as the mainstream high-performance Mustang. Two- and four-barrel 351s were offered, plus the four-barrel 390. Top options were the 428 CJ, or CJ-R with "shaker" hood. Either way, a 428 Mach 1 was the finest Mustang street racer ever. Typical ETs were around 14 seconds at 100 mph.

▲ The "Shelby" link was all but gone, and Ford now built the GT 500 and GT 350 alongside regular Mustangs. The GT 350 gained the new 351-cid Windsor, but sales shrunk. The end neared.

▲ To NASCAR-certify its new 429, Ford put the semi-hemi V-8 into 858 Mustangs. With stock ETs in the low 14s, these 375-bhp Boss 429s never fulfilled their street potential. This is a custom drag car.

▲ The Torino SportsRoof was not a popular shell for a Funny Car, and dapper Phil Bonner's 7.8-second/180-190-mph ride was never a champion.

▲ Cyclone CJ came with the 428 CJ, with the CJ-R optional. Torquey and foolproof with automatic transmission, these were Mercury's finest street racers, with consistent ETs in the high 13s at 100 mph.

▲ A competition handling package was part of the Cyclone CJ's $3224 base price. A Drag Pak option replaced standard 3.50:1 gears with 3.91:1 or 4.30:1, LeMans connecting rods, and an engine oil cooler.

▲ Mercury honored two of its NASCAR drivers with namesake Cyclone Spoilers. The red-on-white "Cale Yarborough Special" (above) was sold by western dealers, while the blue-on-white "Dan Gurney Special" (above right) was sold in the east. Some were built with the aero Torino Talladega nose, and all had a decklid air foil that wasn't used on the race car. Standard was the 290-bhp 351 Windsor V-8 with Cruise-O-Matic and 3.25:1 Traction-Lok.

▲ Adding Ram-Air Induction with hood scoop to a Cyclone CJ cost $138.60. Mercury promised "maximum street get-up-and-go for a modest price."

▼ To qualify for NASCAR, 500 street-going Cyclone Spoilers had to be built and two variations were produced, both for '69 only. As many as 519 were built as the Spoiler fastback (below left) with the conventional Cyclone nose. About 300 were produced as the Spoiler II, with the elongated NASCAR front and a blacked-out grille (below). Both of those pictured are dressed in "Dan Gurney Special" trim.

▲ Mercury answered the Mach 1 Mustang with the Cougar Eliminator. Top engine was the 335-bhp 428 Super Cobra Jet, but choices began with a 290-bhp 351. The facelift retained hidden headlamps.

▲ Eliminator seemed overwhelmed by the 428 CJ. Some got the solid-lifter Boss 302 and were more balanced. They turned 14.8s at 96 mph, but at 3600 pounds, Cougar was more tourer than dragger.

► Eliminator's $3499 base price included a 351 four-barrel. The 290-bhp Boss 302 mill cost $335.50 extra; the 428 Cobra Jet added $283.60; and a 320-bhp 390 also was available. The hood scoop was functional only with the CJ-R. At right is a sample of the over-the-counter hop-ups available through Mercury dealers. They included headers and free-flow exhausts, deep-sump oil pan, special intake manifolds, dual-quads, low-restriction air cleaners, and even a multi-carb Weber setup. Those were the days.

▼ Because the Eliminator was not an XR-7 model, it received the base Cougar's standard vinyl interior, though its instrumentation did include a tachometer. Hurst T-handle lever provided a better grip during power shifts.

1969 MERCURY HIGH-PERFORMANCE ENGINES

TYPE	CID	BORE × STROKE	BHP @ RPM	TORQUE @ RPM	FUEL SYSTEM	COMP. RATIO	AVAIL.
ohv V-8	302	4.00×3.00	290 @ 5800	290 @ 4300	1×4bbl.	10.5:1	Cougar
ohv V-8	351	4.00×3.50	290 @ 4800	380 @ 3400	1×4bbl.	11.0:1	1
ohv V-8	390	4.05×3.78	320 @ 4600	427 @ 3200	1×4bbl.	10.5:1	1
ohv V-8*	428	4.13×3.98	335 @ 5200	440 @ 3400	1×4bbl.	10.6:1	1
ohv V-8	429	4.36×3.59	360 @ 4600	480 @ 2800	1×4bbl.	10.5:1	full size

*Cobra Jet.
1. Cougar, Comet, Cyclone, full size.

▲ Olds authorized the Hurst car as a showroom traffic-builder, but it was no slouch. Again wielding a wicked 455-cid V-8, detuned slightly to 380 bhp, the W-46 Hurst/Olds put down 500 lbs/ft of torque. Zero-60 took 5.9 seconds, the quarter-mile just 13.98 at 101.3 mph.

▲ Hurst and Olds were back with another special 4-4-2, and it was bolder than ever with "Firefrost Gold" striping and a dual-scoop hood. The rear spoiler gave a claimed 15 pounds of downward force at 60 mph. Goodyear Polyglas F60×15 tires rode seven-inch Super Stock II rims. This hardtop has a Rocket rally pack and performance 3.91:1 axle ratio.

▲ About 906 Hurst/Olds were built, but only two were convertibles. The W-46 mill wore W-30 heads and a unique intake manifold. Its scoops worked better than under-bumper units on other hot Oldsmobiles.

▲ The 360-bhp Force-Air version of the standard 400-cid V-8 was again Olds 4-4-2's top gun. Production slipped to 26,357, including 4295 convertibles, despite a new ad campaign headed by "Dr. Oldsmobile."

▲ With three- or four-speed stick, the base 4-4-2 400 had 350 bhp. Turbo Hydra-Matic cut it to 325, but a new W-32 package blended the stronger 350-bhp V-8 and Force-Air with the M40 automatic.

▲ A Hurst/Olds at the '69 Nationals carried Linda Vaughn, Hurst's most famous Miss Golden Shifter.

1969 OLDSMOBILE HIGH-PERFORMANCE ENGINES							
TYPE	CID	BORE × STROKE	BHP @ RPM	TORQUE @ RPM	FUEL SYSTEM	COMP. RATIO	AVAIL.
ohv V-8	400	3.87 × 4.25	325 @ 4600	440 @ 3000	1 × 4bbl.	10.5:1	4-4-2
ohv V-8	400	3.87 × 4.25	350 @ 4600	440 @ 200	1 × 4bbl.	10.5:1	4-4-2
ohv V-8	400	3.87 × 4.25	360 @ 5400	440 @ 3600	1 × 4bbl.	10.5:1	4-4-2
ohv V-8	455	4.13 × 3.25	380 @ 5000	500 @ 3200	1 × 4bbl.	10.25:1	Hurst/Olds

▲ Comedian Dick Smothers piloted this Hurst/Olds in SS/F action at the '70 NHRA U.S. Nationals.

▲ Dickie's Hurst/Olds' ran in the 12s at 110 mph. The Smothers Brothers also sponsored a Top Fuel car.

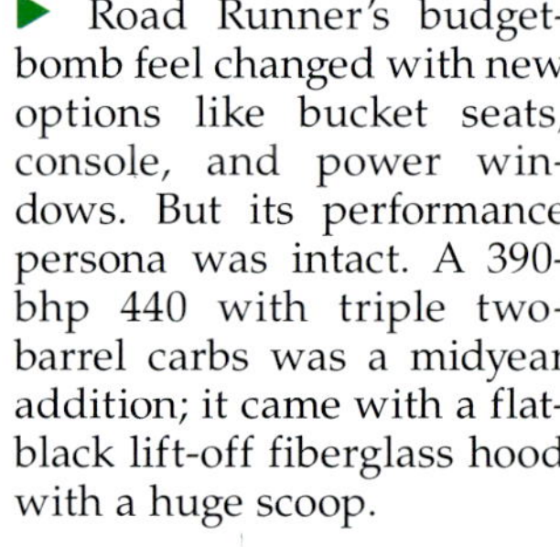

▶ Road Runner's budget-bomb feel changed with new options like bucket seats, console, and power windows. But its performance persona was intact. A 390-bhp 440 with triple two-barrel carbs was a midyear addition; it came with a flat-black lift-off fiberglass hood with a huge scoop.

▲ A 335-bhp 383 was again standard, and the Hemi the top option. Painted steel wheels with taxi-cab hubcaps were standard.

▲ Road Runners remained plenty quick even with the base 383. Five new extra-cost axle packages allowed ratios up to 4.10:1.

▼ Road Runner production peaked at 84,420, nearly doubling the '68 figure. Only 2128 were the new-for-'69 $3313 convertible.

▲ The standard 383 (shown) again delivered 15-second ETs. The 440+6 cost $463 more and included a 4.10:1 Sure-Grip and Hurst shifter. It was nearly as quick as the $813 Hemi, which could turn mid-13s at 105 mph. Hemis went into 788 Road Runners, including 10 ragtops.

▲ Plymouth had the muscle era's most evocative artwork. This one promotes '69's new cool-air induction system option for 383s, 440s, and Hemis.

▲ Plymouth's new "Coyote Duster" cool-air induction system was standard with the Hemi and optional with the 383 and 440+6. The driver could open vents in the standard hood slots to direct air through underhood cowling.

▲ *Motor Trend* ran three '69 Road Runners. Its 383 automatic with 3.23:1 gears turned an ET of 14.7 at 94.6. Its 383 four-speed/4.10:1 turned a 14.3 at 101.5. Its Hemi automatic/4.10:1 cooked a 13.5 at 105.3.

▲ "The Hemi Road Runner has more pure mechanical presence than any other American automobile," said *Car and Driver*. It liked the Hemi's taut suspension, but bemoaned the unavailability of an oil-pressure gauge.

▼ GTX got Plymouth's cartoon treatment, too. Axle-ratio choices expanded to 3.54:1 and 4.10:1 for '69, and the new "Air Grabber" hood was available for the standard Super Commando 440 four-barrel and was included with the $701 Hemi. (The new 440+6 was not a GTX offering.) The GTX hardtop started at $3416 and weighed 3465 pounds, the ragtop based at $3635 and weighed 3590.

▲ GTX four-speeds now had a standard Hurst linkage. TorqueFlite was a no-cost item. GTX ads recommended the Hemi only "if you're serious about sanctioned racing...otherwise the Super Commando delivers more than enough stuff for the average commuter."

▲ Road Runner was *Motor Trend*'s 1969 "Car of the Year," and Glenn White (left), Chrysler-Plymouth general manager, accepted the caliper trophy from *MT* publisher Ray Brock. Brock said it was an exciting, influential car that "everybody here liked to drive."

▲ The 'Cuda name marked a new Barracuda enthusiast package and included the 340 or 383 V-8 and dummy hood scoops. Pressure from rival big-block pony cars prompted midyear availability of the 375-bhp 440 Magnum.

▲ 'Cuda was happiest with the 275-bhp 340. Formula S handling was sharp, but most testers reported high-14s. *Hot Rod* got its 340 four-speed with 3.91:1 gears to turn high-13s.

▲ A 'Cuda with the 440 could run the quarter in 14.01 at 103.81 mph. But some testers still called it an underachiever. Its mandatory TorqueFlite didn't shift crisply, and traction off the line was poor.

▲ A 335-bhp 383 'Cuda was more balanced than a 440. It also was cheaper to insure, and still turned ETs in the low 15s at 92 mph

▲ Stuffing the 440 into the Barracuda gave Plymouth the largest-displacement pony car of the day. But it left no room in the engine bay for power-assisted steering or the booster needed to operate power front disc brakes. Thus, a 'Cuda with the heavy big-block 440 was a bear to park and required lengthy stopping distances. *Car Life* said a 440 'Cuda was at its best on the highway, where abundant power reserves affording effortless passing, and steering and braking shortcomings were minimized.

1969 PLYMOUTH HIGH-PERFORMANCE ENGINES

TYPE	CID	BORE × STROKE	BHP @ RPM	TORQUE @ RPM	FUEL SYSTEM	COMP. RATIO	AVAIL.
ohv V-8	340	4.04×3.31	275 @ 5000	340 @ 3200	1×4bbl.	10.5:1	Barracuda
ohv V-8	383	4.25×3.75	330 @ 5200	410 @ 3600	1×4bbl.	10.0:1	Barracuda
ohv V-8	383	4.25×3.75	330 @ 5000	425 @ 3200	1×4bbl.	10.0:1	1
ohv V-8	383	4.25×3.75	335 @ 5200	425 @ 3400	1×4bbl.	10.0:1	Road Runner
ohv V-8	426*	4.25×3.75	425 @ 5000	490 @ 4000	2×4bbl.	10.25:1	Road Runner
ohv V-8	440	4.32×3.75	350 @ 4400	480 @ 2800	1×4bbl.	10.1:1	full size
ohv V-8	440	4.32×3.75	375 @ 4600	480 @ 3200	1×4bbl.	10.1:1	GTX, Barracuda
ohv V-8	440	4.32×3.75	390 @ 4700	490 @ 3200	3×2bbl.	10.5:1	Road Runner

* Hemi.
1. Belvedere, Satellite.

▲ Pontiac created The Judge for '69 by stirring GTO's hottest performance extras into a single $332 package, slapping on the decals, and giving it the 366-bhp, 400-cid Ram Air III with open hood scoops.

▶ The new 370-bhp Ram Air IV was a $390 Judge option. A four-speed added $195, hood tach, $63. Rear spoiler, beefed suspension, and Rally II wheels were standard on the $3161 hardtop and $3700 convertible. For '69, 6833 Judges were built.

▲ Except for badges, Judge's interior was regular-GTO. "Air" knob to left of the steering wheel opened and closed the Ram Air hood vents.

▲ Judges were no quicker than similarly equipped GTOs. A Ram Air IV four-speed with 3.55:1 gears turned a 14.4 at 97.8 for *Car Life*.

▲ Trans Am, one of Pontiac's most significant performance cars, bowed in midyear as a $725 option group for the Firebird 400. Just 691 T/A hardtops and eight convertibles were built. All were Polar White with blue stripes. Scoops on hood and vents in front fenders were functional.

▲ A 60-inch spoiler was a T/A trademark. High-effort steering, power front discs, and a beefed up suspension were part of the package.

▲ T/As came with a 335-bhp, 400-cid Ram Air III; optional was a 345-bhp Ram Air IV. A Ram Air IV Trans Am with four-speed and 3.90:1 gears turned a 14.1 at 100.7 mph for *Hot Rod*.

1969 PONTIAC HIGH-PERFORMANCE ENGINES

TYPE	CID	BORE × STROKE	BHP @ RPM	TORQUE @ RPM	FUEL SYSTEM	COMP. RATIO	AVAIL.
ohv V-8	350	3.88×3.75	325 @ 5100	380 @ 3200	1×4bbl.	10.5:1	1
ohv V-8	350	3.88×3.75	330 @ 5100	380 @ 3200	1×4bbl.	10.5:1	2
ohv V-8	400	4.12×3.75	330 @ 4800	430 @ 3300	1×4bbl.	10.75:1	Firebird
ohv V-8	400	4.12×3.75	335 @ 5000	430 @ 3400	1×4bbl.	10.75:1	3
ohv V-8	400	4.12×3.75	345 @ 5400	440 @ 3700	1×4bbl.	10.5:1	3
ohv V-8	400	4.12×3.75	350 @ 5000	445 @ 3000	1×4bbl.	10.5:1	4
ohv V-8	400*	4.12×3.75	366 @ 5100	445 @ 3600	1×4bbl.	10.75:1	GTO
ohv V-8	400*	4.12×3.75	370 @ 5500	445 @ 3900	1×4bbl.	10.75:1	GTO

* Ram Air

1. Tempest, LeMans, Firebird. 2. Tempest, LeMans. 3. Firebird, Trans Am. 4.GTO, Gran Prix

▲ Facelifted Firebird returned with 350- and 400-cid V-8s as popular performance engines. Sales slumped to 75,362 coupes, 11,649 ragtops.

1970

Muscle's pinnacle year, with unmatched power and style • AMC issues its strongest engine ever, a 340-bhp 390 for new Rebel Machine • Mopar's first pony cars—Dodge Challenger and Plymouth Barracuda—storm out of the chute • Winged Road Runner Superbird follows shelved Charger Daytona... draws Richard Petty away from Ford and wins the NASCAR crown for Plymouth • FoMoCo unleashes 429-cid Cobra Jet Torinos and Cyclones • Mustang Boss 302 wins Trans Am title • Shelby Mustangs die with little fanfare • GM allows 400-cid-plus engines in intermediates • Buick responds with its quickest-ever car, the GS 455 Stage 1 • Chevelle answers with a 454...LS-6 version threatens all comers • Second-generation Camaro bows with classic Euro styling...Z-28 gets 360-bhp 350 • 455-cid W-30 is baddest Olds 4-4-2 • GTO has effortless 455-cid or raucous 400 Ram Air • Redesigned Trans Am boasts world-class road manners • NHRA creates Pro Stock class...big names flock • Top Fuelers run 6.4s...Funny Cars turn 6.8-7.0s

▲ American Motors made good on its "Machine" prototype (page 200) with this production version based on the fastback Rebel SST intermediate. It had a variation of the paint scheme seen on the now-discontinued '69 SC/Rambler compact, but after the first 1000 or so, any colors were available. List price was a reasonable $3475. Only 2326 were built.

▲ AMC used some late-'60s cliché images to promote its Machine. The car came with a 390-cid V-8, hood scoop with vacuum-activated ducts, front discs, E60×15 tires on seven-inch wheels, and a close-ratio Hurst-shifted four-speed; a three-speed automatic was optional. *Road Test*'s 3.91:1-geared Machine turned a 14.57 at 92.77 mph, but wheel hop from the standard raked suspension hampered traction off the line.

▲ The Machine's four-barrel 340-bhp 390 was AMC's most powerful engine ever. It was delivered with a standard Twin Grip axle and 3.54:1 gears, but ratios up to 5.00:1 were available through the dealer.

▲ Machine instrumentation was scanty, though an 8000-rpm tach was built into the rear of the hood scoop. Optional power steering was overassisted, but *Road Test* said the 3800-pound car handled well.

▲ AMX's forte was high-speed road work, but "Ramblin Man" is typical of one set up for the drags. George Warren's '70 390 AMX won the SS/D class at the NHRA Springnationals with an 11.70-second pass at 118.42 mph.

▲ This Machine 390 has custom headers and valve covers, but retains the stock heavy-duty cooling with flexible fan. AMC ads confided that the Machine was slower than a Hemi, but faster than "your old man's Cadillac."

▲ AMX entered its last season as a two-seater with a larger standard V-8 and a front suspension updated to upper/lower ball joints. New hood scoop could host an optional vacuum-activated Ram Air setup.

▲ This 290-bhp, 360-cid V-8 replaced the 225-bhp 290 as AMX's standard engine. A 390-cid V-8 was still optional, and it now had 325 bhp, up by 10. The new Ram Air setup helped the 390 turn out 340 bhp.

▼ A mild facelift included front-bumper holes that AMC claimed help cool the brakes. Optional "Go" package for the 390 V-8 added power front discs, E70×14 tires, handling components, stainless steel front spoiler, and a Twin-Grip diff. The standard bucket seats were now high-backs with integral head rests. This AMX is finished in Big Bad Green.

▲ Full-width taillamps marked the last of the two-seat AMXs. AMC would make the car a version of the four-place Javelin after this year.

▲ With a Ram Air 390 like this, an AMX could turn mid-to-low 14-second ETs. *Motor Trend* ran its 325-bhp 390 with 3.54:1 gears to a 14.68 at 92 mph. While it combined good scoot with fine handling, AMX never attracted a wide audience. Production sank to 4116 for 1970.

1970 AMC HIGH-PERFORMANCE ENGINES

TYPE	CID	BORE × STROKE	BHP @ RPM	TORQUE @ RPM	FUEL SYSTEM	COMP. RATIO	AVAIL.
ohv V-8	360	4.08×3.44	245 @ 4400	365 @ 2400	1×2bbl.	9.0:1	1
ohv V-8	360	4.08×3.44	290 @ 4800	395 @ 3200	1×4bbl.	10.0:1	2
ohv V-8	390	4.17×3.57	325 @ 5000	420 @ 3200	1×4bbl.	10.0:1	2
ohv V-8	390	4.17×3.57	340 @ 5100	430 @ 3600	1×4bbl.	10.0:1	2

1. Rebel, Javelin, Ambassador. 2. AMX, Javelin, Rebel, Ambassador.

▲ The 1970 GSX with optional 455-cid Stage 1 mill was the ultimate expression of Buick's ultimate supercar. Matching its muscle was extroverted style via Apollo White or Saturn Yellow paint, topped with stripes, spoilers, and scoops.

▲ The $1195 GSX package bowed at midyear and included aero cosmetic pieces, a hood tach, stiffer shocks and suspension pieces, and G60×15 tires on mag-style steel wheels. Only 678 were built for 1970; Buick produced 9948 base GS models, 8732 GS 455 hardtops, and 1416 GS 455 convertibles.

▲ Buick's restyled Skylark again hosted the GS models, which started with a 325-bhp, 350-cid V-8. Replacing the 400-cid V-8 was a big-valve, hot-cam 455. Output was 350 bhp. New top dog was the $199 Stage 1 performance package for the 455. It added a higher-lift cam, even larger valves, and tighter compression for 360 bhp with the same earth-moving 510 lbs/ft of torque as the regular 455. A 3.64:1 Posi-Traction axle was included with either the four-speed or automatic. This is the setup that put the GS 455 on the muscle dream team. *Motor Trend*'s Stage 1 turned a 13.38 at 105.5 mph, prompting the editors to crown it "the quickest American production car we had ever tested."

1970 BUICK HIGH-PERFORMANCE ENGINES

TYPE	CID	BORE × STROKE	BHP @ RPM	TORQUE @ RPM	FUEL SYSTEM	COMP. RATIO	AVAIL.
ohv V-8	350	3.80×3.85	315 @ 4800	410 @ 3200	1×4bbl.	10.25:1	1
ohv V-8	455	4.31×3.90	350 @ 4600	510 @ 2800	1×4bbl.	10.0:1	GS 455
ohv V-8	455	4.31×3.90	360 @ 4600	510 @ 2800	1×4bbl.	10.0:1	GS 455
ohv V-8	455	4.31×3.90	370 @ 4600	510 @ 2800	1×4bbl.	10.0:1	2

1. GS, LeSabre, Skylark, Sportwagon. 2. Wildcat, Estate Wagon, Riviera, Electra, LeSabre 455.

▲ Sheetmetal changes freshened Chevelle and the $445 SS package again came with a 396, but it was now the 350-bhp L-34 version. In January, a 350-bhp, 402-cid V-8 replaced it, but the "396" label stuck.

▲ Super Sports got a beefed suspension with a rear stabilizer bar. Seven-inch sport wheels with F70×14 white-letter tires were included, though the tires on this car are not of the period.

▼ Chevy's response to GM's new displacement rule was to stroke the 427 and create the SS 454 Chevelle. The LS-5 454 had 360 bhp, the LS-6 had 450 bhp and made for one of the quickest supercars ever.

▲ Squarer lines gave SS Chevelles the stance of a street tough. The Super Sport option was available on the coupe, convertible, and El Camino. *Road Test* ran a 350-bhp SS Chevelle with Turbo Hydra-Matic through the quarter in 15.27 seconds at 92.98 mph.

▲ Competition was tough, and Chevelle SS 396 production fell to 53,559. Chevy built 8773 SS 454s, split about evenly between the solid-lifter LS-6, a bargain at $263, and the more manageable LS-5. A limited-slip differential was a $42.15 option.

▲ A popular new option for 1970 was the $147 domed hood. It featured a vacuum-operated cowl-induction flap that opened under full throttle.

◀ *Road Test* said the SS package made a Chevelle "worthy of notice by any serious motorist [and] permits the available power to be utilized with safe handling and braking."

▲ With cowl induction, a soft ring sealed the gap between the hood dome and air cleaner. When the flap opened, outside air entered from the low-pressure area at the windshield's base.

▲ *Road Test* branded cowl-induction a gimmick, saying a Chevelle SS 396 without the cowl setup turned "essentially the same speeds" as one with it. Pictured is the base L-34 396. Available early in the model year were 375-bhp L-78 and aluminum-head L-89 396s. They were dropped when the LS-6 454 entered production.

◀ Super Sport Chevelles shared a revised dash with the new Monte Carlo. A close-ratio four-speed was standard; Turbo Hydra-Matic cost $222, or $290 with the LS-6. Strato-bucket seats added $121, a center console $54, tilt wheel $45, and power steering $105. Special instrumentation, including a tachometer, clock, ammeter, and temperature gauge, totaled $84.30. An AM/FM radio cost $134.

▲ LS-6 ragtop had a beastly beauty. Only the "Rockcrusher" four-speed or heavy-duty M40 Turbo Hydra-Matic could handle its power.

▲ "It has striking performance that you'd never suspect in traffic," said race driver Sam Posey after an LS-6 experience for *Car and Driver*.

► "The past is gone, the future may never see a car like this," *Hot Rod* proclaimed after its LS-6 ran a 13.4 at 108.7 mph. *Car Craft* claimed a 13.1 ET. *Car and Driver* said its automatic with 3.70:1 gears turned a 13.8 at 103.8. Compared to the 10.25:1-compression LS-5, which used a Quadrajet four-barrel, the LS-6 (right) had an 11.0:1 squeeze, an 800cfm Holley, forged steel connecting rods, and forged aluminum TRW pistons. Even with a road-ready weight of 4000 pounds, a Chevelle SS 454 LS-6 carried an astonishingly low 8.9 pounds per bhp.

▲ Camaro was redesigned as a 1970½ model. It also was the foundation for what many Chevy fans regard as the finest Z-28 of all. With its new 360-bhp, 350-cid V-8, a Z-28 with the standard four-speed and a 4.10:1 final drive turned a 14.2 ET at 100 mph for *Road & Track*.

▲ A coupe was now Camaro's only body style. All Camaros handled better this year, but Z-28s benefited further from the stiffer F-41 suspension and F60×15 tires. A Hurst-shifted Muncie four-speed again was standard, but Turbo Hydra-Matic joined as an option. A rear spoiler was included in the $573 Z-28 package price, which made for a $3412 Camaro. Underhood was Corvette's LT-1 350 with solid lifters, hot cam, big valves, extruded aluminum pistons, and a 780cfm Holley four-barrel.

◄▲ Camaro's $168 RS package added a unique nose and soft Endura grille surround. The car pictured is a Z-28 Hurst Sunshine Special, a prototype concept car with a sliding fabric sunroof. GM didn't bite, and just three were built.

◄ While the Z-28 had the LT-1 (left), SS Camaros could get a 300-bhp 350, or a 396 with 350 or 375 bhp. Chevy built 137,455 Camaros for the model year, of which 8733 were Z-28s.

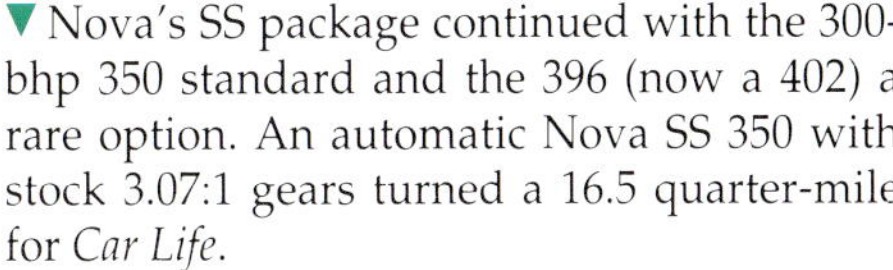

▼ Nova's SS package continued with the 300-bhp 350 standard and the 396 (now a 402) a rare option. An automatic Nova SS 350 with stock 3.07:1 gears turned a 16.5 quarter-mile for *Car Life*.

▲ Pennsylvania Chevy dealer and bowtie hyper-power specialist Don Yenko had offered 425-bhp, 427-cid Rat motors in some '69 Novas. But prohibitive insurance rates forced him to dial back to this 360-bhp LT-1 350 for '70.

▲ Yenko named his hot Nova the Deuce LT-1 and offered it for 1970 only. Just 176 were built. All were two-door sport sedans beefed up with the F-41 suspension and Magnum 500 wheels. Interiors were black and had taxi cab-grade rubber floor mats and vinyl bench seats relieved only by silver Yenko stickers on the door panels.

▲ All Deuce LT-1s got a hood-mounted 8000-rpm tach, but an option put water temperature, amp, and oil pressure gauges under the dash. These cars were delivered with a 12-bolt rear end and a 4.10:1 Positraction differential. Buyers chose between a stock four-speed Muncie or a Turbo Hydra-Matic modified with a Hurst floor-shift unit.

▲ Yenko was never shy about dressing up his mounts, and the Deuce's stripes were in keeping with that policy. Yenko called this Nova his "Mini Muscle" car, and compared to the 450-bhp Camaros and Chevelles he was still turning out, it was. But the Deuce certainly was no slouch and could be expected to turn ETs of around 14 seconds flat right out of the box. Interestingly, Yenko didn't do the engine installation himself. Instead, he was able to order LT-1-equipped Novas (with the 4.10:1 Positraction axle) directly from the factory by working them into a fleet order—and by working some valuable Chevy connections.

1970 CHEVROLET HIGH-PERFORMANCE ENGINES

TYPE	CID	BORE × STROKE	BHP @ RPM	TORQUE @ RPM	FUEL SYSTEM	COMP. RATIO	AVAIL.
ohv V-8	350	4.00 × 3.48	300 @ 4800	380 @ 3200	1 × 4bbl.	10.25:1	1
ohv V-8	350	4.00 × 3.48	360 @ 6000	380 @ 4800	1 × 4bbl.	11.0:1	2
ohv V-8	396	4.09 × 3.76	350 @ 5200	415 @ 3400	1 × 4bbl.	10.25:1	4
ohv V-8	400	4.12 × 3.75	330 @ 4800	415 @ 3200	1 × 4bbl.	10.25:1	3
ohv V-8	402	4.13 × 3.76	350 @ 5200	415 @ 3400	1 × 4bbl.	10.25:1	4
ohv V-8	402	4.13 × 3.76	375 @ 5600	415 @ 3600	1 × 4bbl.	11.0:1	4
ohv V-8	427	4.25 × 3.76	450 @ 6000	460 @ 4000	1 × 4bbl.	11.0:1	5
ohv V-8	454	4.25 × 4.00	345 @ 4400	500 @ 3000	1 × 4bbl.	10.25:1	full size
ohv V-8	454	4.25 × 4.00	360 @ 4400	500 @ 3200	1 × 4bbl.	10.25:1	3
ohv V-8	454	4.25 × 4.00	390 @ 4800	500 @ 3400	1 × 4bbl.	10.25:1	full size
ohv V-8	454	4.25 × 4.00	450 @ 6000	500 @ 3600	1 × 4bbl.	11.25:1	3

1. Camaro, Chevelle, Monte Carlo, Nova, full size. 2. Yenko Nova, Camaro Z-28. 3. Chevelle, Monte Carlo. 4. Camaro, Chevelle, Nova. 5. Yenko Camaro, Chevelle.

▲ Hurst's plushest conversion was the $4200 '70 Chrysler 300-H. All 501 hardtops and two convertibles had a fiberglass hood with air intake.

▲ Rear air foil was fiberglass, too. The 375-bhp 440 hooked to a TorqueFlite and 2.76:1 or 3.23:1 gears, for ETs of 16.8 at 87.3 mph.

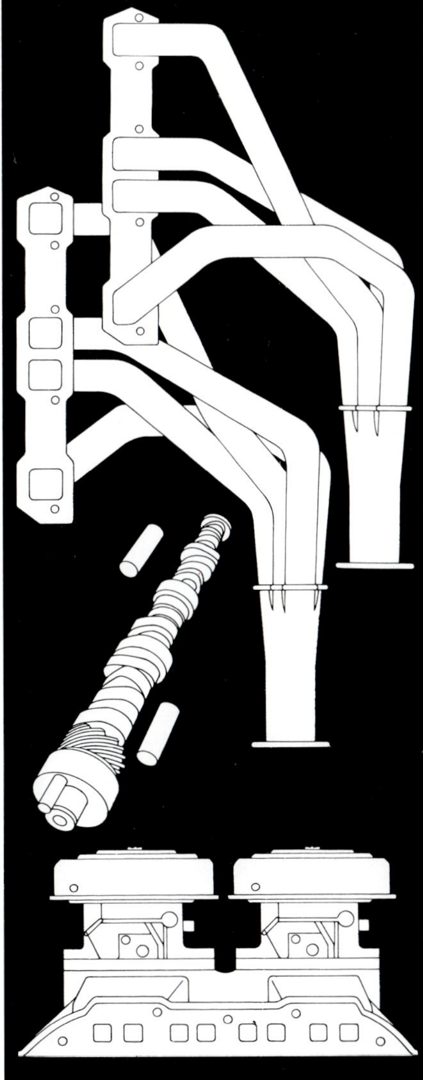

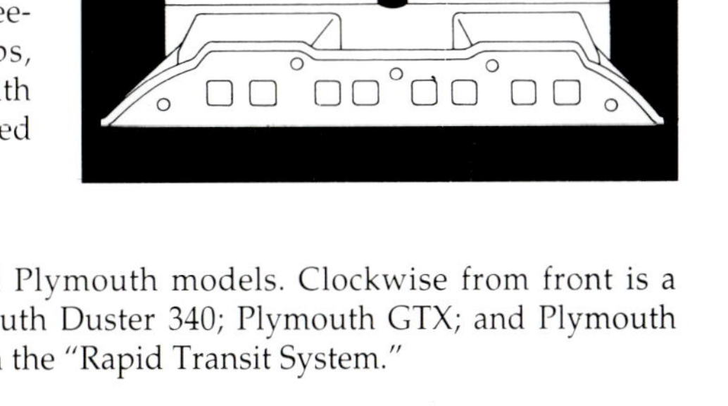

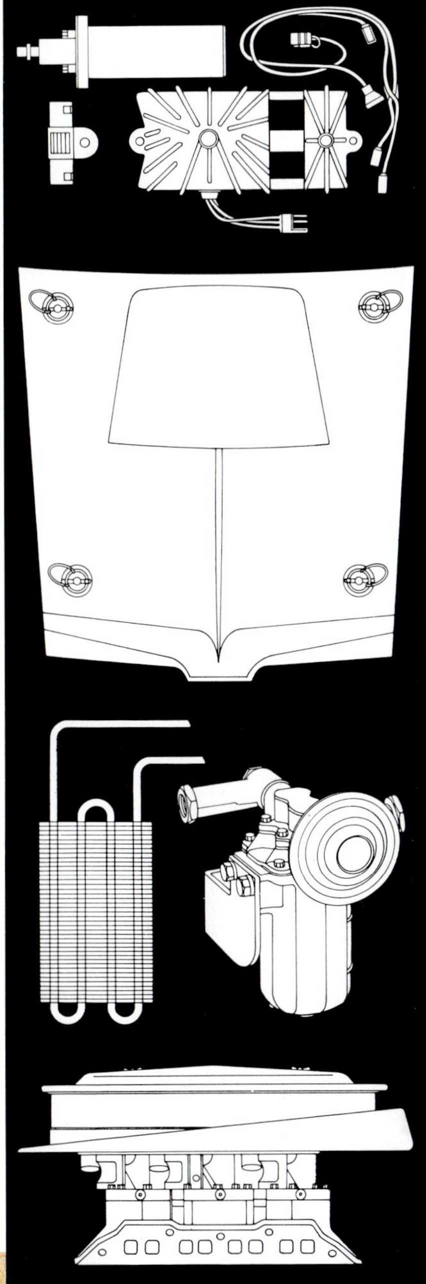

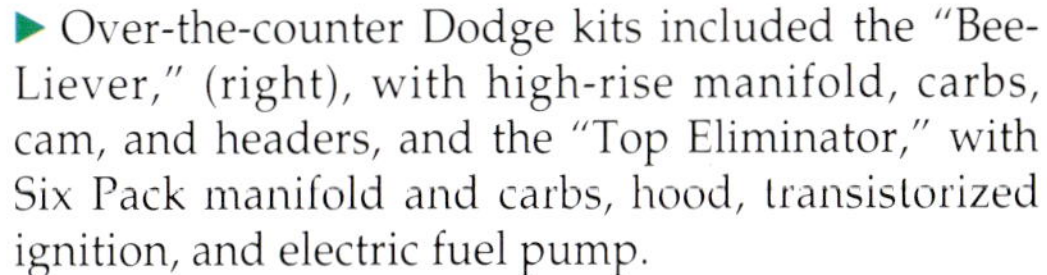

▶ Over-the-counter Dodge kits included the "Bee-Liever," (right), with high-rise manifold, carbs, cam, and headers, and the "Top Eliminator," with Six Pack manifold and carbs, hood, transistorized ignition, and electric fuel pump.

▼ This promotional shot combines Dodge and Plymouth models. Clockwise from front is a Dodge Charger R/T; Dodge Challenger; Plymouth Duster 340; Plymouth GTX; and Plymouth Barracuda. Dodge had the "Scat Pack," Plymouth the "Rapid Transit System."

▲ Super Bee could again get the 440 Six Pack, but now under a scooped steel hood, not the fiberglass lid of '69. Side stripes joined the bee-tail graphics.

▲ Coronet R/T got a split grille and dummy rear vents for '70. The 375-bhp 440 Magnum four-barrel was again standard. Sales fell to 2615, with just 13 getting the extra-cost 426 Hemi, but 210 were ordered with the 440 Six Pack, which was now a Coronet R/T option.

▲ The NHRA created its Pro Stock class in 1970 as a showcase for mechanically-modified stockers. "Dandy" Dick Landy jumped in, running several cars, including this 10-second, 135-mph Hemi Dart.

▲ A new chrome loop grille and fake rear-facing door vents marked the '70 Charger R/T. It again got the 375-bhp 440 four-barrel as standard, but added to the optional Hemi an available 390-bhp, 440-cid Six Pack.

▲ This R/T has a Six Pack, but only Hemis got exterior ID. All had special torsion bars and shocks, extra-heavy rear springs, and a front sway bar. TorqueFlite was standard, Hurst-shifted four-speed optional.

▲ The Daytona was gone. Charger 500 returned, though without the aero grille or flush backlight. This black R/T is combined with the optional SE package, which included leather seat facings.

▲ The 426 Hemi added $648 to the Charger R/T's $3711 list price. Again rated at 425 bhp, it now had hydraulic lifters. It went into about 354 Chargers (R/Ts, 500s, and Daytonas) for 1969, but just 112 Charger R/Ts for '70, as some fans defected to the new Hemi pony cars.

▼ Charger R/T production fell by 50 percent for 1970, to 9509. Skyrocketing supercar insurance rates and increased competition were to blame.

▲ Dodge finally got its pony car: the 1970 Challenger. It used the same unibody platform as Plymouth's new Barracuda, but the Dodge's wheelbase was two inches longer, at 110, to provide slightly more rear-seat room. It was sold in hardtop and convertible form, with the performance model wearing the familiar R/T label. This one's finished in Plum Crazy, one of Dodge's new High Impact hues.

▲ R/Ts came with open hood scoops that didn't feed directly to the engine. Standard was the 335-bhp, 383-cid Magnum. Optional was the 275-bhp 340; the 375-bhp Magnum 440; the 390-bhp 440 Six Pack (shown); and the mighty 425-bhp 426 Hemi. The 440 and Hemi came with a TorqueFlite; ordering the optional four-speed gained them a Hurst shifter and extra-heavy-duty Dana 60 axle with 9¾-inch ring gear. A woodgrain pistol-grip shifter came with the four-speeds. *Motor Trend*'s 383 turned a 15.7 at 90 mph. *Car Craft*'s 440 Six Pack ran a 13.62 at 104. Both were automatics with the standard 3.23:1 axle ratio.

1970 DODGE HIGH-PERFORMANCE ENGINES

TYPE	CID	BORE × STROKE	BHP @ RPM	TORQUE @ RPM	FUEL SYSTEM	COMP. RATIO	AVAIL.
ohv V-8	340	4.04 × 3.31	275 @ 5000	340 @ 3200	1 × 4bbl.	10.5:1	1
ohv V-8	383	4.25 × 3.75	330 @ 5000	425 @ 3200	1 × 4bbl.	9.5:1	2
ohv V-8	383	4.25 × 3.75	335 @ 5200	425 @ 3400	1 × 4bbl.	9.5:1	3
ohv V-8	426*	4.25 × 3.75	425 @ 5000	490 @ 4000	2 × 4bbl.	10.2:1	4
ohv V-8	440	4.32 × 3.75	350 @ 4400	480 @ 2800	1 × 4bbl.	9.7:1	full size
ohv V-8	440	4.32 × 3.75	375 @ 4600	480 @ 3200	1 × 4bbl.	9.7:1	5
ohv V-8	440	4.32 × 3.75	390 @ 4700	490 @ 3200	3 × 2bbl.	10.5:1	4

* Hemi.

1. Dart Swinger 340, Challenger. 2. Coronet, Challenger, full size. 3. Coronet, Coronet Super Bee, Charger, Challenger, Challenger R/T, full size. 4. Charger R/T, Coronet Super Bee and R/T, Challenger R/T. 5. Coronet R/T, Challenger R/T, full size.

▲ Trans Am-series rules required 2500 street versions of a racer. Dodge met that with 2539 Challenger T/As for '70. This one is Panther Pink.

▲ T/As had E60×15 front tires and G60×15 rears. The tail was raised two inches to clear the larger back rubber and standard side-exit exhausts. Front discs, fiberglass hood with working scoop, and ducktail spoiler were standard. This shade of green was "Sublime."

◀ Real race T/As used a 440 bhp 305-cid V-8 with a single four-barrel. Street T/As had a 340 topped with an Edelbrock manifold and three Holley two-barrels (shown). It was rated at 290 bhp, but likely made 350 and was potent enough for low-14-second ETs. Nonstock chrome items on this example include valve covers, hood hinges, breather top, radiator tank, and alternator.

▲ Another of Dick Landy's Pro Stock rides was this outstanding Hemi Challenger. It usually ran high-nines at 140 mph, but its 10.38 at 130.43 was good enough to win the Pro Stock title at the '70 Summernationals. Rules mandated the stock wheelbase and body panels, but allowed some powertrain alterations.

▲The 426 Hemi and associated hardware added $1227 to the R/T's $3226 base. "In return," said *Road Test*, "you get power that can rattle dishes in the kitchen when you start it up in the driveway." *Car and Driver*'s TorqueFlite with 3.23:1 gears turned a 14.1 at 103.2 and got 7 mpg.

▲ Challenger's ram-air setup cost $97 and mounted to the air cleaner, where it vibrated with the engine—hence the "shaker" name. Hemis went into 287 Challenger R/T hardtops, nine convertibles, and 60 R/T SE hardtops.

▲With 58.9 percent of its 3890-pound curb weight on the front tires, a Hemi R/T SE didn't corner very well; neither did one with the 440. But road-race types could always order the well-balanced 340. Despite intense competition, a respectable 83,000 Challengers sold for 1970, nearly 20,000 of them in hot R/T guise.

▲ "Special Edition" package added a vinyl roof with smaller formal backlight, plus leather seat facings, an overhead console, and other extras for $232 over a base R/T hardtop.

▲Boss 302 had new stripes for its second and final year. Its solid-lifter 302 got smaller valves for better driveability, but retained the 290-bhp underrating. Price was $3720. Of 7103 Boss 302s built, 6319 were '70s.

▲ Formerly standard, the "shaker" hood was now a Boss 302 option. Louvers added $65, tail spoiler, $20. *Car and Driver*'s, with a limited slip ($43) and 3.91:1 ($13), ran a 14.9 at 93.4. "Grabber" colors were new.

▲ As did all '70 Mustangs, the Boss 429 got a new twin-lamp face, but it was mechanically unchanged. Its 429-cid engine was a high-rev NASCAR mill, and in stock form, was no quicker than a 428 Cobra Jet on the street.

▲ Rated at 375 bhp, the 429 boasted semi-hemi heads, super-tough internals, and a 735cfm Holly on a high-rise aluminum manifold.

▲ Even with the front suspension altered to fit the big 429, the only room for the battery was in the trunk. It helped weight balance a little.

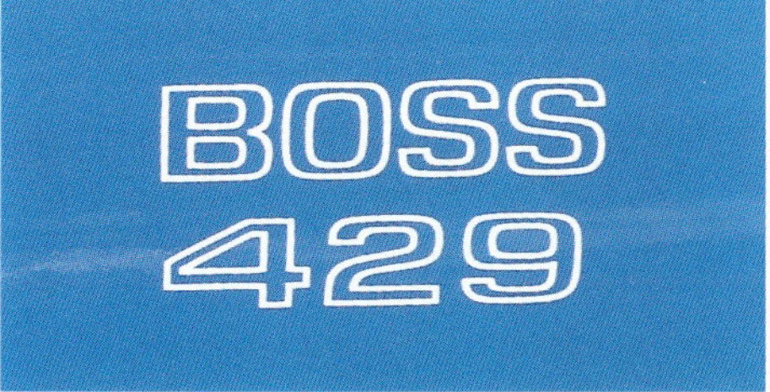

▲ Ford built just 858 Boss 429s for '69 and 489 for '70, but its legend—and unmet promise—live on. It delivered for $4932 in '70.

▲ The $457 428 CJ returned as Mach 1's big gun. A fake hood scoop was standard, but the $522 Ram-Air version got this shaker.

▲ Among the rarest of 1970 Mach 1s are the 96 Twister Specials built for sale by Kansas City dealers.

▲ Mach 1's four-barrel 351 was the new 300-bhp "Cleveland" motor. About half of the Twisters got a fortified 428 called the Super Cobra Jet.

▲ Twisters were Grabber Orange with Traction-Lok and shaker hood. As on all SportsRoofs, spoilers and slats were optional. New rear stabilizer bar aided Mach 1 handling, softer springs improved the ride.

▲ Torino was redesigned on an inch-longer wheelbase (now 117). Its handsome new shape was another venue for the hallowed Cobra name.

▲ New for Ford intermediates was the 429-cid V-8. It replaced the 428 and Boss 429 and came in base, Cobra Jet, and Super Cobra Jet form.

▶ This is the 429 SCJ, which had solid lifters, forged aluminum pistons, and a 780cfm Holley four-barrel. It was variously listed at 370 or 375 bhp, but could be ordered with or without the Ram Air shaker scoop.

▲ The Torino GT came with a 302-cid V-8, fake hood scoop, and steel wheels. Hidden headlamps and Laser side stripe were options. Ford built 56,819 GT SportsRoofs. The GT convertible was Torino's only ragtop, and 3939 were produced. The 390-cid V-8 died, but the better 351-cid Cleveland four-barrel filled its role well.

▲ A 429 CJ Torino Cobra was a comfortable everyday supercar capable of mid-14s at near 100 mph. Black-out hood and grille were standard on Cobra. Shaker scoop was available only with 429 or 351 Cleveland.

▲ Torino Cobra started at $3270 with the 360-bhp 429, competition suspension, ultra-high-rate springs, extra-heavy stabilizer bar, staggered rear shocks, and F70 × 14 tires. Magnum 500 wheels cost $155.

▼ With an elongated front clip on a Torino SportsRoof body, the King Cobra was to succeed the Talladega as Ford's superspeedway tool. Its aerodynamics were disappointing, however, and a change in Ford policy left little money to develop it. Only a handful were built. Regular '70 SportsRoofs did battle on NASCAR's short tracks, while '69 Talladegas and Spoiler IIs ran the big ovals, but neither was enough to beat the Mopars.

► Like the SCJ, the 429 CJ (shown) had 11.3:1 compression, but it used hydraulic lifters, a 700cfm Rochester four-barrel, and made 370 bhp with Ram Air. The base 429 had 360-bhp and a 600cfm Ford quad. The SCJ was combined with a Drag Pack that was otherwise optional. It included a 3.91:1 Traction-Lok or a 4.30:1 Detroit Locker axle.

1970 FORD HIGH-PERFORMANCE ENGINES

TYPE	CID	BORE × STROKE	BHP @ RPM	TORQUE @ RPM	FUEL SYSTEM	COMP. RATIO	AVAIL.
ohv V-8	302	4.00 × 3.00	290 @ 5800	290 @ 4300	1 × 4bbl.	10.5:1	Mustang
ohv V-8	351	4.00 × 3.50	300 @ 5400	380 @ 3400	1 × 4bbl.	11.0:1	1
ohv V-8	390	4.05 × 3.78	320 @ 4600	427 @ 3200	1 × 4bbl.	10.5:1	1
ohv V-8	428	4.13 × 3.98	335 @ 5200	440 @ 3400	1 × 4bbl.	10.6:1	Mustang
ohv V-8	429	4.36 × 3.59	360 @ 4600	480 @ 2800	1 × 4bbl.	10.5:1	2
ohv V-8	429	4.36 × 3.59	370 @ 5400	450 @ 3400	1 × 4bbl.	11.3:1	Fairlane
ohv V-8	429	4.36 × 3.59	375 @ 5200	450 @ 3400	1 × 4bbl.	11.3:1	Fairlane
ohv V-8*	429	4.36 × 3.59	375 @ 5200	450 @ 3800	1 × 4bbl.	10.5:1	Mustang

* BOSS.
1. Fairlane, Torino, Mustang. 2. Fairlane, Thunderbird, full size.

▲ This Torino Cobra has the standard quick-ratio Hurst-shifted four-speed. Its bucket seats cost $133 extra, and front-disc brakes were $65 options. To the left of the steering column is the unusual, rectangular-shaped 8000 rpm tachometer.

▲ The 1970 Shelby Mustangs were actually leftover '69 models with Boss 302-type chin spoilers, hood stripes, and 1970 serial numbers.

▲ The final year's tally: 286 GT-500s; 350 GT-350s. Ford let the Shelbys wither as it concentrated on its own Boss 302 and big-block Mustangs.

▲ Carroll Shelby had ceased direct involvement in the Cobra ponies.

▲ The '70 GT-500 shared Mustang's 335-bhp 428 CJ-R, but GT-350 stayed with the 351 Windsor, not Mach 1's 351 Cleveland.

▲ Costly, with no big performance edge, the Shelby's focus blurred.

▲ Performance versions of Mercury's redesigned Montego started with the base Cyclone, which had the 360-bhp 429 and cost $3238.

▲ Cyclone options included the 370-bhp 429 CJ or the 375-bhp SCJ. Air cleaner flap and rubber ring show the available Ram Air setup.

▲ Top Cyclone was the Spoiler. It came standard with the 429 CJ Ram Air. *Road Test*'s automatic with 3.50:1 Traction-Lok ran a 14.61 at 99.22.

▲ Positioned between Cyclone and Spoiler was the new Cyclone GT. Hidden headlamps and a 250-bhp, 351 two-barrel were standard.

▲ Spoiler's $3530 price included a four-speed with Hurst T-handle, 3.50:1 Traction-Lok, competition handling package, and G70 × 14 tires. The SCJ required a Drag Pack with 3.90:1 or 4.30:1 axle.

▲ Spoiler came with a functional hood scoop and front air dam. The optional Select-Shift automatic upshifted at 5600 rpm during full-throttle runs.

▲ All Spoilers got...a spoiler. Inside were high-back buckets, 140-mph speedo, 8000-rpm tach, and gauges for oil pressure, coolant temp, and amps.

▲ Cyclone's 429 had an "exhaust note which is a solid pleasant roar reminiscent of a NASCAR stocker and highly pleasing...." said *Road Test*.

▲This prototype has a "GT" badge that was never on the Cyclone GT. Similarly, Mercury and Ford said the Boss 429 would be offered in their midsize '70s. None were installed. This is a 351 Cleveland.

▲ Tape stripes and one of six "Grabber" colors (blue, orange, yellow, green, coral, and platinum) could dress up a Spoiler or other Cyclone.

▲ Cougar got a new snout. Eliminator (shown) was back as the performance model with the Boss 302 engine, the 351 Cleveland, or the 428 CJ. The 390 and 351 Windsor were gone. Two racing Eliminators got Boss 429s.

▲ Eliminator's front air dam may have worked, but its rear spoiler was purely decorative. Hood scoop was functional with the 428 CJ only.

▲ Even with the Super Drag Pack's 4.30:1 Detroit Locker, an Eliminator Boss 302's low ET was 15.0 seconds. The 351 was the best overall choice: lighter than the 428, torquier than the 302.

▲ Escape machines, indeed. Like this racer, showroom 4-4-2s took their lead from the Hurst/Olds cars and gained a 455-cid V-8 as standard for '70. It was rated at 365 bhp, or 370 with the W-30 option. With the 365-bhp motor, automatic, and 3.08:1 gears, *Motor Trend* turned a 14.8 at 95 mph. *Hot Rod* got serious. Its W-30 had a Hurst Dual-Gate Turbo Hydra-Matic 400 with a high-performance converter, and a 3.91:1 limited slip. Box stock, it ran a 14.10 at 100.5. Removing the air filter element and adding Autolite A42 plugs got it down to 13.98 at 100.7.

1970 MERCURY HIGH-PERFORMANCE ENGINES

TYPE	CID	BORE × STROKE	BHP @ RPM	TORQUE @ RPM	FUEL SYSTEM	COMP. RATIO	AVAIL.
ohv V-8	302	4.00 × 3.00	290 @ 5800	290 @ 4300	1 × 4bbl.	10.5:1	1
ohv V-8	351	4.00 × 3.50	300 @ 5400	380 @ 3400	1 × 4bbl.	11.0:1	2
ohv V-8	428	4.13 × 3.98	335 @ 5200	440 @ 3400	1 × 4bbl.	10.6:1	1
ohv V-8	429	4.36 × 3.59	360 @ 4600	480 @ 2800	1 × 4bbl.	10.5:1	3
ohv V-8	429	4.36 × 3.59	370 @ 5400	450 @ 3400	1 × 4bbl.	11.3:1	Cyclone
ohv V-8*	429	4.36 × 3.59	375 @ 5200	450 @ 3400	1 × 4bbl.	10.3:1	1
ohv V-8	429	4.36 × 3.59	375 @ 5600	450 @ 3400	1 × 4bbl.	10.5:1	Cyclone

* BOSS.
1. Cougar Eliminator. 2. Cougar, Montego, Cyclone. 3. Montego, Cyclone, full size.

▲ W-30s got fiberglass hood with functional scoops; rear deck spoiler could be deleted.

▲ Chrome bars replaced the black-out grille for '70. Hardtop 4-4-2s started at $3376.

▲ Taillamps were fresh, also. All 4-4-2s got stabilizer bars and Polyglas G70 × 14s.

◀▲ W-30s had air-induction, long-duration cam, aluminum intake manifold, and low-restriction air cleaner. "The 455 W-30 has an almost unholy torque capability," *Hot Rod* said, so launches required "deft throttle work."

▲ Cutlass Supreme shared 4-4-2's interior, though 4-4-2s got a four-spoke steering wheel. Strato bucket seats, optional on Cutlass, were standard on 4-4-2. Note the tach to the right of the steering column. The factory's was combined with a clock; this is an easier-to-read aftermarket item.

▲ Red plastic inner fenders shaved a few pounds from the big-block W-30's nose.

1970 OLDSMOBILE HIGH-PERFORMANCE ENGINES

TYPE	CID	BORE × STROKE	BHP @ RPM	TORQUE @ RPM	FUEL SYSTEM	COMP. RATIO	AVAIL.
ohv V-8	350	4.06 × 3.38	310 @ 4800	390 @ 3200	1 × 4bbl.	10.3:1	1
ohv V-8	350	4.06 × 3.38	325 @ 5400	360 @ 3600	1 × 4bbl.	10.5:1	Cutlass
ohv V-8	455	4.13 × 4.25	365 @ 5000	500 @ 3200	1 × 4bbl.	10.5:1	2
ohv V-8	455	4.13 × 4.25	370 @ 5200	500 @ 3600	1 × 4bbl.	10.5:1	4-4-2
ohv V-8	455	4.13 × 4.25	375 @ 4600	510 @ 3000	1 × 4bbl.	10.3:1	Toronado
ohv V-8	455	4.13 × 4.25	390 @ 5000	500 @ 3200	1 × 4bbl.	10.3:1	full size
ohv V-8	455	4.13 × 4.25	400 @ 5100	500 @ 5100	1 × 4bbl.	10.3:1	Toronado

1. Cutlass, Vista Cruiser. 2. 4-4-2, Vista Cruiser, full size.

▲ A W-30 4-4-2 convertible paced the Indy 500, and Olds assembled 626 Pace Car Replicas; 358 of them were Cutlass ragtops. This Cutlass replica has the 350-cid V-8 with the 325-bhp W-31 package. The W-31 was also offered in the Rallye 350, a budget-muscle version of the Cutlass pillared coupe. Olds built just 3547 Rallye 350s. All were bright yellow with black and orange stripes and turned ETs in the high-14s. No Hurst/Olds was offered for 1970.

▲ "GTX & Road Runner: No brag. Just fact." That was the tag line for this ad shot of Plymouth's reskinned muscle intermediates. They were part of the division's new "Rapid Transit System" approach to performance.

▲ A new vacuum-operated "Air Grabber" scoop slowly rose at the push of a dash switch to reveal a snarling-shark graphic. It was optional on 440 cars, standard with the Hemi. The 426 went into 152 Road Runners and 72 GTXs for '70. Also, the 440+6 was now offered on GTX, and 678 were ordered.

▲ Road Runner (shown) and its GTX cousin were restyled for '70. With the base 335-bhp 383 V-8, the Road Runner started at just $2896, $49 less than in '69—though a three-speed manual had replaced the four-speed as standard for '70. Also, the optional 426 Hemi got hydraulic lifters for easier maintenance and cleaner emissions.

▲ The biggest "Rapid Transit" member was the $3898 Sport Fury GT. It came with the 440 four-barrel or the 440 tri-carb, the latter good for 16-second quarter-miles.

▼ Echoes of the late Dodge Daytona: Plymouth issued a limited-edition, long-snout Road Runner Superbird to meet NASCAR homologation rules. The 25-inch-tall air foil kept NASCAR racers on track at 190 mph.

◀ Plymouth built 1920 Superbirds for this, their lone model year. All NASCAR racers had Hemis; 135 of the street versions got the 425-bhp 426; 716 the 440+6 (shown); and the rest used the 375-bhp 440 four-barrel. All could have TorqueFlite or a four-speed. *Car and Driver*'s Hemi automatic with 3.23:1 gears turned a 13.5 at 105 mph. *Road Test*'s 375-bhp 440 automatic with a Sure-Grip 3.55:1 ran a 14.26 at 103.7.

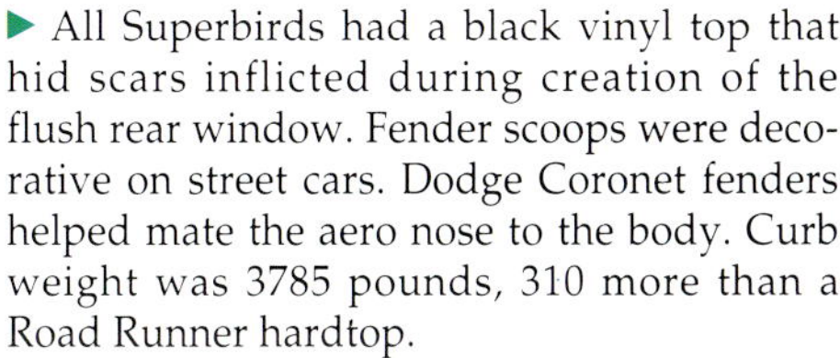

▶ All Superbirds had a black vinyl top that hid scars inflicted during creation of the flush rear window. Fender scoops were decorative on street cars. Dodge Coronet fenders helped mate the aero nose to the body. Curb weight was 3785 pounds, 310 more than a Road Runner hardtop.

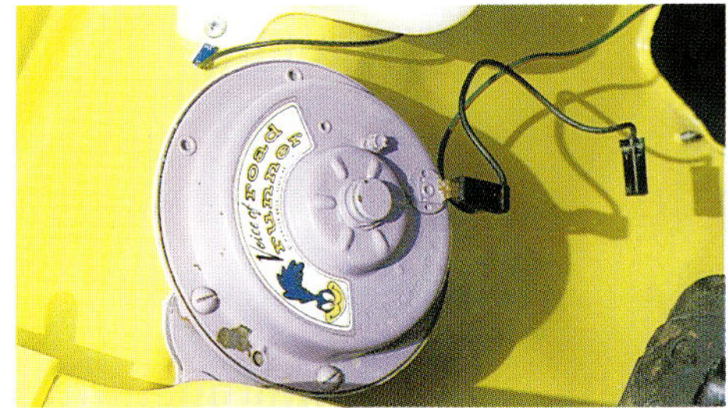

▲As with regular Road Runners, Superbirds had the "beep-beep" horn, which mimicked the cartoon bird's call. "It's cute," remarked *Road Test*, "but absolutely lacks the authority the car deserves."

▲ Road Runners were transformed into Superbirds by Creative Industries, the aftermarket firm that also built the Dodge Charger 500 and Daytona. These weren't cars for those who shunned attention.

▲ Fiberglass hidden-headlamp pods were set into the Superbird's steel beak. The rear wing was aluminum. Heavy-duty suspension gave the nose-heavy car adequate handling, but the ride was harsh.

▲ Power front discs were included in Superbird's $4298 base price, and extra-cost G60×15 tires could replace the usual F70×14s. Buyers were cool to these cars, and many languished on dealers' lots. Now they're coveted.

▲ In its element: Richard Petty's Superbird on the NASCAR banking. Petty had defected to Ford for '69, but Plymouth's new 'bird won him back to the Mopar flock for '70.

▲ The King himself poses with his restored '70 Superbird at the Petty museum in North Carolina. Petty won 18 NASCAR races in '70, but Bobby Isaac, running a Charger Daytona, took the drivers' championship.

▲ NASCAR would outlaw both the Ford and Chrysler aero specials after the '70 season. But Superbirds still ran at the drags, where their wings were of less value. Here's the Sox & Martin car at the '71 NHRA Winternationals.

▲ Ducted and tweaked, Petty's NASCAR Hemi pushed his Superbird to almost 200 mph. Pete Hamilton won the '70 Daytona 500 in a Petty-prepped 'bird, and Mopar took 38 NASCAR wins (21 by Superbirds) to FoMoCo's 10 in 1970.

▲ The Barracuda name was on a redesigned line of pony car hardtops and convertibles for '70. The performance versions were tagged 'Cuda.

▲ They shared a platform, but Barracuda's 108-inch wheelbase was two inches shorter than Challenger's, so it had even less rear leg room.

◀ Only 666 'Cudas had Hemis for 1970, and just 14 went into convertibles. *Motor Trend*'s 4.10:1 automatic Hemicuda coupe turned a 13.7 ET at 101.2 mph. The Rapid Transit System approach matched axle ratios, transmissions, and other gear to the likely use of the car. For example, the factory set suspensions on Hemis and 440s to withstand brutal acceleration, while the 340s and 383s got handling-oriented spring rates.

▲ The 440+6 cost $621 less than a Hemi. *Motor Trend*'s 3.54:1 four-speed stayed with a Hemi to 60 mph, but its 14.04 ET at 100 mph was slower.

▲ Just 635 of the 19,515 'Cudas built for '70 were ragtops. A 383 was standard; the optional 340 was as quick, and gave 'Cuda better balance.

1970 PLYMOUTH HIGH-PERFORMANCE ENGINES

TYPE	CID	BORE × STROKE	BHP @ RPM	TORQUE @ RPM	FUEL SYSTEM	COMP. RATIO	AVAIL.
ohv V-8	340	4.04 × 3.31	275 @ 5000	340 @ 3200	1 × 4bbl.	10.5:1	1
ohv V-8	383	4.25 × 3.75	330 @ 5000	425 @ 3200	1 × 4bbl.	9.5:1	2
ohv V-8	383	4.25 × 3.75	335 @ 5200	425 @ 3400	1 × 4bbl.	9.5:1	3
ohv V-8	426*	4.25 × 3.75	425 @ 5000	490 @ 4000	2 × 4bbl.	10.2:1	4
ohv V-8	440	4.32 × 3.75	350 @ 4400	480 @ 2800	1 × 4bbl.	9.7:1	full size
ohv V-8	440	4.32 × 3.75	375 @ 4600	480 @ 3200	1 × 4bbl.	9.7:1	5
ohv V-8	440	4.32 × 3.75	390 @ 4700	490 @ 3200	3 × 2bbl.	10.5:1	4

*Hemi.
1. Duster 340, 'Cuda. 2. Satellite, Barracuda, full size. 3. Satellite, Road Runner, Barracuda, 'Cuda. 4. Road Runner, GTX, 'Cuda. 5. Road Runner, GTX, 'Cuda, full size.

▲ 'Cuda's functional shaker scoop mounted to the air cleaner though a hole in the hood and quivered with the engine. It was standard with the Hemi, but a $97 option for other 'Cuda mills.

▶ Ronnie Sox (left) and Buddy Martin with the Super Stock Hemicuda that took them to their most successful season. The team won 17 major drag events in '70; Sox was wheelman in 13 of them; Herb McCandless handled the rest. Their Hemi had 13.5:1 compression, Holley dual quads, an experimental camshaft, and transistorized ignition. Valves were stock size: 2.25-inch intake, 1.94-inch exhaust. The car weighed 2980 pounds, ready to rock.

▲ Based on Plymouth's new compact fastback, the Duster 340 was a budget-muscle bull's-eye. Its $2547 base price included the tough 275-bhp 340 four-barrel and a three-speed stick. *Car and Driver*'s had the $188 four-speed, $42 Sure-Grip with 3.91:1 gears, and weighed 3368 pounds. It ran a very respectable 14.39 at 97.2 mph, despite a balky shifter.

▲ A Pro Stock 'Cuda at the Winternationals. This racer has adapted the '69 Six Pack hoodscoop instead of using the stock Shaker scoop.

▲ Elastomeric bumpers and racing mirrors added $94. TorqueFlite was standard with 440 or Hemi; four-speed with Hurst Pistol-Grip was extra.

▲ This illustration shows Plymouth's wild paint palette for '70. Extra-cost High Impact hues were In-Violet, Limelight, Vitamin C Orange, Tor-Red, Lemon Twist, and Moulin Rouge. Far out.

▲ Cousin to Dodge's Challenger T/A was the AAR 'Cuda. Both were built only for 1970 to qualify race versions for the Trans Am series.

▲ Street handling was emphasized, but *Car and Driver*'s AAR 'Cuda, with the standard four-speed and 3.55:1, still ran a quick 14.3 at 99.5.

▲ AAR was raked to clear the big G60 × 15 rear tires and side-exit exhaust. Front tires were E60 × 15s. Ducktail spoiler and a fiberglass hood with working scoop were standard. TorqueFlite was optional.

▲ Named for Dan Gurney's All-American Racers team, the AAR started at $3966, some $800 above a regular 'Cuda coupe. Just 2724 AAR 'Cudas were built.

◀ Race AARs had a 340-cid V-8 destroked to 305 cid and a single four-barrel. Street AARs used the 340, but with three Holley two-barrels, Hemi-grade valve springs, and 290 bhp. It had heavier main webbing and a stronger head casting than regular 340s.

▼ Pontiac GTO wore a new Endura nose for '70, but the big news was behind it. A 455-cid V-8 was available and had 360 bhp (or 370 when hooked to the standard three-speed manual). It joined the carried-over 400 cid, which made 350 bhp in standard tune, 366 with Ram Air III, and 370 with Ram Air IV.

▲ The Judge gained the Ram Air III 400 as standard, with Ram Air IV optional. It could get the 455 V-8 late in the model year. The Judge's air foil was revised, and the heavy-duty suspension was now a $4.21 option.

1970 PONTIAC HIGH-PERFORMANCE ENGINES

TYPE	CID	BORE × STROKE	BHP @ RPM	TORQUE @ RPM	FUEL SYSTEM	COMP. RATIO	AVAIL.
ohv V-8	400	4.12×3.75	330 @ 4800	445 @ 2900	1×4bbl.	10.0:1	1
ohv V-8	400	4.12×3.75	330 @ 4800	430 @ 3000	1×4bbl.	10.25:1	2
ohv V-8	400	4.12×3.75	345 @ 5000	430 @ 3400	1×4bbl.	10.5:1	3
ohv V-8	400	4.12×3.75	350 @ 5000	445 @ 3000	1×4bbl.	10.3:1	4
ohv V-8	400*	4.12×3.75	366 @ 5100	445 @ 3600	1×4bbl.	10.5:1	GTO
ohv V-8	400**	4.12×3.75	370 @ 5500	445 @ 3900	1×4bbl.	10.5:1	5
ohv V-8	455	4.15×4.21	360 @ 4300	500 @ 2700	1×4bbl.	10.0:1	full size
ohv V-8	455	4.15×4.21	360 @ 4600	500 @ 3100	1×4bbl.	10.25:1	GTO
ohv V-8	455	4.15×4.21	370 @ 4600	500 @ 3100	1×4bbl.	10.25:1	6

* Ram Air. ** Ram Air IV.
1. Tempest, LeMans, Firebird, full size. 2. Firebird Formula 400. 3. Trans Am, Formula 400. 4. GTO, Grand Prix, Firebird, Trans Am. 5. GTO, Trans Am, Formula 400. 6. Grand Prix, Catalina, full size.

◀ *Car and Driver* called it "a hard muscled... commando of a car." Trans Am was now a full-fledged model and shared the new Firebird's Euro-styling and Endura nose, but added spoilers and air dams. The $4305 base price included a Ram Air 400 rated at 345 bhp; the optional Ram Air IV 400 had 370. The shaker scoop mated to the motor and Pontiac said it drew in cool air from the windshield base. Fender outlets vented the engine bay. Even with its 3782-pound curb weight split 57/43, handling was sharp. With the base engine, standard Hurst-shifted four-speed, and optional 3.90:1 limited slip, *Sports Car Graphic* turned a 14.6 at 99.5 mph. Turbo Hydra-Matic was optional.

◀ The 455s made their power at lower rpm than the 400s, so they were easier to drive on the street. But an expert driver could wring more from a Ram Air 400. For example, *Car Life*'s base 455 with automatic, 3.55:1 gears, and the $84 Ram Air option turned a 14.76 at 95.9. Its Ram Air III 400 had a four-speed, 3.90:1 axle, and a best ET of 14.6 at 99.5.

▼ The Judge adopted the Goat's fresh metal, plus new multi-hued stripes. The Judge package added $337 to the $3267 price of a base GTO coupe or $3492 GTO convertible. Judge production fell to 3797, of which 168 were ragtops. These cars again were no quicker than similarly equipped GTOs.

▲ Orbit Orange was an exclusive Judge color. "The Judge," observed *Road Test*, "is not for people who are shy about being looked at."

▲ Judge again shared the GTO's interior, except for badging. Buckets were standard; Trans Am steering wheel was a new option. A tach on hood or dash was available. Standard was a three-speed manual, optional was a Hurst-shifted close-ratio four-speed—both with Hurst T-handle shifter. Turbo Hydra-Matic also was an option.

▲ Foam gasket mated Ram Air engines to the hood scoops; underdash knob could cut the air flow. Air conditioning was unavailable with the Ram Air IV engine.

1971

The beginning of the end for the age of muscle... emissions regulations, high insurance costs, changing social climate take their toll • High compression engines fade...all GM cars and some Mopars run on regular fuel...Ford not so quick to surrender • Net horsepower ratings reflect power of engines as installed in cars • Baby muscle cars like AMC Hornet SC/360 and Dodge Demon 340 proliferate • Chevelle's 402-cid V-8 loses "396" designation, drops to 300 bhp; 454 sinks to 365 bhp • Hemis and 440 Six Packs still available in Dodge and Plymouth pony cars and intermediates, but very rare • Bloated new Mustang bows...Boss 351 the last of the Boss line...Ford/Mercury 429 still available with Ram Air for 370 bhp • At NHRA Nationals, Top Fuel ET Falls to 6.21; Funny cars run 6.64; Ronnie Sox captures Pro Stock with 9.58 in Hemi Cuda • King Richard Petty takes 21 NASCAR wins for Plymouth, scores his third national championship • NASCAR nixes Ford Talladega, winged Dodge/ Plymouths, and Mercury Cyclone Spoiler II

▲ Full-bore muscle machines were under attack on many fronts. So Detroit turned to less-obvious performance cars. A 304-cid V-8 had been offered in the 1970 Hornet compact, but it was the underrated '71 Hornet SC/360 that was AMC's real boy racer.

▲ The SC/360's 360-cid V-8 made 245 bhp with a two-barrel. A $199 "Go" package added a Ram-Air four-barrel for 285 bhp. A three-speed or Hurst shifted four-speed, or an automatic, were offered. SC/360s turned modest 14.9s at 95.3 in the quarter, but handled well.

▲ Starting at just $2663, this was affordable sportiness. Still, of nearly 75,000 Hornets sold for '71, just 667 were SC/360s. Body stripes were standard; dual exhausts, tachometer, handling package, and white-letter tires were optional.

▲ The second-generation AMX was no longer a two-seater or a distinct model. It was now an option package for the Javelin, itself bigger for '71. A new available 401-cid four-barrel had 330 bhp and pulled the heavier AMX to mid-14 quarters at around 93 mph.

▲ The Javelin AMX started at $3432 and weighed 3244 pounds, 100 pounds more than its two-seat predecessor. Front and rear spoilers were standard. Optional were a reverse-flow cowl induction setup and a "Go" pack with power front discs and E60 × 15 tires.

▲ Production versions of the subcompact Gremlin could have a 150-bhp six-cylinder, at most. With a modified big-block V-8, however, the Gremlin was a decidedly different creature. This full-race variant was AMC's first foray into pro-stock dragging. Painted in the distinctive AMC livery of the day, it was driven by Wally Booth of Amarillo, Texas. He turned consistent 9.40s at 140 mph. Note the narrowed rear axle needed to fit the fat slicks within the stock fender lines, and the castors needed to keep the wheelies in check.

1971 AMC HIGH-PERFORMANCE ENGINES

TYPE	CID	BORE × STROKE	BHP @ RPM	TORQUE @ RPM	FUEL SYSTEM	COMP. RATIO	AVAIL.
ohv V-8	360	4.08 × 3.44	245 @ 4400	365 @ 2600	1 × 2bbl.	8.5:1	1
ohv V-8	360	4.08 × 3.44	285 @ 4800	390 @ 3200	1 × 4bbl.	8.5:1	1
ohv V-8	401	4.17 × 3.68	330 @ 5000	430 @ 3400	1 × 4bbl.	10.2:1*	2

* Early 1971, 9.5:1 late 1971.

1. Hornet, Matador, Ambassador, Javelin. 2. Matador, Ambassador, Javelin, AMX.

▲ AMC built 2054 AMXs for '71—just seven percent of Javelin production—and only 745 were equipped with the 401 V-8. The nation was rapidly switching over to low-octane, low-lead gas as 1971 unfolded, and the 401's tepid 9.5:1 compression ratio was a sign of the times.

▲ As with most muscle cars that survived to see 1971, the Buick GS seemed a little defused. Stricter exhaust-emissions standards and the movement toward low-lead regular-gas were strangling engine outputs. Plus, soaring insurance rates were depressing the demand for performance models.

▼ GS 455 buyers got either the four-speed manual or the THM 400 Turbo Hydra-Matic. The 3.61:1 axle ratio was dropped and the 3.42:1 took over as the top gear. GS models still got functional hood scoops, dual exhaust, heavy-duty suspension, and G60×15 bias-belted tires, though.

▲ GS sales fell more than 50 percent for '71, to 9170. This Bittersweet Mist GS 455 is one of just 902 GS ragtops built that year.

▲ The Stage 1 package was ordered on only 801 GS coupes and 81 convertibles for '71.

▲ Compression, 10.0:1 or more in 1971, was now 8.5:1 for all GS mills. The GS350's 350-cid four-barrel dropped from 315 bhp to 260; the regular 455 (shown) fell from 350 bhp to 315; and the 455 Stage 1 slipped from 360 bhp to 345. *Motor Trend*'s Stage 1 turned a 14.7 ET at 92.5 mph, down 1.3 seconds and 12.5 mph from '70. Still, with more than 450 lbs/ft of torque, the 455s were plenty strong enough to avoid embarrassment.

▲ The Turbo Hydra-Matic's shift points dropped several hundred rpm, to 5000, to keep the retuned V-8 in its best range.

1971 BUICK HIGH-PERFORMANCE ENGINES

TYPE	CID	BORE × STROKE	BHP @ RPM	TORQUE @ RPM	FUEL SYSTEM	COMP. RATIO	AVAIL.
ohv V-8	350	3.80 × 3.85	260 @ 4600	360 @ 2300	1 × 4bbl.	8.5:1	Skylark GS, full size
ohv V-8	455	4.31 × 3.90	315 @ 4400	450 @ 2800	1 × 4bbl.	8.5:1	1
ohv V-8	455	4.31 × 3.90	330 @ 4600	455 @ 2800	1 × 4bbl.	8.5:1	Riviera GS, full size
ohv V-8	455	4.31 × 3.90	345 @ 5000	460 @ 3000	1 × 4bbl.	8.5:1	Skylark GS

1. Skylark GS, Riviera, full size.

▲ NHRA's new-for-1970 Pro Stock class was designed to give factory-backed racers a place to compete heads-up with one another instead of racing on handicap indexes against amateur competitors. In 1971, Pro Stockers such as Butch Leal's 427 Camaro, shown here, still resembled factory muscle cars. Changes in rules for 1972 would bring economy compacts like Vegas and Pintos into the class.

▲ Pro Stock allowed engine cross-breeding, so Rich Mirarcki and Bill Blanding put a 327-cid Chevy small-block in a Vega and ran 9.5s at 140.

▲ Chevy apparently planned to offer the 425-bhp LS-6 454 in Chevelles for '71, but none were actually built with it. However, about 19,000 of the estimated 80,000 '71 SS Chevelles had the LS-5 454.

▲ In 1970, Bill "Grumpy" Jenkins was Pro Stock's first top eliminator. He was back for '71 with a 427 Camaro that turned 9.7s at 138 mph.

▲ This is Ray Allen's tough automatic-transmission SS Chevelle ragtop defending its 1970 SS/E world championship. Allen ran in the 12.20s.

▲ Most performance engines were revamped to run on regular fuel for '71. The Camaro Z-28's 350-cid LT-1 got new pistons that dropped compression from 11.0:1 to 9.0:1, and horsepower from 360 to 300. Power now concentrated between 3000 and 5500 rpm, hampering hole shots. A good one could turn a 14.9 quarter.

▲ The base Chevelle SS dropped its celebrated "SS 396" badge for '71, but the domed hood was again standard and cowl induction returned as an option.

▲ Compression of the optional 454 LS-5 fell from 10.25:1 to 8.5:1, but it gained 5 bhp to 365. SS Chevelles came with larger tires, now F60×15, for '71.

▲ Available on coupe and convertible Chevelles, the basic SS Package now cost $357.

◀ A 402-cid V-8 replaced the SS Chevelle's 396-cid mill during '70. It returned for '71 under the Turbo-Jet 400 tag with 8.5:1 compression instead of 10.25:1 and 300 bhp instead of 350. A 350-cid V-8 with 245 or 270 bhp also was offered on SSs.

▲ Monte Carlo, Chevy's "personal-luxury" coupe, bowed for '70. It used the Chevelle platform, but had the 116-inch wheelbase of the sedan and wagon, not the 112-inch span of the coupe and convertible. As in '70, regular Monte Carlos came standard with a 350-cid V-8 and could be ordered with the 400-cid V-8, which had up to 330 bhp. Enthusiasts could opt for the SS 454 iteration, which made it Chevy's "personal luxury/performance" coupe. About 127,000 Monte Carlos were built in each year, but there were only 3823 SS 454 versions for '70; this is one of just 1919 built for '71.

▲ As in the Super Sport Chevelle, the big block in the '71 Monte Carlo SS 454 had 365 bhp (That was the gross power rating. When Chevrolet switched to more realistic net measurements, the 454's rating dropped to 285 bhp.) Also, the hot LS-6 variant was unavailable in Monte Carlos for '71. *Motor Trend*'s '71 automatic SS 454 Monte did 0-60 mph in 7.1 seconds and the quarter mile in 15.0 at 91.5.

1971 CHEVROLET HIGH-PERFORMANCE ENGINES

TYPE	CID	BORE × STROKE	BHP @ RPM	TORQUE @ RPM	FUEL SYSTEM	COMP. RATIO	AVAIL.
ohv V-8	350	4.00×3.48	270 @ 4800	360 @ 3200	1×4bbl.	8.5:1	1
ohv V-8	350	4.00×3.48	330 @ 5600	360 @ 4000	1×4bbl.	9.0:1	Camaro Z-28
ohv V-8	400	4.13×3.75	255 @ 4400	290 @ 2400	1×2bbl.	8.5:1	Monte Carlo, full size
ohv V-8	402	4.13×3.76	300 @ 4800	400 @ 3200	1×4bbl.	8.5:1	2
ohv V-8	454	4.25×4.00	365 @ 4800	465 @ 3200	1×4bbl.	8.5:1	3
ohv V-8	454*	4.25×4.00	425 @ 5600	475 @ 4000	1×4bbl.	9.0:1	4

* LS-6

1. Camaro, Chevelle, Monte Carlo, Nova, full size. 2. Chevelle SS, Monte Carlo. 3. Chevelle SS, Monte Carlo SS, full size. 4. Corvette.

◀ SS 454s got stouter suspension pieces than other Monte Carlos, but exterior ID was confined to discreet rocker-panel lettering. Testers praised the car's ride and quietness, but said the Turbo Hydra-Matic was dangerously slow to kick down for passing. The rare SS 454 Monte Carlo would not return for '72.

▲ A revised grille marked the '71 Dodge Challenger. Base coupes like this one could get the 383-cid four barrel. It now had 300 bhp, down from 335.

▲ Challenger R/T got new stripes. The 383 was again standard, the 275-bhp 340 and 385-bhp 440 Six-Pack optional. Just 71 of the 4630 R/Ts built got Hemis.

▲ The R/T convertible died, so the only '71 ragtops were base models. A 383 Challenger soft top paced the Indy 500; this replica has the 340, however.

▲ In June 1970, LeRoy Goldstein's Ramchargers Challenger became the first sub-7-second Funny Car. By '71, his Dodge was into the 6.70s at 220 mph.

▲ This colorful Pro-Stock Hemi Challenger was owned by Billy Stepp of Dayton, Ohio. Driven by Stu McDade, it was typical of a host of cars that were very competitive in the NHRA's regional action, but never put together the right run at the right time to win a national championship. This car ran in the 9.70s at 140 mph.

▶ Dick Landy continued his hard-charging ways in this '71 Hemi Challenger. This car wears the fiberglass hood first seen on the '70 Challenger T/A. Landy was a key participant in the Dodge Performance Clinics, in which factory-supported racers toured local Dodge dealerships, dispensing go-fast tips to amateur racers and promoting Mopar hop-up parts and accessories.

▲ This Hemi-powered Dart was among the many cars sponsored by Gratiot, a Michigan high-performance parts dealer. With driver Ron Mancini at the wheel, this car ran in the 10.50s at around 131 mph.

▲ Big-time drag racing was a hot sport in Canada, as demonstrated by this Hemi Demon run by popular Canadian Mopar competitor John Petrie.

▲ Dodge followed Plymouth's successful '70 Duster 340 into the junior-muscle market with the '71 Demon 340. Starting at just $2721, it was a devilish value. Optional hood with fake scoops had trendy tie-down pins.

▲ Chrome exhaust tips and optional rally wheels dressed out the Demon 340. Standard Rallye suspension had heavy-duty components; drum brakes were larger than on other Demons, as were the E70×14 Goodyear Polyglas GT tires.

▼ Dodge chose the "Demon" name after rejecting "Beaver." Of 79,757 Demons built in '71, 10,098 were 340s.

▲ As in other Mopars, Demon's 340-cid four-barrel was rated at 275 bhp. It mated with a three- or four-speed manual or TorqueFlite. A range of axle ratios, from 2.94:1 to 4.10:1, was available. Tipping the scales at just 3165 pounds, the scrappy Demon 340 had a pretty decent power-to-weight ratio. A well-driven three-speed with the 3.23:1 gear could do 0-60 mph in 6.5 seconds and the quarter-mile in 14.5.

1971 DODGE HIGH-PERFORMANCE ENGINES

TYPE	CID	BORE × STROKE	BHP @ RPM	TORQUE @ RPM	FUEL SYSTEM	COMP. RATIO	AVAIL.
ohv V-8	340	4.04×3.31	275 @ 5000	340 @ 3200	1×4bbl.	10.2:1	1
ohv V-8	383	4.25×3.75	275 @ 4400	375 @ 2800	1×2bbl.	8.5:1	2
ohv V-8	383	4.25×3.75	300 @ 4800	410 @ 3400	1×4bbl.	8.5:1	2
ohv V-8	426*	4.25×3.75	425 @ 5000	490 @ 4000	2×4bbl.	10.2:1	Challenger, Charger
ohv V-8	440	4.32×3.75	335 @ 4400	460 @ 3200	1×4bbl.	8.8:1	full size
ohv V-8	440	4.32×3.75	370 @ 4600	480 @ 3200	1×4bbl.	9.5:1	Charger, full size
ohv V-8	440	4.32×3.75	385 @ 4700	490 @ 3200	3×2bbl.	10.3:1	Challenger, Charger

* Hemi.
1. Demon 340, Challenger, Charger. 2. Challenger, Charger, full size.

▲ This was the final year for factory-installed 426 Hemi V-8s. Among the last Dodges to get them was the redesigned Charger. The legendary engine was offered on the R/T and Charger Super Bee models, and added $883.55, not including required extras such as the Sure-Grip differential. Just 85 '71 Hemi Chargers were built.

▶ Charger wore its new Coke-bottle shape on a 115-inch wheelbase, down two inches from '70. R/Ts got a blackout louvered hood, special door skins with simulated air extractors, and Rallye wheels. Spoilers on rear deck and chin were optional.

▲ The R/T came standard with the 440-cid V-8; the four-barrel had 370 bhp, the Six Pack 385.

▲ Vacuum-operated hood scoop helped feed Hemi's dual quads. It was a stock item, unlike the hood-mounted tach.

◀ For '71, the R/T was still Charger's image leader, but it cost $3777, and was outsold by the $3271 Super Bee model, 5054 units to 3118. The only Charger to retain the car's trademark hidden headlamps was the luxury SE model, which started at $3422.

▲ R/Ts and Super Bees with the 383, 440, or Hemi used the four-speed manual with Hurst pistol-grip shifter or the slap-stick TorqueFlite automatic.

▲ Both the 440 Magnum and 426 Hemi could still turn high 13s at over 100 mph—good numbers for any era.

▲ The mighty Hemi still packed a punch. *Motor Trend*'s turned a 13.7 quarter at 104 mph with a 4.10:1 gear.

▲ Hawaiian Roland Leong's Funny Cars were colorful and quick. Butch Maas drove this blown Hemi in the 6.90s at 220 mph.

▼ Super Bee came standard with the 300-bhp four-barrel 383 detuned to run on regular fuel. It also had a bumble-bee graphic hood bulge.

▲ The last Boss was built from the restyled SportsRoof Mustang. It was kin to the 351-cid four-barrel Mach 1, but the Boss 351 had 330 bhp on 11.7:1 compression and mechanical lifters. The Mach 1 had 285 bhp, 10.7:1, and hydraulic lifters. With its larger tires and a fatter sway bar, the Boss handled better, but it cost $4124, to $3268 for the Mach. Just 1806 Boss 351s were built.

▲ With a four-speed and 3.91:1 gear, the Boss 351 ran 0-60 mph in 5.8 seconds and turned the quarter in 14.1 at 100.6 for *Car and Driver*. Top speed was 117 mph.

▲ The new Mustang's added heft compelled some Pro-Stockers to stick with the svelter '70 models. The Polaris drag team did. Here, its coupe is launched by Jerry Baker at the '71 Winternationals.

▶ Fred Stone, Leonard Woods, and Doug Cooke ran a series of successful A/GS Willys in the '60s, but their Funny Cars never won a national event. Mike Van Sant drove this one.

▼ Boss 351 was quicker and more tractable than the earlier Boss 302, but had less character. Ram Air, F60 × 15 tires were standard. Magnum 500 wheels, rear spoiler were options.

▲ Mustang's muscle mainstay for '71 was the new Mach 1, offered with six V-8s that required premium fuel. The fun started with the 285-bhp 351 four-barrel and got serious with the 370-bhp 429 Cobra Jet or 375-bhp Super Cobra Jet. "Drag Pack" editions of both 429s had mechanical lifters, a high-lift cam, and 3.91:1 Traction-Loc or 4.11:1 Detroit Locker. The 429 put more than 850 pounds over the Mach's nose, however, and both handling and traction off the line were problems. A Cobra Jet spun 'em badly out of the hole and ran 0-60 in 6.3 seconds with a 14.6 ET at 99.4 for *Sports Car Graphic*. It had the four-speed and 3.50:1 gears.

1971 FORD HIGH-PERFORMANCE ENGINES

TYPE	CID	BORE × STROKE	BHP @ RPM	TORQUE @ RPM	FUEL SYSTEM	COMP. RATIO	AVAIL.
ohv V-8	351	4.00 × 3.50	285 @ 5400	370 @ 3400	1 × 4bbl.	10.7:1	Torino, Mustang
ohv V-8	351	4.00 × 3.50	330 @ 5400	370 @ 4000	1 × 4bbl.	11.1:1	Mustang Boss 351
ohv V-8	429	4.36 × 3.59	370 @ 5400	450 @ 3400	1 × 4bbl.	11.3:1	Torino, Mustang
ohv V-8	429	4.36 × 3.59	375 @ 5600	450 @ 3400	1 × 4bbl.	11.3:1	Torino, Mustang

▲ Wheelbase was up only one inch, but the '71 Mustang was eight inches longer overall, six inches wider, and 600 pounds heavier than the '70 version. Mach 1 came with a "competition suspension" and F70 × 14 tires. Mag wheels and Ram Air were optional. Note the flexible, body-colored front bumper compared to the Boss 351's chrome piece.

▲ NASCAR banned Mercury's droop-nose Cyclone Spoiler II for '71 (along with the similar Talladega and winged Mopars). But the street Cyclone Spoiler was back with few changes. It was essentially a grand-touring coupe with an attitude. The Spoiler "can best be described as a gentleman's muscle car," concluded *Car and Driver*. Despite its "competition-oriented external appearance [the Spoiler] was carefully developed for minimum intrusion on the occupants' senses," it said.

▲ The senses were in for a rush when the Spoiler had a 429 Cobra Jet (shown). Ford was slower than GM to lower compression ratios, so the CJ still had an 11.3:1 squeeze and 370 bhp. The Super Cobra Jet had an 11.0:1 ratio, mechanical lifters, and 375 bhp. A 370-bhp Cyclone GT did 0-60 mph in 6.4 seconds and the quarter-mile in a respectable 14.5. Standard in the Spoiler was the 285-bhp, 351-cid Cleveland four-barrel. Like the 429s, it required premium gas.

1971 MERCURY HIGH-PERFORMANCE ENGINES

TYPE	CID	BORE × STROKE	BHP @ RPM	TORQUE @ RPM	FUEL SYSTEM	COMP. RATIO	AVAIL.
ohv V-8	351	4.00 × 3.50	300 @ 5400	380 @ 3400	1 × 4bbl.	10.7:1	1
ohv V-8	429	4.36 × 3.59	370 @ 5400	450 @ 3400	1 × 4bbl.	11.3:1	Cougar, Cyclone
ohv V-8	429	4.36 × 3.59	375 @ 5600	450 @ 3400	1 × 4bbl.	11.0:1	Cougar, Cyclone

1. Cougar, Montego, Cyclone.

▲ This pre-production Spoiler photographed at Ford's proving grounds borrows hidden headlamps from the Cyclone GT and has a deep, non-production air dam.

▲ Rear spoiler, side stripe, G70×14 tires, a Hurst-shifted four-speed, and 3.25:1 Traction-Lok axle were standard on Cyclone Spoiler.

◀ Olds followed GM's lead and detuned its engines for '71, but the 4-4-2 W-30 package still meant a factory-blueprinted 455-cid with air-induction hood. Note the weight-saving red plastic fender liners on this W-30.

▼ *Motor Trend* ran two '71 W-30s, both with 3.42:1 gears. The automatic did 0-60 in 6.1 seconds and turned a 14.4 ET at 97 mph. The wide-ratio four-speed hit 60 mph in 6.6 seconds and turned a 14.7 at 97.

▲ 4-4-2s now came only as a $3552 coupe weighing 3688 pounds or as a $3743 convertible at 3731 pounds. The W-30 package added $369. The W-32 and the 350-cid W-31 died.

▲ The 455 still was standard on 4-4-2, but under Olds' net horsepower system (measuring output with all accessories in place), the base 455 got a rating of 260 bhp and the W-30 a rating of 300 bhp.

▲ Regular fuel meant a compression drop to 8.5:1. The base 455 four-barrel (shown) had 340 gross bhp, down 25; the W-30 made 350 gross bhp, down 20.

▲ 4-4-2 cabins bespoke upscale sportiness. A Hurst-stirred four-speed was standard. A Turbo Hydra-Matic 400 was optional—and this one has a Hurst dual-gate shifter.

▲ *Motor Trend* said the 4-4-2 seemed less affected by the switch to regular fuel than many other '71 models, but its acceleration above 60 mph was noticeably weakened.

▲ *Motor Trend* achieved its best launches with the automatic W-30 by "walking" into the throttle, keeping the tires on the verge of spinning, and manually shifting at 5200 rpm. The performance was still there, but '71 4-4-2 production fell to just over 7500 units, 1304 of them ragtops.

1971 OLDSMOBILE HIGH-PERFORMANCE ENGINES

TYPE	CID	BORE × STROKE	BHP @ RPM	TORQUE @ RPM	FUEL SYSTEM	COMP. RATIO	AVAIL.
ohv V-8	350	4.06 × 3.39	260@ 4600	360 @ 3200	1 × 4bbl.	8.5:1	Cutlass
ohv V-8	455	4.12 × 4.25	320 @ 4400	460 @ 2800	1 × 4bbl.	8.5:1	Cutlass, full size
ohv V-8	455	4.12 × 4.25	340 @ 4600	460 @ 3200	1 × 4bbl.	8.5:1	4-4-2
ohv V-8	455	4.12 × 4.25	350 @ 4700	460 @ 3200	1 × 4bbl.	8.5:1	4-4-2

▶ Plymouth's hot little Duster 340 lost none of its performance, but relinquished a little of its sleeper quality for '71. The grille was flashier, and the side stripe now culminated with "340" numerals on the rear fender. The little hummer's cover could be blown completely by ordering an optional flat-back hood treatment emblazoned with "340" script that had the word "Wedge" stenciled within. Groovy.

▲ Plymouth's popular Duster proved a versatile venue for Mopar power and the NHRA seemed to have a class to accommodate it, regardless of the engine.

▲ Even a near-stock 340-cid Duster could find a home—the 1970 "Devil Wind" example shown here ran in G/Stock. It was typical of the locally sponsored cars that were the back-bone of the sport.

▶ Capitalizing on the popularity of the original Duster 340 was the new Duster Twister. Pictured here with a "Curious Yellow" 340 is a "Sassy Grass Green" example. Twister got the 340's grille, mirrors, and wheels (without trim rings). The blackout, strobe-stripe hood was standard, but the non-functioning scoops were optional. Twisters were offered with a pair of six-cylinder engines or the 230-bhp 318-cid two-barrel V-8, which, Plymouth noted, made it easier to insure and cheaper to fuel than the 340.

▲ Duster sales increased 21 percent in '71, but muscle was waning and sales of the 340 fell by half, to 12,866.

▲ Compression slid fractionally from 10.5:1 to 10.2:1, but Plymouth's 340 four-barrel kept its 275-gross-bhp rating. Its net rating was 235 bhp.

▼ The spare beauty of the 1970 'Cuda gave way to a busy grille and fake fender vents, but V-8s from the taut 340 up to the thundering Hemi could still shake things up.

▲ Road Runner was radically restyled for '71. Wheelbase dropped an inch, to 115, rear track widened by three inches for better handling, and the convertible and pillared coupe were retired. With a base price of just $3147, it was still a good muscle value.

▲ The 383 four-barrel fell 35 bhp, to 300, as compression dipped one point, to 8.50:1. Still, *Motor Trend* said the 383 was an all-round better value than the 440 V-8.

▲ *Motor Trend*'s triple-deuce 440 was not as easy to drive in fluctuating traffic as the 383. The larger engine averaged 10.8 mpg, the 383, 11.1, both with automatic.

▲ A reconfigured interior featured improved ergonomics. This Road Runner has the optional tachometer and 14½-inch diameter Tuff steering wheel.

▲ The burly 440 six-barrel resisted major detuning, dropping only five bhp, to 385 (330 net), and losing just a fraction of compression, now at 10.3:1.

▲ The six-barrel 440 added $262, the Air Grabber hood $69, and TorqeFlite $262 to the Road Runner's price. Despite the new skin and the minimally diminished V-8s, Road Runner sales plummeted from 41,484 to 14,218 in '71.

▲ Grabber graphics played to Road Runner's cartoon theme. Performance varied by car and condition. For example, in a heads-up match of '71 automatics, *Motor Trend*'s 383, which cost $4324 with options and had a 3.91:1 gear, turned a 14.84 at 94.5. A 440 six-barrel cost $4638, had a 4.10:1, and managed a 15.02 at 96. In another test, *MT*'s air-conditioned 383 with a 3.23:1 gear and TorqueFlite snoozed to a 15.9 at 84 mph, while a 440 blew its doors with a 14.3 at 100.

▲ This was the final year for the GTX, but it died with its big-cube boots on. The 440 was again standard, the Hemi was optional, and competitive ETs were guaranteed.

▲ This also was the mighty Hemi's swan-song season. It still ruled with 425 bhp, but times had changed. Only 55 were installed in Road Runners, 30 in GTXs.

1971 PLYMOUTH HIGH-PERFORMANCE ENGINES

TYPE	CID	BORE × STROKE	BHP @ RPM	TORQUE @ RPM	FUEL SYSTEM	COMP. RATIO	AVAIL.
ohv V-8	340	4.04×3.31	275 @ 5000	340 @ 3200	1×4bbl.	10.2:1	1
ohv V-8	383	4.25×3.75	300 @ 4800	410 @ 3400	1×4bbl.	8.5:1	2
ohv V-8	426*	4.25×3.75	425 @ 5000	490 @ 4000	2×4bbl.	10.2:1	3
ohv V-8	440	4.32×3.75	335 @ 4400	460 @ 3200	1×4bbl.	8.8:1	full size
ohv V-8	440	4.32×3.75	370 @ 4600	480 @ 3200	1×4bbl.	9.5:1	GTX, full size
ohv V-8	440	4.32×3.75	385 @ 4700	490 @ 3200	3×2bbl.	10.3:1	4

* Hemi.
1. Duster 340, Barracuda, Road Runner. 2. Barracuda, Satellite, full size. 3. Barracuda, Road Runner, GTX.
4. Barracuda, Road Runner, GTX, Sport Fury GT.

▲ Plymouth advertising was among the most creative of the era and, as this promotional shot shows, whimsy was still afoot in '71.

◀ Plymouth's slice of the full-size muscle-car pie was the Sport Fury GT. It bowed for '70 as a member of the Rapid Transit System and returned virtually unchanged for '71. The 440 four-barrel was standard and the six-barrel optional. All had the high-upshift TorqueFlite, dual exhausts with 2¼-inch-diameter tail pipes, heavy-duty suspension with six-leaf rear springs, and meaty H70 × 15 fiberglass-belted tires. The GT went for around $4000 and weighed about 4000 pounds. Few were sold, and the big coupe died after a 1971 production run of just 375.

▲ Firebird changed little after its short '70 model year, though Formula 350 and 455 models joined the Formula 400.

▲ Trans Am's rear spoiler was now an option on all Firebirds. This is a Formula, which started at $3445.

▲ Firebird's 400-cid now made 300 bhp, down 30, after a two-point drop in compression, to 8:2:1. The Ram Air option was back, and the 455 and 455 H.O. were new.

▲ Trans Am's only change was that the 455 H.O. V-8 was now standard. This mill was offered in the cheaper Formula, however, and sales of the $4590 T/A fell to just 2116.

▼GTOs got a revised fascia for '71, and so did The Judge, though the 455 H.O. was now The Judge's only engine. It had 335 bhp, down from the 360 bhp it made in '70.

▲The Judge ran the quarter in 14.9 at 95 mph for *Motor Trend*, compared to a 15.4 at 92 mph for a 300-bhp 400-cid GTO. Zero-60 times were 7.0 for The Judge, 7.1 for the Goat. Both were '71s with a four-speed and 3.55:1 rear axle.

1971 PONTIAC HIGH-PERFORMANCE ENGINES

TYPE	CID	BORE × STROKE	BHP @ RPM	TORQUE @ RPM	FUEL SYSTEM	COMP. RATIO	AVAIL.
ohv V-8	400	4.12 × 3.75	300 @ 4800	400 @ 2400	1 × 4bbl.	8.2:1	1
ohv V-8	455	4.15 × 4.21	325 @ 4400	455 @ 3200	1 × 4bbl.	8.2:1	1
ohv V-8	455	4.15 × 4.21	335 @ 4800	480 @ 3600	1 × 4bbl.	8.4:1	2

1. Grand Prix, GTO, LeMans, Firebird, full size. 2. GTO, LeMans, Trans Am.

▼▶ Judges equipped with the new optional Road Package suspension got 1.25-inch-diameter Trans Am-type front and rear stabilizer bars, the Trans Am steering ratio, 60-series tires on 15×7-inch wheels, and front disc brakes. "The result, when coupled with the coarse pitch M-22 close ratio four-speed, is a very well-behaved package that comes within a whisker of the Trans Am's lateral G capability in cornering," said *Motor Trend*. Braking was excellent, the editors said, but the downside was a very harsh ride.

▲ Court adjourned: Insurance rates and changing tastes retired The Judge in midyear after just 357 hardtops and 17 convertibles had been built.

◀ The '71 Ram Air 455 had fewer horses than the previous optional Ram Air 400 IV, but it had much more torque at lower rpm. Not exactly tractable, it was still better behaved on the street than the high-strung 400 IV.

▲ The GTO's standard 400-cid V-8 was rated at 300 bhp. This is one of only 661 GTO convertibles built for '71; 9497 hardtops were produced.

▲ Royal Pontiac had been at it for nearly a decade by '71, and its Ponchos, including this Firebird, were just as formidable in Super Stock as they were on the street.

▲ Nose elevated as the weight transfers; low-pressure slicks wrinkling as they bite; driver hunched forward in concentration—a classic car in a classic pose.

▲ Linda Vaughn, "Miss Hurst Golden Shifter," with the SSJ Hurst. Adding $1150 to a Pontiac Grand Prix J, the conversion included Fire Frost Gold accents, a landau top, a Cadillac Eldorado sunroof, and American Racing wheels. About 450 1970-72 SSJs were built.

1972

Just two years after its peak season, muscle is on the run...All manufacturers now give net horsepower and torque ratings—and even net bhp is down • Nearly all engines now must use low-lead regular gas • Buick GSX is gone...GS 455 Stage 1 continues with 270 bhp • 454-cid V-8 still available in Chevelle and Monte Carlo, but deflated to 270 bhp • Mopar's Hemi and 440 six-barrels are gone • Dodge Charger R/T and Super Bee are gone...meeker Rallye remains • Dodge Challenger R/T is gone...340-cid V-8 is now biggest Challenger/ Barracuda mill • Ford's Torino Cobra is gone...GT Sport with 205-bhp 429 is a pale imitation • Mustang big-blocks and Boss 351 are gone...351 H.O. tops out at 275 bhp • Olds demotes 4-4-2 to an option...W-30 package sticks with 455 V-8 • Plymouth GTX is gone... Road Runner continues with 400- and 440-cid V-8s • GTO demoted to Pontiac LeMans option; available with Trans Am's 300-bhp, 455-cid V-8 • Mike Snively turns record 5.97-second ET in rail dragster at Supernationals • Funny Car hits 235 mph for first time at Supernationals

▲ Javelin AMX wasn't as sharp for '72. Base power was downgraded to the 304-cid V-8, and the previous 360 joined the 401 on the options sheet. All '72 Javs got new taillamps, but the basic '71 styling was unaltered.

▲ Post-1970 Javelins had a curved gauge cluster. Pontiac's 1969-72 Grand Prix had something similar—purely coincidence. Unusual concentric clock/tachometer sat to the right of the central speedometer.

1972 AMC HIGH-PERFORMANCE ENGINES

TYPE	CID	BORE × STROKE	BHP @ RPM	TORQUE @ RPM	FUEL SYSTEM	COMP. RATIO	AVAIL.
ohv V-8	360	4.08×3.44	195 @ 4400	295 @ 2900	1×4bbl.	8.5:1	1
ohv V-8	360	4.08×3.44	220 @ 4400	315 @ 3100	1×4bbl.	8.5:1	1
ohv V-8	401	4.17×3.68	255 @ 4800	345 @ 3300	1×4bbl.	8.5:1	1

1. Matador, Ambassador, Javelin.

▲ Javelin's 401 V-8 option cost $162 and made 255 *net* bhp for '72, as AMC gave up on gross ratings.

▼ Stage 1 455 was down to 270-net bhp for Buick GS. New fabric sunroof was a rare option.

▲ NHRA founder Wally Parks (right) congratulates David Benisek on winning Stock honors at the '72 Winternationals. A TV was part of his prize.

▲ David Benisek's Buick GS copped Stock Class honors at the 1972 NHRA Winternationals in Pomona with a quarter-mile of 13.39 seconds at 87.97 mph.

1972 BUICK HIGH-PERFORMANCE ENGINES

TYPE	CID	BORE × STROKE	BHP @ RPM	TORQUE @ RPM	FUEL SYSTEM	COMP. RATIO	AVAIL.
ohv V-8	350	3.80×3.85	195 @ 4000	290 @ 2800	1×4bbl.	8.5:1	1
ohv V-8	455	4.31×3.90	225 @ 4000	260 @ 2800	1×4bbl.	8.5:1	2
ohv V-8	455	4.31×3.90	250 @ 4000	375 @ 2800	1×4bbl.	8.5:1	3
ohv V-8	455*	4.31×3.90	360 @ 4000	375 @ 2800	1×4bbl.	8.5:1	4
ohv V-8	455*	4.31×3.90	270 @ 4400	390 @ 3000	1×4bbl.	8.5:1	GS 455

* Stage 1.
1. GS, Skylark, LeSabre. 2. GS 455, Centurion, Electra 225, Riviera, Estate Wagon, LeSabre.
3. Riviera, LeSabre, Centurion, Electra 225. 4. Riviera GS, Centurion.

▲ Optional column-mounted automatic and factory 8-track dressed out the already plush GS cabin.

▲ The GSX died, and Buick built just 8575 GS models for '72. Their hood scoops were functional.

▲ Buick cut prices $60-$70 to spur 1972 GS sales. The hardtop started at $3225. The convertible started at $3406, but just 852 ragtops were built.

▲ Despite lower rated power, the '72 Stage 1 GS was still quick. *Motor Trend* clocked 0-60 in 5.8 seconds and 14.1 at 97 mph for the quarter.

◀▲ This was the last year for true Chevelle Super Sport muscle. The top power option, the 454 LS-5, was down to 270 net bhp; the Turbo-Jet "400" fell to 240. The LS-5 went into just 5333 cars, mostly hardtops. Base SS power was a 130-bhp 307, and docile 165- and 175-bhp 350 small-blocks were optional. Another sign of worsening muscle-car times: The "performance" axle was a 3.31:1. LS-5s again came only with a "Rockcrusher" four-speed. Other V-8s offered three- and four-speed manuals, Hydra-Matic, and even a revived Powerglide option.

1972 CHEVROLET HIGH-PERFORMANCE ENGINES

TYPE	CID	BORE × STROKE	BHP @ RPM	TORQUE @ RPM	FUEL SYSTEM	COMP. RATIO	AVAIL.
ohv V-8	350	4.00×3.48	175 @ 4000	280 @ 2400	1×4bbl.	8.5:1	Monte Carlo, Chevelle
ohv V-8	350	4.00×3.48	200 @ 4400	300 @ 2800	1×4bbl.	8.5:1	Camaro SS, Nova
ohv V-8	350	4.00×3.48	255 @ 5600	280 @ 4000	1×4bbl.	9.0:1	Camaro Z-28
ohv V-8	402	4.13×3.76	210 @ 4400	320 @ 2400	1×4bbl.	8.5:1	full size
ohv V-8	402	4.13×3.76	240 @ 4400	345 @ 3200	1×4bbl.	8.5:1	1
ohv V-8	454	4.25×4.00	270 @ 4000	390 @ 3200	1×4bbl.	8.5:1	2

1. Camaro, Chevelle, Monte Carlo. 2. full size, Chevelle, Monte Carlo.

▶ Chevelle SS lost its prominent central grille bar, but '72 styling was mostly a 1970-71 repeat. The Super Sport package itself was also little changed. Total SS production fell to 24,946, out of 370,000 Chevelles. Overall, though, Chevy built 296,000 SS 396s and 454s for 1968-72. No muscle car enjoyed a better five-year run.

▲ Only 5333 LS-5s went into these last true SS Chevelles; included were a handful of SS 454 convertibles.

◀ Air cleaner decal says "400," but this V-8 was still really the 402-cid extension of Chevy's original mid-'60s 396-cid big-block.

▲ This Cream Yellow SS has the popular optional black vinyl top and stripe group. Five-spoke, mag-type wheels were again part of the SS package, and the cowl-induction hood could still be ordered.

▲ Top mill for Dodge's Charger was a 280-bhp 440 four-barrel. R/T Super Bee, and Hemi died.

▲ *Motor Trend*'s 340 four-barrel/automatic Charger turned an ET of 16.2 seconds at 89 mph.

▼ Dodge built 45,361 of its basic '72 Charger hardtops. Wire wheels and vinyl roof shown here were extras. So was V-8 power in lieu of standard Slant Six.

▼ Rallye option with blackened hood bulge was now the performance Charger. The 340 adjusted to its smog gear and ran better than in '71.

1972 DODGE HIGH-PERFORMANCE ENGINES

TYPE	CID	BORE × STROKE	BHP @ RPM	TORQUE @ RPM	FUEL SYSTEM	COMP. RATIO	AVAIL.
ohv V-8	340	4.04 × 3.31	240 @ 4800	290 @ 3600	1 × 4bbl.	8.5:1	1
ohv V-8	400	4.34 × 3.38	225 @ 4800	340 @ 3200	1 × 4bbl.	8.2:1	Charger SE
ohv V-8	400	4.34 × 3.38	255 @ 4800	340 @ 3200	1 × 4bbl.	8.2:1	Charger, Coronet
ohv V-8	440	4.32 × 3.75	230 @ 4400	355 @ 2800	1 × 4bbl.	8.2:1	Monaco
ohv V-8	440	4.32 × 3.75	280 @ 4800	375 @ 3200	1 × 4bbl.	8.2:1	2

1. Demon 340, Challenger, Charger. 2. Charger, Charger SE.

▲ Rallye's instrument panel had simulated wood and a 150-mph speedometer. An AM/FM stereo radio with 8-track tape player was a $358 option.

◀ Challenger entered its third model year with a more extensive facelift. New Rallye model replaced the hot R/T. Black grille, dummy air vents on hood and front fenders, and bodyside stripes identified it. Only 8123 '72 Rallyes were built, reflecting the fast-falling demand for performance and pony cars. Rallye bowed with a mild 318 V-8 as base power, but some were equipped with the optional four-barrel 340, rated at 240 bhp in that year's newly adopted net measure.

▲ Mustang still offered the Mach 1, but graphics were counted on more and more to signal sportiness. A good example was the new Sprint Decor Option, which had white paint, blue hood and rocker stripes, American flag decals on rear fenders, and color-keyed interior.

▶ The redesigned Torino put on pounds and inches. The hot model was this GT Sport fastback on a new 114-inch wheelbase. It was offered with the 429, re-rated to 205 net bhp, but the 248-bhp 351 four-barrel was the best choice. A 161-bhp two-barrel 351 turned an ET of 17.9 at 80 mph for *Motor Trend*.

▲ The Boss retired, and Mach 1 lost its big-block options. Base power was now a lowly 302 with 136 net bhp; the top option was a new 275-horse four-barrel 351 High Output with mandatory four-speed. *Car and Driver*'s did the quarter in 15.1 seconds at 94 mph.

◀ Mach 1's base price was $3053, and 27,675 were built. Overall Mustang volume was well down even from the depressed '71 total, at a bit over 125,000. Big NACA hood ducts were functional with the $985 351 H.O./four-speed combo.

▲ Mercury's Maverick-clone Comet returned for '72 with new four-door models. The GT option shown here remained exclusive to the two-door and cost $173. Hood scoop was fake, but sporty features mated well with optional 302 V-8.

1972 FORD HIGH-PERFORMANCE ENGINES

TYPE	CID	BORE × STROKE	BHP @ RPM	TORQUE @ RPM	FUEL SYSTEM	COMP. RATIO	AVAIL.
ohv V-8	351	4.00×3.50	248 @ 5400	299 @ 3600	1×4bbl.	8.6:1	Torino
ohv V-8	351	4.00×3.50	262 @ 5400	299 @ 3600	1×4bbl.	8.6:1	full size
ohv V-8	351	4.00×3.50	266 @ 5400	301 @ 3600	1×4bbl.	8.6:1	Mustang
ohv V-8	351	4.00×3.50	275 @ 6000	286 @ 3800	1×4bbl.	9.2:1	Mustang
ohv V-8	400	4.00×4.00	172 @ 4000	298 @ 2200	1×2bbl.	8.4:1	full size
ohv V-8	429	4.36×3.59	205 @ 4400	322 @ 2600	1×4bbl.	8.5:1	Torino
ohv V-8	429	4.36×3.59	212 @ 4400	327 @ 2600	1×4bbl.	11.3:1	Thunderbird

▶ Mid-size Mercurys were remodeled along Torino lines for '72. Cyclone was gone with the wind, leaving a new Montego GT fastback as the "muscle" model. Base price was $3346 with standard 302 V-8. The hottest power options included the 351 H.O. and big-block 429.

1972 MERCURY HIGH-PERFORMANCE ENGINES							
TYPE	CID	BORE × STROKE	BHP @ RPM	TORQUE @ RPM	FUEL SYSTEM	COMP. RATIO	AVAIL.
ohv V-8	351	4.00×3.50	262 @ 5400	299 @ 3600	1×4bbl.	8.6:1	Cougar
ohv V-8	351	4.00×3.50	266 @ 5400	301 @ 3600	1×4bbl.	8.6:1	Cougar
ohv V-8	400	4.00×4.00	172 @ 4000	298 @ 2200	1×2bbl.	8.4:1	full size
ohv V-8	429	4.36×3.59	205 @ 4400	322 @ 2600	1×4bbl.	8.5:1	Montego
ohv V-8	429	4.36×3.59	212 @ 4400	327 @ 2600	1×4bbl.	11.3:1	full size
ohv V-8	460	4.32×3.85	224 @ 4400	357 @ 2800	1×4bbl.	8.5:1	full size

▼ Oldsmobile's 4-4-2 reverted to its original status as an option package and was in fact a Cutlass trim/handling group. Even so, production rose a bit over '71, ending at 9845 units. Among them were the final 4-4-2 convertibles.

▲ A special grille was again part of the 4-4-2 package. This example carries the optional four-barrel 350 V-8, rated now at 180 bhp.

▲ All 4-4-2 engines, this 350 included, had lower compression for '71 to run on low-lead gas. FE2 suspension was part of the 4-4-2 package.

1972 OLDSMOBILE HIGH-PERFORMANCE ENGINES							
TYPE	CID	BORE × STROKE	BHP @ RPM	TORQUE @ RPM	FUEL SYSTEM	COMP. RATIO	AVAIL.
ohv V-8	350	4.06×3.39	180 @ 4000	275 @ 2900	1×4bbl.	8.5:1	1
ohv V-8	455	4.13×4.25	225 @ 3600	360 @ 2600	1×4bbl.	8.5:1	full size
ohv V-8	455	4.13×4.25	250 @ 4000	375 @ 2800	1×4bbl.	8.5:1	Toronado, full size
ohv V-8	455	4.13×4.25	270 @ 4400	370 @ 3200	1×4bbl.	8.5:1	Cutlass, Hurst/Olds
ohv V-8	455	4.13×4.25	300 @ 4700	410 @ 3200	1×4bbl.	8.5:1	Cutlass, Hurst/Olds

1. Supreme, Cutlass, F-85, full size.

▲ Blueprinted four-barrel 455-cid W-30 with 300 net bhp remained 4-4-2's top power option. Priced at $599, it again included Cold-Air induction hood.

▲ After a two-year absence, the Hurst/Olds returned as a Cutlass Supreme-based hardtop and convertible. Respective production was 499 and 130.

▲ The '72 H/O convertible paced the Indy 500. W-30 engine and special white paint with gold striping were included on all '72 H/Os.

◀ Olds ads stressed the more affordable 4-4-2. It was available on base Cutlass coupe, S coupe and hardtop, and Cutlass Supreme hardtop and convertible. Package price depending on model was $71-$150—not a bad deal.

▲ Winged wheel insignia of the Indy 500 graced the Hurst/Olds pace car. All '72 H/Os included firm Rallye suspension, dual exhausts, and power front-disc brakes.

▲ Hurst/Olds badge marked the very rare but still very hot limited-edition 4-4-2 hardtop and convertible. Hurst conversions were carried out at the firm's Southfield, Michigan, Headquarters.

▲ "Twister" and "340" versions were back for Plymouth's little-changed Duster. This catalog-illustration car has both. The 340 had a 235-bhp two-barrel and 15,681 went out of the factory.

◄▼ Plymouth quarter-mile veteran Butch Leal campaigned this "California Flash" Duster in NHRA's Pro-Stock Class during '72. A Hemi was under the special domed hood. On the street, *Car and Driver*'s 340 with TorqueFlite and 3.23:1 gears did the quarter in 15.6 at 89.5 mph. It cost $4213 with options and averaged 10-12 mpg on 91-octane gas.

▲ Rear-deck stripes and Air Grabber hood were among the options on the '72 Road Runner, but sales declined to just 7628 for the model year.

▲ Road Runner hardtop started at $3095 with a 255-bhp, 400-cid four-barrel. Hemi, 383, and the 440+6 all succumbed to stricter smog laws.

▲ Step-down power for the Road Runner was the 240-bhp (net) 340 small-block, which used a new Carter Thermo-Quad plastic-bodied four-barrel carb.

1972 PLYMOUTH HIGH-PERFORMANCE ENGINES

TYPE	CID	BORE × STROKE	BHP @ RPM	TORQUE @ RPM	FUEL SYSTEM	COMP. RATIO	AVAIL.
ohv V-8	340	4.04 × 3.31	240 @ 4800	290 @ 3600	1 × 4bbl.	8.5:1	1
ohv V-8	400	4.34 × 3.38	255 @ 4800	340 @ 3200	1 × 4bbl.	8.2:1	2
ohv V-8	440	4.32 × 3.75	230 @ 4400	355 @ 2800	1 × 4bbl.	8.2:1	Fury
ohv V-8	440	4.32 × 3.75	280 @ 4800	375 @ 3200	1 × 4bbl.	8.2:1	Road Runner

1 Duster 340, Barracuda, 'Cuda, Road Runner. 2 Satellite, Road Runner, Fury.

▶ Optional "strobe stripes" spilled from side-facing dummy hood scoops. Though Plymouth's plush GTX was gone, the '72 Road Runner offered a "GTX option"—a four-barrel 440 making 280 net bhp. New two-slot grille was unique to the Road Runner.

▲ Barracuda reverted to a 1970-type grille for '72. Twin-scoop black-finish hood was optional.

▲ Four-barrel 340 with 240 net bhp was the top power option for Plymouth's 1972 Barracuda. Vinyl top and bodyside tape stripes returned at extra cost. 'Cuda production fell to 7828 for the model year.

▲ In the '70s, the late Don Carlton drove a series of "Motown Missile" Plymouths. This is the '72 version. Hoodscoops were evolving to accommodate bigger intakes and carbs.

▲ As before, the Road Runner's front parking/directional lamps were styled to resemble driving lights. The base 400 was essentially a bored-out 383 and like the 340, it breathed through Carter's novel plastic-bodied Thermo-Quad carb. Road Runners still came with a heavy-duty suspension and brakes, three-speed floor-mounted stick, F70×14 tires, and 150-mph speedometer; a tach was optional. This would be the last year for a Road Runner with anything like the original's sizzle. At least the horn still went "beep-beep."

▼ As with the Olds 4-4-2, Pontiac's GTO was demoted to option status and looked all but identical to the '71 models. No '72 Goat ragtops are known.

▲ GTO production fell to just 5807, but body-color Endura nose remained neat and functional. Wide hood "nostrils" are also functional on this car, which carries the 455 High Output four-barrel with Ram Air, a combo good for 300 net bhp.

▲ *Motor Trend*'s 455 H.O. four-speed with 3.55:1 gears turned a 15.4 at 92 mph. *MT* said the 455's cam shook the whole car at idle. The engine tended to bog so it had to be launched at 3400 rpm, thereby incurring massive wheelspin.

1972 PONTIAC HIGH-PERFORMANCE ENGINES

TYPE	CID	BORE × STROKE	BHP @ RPM	TORQUE @ RPM	FUEL SYSTEM	COMP. RATIO	AVAIL.
ohv V-8	400	4.12×3.75	200@4000	295@2800	1×4bbl.	8.2:1	LeMans, Catalina
ohv V-8	400	4.12×3.75	250@4400	325@3200	1×4bbl.	8.2:1	1
ohv V-8	455	4.15×4.21	220@3600	350@2400	1×4bbl.	8.2:1	full size
ohv V-8	455	4.15×4.21	230@4400	360@2800	1×4bbl.	8.2:1	LeMans, GTO
ohv V-8	455	4.15×4.21	250@3600	375@2400	1×4bbl.	8.2:1	2
ohv V-8	455	4.15×4.21	300@4000	415@3200	1×4bbl.	8.4:1	3

1. Grand Prix, GTO, Formula 400, LeMans, Catalina. 2. LeMans, GTO, Grand Prix, full size. 3. Trans Am, LeMans, GTO, Firebird Formula 455.

▲ A 300-bhp 455 H.O. topped a limited '72 GTO power slate. That year's base 400 and "regular" 455 option both made 250 net bhp; the latter required automatic. Axle ratios ranged from 3.08 to just 3.55:1.

▲ Firebird Trans Am continued as racy as ever, and the price was cut $340 to $4256 list, presumably to spark sales. But the public's continued drift away from performance combined with a factory strike to hold T/A production to just 1286 for the model year.

▶ Trans Am's shaker-hood 455 H.O. returned with 300 net bhp, down from 1971's 335 gross figure. Torque also fell. A four-speed manual replaced a three-speed as standard. *Car and Driver* ran one with 3.42:1 gears to 60 mph in just 5.4 seconds and through the quarter in 13.9 at 104.6 mph.

1973

Horsepower, torque, and compression ratings continue downward spiral ... muscle cars going, going—most are gone • OPEC oil embargo leads to severe fuel shortage, with long lines, price hikes, and threat of rationing • Big blocks hold out against the tide • A 429 is still available in the Ford Torino, but at 201 bhp • 455s survive in Pontiac Firebird Formula and Trans Am with up to 310 bhp • Final season for Chevelle's 454, now 245 bhp; 400- and 402-cid engines gone, SS option survives • Mopar allows 280-bhp 440 four-barrels into Charger and Road Runner • GM's "Colonnade" styling helps kill off pillarless hardtops and convertibles • Buick Gran Sport option returns with 270 bhp in Stage 1 • Big-cube and SS options depart from Camaro; Z-28 drops to 245 bhp from hydraulic-lifter 350 V-8 • John Wiebe's Top Fuel ET is 6.49 at 227.27 mph...Funny Cars are not far behind: "Soapy Sales" Dodge is quickest at 6.71 (222.77 mph) • Super Stockers run in the mid-10s; "Grumpy" Jenkins's Pro Stock Camaro turns a 9.02 at 150.25

▲ Javelin AMX was mostly a carryover, but tail/backup lamps were slightly different. Brochures still touted Jav's racing successes, and the 401 V-8 option was back with 255 bhp (net), but comfort, rear-seat room, and even warranty coverage received increasing ad emphasis.

▲ Despite few changes, the Javelin AMX recorded its highest model-year production for 1973, with 4737 units, about 18 percent of the Javelin total. AMC design chief Dick Teague had penned a two-seat AMX with this same basic design, but it was shot down for lack of sufficient anticipated sales.

1973 AMC HIGH-PERFORMANCE ENGINES

TYPE	CID	BORE × STROKE	BHP @ RPM	TORQUE @ RPM	FUEL SYSTEM	COMP. RATIO	AVAIL.
ohv V-8	360	4.08×3.44	195 @ 4400	295 @ 2900	1×4bbl.	8.5:1	1
ohv V-8	360	4.08×3.44	220 @ 4400	315 @ 3100	1×4bbl.	8.5:1	1
ohv V-8	401	4.17×3.68	255 @ 4800	345 @ 3300	1×4bbl.	8.5:1	1

1. Matador, Ambassador, Javelin.

▲ Dark blue paint and discreet "PC" front-fender badge identifies this '73 Javelin AMX as having that year's new Pierre Cardin trim package. Mesh over headlamps on car below is not stock.

▲ The 401 four-barrel teamed with a four-speed manual or optional Torque Command automatic. A 195-bhp 360 four-barrel also was a popular AMX choice.

◄▲ Tri-color interior trim dressed out Pierre Cardin-equipped AMX. "Designer editions" were a relatively cheap way to put new sparkle in aging models. Note the matching headliner (left). For more substance, "Go" suspension/axle packages were still available at $428 for the 360 V-8 and $476 for the 401. Power front disc brakes added $79 to Javelin AMX's $3191 base price.

▲ Though not as potent as earlier Stage 1 Gran Sports, Buick's new Century-based 1973 edition was among the rarest: just 728 built. Basic GS package added $173 to Century coupe's $3057 list.

▲ The 455 was available on all Century coupes, but the Stage 1 was a GS exclusive. Priced at $546, it had 270 net bhp via hotter cam and heads, Quadra-Jet carb, twin-snorkel air cleaner, and dual exhausts. Only seven were built with manual transmission; all others had THM 400 automatic.

▲ Black-finish grille and headlamp bezels identified the '73 Gran Sport. Standard 14×7 five-spoke wheels wore low-profile bias-belt tires.

▲ Gran Sport came standard with the same 150-bhp, 350-cid two-barrel as other Centurys, though only GS models could get the 190-bhp four-barrel 350.

▲ All the General Motors intermediates were restyled for '73, but retained the 116-inch wheelbase. Buick resurrected the Century name for its version, and the GS built upon the Colonnade coupe.

▲ "Stage 1" front-fender badge signaled that 390 pounds/feet of torque awaited. A good thing the '73 Stage 1 package included a limited-slip rear differential.

1973 BUICK HIGH-PERFORMANCE ENGINES

TYPE	CID	BORE × STROKE	BHP @ RPM	TORQUE @ RPM	FUEL SYSTEM	COMP. RATIO	AVAIL.
ohv V-8	350	3.80 × 3.85	190 @ 4000	285 @ 2800	1×4bbl.	8.5:1	1
ohv V-8	455	4.31 × 3.90	250 @ 4000	375 @ 2800	1×4bbl.	8.5:1	2
ohv V-8	455*	4.31 × 3.90	260 @ 4400	380 @ 2800	1×4bbl.	8.5:1	3
ohv V-8	455*	4.31 × 3.90	270 @ 4400	390 @ 3000	1×4bbl.	8.5:1	4

* Stage 1.
1. Gran Sport, Century, LeSabre Centurion. 2. Century, LeSabre, Centurion, Electra 225, Riviera. 3. Riviera, Centurion. 4. Century Gran Sport.

▲ New Chevelle Laguna was Chevy's mid-size. The SS group returned on 28,647 cars at $243; 2500 also had the 454 V-8, another $235.

▲ Chevy's Camaro aimed more toward luxury touring with 1973's new Type LT. RS and Z-28 were still around, but as packages. LT started at $3268.

1973 CHEVROLET HIGH-PERFORMANCE ENGINES							
TYPE	CID	BORE × STROKE	BHP @ RPM	TORQUE @ RPM	FUEL SYSTEM	COMP. RATIO	AVAIL.
ohv V-8	350	4.00 × 3.48	175 @ 4000	260 @ 2800	1 × 4bbl.	8.5:1	1
ohv V-8	350	4.00 × 3.48	245 @ 5200	280 @ 4000	1 × 4bbl.	9.0:1	Camaro Z-28
ohv V-8	400	4.13 × 3.75	150 @ 3200	295 @ 2000	1 × 4bbl.	8.5:1	full size
ohv V-8	454	4.25 × 4.00	245 @ 4000	375 @ 2800	1 × 4bbl.	8.5:1	2

1. Camaro, Chevelle, Monte Carlo, Nova, full size. 2. Chevelle, Monte Carlo, full size.

▲ Rallye became a $182 option on Dodge's $3011 Challenger. The 240-bhp 340 four-barrel returned as the top mill and added $181.

▲ Chevelle Laguna shows the new Colonnade look of all '73 GM intermediates. Besides this "hardtop," Laguna also came as a sedan and wagon.

▼ The Dodge Demon was facelifted for '73 to become the Dart Sport. Hot 340 V-8 was standard, again with 240 bhp.

▲ Dodge built only 11,315 Dart Sport 340s for 1973, despite a base price of just $2793. Sunroof and fold-down rear seat were new extras.

▶ Chrysler's small-block 340 was in its final year for '73, but would return as an upsized 360. Dodge put it in the Dart Sport and in the Rallye versions of the Challenger and Charger. Times had changed since the "Scat Pack" days.

▲ Charger changed little for '73. Luxury SE got hammy triple opera windows, but outsold standard hardtop and coupe. Rallye option ($182), now available with any V-8, again included a beefed chassis and "power bulge" hood.

1973 DODGE HIGH-PERFORMANCE ENGINES

TYPE	CID	BORE × STROKE	BHP @ RPM	TORQUE @ RPM	FUEL SYSTEM	COMP. RATIO	AVAIL.
ohv V-8	340	4.04×3.31	240 @ 4800	295 @ 3600	1×4bbl.	8.5:1	1
ohv V-8	400	4.34×3.38	260 @ 4800	335 @ 3600	1×4bbl.	8.2:1	2
ohv V-8	440	4.32×3.75	220 @ 3600	350 @ 2400	1×4bbl.	8.2:1	full size
ohv V-8	440	4.32×3.75	280 @ 4800	380 @ 3200	1×4bbl.	8.2:1	2

1. Demon 340 Sport, Challenger, Charger. 2. Charger, Charger SE, Coronet.

1973 FORD HIGH-PERFORMANCE ENGINES

TYPE	CID	BORE × STROKE	BHP @ RPM	TORQUE @ RPM	FUEL SYSTEM	COMP. RATIO	AVAIL.
ohv V-8	351	4.00×3.50	246 @ 5400	312 @ 3600	1×4bbl.	8.0:1	full size, Torino
ohv V-8	351	4.00×3.50	259 @ 5600	292 @ 3400	1×4bbl.	7.9:1	Mustang
ohv V-8	429	4.36×3.59	201 @ 4400	322 @ 2600	1×4bbl.	8.0:1	full size, Torino

▲ Mach 1 was again the hottest Ford Mustang for '73, but that only meant a standard 302 V-8 with 136 net bhp. "Fat" generation was in its final year.

▲ Ford's mid-engine GT40 and Mark IV racers allegedly inspired the sweeping roofline of 1971-73 Mustang fastbacks. This one has optional aluminum wheels, customized by painting the slots body color.

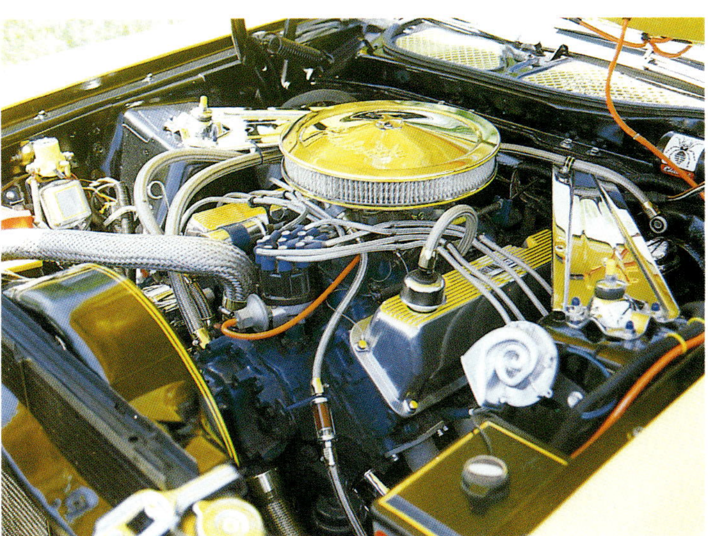

▲ Top Mustang engine for '73 was still the four-barrel 351 Cleveland, shown here. Output was down to about 260 net. This one has abundant custom touches, including chrome accessories and body-color accents.

▲ With real muscle nearly extinct, the '73 Hurst/Olds was a standout. A 455 V-8, Hurst Dual-Gate shifter, "wet look" all-vinyl interior, and heavy-duty suspension were included, said Hurst, "for the man in motion."

▲ Note tiny "opera" windows on this handsome '73 Hurst/Olds. The H/O was technically an option package W-45 for that year's Cutlass S coupe.

▲ Hurst built 1097 of the '73 H/Os, all with gold accents. About 40 percent had black paint, the rest were Cameo White. Car shown here also has the rare factory sunroof option. Olds also offered a 4-4-2 for '73, but it was just a $121 cosmetic package with heavy-duty suspension thrown in. Production isn't available, having been lumped in with workaday Cutlass coupe figures.

▲ If real Olds muscle was a thing of the past, at least the Hurst/Olds still looked the part—though the standard half-vinyl top clashed with the image. Still, this was an executive hot rod, not a bad-boy street sweeper. Hurst-brand options included a digital tachometer, air shocks, and anti-theft alarm.

◀ Hurst declined to state horsepower for the '73 H/O, but the figure was likely in the region of 250 net for the "L77" Olds 455. That big-block mated only to a Turbo Hydra-Matic 400 with Hurst dual-gate shifter. Other functional '73 standards were power front-disc brakes, Rallye suspension, Super Stock III wheels, GR60-14 Goodrich Radial T/A tires, and the louvered "Nassau" hood duct. Options included a digital tach, air shocks, alarm system, and "loc lugs," all courtesy of Hurst.

1973 OLDSMOBILE HIGH-PERFORMANCE ENGINES

TYPE	CID	BORE × STROKE	BHP @ RPM	TORQUE @ RPM	FUEL SYSTEM	COMP. RATIO	AVAIL.
ohv V-8	350	4.06 × 3.39	180 @ 3800	275 @ 2800	1 × 4bbl.	8.5:1	1
ohv V-8	455	4.13 × 4.25	250 @ 4000	370 @ 2100	1 × 4bbl.	8.5:1	1
ohv V-8	455	4.13 × 4.25	250 @ 4000	375 @ 2800	1 × 4bbl.	8.5:1	Toronado
ohv V-8	455	4.13 × 4.25	275 @ 3600	360 @ 2600	1 × 4bbl.	8.5:1	2

1. Supreme, Cutlass, Vista-Cruiser. 2. Delta 88, Delta 88 Royale, Custom Cruiser, 98, 98 Luxury.

▲ Recalling Chrysler circa 1960, Olds offered swivel front bucket seats as a '73 Cutlass option. That year's Hurst/Olds had them standard. H/O dash was pretty much stock Cutlass, so instrumentation wasn't generous.

1973 PLYMOUTH HIGH-PERFORMANCE ENGINES

TYPE	CID	BORE × STROKE	BHP @ RPM	TORQUE @ RPM	FUEL SYSTEM	COMP. RATIO	AVAIL.
ohv V-8	340	4.04 × 3.31	240 @ 4800	295 @ 3600	1 × 4bbl.	8.5:1	1
ohv V-8	400	4.34 × 3.38	260 @ 4800	335 @ 3600	1 × 4bbl.	8.2:1	2
ohv V-8	440	4.32 × 3.75	220 @ 3600	350 @ 2400	1 × 4bbl.	8.2:1	Fury
ohv V-8	440	4.32 × 3.75	280 @ 4800	380 @ 3200	1 × 4bbl.	8.2:1	Road Runner

1. Duster 340, Barracuda, 'Cuda, Road Runner. 2. Satellite, Road Runner.

▲Plymouth's Duster 340 lost compression, but survived with 240 bhp. Price was $2822; 15,731 were built.

▲"Pistol grip" four-speed shifter by Hurst was popular on '70s Plymouths.

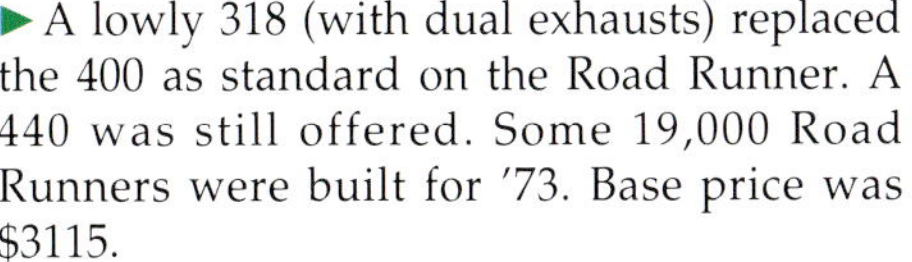

►A lowly 318 (with dual exhausts) replaced the 400 as standard on the Road Runner. A 440 was still offered. Some 19,000 Road Runners were built for '73. Base price was $3115.

▲Things were hotter than ever at the drags. Here, Mickey Thompson's '73 Pontiac Grand Am Funny Car smokes away at the Winternationals in Pomona.

▲Firebird bucked the trend: Sales of the Trans Am (shown) nearly quadrupled, to 4802, while sales of the Formula nearly doubled, to 10,166.

◀ The '73 Firebirds were the first to wear the giant "screaming chicken" hood decals, but the real news was underneath. Trans Am retained 455-cid power. The base unit had 250 bhp. Available was the big-port 455 Super Duty, which started the year rated at 310 bhp, but was revised to 290.

▲ Standard on the Formula was a 350-cid two-barrel, but a 400 and both 455s were offered. Both T/A and Formula were among the few really hot cars left.

▲ Formulas with the Ram-Air option got the fiberglass hood with lovely functional scoops. The 455 SD brought the Trans Am hood and rear-facing air inlet, regardless of model.

◀ Both Formula and T/A balanced their big blocks with wide tires and stiff suspensions, so handling was quite competent. Formula came with a three-speed manual, Trans Am a four-speed. Automatic was optional with any mill.

1973 PONTIAC HIGH-PERFORMANCE ENGINES

TYPE	CID	BORE × STROKE	BHP @ RPM	TORQUE @ RPM	FUEL SYSTEM	COMP. RATIO	AVAIL.
ohv V-8	400	4.12×3.75	200 @ 4000	310 @ 2400	1×4bbl.	8.0:1	full size
ohv V-8	400	4.12×3.75	230 @ 4400	325 @ 3200	1×4bbl.	8.0:1	1
ohv V-8	455	4.15×4.21	215 @ 3600	350 @ 2400	1×4bbl.	8.0:1	full size
ohv V-8	455	4.15×4.21	250 @ 4000	370 @ 2800	1×4bbl.	8.0:1	2
ohv V-8	455	4.15×4.21	290 @ 4000	390 @ 3600	1×4bbl.	8.4:1	3

1. Grand Prix, GTO, Formula 400, LeMans, Grand Am, Formula 400, Catalina, Bonneville. 2. Trans Am, Grand Prix, full size, GTO, LeMans, Formula 455. 3. Trans Am, Formula 455.

▲ Second-generation Firebird styling, always good, was purest through '73, the last year before safety bumpers.

1974

Fuel crisis eases, but the die is cast for the end of the muscle-car era • GTO nameplate returns for one final season, but on an embarrassing Nova-like Pontiac Ventura compact • Pontiac's Super Duty 455-equipped Firebirds carry the torch with 290 bhp...sales soar • No V-8 is available on the new downsized Mustang II...four-cylinder and V-6 are only engines • Buick's top Gran Sport 455 enters its final model year, slips to 255 horsepower • Camaro Z-28 goes into hibernation at the end of the model year • Laguna Type S-3 replaces the Super Sport Chevelle • Dodge Challenger enters last season with Mopar's new 360 as top V-8 • Dodge Charger Rallye can still have 400- or 440-cid V-8 • Dodge Dart and Plymouth Duster get 360-cid V-8 choice ... Barracuda built for last time • Road Runner is sole Plymouth with top (275-bhp) 440 option • Olds 4-4-2 loses solid-lifter V-8 and four-speed; cold air induction remains as an option • Hurst/Olds paces Indy 500 • Wayne Gapp's Pro Stock Maverick turns an 8.95 at 153.06 mph • Top Fuel dragsters hit 5.98 at 247.25

▲ Javelin's swan-song '74s: the base model (background) and sportier AMX. The latter retained its standard 304 V-8, as well as 360- and 401-cid options. AMX production came to only 4980 of nearly 25,000 Javelins built.

▲ AMC never had a well-financed factory drag-racing effort, and its Hornet was an unlikely competitor even in Pro Stock. But the compact did wage war on the strip, including this hatch coupe at the 1974 Gatornationals in Gainesville, Florida.

▲ Another Hornet that aimed its sting at the strip was Maskin and Kanner's 1974 hatch coupe. Here, it approaches the Christmas tree for a qualifying run at that year's NHRA Winternationals in Pomona.

▲ AMX held out to the end with an available big-block in the 255-bhp 401. Starting price was $3299, and improved compatibility with emissions hardware allowed the 3350-pound coupe to turn quarter-miles in the mid-15s.

▲ Go-Packages also survived, and included Rally-Pac gauges with a tach and power front disc brakes. A four-speed with Hurst shifter was offered on AMX.

1974 AMC HIGH-PERFORMANCE ENGINES

TYPE	CID	BORE × STROKE	BHP @ RPM	TORQUE @ RPM	FUEL SYSTEM	COMP. RATIO	AVAIL.
ohv V-8	360	4.08 × 3.44	195 @ 4400	295 @ 2900	1×4bbl.	8.25:1	1
ohv V-8	360	4.08 × 3.44	220 @ 4400	315 @ 3100	1×4bbl.	8.25:1	2
ohv V-8	401	4.17 × 3.68	255 @ 4800	345 @ 3300	1×4bbl.	8.25:1	2

1. Hornet, Matador, Ambassador, Javelin. 2. Matador, Ambassador, Javelin.

▲ With the proud Super Sport gone for '74, the Laguna Type S-3 carried Chevelle's performance flag with two- or four-barrel 350-cid V-8s, or the available 454 with 235 bhp, the latter capable of high-15-second ETs.

▲ Starting at $3951, the Type S-3 came with a body-colored rubberized front grille, swivel bucket seats, 15×7 Rallye wheels, and special shocks. Chevy built 15,792 for 1974.

▲ With Mustang gelded, Camaro sales boomed. The $600 Z-28 package returned for its last year with a 245-bhp 350 and ETs in the mid-15s.

▲ Ironically, the only SS Chevy for '74 was a version of the Nova. Trim packages like this "Spirit of America" were more indicative of the times, though.

1974 CHEVROLET HIGH-PERFORMANCE ENGINES							
TYPE	CID	BORE × STROKE	BHP @ RPM	TORQUE @ RPM	FUEL SYSTEM	COMP. RATIO	AVAIL.
ohv V-8	350	4.00×3.48	185 @ 4000	270 @ 2600	1×4bbl.	8.5:1	1
ohv V-8	350	4.00×3.48	245 @ 5200	280 @ 4000	1×4bbl.	9.0:1	Camaro Z-28
ohv V-8	400	4.13×3.75	180 @ 3200	290 @ 2000	1×4bbl.	8.5:1	2
ohv V-8	454	4.25×4.00	235 @ 4000	375 @ 2800	1×4bbl.	8.5:1	3

1. Camaro, Chevelle, Monte Carlo, Nova, full size. 2. Chevelle, Monte Carlo, full size. 3. Chevelle, Monte Carlo, full size.

▼ Mopar enlarged its well-regarded 340-cid V-8 to 360 cubes and used the 245-bhp small-block as the Dodge Challenger's top option. The basic Rallye package shown here cost $190 and included fake fender scoops. Challenger wouldn't answer the bell for the '75 round, and hung it up after '74 with a final run of 16,437 units.

▲ A 318-cid V-8 was standard in Challenger, which started at $3143. The 360 V-8 added $259 and was also offered on the base model. A three-speed manual was standard, with a four-speed and TorqueFlite optional. This Rallye package-equipped example wears an optional vinyl roof ($84). Bumper guards were larger this year to comply with the federal 5-mph protection decree.

▲ Rallye trim included side strobe stripes, fake hood scoops, and F70×14 white-letter tires on special cast wheels with trim rings.

▲ Dodge's Dart Sport 340 became a 360 for '74—if you ordered that newly enlarged four-barrel V-8. Few people did: just 3951 for the model year.

1974 DODGE HIGH-PERFORMANCE ENGINES							
TYPE	CID	BORE × STROKE	BHP @ RPM	TORQUE @ RPM	FUEL SYSTEM	COMP. RATIO	AVAIL.
ohv V-8	360	4.00×3.58	200 @ 4000	290 @ 3200	1×4bbl.	8.4:1	1
ohv V-8	360	4.00×3.58	245 @ 4800	320 @ 3600	1×4bbl.	8.4:1	2
ohv V-8	400	4.34×3.38	205 @ 4400	310 @ 3400	1×4bbl.	8.2:1	3
ohv V-8	400	4.34×3.38	250 @ 4800	330 @ 3400	1×4bbl.	8.2:1	3
ohv V-8	440	4.32×3.75	230 @ 4000	350 @ 3200	1×4bbl.	8.2:1	full size
ohv V-8	440	4.32×3.75	275 @ 4400	375 @ 3200	1×4bbl.	8.2:1	4

1. Coronet, Charger, full size. 2. Dart 360 Sport, Challenger, Charger. 3. Coronet, Charger, full size. 4. Charger, Coronet.

▲ Charger got a minor facelift, but the 150-bhp 318 V-8 returned as standard. The four-barrel 440 was still around as the top power option, delivering a healthy 275 net bhp, good for ETs in the mid-15-second range. This is the top-line SE model. The Rallye option returned for the base coupe and hardtop; it cost only $100.

◀ Richard Petty won his second straight Daytona 500 in a '74 Charger, and accounted for all 10 of Dodge's NASCAR victories on his way to the driver's title. His mount was a far cry from this SE, which, despite its $3742 base price, was the top-selling model with 36,399 built out of 74,376 Chargers.

▲ Still going strong—or what passed for it in 1974—was the jazzy Hurst/Olds, which was patterned on the '74 Indy 500 pace car. Many of the 380 built were actually used in the Indy fleet, though not necessarily on the track.

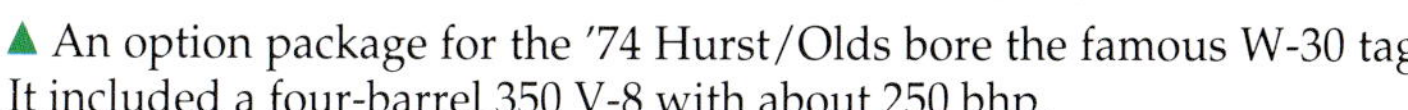

▲ An option package for the '74 Hurst/Olds bore the famous W-30 tag. It included a four-barrel 350 V-8 with about 250 bhp.

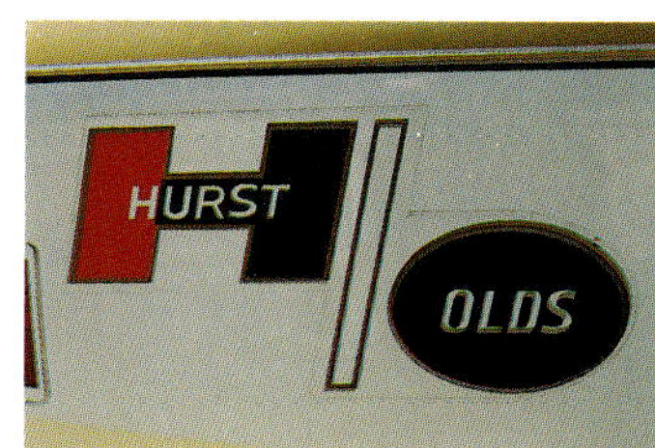

▲ The basic Hurst/Olds package was similar to 1973's save the W-30 engine option and modified styling shared with its Cutlass S "parent."

▼ Road Runner was demoted to an option on the base Plymouth Satellite for '74. It still came with a "power bulge" hood—but no more power. New 360 small-block replaced the 340 option, but the 440 four-barrel was back. Base price that year was $3444—again with 318 V-8.

1974 OLDSMOBILE HIGH-PERFORMANCE ENGINES

TYPE	CID	BORE × STROKE	BHP @ RPM	TORQUE @ RPM	FUEL SYSTEM	COMP. RATIO	AVAIL.
ohv V-8	455	4.13×4.25	230 @ 4000	370 @ 2100	1×4bbl.	8.5:1	Toronado
ohv V-8	455	4.13×4.25	250 @ 4000	375 @ 2800	1×4bbl.	8.5:1	1
ohv V-8	455	4.13×4.25	275 @ 3600	360 @ 2600	1×4bbl.	8.5:1	1

1. Cutlass, Vista Cruiser.

▼ Bird decals continued on '74 Road Runners, but former standards like a performance-axle and heavy-duty suspension were now options. Only 11,555 were built for the model year.

▲ Duster remained the most popular Plymouth, but most were the garden variety like this, not the sporty new $3288 Duster 360, which replaced the familiar 340 package and could turn 15.8-second ETs.

▲ Plymouth's Barracuda was beached after a '74 output of just 11,734; only 4989 were 'Cudas (foreground). The 340 was supplanted by the new 245-horse 360 as the "performance" V-8 option.

1974 PLYMOUTH HIGH-PERFORMANCE ENGINES

TYPE	CID	BORE × STROKE	BHP @ RPM	TORQUE @ RPM	FUEL SYSTEM	COMP. RATIO	AVAIL.
ohv V-8	360	4.00 × 3.58	200 @ 4000	290 @ 3200	1 × 4bbl.	8.4:1	1
ohv V-8	360	4.00 × 3.58	245 @ 4800	320 @ 3600	1 × 4bbl.	8.4:1	2
ohv V-8	400	4.34 × 3.38	205 @ 4400	310 @ 3400	1 × 4bbl.	8.2:1	1
ohv V-8	400	4.34 × 3.38	250 @ 4800	330 @ 3400	1 × 4bbl.	8.2:1	3
ohv V-8	440	4.32 × 3.75	230 @ 4000	350 @ 3200	1 × 4bbl.	8.2:1	full size
ohv V-8	440	4.32 × 3.75	275 @ 4400	375 @ 3200	1 × 4bbl.	8.2:1	3

1. Satellite, full size. 2. Duster 360, 'Cuda, Road Runner. 3. Satellite, Road Runner.

1974 PONTIAC HIGH-PERFORMANCE ENGINES

TYPE	CID	BORE × STROKE	BHP @ RPM	TORQUE @ RPM	FUEL SYSTEM	COMP. RATIO	AVAIL.
ohv V-8	350	3.88 × 3.75	170 @ 4000	290 @ 2400	1 × 4bbl.	7.6:1	1
ohv V-8	350	3.88 × 3.75	200 @ 4400	295 @ 2800	1 × 4bbl.	7.6:1	2
ohv V-8	400	4.12 × 3.75	200 @ 4000	320 @ 2400	1 × 4bbl.	8.0:1	full size
ohv V-8	400	4.12 × 3.75	225 @ 4000	330 @ 2800	1 × 4bbl.	8.0:1	3
ohv V-8	455	4.15 × 4.21	215 @ 3600	355 @ 2400	1 × 4bbl.	8.0:1	full size
ohv V-8	455	4.15 × 4.21	250 @ 4000	370 @ 2800	1 × 4bbl.	8.0:1	4
ohv V-8	455	4.15 × 4.21	290 @ 4000	390 @ 3600	1 × 4bbl.	8.4:1	5

1. Ventura, LeMans. 2. GTO, Ventura, LeMans. 3. Grand Prix, Trans Am, Formula 400, LeMans, Grand Am. 4. Grand Am, Grand Prix, full size. 5. Trans Am, Formula 455.

▼ Pontiac's 1974 Firebird was deftly restyled to accommodate new federal "crash bumpers" without ruffling its great-looking feathers. Trans Am remained top of the line with a $4446 base price; 10,255 were built for the model year.

▲ This Buccaneer Red 1974 T/A shows off that year's newly optional "honeycomb" body-color wheels. Just visible is the "screaming chicken" hood decal, which cost $55. Front- and rear-wheel "spats" remained standard for all T/As.

▲ Early second-generation Firebirds had these high-back "Strato" front buckets. Shift console was a separate extra.

▲ T/A's Super-Duty 455 again made 290 net bhp for '74.

1975-81

Performance hibernates . . . safety, environmental, and fuel issues alter automotive landscape • Big-inch engines fade . . . Chevy drops 454 after '76 . . . Firebird loses 455 after '76, 400 after '79 . . . Mopar's 440 goes away after '78 • Horsepower mostly declines . . . highest in '75 is 235 in Mopar 440 . . . by 1980 only turbocharged Firebird tops 190 • Manufacturers attempt to replace lost performance with flashy visuals . . . an era of bulky tacked-on body panels and gaudy graphics emerges • Legendary muscle car models disappear . . . most that survive are weak, name-only versions • Camaro Z-28 and Firebird Trans Am are considered to be last somewhat credible holdouts . . . they sell briskly, but merely hint at the performance of their forebears • Mustang is redesigned for '79 . . . clean styling and sophisticated chassis offer hope for enthusiasts . . . but weak 140-bhp 302-cid V-8 continues, then is replaced by a 115-bhp 255-cid V-8 for '80

▲ For '75, Road Runner was an option on Plymouth's new midsize Fury line. Blocky facelift was a snooze, but a hint of performance remained in 180-bhp, 360-cid and 260-bhp, 440-cid four-barrel options.

▲ Trans Am lost its 455 V-8 for '75, regained it for '76, then dropped it for good after that. Base price for this '76 T/A was $4987. The 455 was a $150 option. The top engine provided decent performance, with *Motor Trend* driving a '76 455 T/A to low 16-second ETs and a 120-mph top speed. Sales steadily grew as Trans Am's rivals disappeared; 46,701 were built for '76, 68,745 for '77, and 93,341 for '78.

▶ Redesigned Chrysler Corporation compacts were introduced for '76, carrying Plymouth Volare and Dodge Aspen nameplates. Performance versions were Road Runner and R/T, respectively, which differed mainly in their trim. Standard engine on both was a six, but 318- or 360-cid V-8s were optional, the latter producing 175-bhp. This '77 Aspen R/T sports the "Super Pack" decor option, which included front and rear spoilers and louvered quarter windows.

◀ Brisk Trans Am sales encouraged Chevy to bring back the Z-28, which wasn't offered for '75 and '76. The new version, introduced midyear '77, stressed handling over pure muscle. Included were unique front stabilizer bars, stiffer springs, different shock-absorber valving, performance tires, and quicker steering ratio. The combination elicited considerable praise from automotive journalists. *Motor Trend* called the revived Z-28, "Nothing short of incredible." Sole engine was a 170-bhp 350 V-8 teamed with standard four-speed manual or optional automatic. Quarter-mile times ranged from *Car and Driver's* 16.3 ET at 82 mph, to *Hot Rod's* 15.35 at 91. The '77 Z-28 started at $5170. Production for its short 1977 model year totaled just 14,347, but overall Camaro sales topped Mustang for the first time, 198,755 to 161,654.

▲ Aspen R/T was little changed for '78, but got revised taillights and striping. With 360 V-8 and optional 3.21 gear, R/Ts went 0-60 in 8.5-9.0 seconds and did 17-second quarters.

▲ The "Super Coupe" package with a 360 V-8 added $1351-$1420 to the '78 Aspen coupe's $3783 base price. As with the Volare's like-named option, it included firm suspension and lots of body add-ons.

▼ Ford's Mustang II offered a new King Cobra package for 1978. It included a 139-bhp 302 V-8 and four-speed manual transmission. *Motor Trend* posted a lethargic 17.7 ET at 77.6 mph in its test of a '78 Cobra II. Nonetheless, Mustang sales that year totaled 192,410.

▲ Road Runner ran its last in 1978—again as a collection of trim options for Plymouth's $3771 Volare coupe. This is the $499 "Sport Pack" version. Also offered were "Super Coupe" ($1417) and "Street Kit Car" ($1085) groups.

▶ For '78, the second-generation Camaro series received its third and final facelift. All got a redesigned front and rear fascia, to which the Z-28 added fender flares and a nonfunctional hoodscoop. This '78 has the new optional alloy wheels, too. Along with the revised styling, Z-28's standard 350 V-8 gained 10 horsepower, to 185, despite a compression drop from 8.5:1 to 8.2:1. Sales were gaining strength by this time, with 54,907 Z-28s sold in the '78 model year.

▲ Dodge's Li'l Red Truck had good performance, largely because of looser emissions standards for pickups. Its 225-bhp 360-cid V-8 was essentially the E58 Police unit with a Holley four barrel and minimal pollution controls. *Hot Rod* magazine drove a '78 to 15.71 ETs at 88.06 mph. Production was low at 2188 '78s, and 5188 '79s such as this one.

▲ An all-new Mustang bowed for '79. Its available 140-bhp 302 V-8 and four-speed manual trans were good for high-16-second ETs. Prices started at $4071. This Cobra package added high-performance TRX suspension and "Cobra" stickers, but the hood decal was optional. Mustang's 369,936 sales total for '79 nearly doubled that of '78.

▲ Mercury's '79 Capri was based on the new Mustang, but differed in its front and rear fascia design, creased fender bulges, and other styling details. *Motor Trend* said lighter, turbo four-cylinder versions such as this Capri RS went about a second quicker than the 8.7-second 0-60 mph time its testers got from a V-8 Mustang. Capri sales totaled 110,144 for '79. Prices started at $4872.

◀ With its $10,619 base price, the '79 Tenth Anniversary Trans Am was the first Firebird to start above $10,000. Included in the Anniversary package were unique alloy wheels, four-wheel disc brakes, silver leather seats, and silver tinted T-tops. A total of 7500 were built. Pontiac pony-cars increasingly used engines from other divisions, such as the 185-bhp 403-cid Oldsmobile V-8 standard on Trans Am for '79. Top T/A powerplant was an optional 220-bhp 400-cid Pontiac V-8. In a four-speed Formula, it was strong enough for 16.1 ETs in *Motor Trend*'s hands.

▶GM's second-generation Camaro and Firebird entered their final year in 1981. Z-28 was little changed although power was down somewhat from its previous 190 bhp. The '81's standard engine was a 165-bhp 5.0-liter (305-cid) V-8 teamed with four-speed manual transmission. Optional at no extra cost was a 174-bhp 5.7-liter (350-cid) V-8 with automatic transmission. Four-speed manual was unavailable with the larger engine. Z-28 production for '81 was a respectable 43,272. But that was still a considerable drop from its 84,877 high to this point, achieved in the '79 model year. The '81 Z-28 had a base price of $8263.

1982-92

Energy crisis eases then gradually turns into a gas glut, paving the way for a return to performance • Mustang GT is revived for '82; its 157-bhp 302 and 4-speed manual transmission help restore lost credibility • '83 Hurst/Olds Cutlass has 180-bhp 307 V-8 . . . for '85 it's replaced by a 4-4-2 with similar equipment • Chevy restores the Super Sport name, on an '83 Monte Carlo variant intended to strengthen the division's chances in NASCAR competition . . . included are a more aerodynamic front fascia and a 180-bhp, 305-cid V-8 • Horsepower generally increases through the mid Eighties . . . by 1987 Camaro and Mustang both pack 225-bhp V-8s, making them once again capable of high-14-second ETs • Manufacturers offer performance cars with small turbocharged engines . . . best is Buick's Regal Grand National; '87 GNX version runs quarter mile in mid-13-second range • Electronic fuel injection proliferates in the late Eighties . . . power increases little, but fuel economy, emissions, and drivability are improved

▲ Third-generation GM F-Bodies bowed for '82. Compared with the '81, the '82 design was 9.8-inches shorter, on a 7-inch shorter wheelbase. Weight was down by 500 pounds. Z-28 was still the hottest Camaro, with its available 165-bhp 305-cid V-8. Base price for the '82 Z-28 was $9700. Some 65,000 were sold. A five-speed '82 went 17.5 in the quarter mile for *Road & Track.*

▲ Firebird shared Camaro's redesign for '82. Trans Am had the same power choices as Z-28. Among the changes incorporated into the redesigned GM ponycars was MacPherson strut instead of A-arm front suspension, along with a greater emphasis on handling. Sticker price for the '82 T/A started at $9658, and 52,960 were sold that year.

▲ Ford for '82 replaced Mustang's weak 115-bhp 255-cid V-8 with a 157-bhp 302. The following year, the GT returned. The '83 GT, shown here, had a standard 175-bhp 302 and started at $9328. *Road & Track's* four speed '83 GT ran a 16.3 at 84 mph.

◀ After taking a few years off, the Hurst/Olds returned for 1983 as a limited edition Cutlass Supreme coupe. The revived '83 marked 15 years of Hurst/Oldsmobiles. Just 3000 were built that model year. While not quite as athletic as its lighter ponycar contemporaries, the H/O could hold its own in a straight line, going 0-60 mph in around eight seconds and doing the quarter in 16. Standard engine was a 180-bhp 307 V-8 with a four-barrel. Automatic transmission was standard, topped with Hurst's unusual Lightning Rod shifter. It had three levers: a main one, along with two separate sticks for manual shifting of first and second.

▲ Carroll Shelby masterminded the unassuming 1984 Dodge Omni GLH. It used the same 110-bhp 2.2-liter 4-cylinder engine and five-speed manual transmission as the Shelby Charger sports coupe, which went 0-60 mph in a respectable 9.62 seconds for *Car and Driver.*

▲ The GLH monicker stood for "Goes Like Hell," which the limited-production front-drive car did. Alloy wheels and firm suspension were included in the $7350 base price. GLH production for '84 totaled 3285.

▲ ▶ Ford's Special Vehicle Operations brewed up a 2.3-liter intercooled 175-bhp turbo four for the new '84 Mustang SVO. It went 0-60 mph in 7.5 seconds and ran the quarter mile in just under 16. The car aimed for a Euro-style blend of performance and high-speed handling. However, its sticker started at $15,596 versus $9578 for the GT, a factor that helped limit '84 SVO sales to just 4508.

▲ Chevy's '83 Monte Carlo got a reborn SS option. This similar '85 included a 180-bhp 305 V-8 and started at $11,380.

▲ The 5.0-liter High-Output V-8 on manual trans Mustang GTs for '85 gained 35 horsepower, to 210. ETs dipped into the high 14s.

▲ Mustang GT for '85 got articulated sport seats and an aircraft-inspired matte-grey instrument panel surround.

▲ The '85 GT was the last with a Holley four barrel. Increased power that year was due in part to new roller cam and stainless-steel headers.

▲ Buick used turbocharging to give V-6 Regals true V-8 punch. With a $13,714 base price for '86, these were hardly budget muscle cars, but their performance justified the cost. *Car and Driver* drove one to 13.4-second ETs, and a top speed of 124 mph. It produced a stout 330 pounds/feet of torque at just 2400 rpm. The turbo V-6 was available in T-Type trim, shown on this '86, or the monochrome black Grand National.

▲ Buick turbo V-6s got an intercooler for '86, boosting output by 35 bhp. The '87 T-Type/Grand National V-6 made 245 bhp.

▶Ford's Mustang SVO never sold as expected. This is one of 1954 built for '85. The turbo four-cylinder Mustang vanished after a final 3382 copies for 1986.

▲ Monte Carlo SS Aerocoupe bowed for '86. Its primary purpose was to homologate a more aerodynamic back window for use in NASCAR superspeedway racing. The fastback-style rear glass is evident when shown in front of a standard SS. Just 200 Aerocoupes were built for '86. They used the same 180-bhp 305 V-8 of the regular Monte SS, and thus had similar low-16-second quarter mile performance.

▲ Only 6052 Aerocoupes were sold for '87, the model's second and final year.

▲ El Camino pickups such as this '86 could get a Monte Carlo SS-type package, with a 150-bhp 305 V-8. Available options included these nonfunctional sidepipes and unique alloy wheels.

◀ Camaro's use in the International Race of Champions series prompted the IROC-Z for 1985-90. All had a 350 V-8, which produced 225-bhp in 1985-86 versions. This is an '86, which could do 0-60 in 8.1 seconds, and the quarter mile in 16.5. For '87, the 350's output increased to 245-bhp, and a convertible was added, the first production ragtop Camaro in 18 years. Base sticker for the coupe ranged from $11,739 to $14,555. Convertible IROC starting prices went from $17,917 to $20,195. IROCs sold well most years, peaking at 49,585 for 1986.

◀ ▲ Dodge Omni GLH (left) gained a turbocharger for 1985-86, lifting horsepower to 142. In 1986, Carroll Shelby introduced the GLHS, which added an intercooler and more boost to the GLH 2.2-liter four, bringing horsepower to 175. *Car and Driver* clocked a 14.9-second quarter in a stock GLHS, laying aside any doubts as to its muscle-car credentials.

▲ Like its Omni GLH and GLHS sisters, This '86 Dodge "Shelby" Charger got a turbo and 146-bhp for 1985-86, and Carroll Shelby's "Shelby" Charger got 175 bhp. Shelby's version also shared GLHS's sub 15-second quarter mile performance.

▲ Front-wheel drive became prevalent on the street in the mid-'80s, and showed up on the strip, too. Witness this '86 Shelby Charger at Indianapolis.

▲ Mustang GT's 5.0-liter V-8 was offered in the lighter, less-expensive LX. The coupe's more rigid body made it top pick for enthusiasts. Also favoring it were law enforcement agencies; many used 5.0 coupes; such as this '86, for pursuit vehicles.

▲ Mustang GT's 5.0-liter V-8 gained fuel injection for '86, but output dropped by 10-bhp, to 200, mostly due to revised cylinder heads.

▶ Pontiac's third-series Trans Am got a smoother nose for '85. Its base engine that year was a 160-bhp 305 V-8. Top power option was a 205-bhp 305 with GM's Tuned Port fuel injection. It teamed with automatic transmission only. *Motor Trend*'s fuel injected '85 T/A went 16.07 at 84.5 mph in the quarter. The '86, shown here, was little different, although its injected 305 gained 5 bhp, to 210. The '86 T/A had a base price of $12,395. Like Chevy's Z-28, Trans Am sales were good during this period, with 44,028 sold for '85, 48,870 for '86.

◀ Pontiac revived the "2+2" tag for this '86 Grand Prix. As with Chevy's Monte Carlo SS Aerocoupe, the 2+2 was intended to improve the division's chances in NASCAR competition by allowing a more aerodynamic sloping rear window and rounded front fascia. The 200 street 2+2s built for '86 had a fuel-injected 305-cid V-8 that made just 165 bhp, limiting the car to 17.6-second ETs at 80 mph, according to Pontiac. But lack of power was offset somewhat by handling enhancements that included gas-filled shock absorbers, stiffer springs, beefier sway bars, and performance tires.

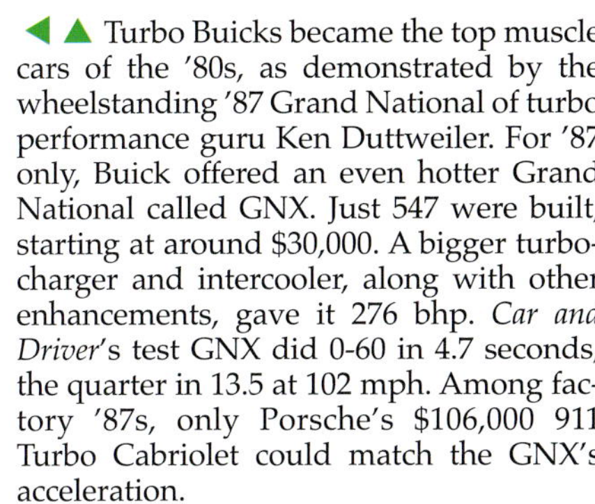

◀ ▲ Turbo Buicks became the top muscle cars of the '80s, as demonstrated by the wheelstanding '87 Grand National of turbo performance guru Ken Duttweiler. For '87 only, Buick offered an even hotter Grand National called GNX. Just 547 were built, starting at around $30,000. A bigger turbocharger and intercooler, along with other enhancements, gave it 276 bhp. *Car and Driver*'s test GNX did 0-60 in 4.7 seconds, the quarter in 13.5 at 102 mph. Among factory '87s, only Porsche's $106,000 911 Turbo Cabriolet could match the GNX's acceleration.

◀ ▲ The Hurst/Olds was replaced by a reborn 4-4-2 after 1984. The same 307-cid V-8 carried over, with power ratings little changed at 170-180 bhp. *Car and Driver* drove an '85 4-4-2 to a 16.6-second ET at 83 mph, and went 0-60 mph in 9.1 seconds. The swan-song '87, shown here, was a $2577 option on the Cutlass Supreme coupe. About 4210 were sold.

▲ Mustang's 5.0-liter V-8 for '87 gained 25 bhp, to 225. The year before, its four-barrel carburetor was replaced with fuel injection, which many feared wouldn't allow modification. To the contrary, the system proved flexible enough to accept considerable change, and aftermarket 5.0 parts soon flooded the market.

▲ ▼ Carroll Shelby worked his magic on 1500 '89 Dodge Dakota compact pickups. The vehicles were originally built with V-6s then shipped to Shelby's facility, where 175-bhp fuel-injected 318-cid V-8s were installed. The Shelby Dakota started at $15,813, versus $11,058 for a stock V-6 Dakota Sport. *Car and Driver*'s test Shelby Dakota did the quarter mile in 16.5 seconds.

▲ Since 1984, Saleen Autosport had offered modified Mustangs through Ford dealerships. The '89, shown here, retained its stock 5.0 V-8, but got chassis mods that included a strut-tower brace, Koni shocks, urethane bushings, and lower, stiffer springs. An '89 Saleen went 15.2 in the quarter, and had a top speed of 136 mph for *Car and Driver.* Base price was $19,900, compared to $13,272 for a regular Mustang GT.

▲ For 1984, Dodge replaced the Charger with the similar front-drive Daytona. As with its predecessor, Shelby also offered a modified version. The '89, shown here, got 174 horsepower from its turbocharged 2.2-liter four cylinder, good enough to propel it to 16.0 second ETs at the hands of *Road & Track* editors.

▲ For '89, Saleen added the SSC to its line. Engine mods included a revised intake plenum, enlarged throttle body, and ported heads, boosting output by 67 horsepower over the stock Mustang's 225-bhp. Roughly 250 were built for '89, starting at around $35,000. *Car and Driver* got a 14.2 ET from an '89 SSC.

◀ Oldsmobile stopped building traditional V-8 muscle cars after '87. This front-drive '89 Calais with 185-bhp "Quad-4" four cylinder didn't have the brawn of the late 4-4-2, but *Road & Track* managed a 16.5-second ET with one.

▲ Camaro IROC-Z coupe rolled into 1990 with newly standard 16-inch wheels and limited-slip differential. A 230-bhp 350 V-8 repeated as the top power option.

▶ For 1990, Chevy introduced the 454 SS, a true muscle truck. The two-wheel-drive, full-size pickup had a fuel-injected 454-cid big-block V-8 with 230 bhp. Base price for the '90 SS was $18,295, which included Bilstein shocks, quicker steering, and styled chrome wheels shod with 275/60R15 tires. SS production that model year was 13,748.

▲ Camaros had always been hot in quarter-mile action. Here, Joe Scott launches at Heartland Park, Topeka.

▲ From 1983-87, Ford offered the Thunderbird Turbo Coupe, powered by a turbocharged four-cylinder similar to that used in the Mustang SVO. T-Bird was redesigned for '89, at which time the Turbo Coupe was replaced by the Super Coupe, with a 210-bhp supercharged 3.8-liter V-6. This '90 Super Coupe started at $20,390 and could do 0-60 in 7.5 seconds.

▶ Camaro dropped its IROC-Z name for '91, and Z-28 returned as the top version. Standard V-8 was a 230-bhp 305. The optional 245-bhp 350 was potent enough for 14.9-second ETs in the hands of *Car and Driver.* Z-28 coupes for '91 started at $15,445, convertibles $20,815.

◀ ▲ New for 1991, the Dodge Spirit R/T was a real "Q-ship." Its unique 224-horse, turbocharged, 2.2-liter four had a Lotus designed twincam cylinder head. Also included were stiffer suspension and bigger tires. Sole transmission was a five-speed manual. *Car and Driver* drove a Spirit R/T to 14.5-second quarters at 97 mph, and went 0-60 mph in 5.8 seconds. Base price was $17,820.

▲ V-8 Mustangs had by the late '80s become the dominant low-buck performance car. Changes were few from year to year, but V-8 'Stangs for '91 got these five-spoke alloy wheels. This LX hatchback started at just $14,055. Its 225-bhp 5.0 V-8 was good for high-14-second ETs.

▲ Mustang sales had been in decline for several years, falling from 209,769 for '89 to 90,460 for '91. This '91 GT convertible had a base price of $19,864.

◀ For '91, GMC introduced the Syclone, a compact pickup with a 280-bhp, turbocharged, 262-cid V-6 and standard full-time all-wheel drive. Black was the sole body color choice. Despite it being a truck, Syclone was not very useful for hauling; warnings inside the tailgate and owners manual expressly warned against carrying a load of more than 500 pounds in the bed, so as not to damage the lowered suspension. *Car and Driver*'s test Syclone ran 0-60 mph in 5.3 seconds and turned the quarter in 14.1. Prices for the 3000 built started at $25,970.

▲ Marking Camaro's 25th birthday in 1992 was this $175 "Heritage Appearance Package." It included '60s-style stripes, special emblems, and body-color grille.

▲ Chevy served up a Z-34 coupe for '92, based on the front-wheel-drive Lumina. Included was a 210-bhp twin-cam V-6. *Car and Driver* wheeled one to a 15.58 quarter. The '92 Z-34 started at $17,500.

◀ ▼ Mustang and Camaro/Firebird continued their rivalry unabated on the strip. Small-block-powered ponycars of this period could be modified to compete in a number popular drag-race sanctioning bodies. Combinations ranged from almost showroom-condition 14-second cars, to blown, tube-frame machines capable of sevens. Occupying somewhat of a middle ground were 10- and 11-second racers such as these.

▲ Trucks were hot in the '90s, and, like GMC's Syclone, the division's $29,000 Typhoon sport-utility had a turbocharged 262-cid V-6 and permanently engaged all-wheel drive. Tires were 245/50VR16 performance rubber, specially developed by Firestone for Typhoon. Also included were full antilock brakes, instead of rear-only as used on regular GMC Jimmy SUVs. Performance was on par with Syclone, with *Road & Track* running a Typhoon through the quarter mile in 14.3 seconds, at 93 mph. Just 3000 were built for '91, 500 for '92.

1993-2002

Performance is on the rise as another horsepower race begins • New Camaro and Firebird debut for '93, gain 30 bhp to 275 • Ford's response to GM ponycar power is delayed, but '96 Cobra matches GMs with its 305-bhp 5.0 V-8 • Full-size cars again become muscle car fodder when Chevy introduces the Impala SS for '94; it features a 260-bhp small block similar to Corvette's LT-1 • Trucks jump in popularity . . . Ford's '99 Lightning packs a 360-bhp supercharged 5.4-liter V-8 • Z-28 and Trans Am for '98 top Cobra's 305-bhp . . . all are capable of 13-second ETs, quicker than most Sixties muscle cars • Ford for '93, '95, and 2000 offers special road-race-intended Mustang Cobra "R" variants . . . strongest is the 2000, which includes a 385-bhp 5.4 V-8; its 12-second ETs place it among the quickest muscle cars ever • For 2001, Ford releases the Bullitt Mustang, a 300-bhp GT with styling cues from the famous movie car • 2002 is the final year for Firebird and Camaro, but muscle is far from dead

▲▶ Camaro was redesigned for '93. Its wheelbase stayed the same, but the car was slightly heavier despite more extensive use of plastics. The interior was all new, and got vastly improved ergonomics. Big news underhood was 30 more horses for Z-28's standard 5.7 V-8, which brought it to 275 bhp. *Motor Trend* drove a six-speed '93 Z-28 to a 14.0-second ET at 98.8 mph. Sticker prices started at $16,779.

▲ Chevrolet took advantage of the redesigned F-body platform to build this "ZL-1" version, a one-off engineering exercise named for the famed 500-plus horsepower 1969 Corvette/Camaro race-only big-block.

◀▲ Unlike the original 427-cid ZL-1, the 1993 namesake displaced 572 cubic inches, and produced a whopping 650-bhp and 700 pound-feet of torque. The new fourth-generation F-body's short, steep hood forced even the production small block to be mounted nearly halfway under the cowl, making this big block a tight fit.

▲ Mustang's 1979 design hit the end of the road in '93. Available that year was this special LX appearance package, which featured white leather interior and alloy wheels. Also available was a yellow version with chrome rolling stock.

▲ New for '93 was this Mustang Cobra and the first of the race-ready Cobra Rs. Both used a 240-bhp 5.0 V-8, but the R had stiffer suspension and a pared-down interior. Only 107 '93 Rs were built. Regular Cobras started at $19,990 and did 0-60 in 5.9 seconds, according to Ford.

▲ Ford's answer to Chevy's SS 454 pickup was this F-150 Lightning and its 250-bhp 351 V-8. It listed for $21,655 and came in two-wheel drive only. Some 10,000 Lightnings were built for '93. *Car and Driver*'s best ET with one was 15.8 at 110 mph.

◀ Oldsmobile continued to play with small front-drive cars, offering this hotter SCX version of its Achieva compact for '93. It started at $15,524, and production was limited to around 500. Light weight and standard 175-bhp V-6 made for respectable 16.1 ETs in the hands of *Car and Driver.* But the little Olds was no bargain as a muscle car. That year's 5.0 Mustang LX coupe had 30 more horsepower and cost some $1500 less. Equally compelling was the '93 Camaro Z-28, which had a 100-horse advantage over the SCX and cost only a grand more.

▶ All-new Firebirds arrived with the same basic design as Chevy's '93 Camaros, but retained unique Pontiac style. Both for '93 came in hatchback coupe form only; a convertible wasn't offered until '94. Here's the Trans Am, which used Z-28's 275-bhp 5.7 V-8. Also shared between GM's top ponycars were new standard antilock brakes and six-speed manual transmission. Base price for the '93 Firebird Formula was $17,995, Trans Am was $21,395. Overall Firebird production for '93 was a low 19,068.

▲ Chevy resurrected the Impala SS for '94, based on the full-sized Caprice sedan. Exterior cues included a rear spoiler, restyled rear quarter windows, and a unique blacked-out grille.

▲ Standard on Impala SS were alloy wheels shod in wide performance rubber, and rear disc brakes instead of drums. The '94 was offered in black only, with a base price of $21,920.

◀ Impala SS had a 350 LT-1 small block and chassis improvements that included quicker steering, a rear stabilizer bar, and a 3.08:1 rear gear instead of the Caprice's 2.93:1. *Car and Driver* got a 15.0 ET.

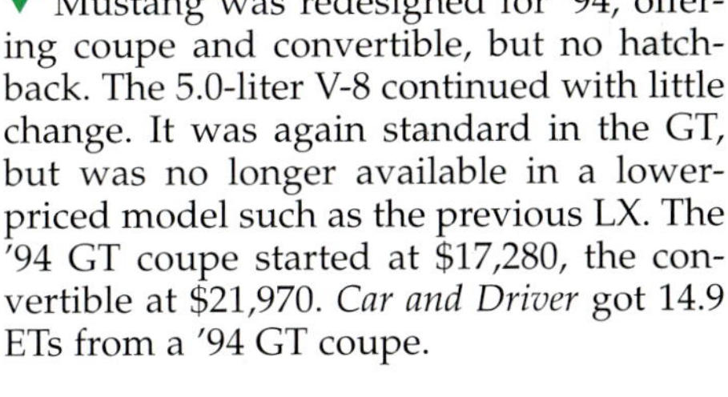

▼ Mustang was redesigned for '94, offering coupe and convertible, but no hatchback. The 5.0-liter V-8 continued with little change. It was again standard in the GT, but was no longer available in a lower-priced model such as the previous LX. The '94 GT coupe started at $17,280, the convertible at $21,970. *Car and Driver* got 14.9 ETs from a '94 GT coupe.

▲ Mustang Cobra returned in midyear '94, with a 240-bhp 5.0 V-8. Production was set at 5000 coupes, starting at $22,425, and 1000 ragtops with a $23,535 base price. *Car and Driver*'s best ET with a '94 Cobra coupe was a 14.7 at 96 mph.

▲ Although the '94 Mustang's styling was markedly different from that of the 1979-93 design, it was built on basically the same "Fox" platform. However, the new car was more rigid and got numerous revisions aimed at increased overall refinement.

▶ Trans Am gained a plush GT version for '94. Available on the new model was this 25th Anniversary package. The $995 option included white alloy wheels and leather upholstery, blue stripes, and unique badges. Anniversary Trans Ams started at $22,504 for the coupe, $27,964 for the convertible. Production of the limited edition cars is estimated at 1250 coupes and 250 convertibles. Among Trans Am drivetrain revisions for '94 were a forced one-to-four skip shift on the manual trans and, in late model year, optional traction control. In tests of an automatic transmission 25th Anniversary Trans Am convertible, *Car and Driver* did the quarter mile in 14.6 seconds and clocked top speed at 153.

▲ For '95, Ford offered another race-intended R version of the Cobra. The cars were immediately recognizable by their bulged fiberglass hood, fitted to clear the tall intake manifold. Also included were unique five-spoke alloy wheels with wide performance tires.

▲ The '95 Cobra R was fully street legal, but Ford required buyers to show a current competition license from a race sanctioning body. Production was a low 252 units. Visible below the rear fascia is the R's standard 20-gallon fuel cell.

◀▲ Rs packed a 300-bhp 5.8-liter V-8, instead of the regular Cobra's 240-bhp 5.0. The only transmission was a heavy-duty Tremec five-speed manual. Inside, the front seats were base V-6 units that had very little side bolstering, the assumption being that owners would replace them with a single racing bucket. The rear seat was deleted, as was the radio and air conditioning. Top speed was 151 mph, ETs were in the low- to mid-13s.

▲ Impala SS changed little for '96, its last year in V-8, rear-drive form. A console-mounted shifter replaced the previous column unit, and gauges were now analog instead of digital. Base price was $24,405.

▲ Chevy introduced a 305-bhp SS option on the '96 Z-28. The package added $3999 to the base 285-bhp Z-28, which started at $19,390 for the coupe, $24,490 for the convertible.

▲ Ford met Camaro's increased power, giving the '96 Cobra a 65-horsepower boost, to 305. It was good for 14.2 ETs, according to Ford. Part of the increase was due to Mustang's new dohc 4.6-liter V-8. GTs that year got a 225-bhp sohc variant.

▲ V-8 Firebirds for '96 were also available with a new high-performance package, in this case called Ram Air WS6, offered on coupes only.

◀▲ Top performance packages for '96 Camaros and Firebirds included a functional hood scoop, stiffer springs, unique shock valving, and wide 275/40ZR17 performance tires on unique five-spoke alloy wheels. Ram Air Pontiacs also shared Camaro SS's 305-bhp small block, which was good for 14.3-second ETs in a '96 Ram Air Trans Am tested by *Motor Trend.* Meanwhile, regular Formulas, Trans Ams, and Camaro Z-28s weren't left out that year; they got a less-restrictive exhaust system that increased output by ten horsepower, to 285. The Ram Air package added $2995 to the $19,464 Firebird Formula or $21,414 Trans Am.

▲ Chevy celebrated Camaro's 30th anniversary in 1997 with this commemorative option package. It included white alloy wheels, houndstooth seat inserts, and stripes inspired by the '69 Z-28.

▲ Camaro for '98 got a facelift that featured a larger, more menacing grille opening. The SS option package continued to be available on coupes and convertibles.

▶ Revised Firebird styling bowed alongside that of Camaro for '98. Among the changes were a meaner, more sculpted front fascia and taller hood scoop.

▲ The biggest news for '98 GM ponycars was the LS1 V-8. This aluminum 5.7-liter engine was introduced the previous year in the Corvette, replacing the original 1955-design Chevrolet small-block V-8. Although an overhead-valve design as its predecessor was, the LS1 had practically nothing else in common with it. Along with the engine change came another boost in power for Camaro Z-28, Firebird Formula, and Trans Am; all gained 20 bhp, to 305. Power increased the same amount for Ram Air and SS packages, to 320 bhp. With the new engine, the top '98 F-body models took their place among the quickest muscle cars ever. A '98 Camaro SS did the quarter mile in 13.6 seconds at 106.5 mph for *Motor Trend*'s testers. Better yet was the 13.4 ET at 107.3 the magazine got from a '98 Ram Air Trans Am.

▲ Firebird's facelift for '98 also included honeycomb taillights with round back-up lights. The '98 Firebird Formula coupe had a base price of $22,865. Trans Ams that year started at $25,975 for the coupe, $29,715 for the convertible.

◀▲ Mustang got an extensive facelift for '99, while Cobra added independent rear suspension and 15 more horsepower—enough for 13.9 ETs in *Road & Track*'s hands. Some '99 Cobras put out far less than the rated 320 bhp, which was found to be caused by faulty intake parts. As a result, no Cobras except R models were built for 2000, and Ford repaired the '99s at no charge. Cobra coupes for '99 started at $27,470, convertibles at $31,470.

▲ Ford's SVT F-150 Lightning pickup returned for '99, after a three-year hiatus. The '99 included sport suspension tuning, four-wheel disc brakes from the F-250 Super Duty pickup, and massive 295/45ZR18 tires mounted on unique five-spoke alloy wheels. Further distinguishing it from regular Ford trucks was a special front fascia and rocker sill extensions with side-exit exhaust.

▲ Lightning's sohc 5.4-liter V-8 produced 330 bhp with the help of a supercharger and an intercooler. *Car and Driver* got a '99 through the quarter mile in 14.4 seconds. But the numbers didn't really show the big-block style punch of Lightning's 440 pound-feet of torque. The '99 started at $29,355, and 4000 were built.

▲ Mustang GT's sohc V-8 for '99 got hotter cams, bigger valves, and revised intake manifold, boosting horsepower by 35, to 260. *Car and Driver* got 14.2 ETs and a 138 mph top speed from a '99 GT.

▲ Along with drivetrain improvements, the '99 Mustang was given new-design alloy wheels and a 1.4-inch wider rear track. GT coupes that year started at $20,870, convertibles at $24,870.

▲▶ Trans Am celebrated its 30th anniversary with this special edition 1999 T/A that featured a color scheme reminiscent of the original 1969 version.

▼ Ford for 2000 offered the third of its race-bred Cobra Rs. Only 300 were built, all in red, starting at $54,995. Power came from a 385-bhp 5.4-liter V-8 teamed with a beefy Tremec T-56 six-speed manual transmission. As in previous Rs, the interior had no radio, backseat, or sound deadening. However, the 2000 model included Recaro seats up front. Performance was torrid, with *Motor Trend* driving one to a 12.9-second quarter at 110.8 mph.

▲ Pontiac's 1999 GTO concept car wasn't destined for production, but showed the division's interest in its muscle heritage.

◀ NASCAR star Rusty Wallace poses after driving some fast laps at Road Atlanta in the FR 500, a Ford engineering exercise aimed at showing Mustang's ultimate performance potential. Its dohc 4.6-liter V-8 had high-flow heads, variable-geometry intake manifold, and dual 70mm throttle bodies. Chassis modifications included dual A-arm front suspension instead of MacPherson struts, on a wheelbase stretched by five inches. Ford said the FR 500 put out 415 bhp, did the quarter mile in 12.7 seconds, and had a top speed of 175 mph.

◀▲ In 2000, Ford showed a concept car commemorating the 1968 Mustang GT 390 used in the movie *Bullitt.* For 2001, the package was put into production as the Bullitt edition for the GT coupe. It used the GT's 4.6-liter sohc V-8, but added a freer-flowing induction system. The engine mods gave it only five horsepower more than the base 260-bhp GT, but also provided more readily available power at lower rpms. Other enhancements included a lower ride height, Brembo front brakes, and Tokico high-performance shocks and struts. Inside were aluminum pedals, along with seat stitching and instrument faces reminiscent of '60s 'Stangs. Standard on Bullitt and optional on the GT were 17-inch alloy wheels styled after the movie car's American Racing Torq Thrusts. The Bullitt package added $3695 to the $22,535 base price of an '01 GT coupe. A total of 6500 were built, most in Dark Highland Park Green, though black and dark blue were also available.

▼▶ While 2002 marked the 35th anniversary of the Chevrolet Camaro, it was also the last production year for both of the General Motors F-body cars. Sales of the Camaro had slumped from 136,000 in 1995 to just over 29,000 in 2001. The 35th anniversary edition Camaro SS had silver checkered-flag pattern stripes and special fender badges, among other touches. Commemorative coupes came with T-tops. The special edition cars were powered by a Ram Air-inducted 5.7-liter aluminum V-8 that made 325 bhp.

◀ By 2001, sales of the Pontiac Firebird had fallen to about 21,000 units annually. The Ford Mustang was outselling both the Camaro and Firebird better than three to one, and General Motors wasn't putting much further development into its ponycars. These factors led GM to make 2002 the last year for the Firebird. To commemorate the Firebird's 35th anniversary, Pontiac offered the 2002 Trans Am Collector Edition coupe or convertible, both of which had the 325-bhp WS6 Ram Air engine, unique wheels, and yellow paint. Buyers who chose the SLP Firehawk package got an extra 20 horsepower.

2003-06

Muscle is back in a big way Dodge turns the Neon into a 215-bhp pocket rocket called SRT-4 • Pickup trucks become increasingly popular among the performance set . . . Ford offers a 380-bhp Lightning regular-cab pickup for 2003, as well as a 340-bhp supercharged Harley-Davidson SuperCrew . . . Dodge introduces the 500-bhp V-10-powered Ram SRT-10 in 2004 . . . Chevrolet enters the fray with a 300-bhp roadster pickup called SSR • Mustang gets two new performance models in 2003, with the 310-bhp Mach I and 390-bhp supercharged SVT Cobra • The legendary GTO name returns for 2004 as a 350-bhp Australian import; it has the power but not the looks • Cadillac builds a high-end muscle car called CTS-V; this 400-bhp burner is based on Caddy's entry-level model • DaimlerChrysler revives the Hemi as a 340-bhp 5.7-liter V-8 and installs it in the 2005 Chrysler 300C and Dodge Magnum RT; 425-bhp 6.1-liter versions follow in several SRT-8-badged Chrysler, Dodge, and Jeep models

◀ ▼ Chevrolet built a concept called the SSR for the 2000 auto show circuit that evoked both the styling of a modern roadster and Chevy's own 1947-53 pickups. Press and public reaction was so favorable that Chevy pushed it through to production almost entirely unchanged—except for the 300-bhp 5.3-liter V-8 that replaced the 6.0 shown in the concept.

◀ Chevrolet used the chassis and 5.3-liter V-8 from its TrailBlazer midsize SUV as the basis for the SSR. A rumbling exhaust note made it sound fast, but the 4765-pound curb weight and four-speed automatic contributed to mediocre performance. *Motor Trend* pushed the SSR from 0 to 60 mph in 7.4 seconds—not bad, but not in keeping with its $41,370 price tag. Sales were slow, too. Chevy sold fewer than 2000 SSRs in 2003 and 2004.

▲ The second-generation Ford SVT F-150 Lightning bowed in 1999 with a supercharged 5.4-liter V-8 that made 360 bhp and 440 pound-feet of torque. For 2001, those numbers rose to 380 and 450, respectively. New wheels and a reworked front fascia with a new grille were also added in '01. The 2002 and '03 models remained virtually unchanged visually, but the '03s got significant revisions below the skin. Ford retuned and lowered the chassis, allowing for a higher top speed and increased payload capacity from 800 to 1400 pounds. These updates prompted Ford to add larger front vented brake rotors.

◀ The most basic quality of the muscle car is big power in a small package. Dodge surely had that in mind when it created the feisty SRT-4 by installing a cast-aluminum turbocharged 2.4-liter four-cylinder engine, underrated in 2003 at 215 bhp, in the compact Neon. The car hurtled from 0 to 60 mph in 5.8 seconds, backing up Dodge's claim that the SRT-4 was not only the second-fastest car in the its line, but also the quickest production car available for under $20,000. Made "for tuners by tuners," the SRT-4 proved America could compete in the import-dominated sport-compact market.

▲ In keeping with the muscle car mentality, the strictly performance-oriented SRT-4 was only offered with a five-speed manual transmission. The spartan-but-racy interior also featured sport seats, a 160-mph speedometer, white gauge faces, silver and carbon-fiber accents, and a boost gauge.

▲ In 2004, DaimlerChrysler engineers recalibrated the SRT-4's engine and gave it larger injectors to boost output to 230 bhp. More importantly, they gave it a front-wheel limited-slip differential that diminished torque steer and vastly improved handling characteristics. SCCA racers across the country were pleased.

▲ The 2003 Ford SVT F-150 Lightning's 5.4-liter Triton V-8 featured an Eaton Gen-IV supercharger. Power was delivered to the wheels through a four-speed automatic transmission. So equipped, the 2003 SVT Lightning sprinted from 0-60 mph in 5.2 seconds. The $33,310 sticker price may have seemed high compared with other regular-cab short-bed pickups, but it was a performance bargain.

▲ On Aug. 13, 2003, at Ford Motor Company's (Dearborn) Michigan Proving Grounds, the 2003 Ford SVT F-150 Lightning earned the title of "The World's Fastest Production Pickup Truck" from Guinness World Records, Ltd. The Lightning achieved an average speed of 147.7 mph after two runs, one in each direction, around the Proving Grounds' five-mile high-speed oval track. The only modifications Guinness allowed were removal of the radio antenna and folding in the side mirrors. Dodge's Ram SRT-10 would break the record less than a year later.

▲▶ Ford commemorated Harley-Davidson's 100th anniversary with the 2003 Harley-Davidson F-150, available in black and silver or just black. Chrome accents and Harley-Davidson badging paid homage to the mighty hogs for which the SuperCrew crew-cab pickup was named. Under the hood, Ford installed a detuned version of the SVT Lightning's supercharged 5.4-liter V-8, this one making 340 bhp. *Motor Trend* clocked its 0-60-mph time at six seconds flat.

◀▲ During most of the last decade, the Chevrolet Camaro and Pontiac Firebird outperformed the Ford Mustang. After the demise of General Motors' ponycars, however, Ford's Special Vehicle Team gave the Mustang some serious muscle credibility with the release of the 2003 Ford SVT Cobra. A 32-valve, 390-bhp supercharged 4.6-liter DOHC V-8 was the star of the show. *Motor Trend* timed a 2003 Cobra at 4.9 seconds 0 to 60 mph and 13.3 seconds at 109.58 mph in the quarter mile.

▶ Ford SVT Cobra Mustang coupes and convertibles were released together at $34,750 and $38,995, respectively. Even taking into account the $1000 Gas-Guzzler tax, Cobras were more affordable than other production cars with similar performance. Ragtops received their own suspension tuning to compensate for their inherent decreased body rigidity. The SVT Cobra was the only Mustang offered with independent rear suspension, and its lone transmission was a six-speed manual. Dual hood scoops, unique front and rear fascias, round fog lamps, and larger wheels distinguished Cobras from other Mustangs. The convertible shown features the unique wheels and two-tone leather seats included with the $1495 Anniversary Package that Ford offered to commemorate 10 years of SVT performance.

▲ Ford released the new Mach 1 for 2003 as a limited-production coupe, reviving a Mustang badge born in 1969 and last seen in '78 on a Mustang II. The "shaker" scoop mounted to the 4.6-liter V-8 helped the engine breathe freely. It combined with performance cams and exhaust to produce 300 bhp, 40 more than a stock Mustang GT. The interior featured aluminum accents on the shifter boot and pedals.

▲ Ford incorporated 1969 Mach 1 styling cues into its 2003 edition. Just look for the Magnum 500-style wheels and raised "powerdome" hood with its functional scoop protruding from a black center stripe. Also unique to the Mach 1 were the front air dam, rear spoiler, huge 13-inch front brake rotors, and lowered suspension on Tokico shocks and struts.

▶ In 2001, Mercury officials announced that the Marauder, a full-size performance machine based on the Grand Marquis four-door sedan, would go on sale as a 2003 model. With big rear-drive-sedan underpinnings and a 300-bhp 4.6-liter V-8 engine, Marauder was undeniably old school. But the excitement waned when performance didn't live up to the hype. Production ended after two years and 7608 sales. At the end of its run, an anonymous benefactor donated 18 Marauders to the Florida Highway Patrol.

▲▶ Cadillac replaced the poor-selling midsize Catera in mid 2002 with the 2003 CTS. Benchmarked against European luxury sports sedans, the rear-drive CTS's chassis was tuned on Germany's infamous Nurburgring road course. While handling was exemplary, the 3.2-liter V-6 was underwhelming. Then, for 2004, Cadillac installed its new 245-bhp 3.6-liter V-6 and the CTS was transformed into a world-class sports sedan. General Motors took the concept a step further with the 2004 CTS-V (shown), a sport-tuned CTS with true muscle in the form of a 400-bhp version of the Chevrolet Corvette's 5.7-liter LS2 V-8 linked to a six-speed manual. *Road & Track* launched it from 0 to 60 mph in 5.0 seconds.

◀ Aiming to redefine its conservative image, Cadillac campaigned CTS-V race cars on the SCCA race circuit. Featuring a bored-and-tuned version of the production car's 5.7-liter V-8, the CTS-V made upward of 500 bhp. In their first race, held March 19, 2004, at the historic Sebring International Raceway, Cadillac's two entries finished first and second in the GT class against competition that included Chevrolet Corvettes, Vipers, and Porsche 911s.

▲▼ "If it's worth doing, it's sometimes worth overdoing." This was the school of thought for the Chrysler Performance Vehicles Operations engineers who worked on the limited-production 2004 Dodge Ram SRT-10. No other performance pickup compared to the astronomical numbers of this Viper-powered truck with its 500 bhp, 525 pound-feet of torque, and $45,795 price tag. Huge 305/40ZR22 tires transferred all that V-10-produced power to the ground. Dodge quoted a quarter-mile time of 13.8 seconds.

◀▲ Chrysler's PVO team set out to build the fastest, most powerful pickup truck in the world. On Feb. 2, 2004, PVO proved it had succeeded. The Ram SRT-10 shattered the Land Speed Record for a production pickup previously held by Ford's SVT F-150 Lightning. Brendan Gaughan, six-time NASCAR Craftsman Truck Series winner in 2003, drove the Ram SRT-10 to a two-way average of 154.587 mph in the measured kilometer at DaimlerChrysler's Chelsea (Michigan) Proving Grounds. The successful record attempt was moderated by SCCA and officials from Guinness World Records, Ltd. With its 500-cid V-10, the Dodge Ram SRT-10 proved once again that there's no replacement for displacement.

▼▶ The 40th anniversary of the Ford Mustang heralded the end of an era, as 2004 was the final year for the Fox platform, a chassis that traced its roots back to 1978. All 2004 models wore a commemorative anniversary badge, but were otherwise visually unchanged from the previous year. A limited number were offered with "Mystichrome" paint (below), a paint that changes color depending on the angle of view. To send the Foxes out in style, Roush Racing offered a limited run of 40 high-performance 440A Mustangs (right). The 440A nameplate decodes like this: 400 horsepower, 40th production year, anniversary edition.

◀▼ Bob Lutz, General Motors' product development czar, unveiled the reborn Pontiac GTO at the 2003 Los Angeles Auto Show. Lutz was the main force behind GM's revival of the revered GTO badge, attaching it to the Australian Holden Monaro, and bringing it to the United States. The announcement piqued the interest of enthusiasts. Upon the car's release, however, many were dismayed with the car's styling, decrying its lack of retro design elements.

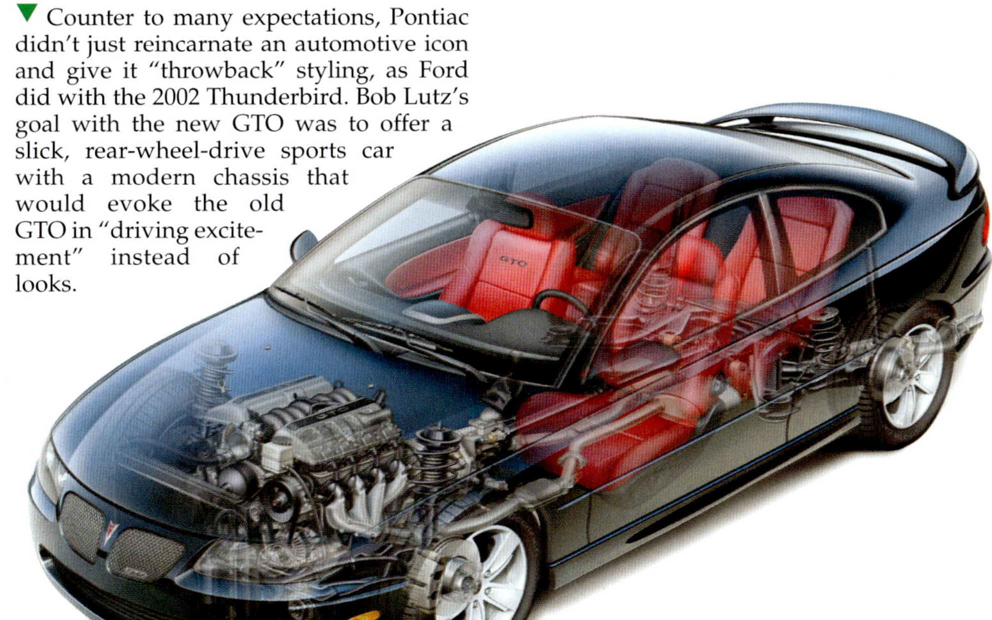

▼ Counter to many expectations, Pontiac didn't just reincarnate an automotive icon and give it "throwback" styling, as Ford did with the 2002 Thunderbird. Bob Lutz's goal with the new GTO was to offer a slick, rear-wheel-drive sports car with a modern chassis that would evoke the old GTO in "driving excitement" instead of looks.

▲ The 2004 Pontiac GTO came with a 350-bhp 5.7-liter V-8 engine. *Motor Trend* posted a 0-60-mph time of 5.3 seconds and a 13.62 quarter mile—times that not even die-hard Goat fans could complain about. Still, sales were below Pontiac's expectations; fewer than 14,000 were sold in 2004.

▼ ▶ Rhys Millen, accomplished rally driver and son of Pikes Peak legend Rod Millen, approached Pontiac with the idea of making the powerful, rear-wheel-drive GTO a drift car. Aiming to benefit from the growing popularity of a motorsport new to the U.S., Pontiac agreed and sponsored Millen's GTO drifting program. Drifting, which was born on Japanese back roads and involves high-speed controlled oversteer, is judged on style rather than speed. Driving an extensively modified '04 GTO, Millen slid the car through the corners to a first-place finish at Irwindale, California, in the last event of 2004's SCCA-sanctioned Formula D series.

▲ When it was first released in 2003, the Chevrolet SSR was an attention-grabbing cruiser with more show than go. For the 2005 model year, it made the transition to honest-to-goodness muscle truck. The first-time availability of a six-speed manual transmission added to the driving excitement, but it was the 390-hp version of the Corvette's LS2 small-block V-8 that transformed the SSR into a hot rod. Otherwise, the Super Sport Roadster remained unchanged. It had a live rear axle and independent front suspension. The standard rigid tonneau covered a bed of about 5 × 3 ft. And the power hardtop retracted with the touch of a button.

◀▲ Previous model-year SSRs sounded a lot meaner than they were, but the 2005 SSR got a bite to match its bark in the form of a new 390-bhp 6.0-liter V-8. More powerful than its 5.3-liter predecessor by 90 horses, the new engine helped six-speed manual versions sprint from 0 to 60 mph in 5.3 seconds. Even automatic-equipped models ran 0-60 mph in 5.5 seconds, two seconds faster than the SSR at its debut. A sizable price increase usually accompanies such a dramatic power gain, but with a price of $42,245, the 2005 SSR cost only $1000 more than it had two years earlier. Note the console-mounted torque gauge in the photo at the left.

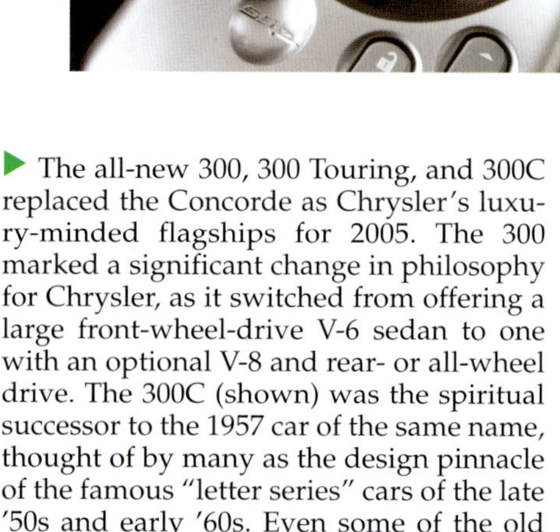

▶ The all-new 300, 300 Touring, and 300C replaced the Concorde as Chrysler's luxury-minded flagships for 2005. The 300 marked a significant change in philosophy for Chrysler, as it switched from offering a large front-wheel-drive V-6 sedan to one with an optional V-8 and rear- or all-wheel drive. The 300C (shown) was the spiritual successor to the 1957 car of the same name, thought of by many as the design pinnacle of the famous "letter series" cars of the late '50s and early '60s. Even some of the old 1957 design cues were faintly echoed in the front fascia of the '05 version (just imagine the grille flipped upside-down).

▲ Prior to resurrecting the 300C nameplate, Chrysler had also brought back the legendary Hemi engine. The 300C came equipped with a 340-bhp 5.7-liter Hemi V-8. This engine first saw production use in the 2003 Dodge Ram Heavy Duty.

◀ Every Chrysler 300 was equipped with an automatic transmission; base models had a four-speed, all-wheel drive, and V-8 versions came with a five-speed automatic with manual shift gate. The 2005 300C started at $33,720, and all-wheel versions cost $35,045. With its unique combination of room, comfort, and available power, the 300 was a bargain buy.

▲ The 300C SRT-8 debuted mid-model year as an even higher performance version of the 2005 300C. Available in Bright Silver or Brilliant Black, Chrysler's new flagship rolled on 20-inch wheels with Brembo brakes and a sport-tuned suspension. It was the newest entry in an expanding line of SRT vehicles. SRT, for "Street and Racing Technology," was the label given by Chrysler's PVO (Performance Vehicles Operations) engineers to cars they had tuned. The others were the Dodge Viper SRT-10, the Neon-based SRT-4, and the Ram SRT-10, as well as the Chrysler Crossfire SRT-6. The numbers denote the number of cylinders in that model's engine.

▲ Chrysler's new 5.7-liter Hemi V-8 served as the starting point for the engine that would be developed for the 300C SRT-8. The Chrysler PVO team re-bored all eight cylinders by 3.5 mm and raised the compression ratio from 9.6:1 to 10.3:1. They gave it bigger valves and ports, performance cams, headers, and all-around wider intake and exhaust components. They even painted the engine block orange, like the Hemis of old. The result was an incredible 425-bhp 6.1-liter V-8 engine that could push the 4200-lb car to a *Car and Driver*-estimated 0-60-mph time of 5.0 seconds.

▲ Dodge replaced its Intrepid sedan with the 2005 Magnum station wagon. The Magnum came in three trim levels: SE with a 2.7-liter V-6, SXT with the 2.7- or 3.5-liter V-6, and RT (shown) with the Hemi V-8. Like its Chrysler 300C cousin, the Magnum RT was a muscular daily driver with either rear- or all-wheel drive and an independent rear suspension patterned on the design used for the Mercedes-Benz E-Class.

▲ Ford redesigned the Mustang from the ground up for 2005, effectively re-committing itself to the future of the iconic American ponycar. It was the first ever Mustang on its own chassis. Even the 1964 Mustang was based on the Ford Falcon. Clearly, Ford's designers used styling cues from the popular Mustangs of the late 1960s.

▲ Base 2005 Mustangs got a 210-bhp 4.0-liter V-6 that replaced a 193-bhp 3.8 V-6. GTs kept the 4.6-liter V-8 from previous years, but horsepower was up 40 to 300. *Motor Trend* launched a GT from 0 to 60 mph in 5.1 seconds.

▲▶ Ford's modern-retro styling theme continued into the interior with simple circular instrumentation that recalled an era of less-busy cockpits. Out back, the triple-element taillamps were an honored Mustang styling cue, the trunklid badge recalled the fuel-filler cap on late Sixties and early Seventies models, and the rear quarter windows aided driver vision while evoking bygone styling.

▲▶ The new Mustang was almost six inches longer in wheelbase than the previous version, yet only about 100 pounds heavier, and a new front suspension design gave it a smaller turning radius. Ford kept the solid rear axle, but promised an upcoming SVT version with an optional independent rear suspension. A five-speed manual was standard, though an optional five-speed automatic, exclusive to the Mustang, was offered. Convertible versions were released in the spring. Premium packages in coupes and convertibles alike included colored leather upholstery and accents. The new Mustang offered a lot of bang for the buck. Deluxe Base 2005 Mustangs sold for $19,410, and pricing topped out at $31,175 for the Premium GT convertible.

▲ Soon after the 2005 Mustang coupe's debut, a spate of tuners released their own versions before the stock convertible even hit showroom floors. Roush Performance, one of a few aftermarket firms that grew from bolt-on parts supplier into car producer, offered the 2005 Roush Mustang with the Stage 1 package for $8700 over the price of a stock GT. The Stage 1 package included performance tires, wheels, fog lamps, exhaust, and an aero kit.

▶ Specializing in aftermarket performance parts for Ford vehicles, Steeda Autosports built a reputation for offering such items as suspension kits, spoilers, intake and exhaust setups, shifters, superchargers, wheels, and brake rotors. Shown here is Steeda's $32,484 Torch Red Q Mustang. Steeda Sport springs, a strut tower brace, and 18-inch wheels and tires were added to aid handling. Other Steeda features included the front air splitter, rear wing, cold-air intake, performance exhaust, and Tri-Ax shifter. According to Steeda, the shifter, "makes the job of swapping cogs less like rowing a boat, and more like flipping a switch."

◀ Designed as a nod to the famous Boss 302 Trans-Am racers of 1969-'70, the Ford Mustang GT-R Concept was also built to serve as a showcase for Ford Racing Performance Parts. The 5.0-liter V-8 crate engine (a bored-out 4.6) was chosen in part because it matched the displacement of the Boss 302 Trans-Am cars, but also because it put out a whopping 440 bhp. Customers could buy the engine for $14,995, but the GT-R Mustang didn't make it to production or to the race track in any official capacity.

▶ The 2005 Saleen S281 came in two forms: the $39,043 3-Valve and the $46,134 Supercharged. Both used the Ford Mustang's 4.6-liter V-8. The 3-Valve boasted an output of 325 bhp, while the Supercharged engine (shown) used a Saleen Series VI supercharger to achieve 400 bhp. Saleen hinted that it would build an S281 Extreme with 500 bhp.

◀ 2005 marked 21 years since Saleen offered its first car, which was also based on the Ford Mustang. Unlike other tuners specializing in Mustangs, Saleen was founded as an original equipment manufacturer. All of its cars met EPA and crash test regulations. Over the years, Saleen's modifications typically focused on handling and style more than power.

▲ Pontiac installed a V-8 in the Grand Prix for the first time since 1987 with the release of the 2005 Grand Prix GXP. The performance-oriented GXP's 303-bhp 5.3-liter V-8 was mounted transversely for a front-wheel-drive configuration. With all that power running to the front wheels, the car featured P255/45R18 tires up front and P225/50R18s out back. The GXP was also equipped with a sport-tuned suspension, big brakes, and manual shift-paddles on the steering wheel. The retail price was $29,995.

▲▼ Sales were below expectations in the resurrected GTO's debut year of 2004, so Pontiac juiced up both the looks and power for 2005. Dual hood scoops became standard on '05s, addressing one of the styling complaints voiced by enthusiasts. The scoops were functional only in that they helped ventilate the engine compartment, which contained a modified LS2 from the Corvette. Pontiac also added a new split-dual exhaust system, giving the car a deeper burble. To make way for the new pipes, Pontiac designers revamped the rear fascia as well. Brakes and rotors grew for 2005, and the front calipers were painted red and given the GTO logo.

▲ The GTO's new 6.0-liter LS2 engine produced 400 bhp, a full 50 more than the previous year's 5.7-liter LS1. Torque was up to 395 pound-feet from 365. *Motor Trend* magazine reported times of 5.0 seconds from 0 to 60 mph and 13.3 seconds in the quarter mile.

◀ The Monte Carlo SS of 1983-88 was one of the few muscle cars of its day. That all ended in 1989 with the release of the Lumina and the temporary end of the Monte Carlo's run. When the Monte Carlo returned in 1995, the front-wheel-drive layout and V-6 power indicated the muscle was gone. When Chevrolet freshened the looks for 2006, V-8 power returned in the SS model, but the front-drive layout prevented purists from accepting it as a true muscle car. Still, the 303-bhp LS4 V-8 was a more viable attempt at an SS model than the previous normally aspirated and supercharged 3.8-liter V-6 versions.

▶ Chevrolet added muscle to the sport utility vehicle with the release of the 2006 TrailBlazer SS. Unveiled at the 2005 New York International Automobile Show, the TrailBlazer SS used a modified version of the LS2 small-block V-8 from the Corvette, this one making 390 bhp. Chevrolet estimated a 0 to 60 mph time of 6.0 seconds. The new SUV marked the second high-performance application for the TrailBlazer platform. It had also been used for the Chevy SSR roadster pickup. Neither vehicle offered handling commensurate with the LS2's copious power.

▲ After a year without a full-size four-door sedan, Dodge resurrected the legendary Charger nameplate as a 2006 model year sedan based on the Magnum wagon. Aware that muscle car purists would balk at the body style, Dodge called it a "coupe-styled sedan." The previous Charger was a front-drive compact, but Dodge called this one an "homage to muscle cars of the '60s." Dodge tapped further into muscle car lore with the 2006 Charger Daytona (shown). It was offered in two "High Impact"-inspired colors: Top Banana and Go ManGo.

◀ Base Chargers had a 250-bhp 3.5-liter V-6, and the RT model got the 340-bhp 5.7-liter Hemi V-8. Even toting 4031 lb, the Hemi could launch the Charger from 0 to 60 mph in about six seconds. Charger Daytona models had special Hemi Orange engine covers (shown) and tweaked intake and exhaust systems, giving them 350 bhp. Both V-8s featured Dodge's Multiple Displacement System, which shut down four cylinders while cruising and idling to improve fuel economy.

▼ All 2006 Dodge Chargers had a five-speed automatic transmission with a manual shift gate. Dodge designers took inspiration from the Viper in the dash gauge treatment. RT and Daytona versions received sport-style bolstered seats. The Daytona also featured body-color accents on the headrest stitching, center console bezels, and shifter bezel.

▲ Flat black exterior cues delineated the Daytona from other Chargers, including the chin and deck spoilers, the accents on the hood and trunk panels, and the rear fender stripes with their Daytona lettering. Eighteen-inch wheels and split-dual exhaust were standard on the Daytona and RT, though the Daytona featured a different exhaust and old-school "R/T" badges.

▶ Already quite capable with its 5.7-liter Hemi V-8, the Dodge Magnum got even stronger when DaimlerChrysler's Performance Vehicles Operations team released the SRT-8 version as a 2006 model. Dodge's goal was to create "a vehicle that can cover a quarter mile in the high 13-second range and haul home a brand-new 27-inch TV." PVO equipped the Magnum SRT-8 with the same 425-bhp 6.1-liter Hemi V-8 found in the Chrysler 300C SRT-8. The appearance of the Magnum SRT-8 differed slightly from other Magnums; it featured SRT-8 badging and a different front fascia with wider air ducts. Magnum SRT-8s also had large Brembo brakes with red calipers, a sport-tuned suspension, and 20-inch wheels.

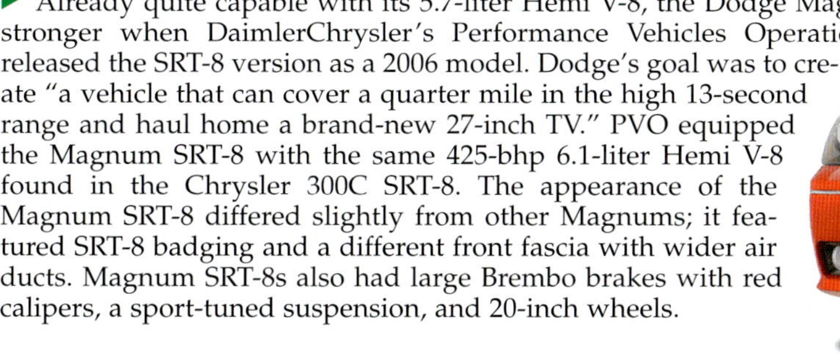

▲ Given the muscle car heritage of the Charger name, it came as no surprise when Dodge gave the new Charger its own SRT version. The 2006 Charger SRT-8 wore several visual and performance mods, including a new front fascia, a functional hood scoop, giant 20-inch alloy wheels, and, of course, 425 horses in the 6.1-liter Hemi V-8.

◀ With the release of the 2006 Jeep Grand Cherokee SRT-8, Chrysler had a performance vehicle in every marque under its banner. In this application, the 6.1-liter Hemi made 415 bhp, and Jeep claimed it could romp from 0 to 60 mph in under five seconds. Vehicles like this, the Chevrolet TrailBlazer SS, and the Ford F-150 Lightning pickup illustrated that muscle wasn't just for cars anymore.

▲ At the 2005 New York Auto Show, Ford unveiled the Shelby Cobra GT500 show car. Released in 2006 as an early 2007 model, the GT500 was the first production Ford to bear the Shelby name since 1970. It was also the most powerful Mustang yet, putting out more than 450 bhp and 450 pound-feet of torque. The supercharged, 32-valve 5.4-liter V-8 had first seen Mustang duty in the 2000 Cobra R, but now benefited from technology developed for the Ford GT supercar.

◄▲ Inside, the Shelby Cobra GT500 show car featured red leather seat inserts, leather on the dash and door panels, the Shelby Cobra on the steering wheel hub, and a manual shifter linked to Ford's T56 six-speed manual transmission. Despite speculation that a performance Mustang would have an independent rear suspension, the Shelby still used a solid rear axle. It did have special 19×9.5-inch alloy wheels and a performance-tuned suspension, though.

► The man himself, Carroll Shelby, pilots a prototype 2007 Shelby Mustang GT500 convertible. The rush of the wind and the whine of the supercharger made a symphony for every muscle-car fan. Ford said the goal was "to build the most powerful, most capable Mustang ever." That goal was reached, though at the cost of an additional 150 pounds—most of it in the nose, which could exhibit plow in hard cornering.

▲ Top GM execs (from left) Rick Wagoner, Bob Lutz, and Ed Welburn pose with the freshly unveiled Camaro Concept on January 6, 2006, at the Detroit Auto Show. Fans cheered when Wagoner announced in August '06 that GM would build a production version.

▲ GM worldwide design VP Ed Welburn brought in his own 1969 Camaro SS to pose with a late mockup of the 2006 Camaro Concept. Designers were careful to avoid a straight-up rehash of the '69's classic lines, opting instead for a sleeker, more rakish feel.

▲▶ Also debuting at the 2006 Detroit Auto Show was the Dodge Challenger Concept, a new-millennium re-imagining of the legendary 1970 original. As with the Camaro Concept, enthusiasts said, "Build it!" and Dodge announced in July that it would. The production version that debuted for 2008 stayed remarkably true to the concept, though details such as the rear-fender name badge and "gun sight" grille didn't make the cut.

▶ While the Camaro and Challenger concepts were dazzling crowds on the 2006 auto show circuit, many Pontiac GTOs were going begging in new-car showrooms. In the case of the reborn GTO, the sizzle was apparently as important as the steak. Despite world-class performance numbers from its 6.0-liter V-8, the reborn Goat's modern, understated styling simply left most traditional fans cold. After a run of 11,268 cars for the 2006 model year, Pontiac pulled the plug.

2007-12

Despite heightening concerns over the environment and Middle East oil supplies, automakers continue to manufacture a variety of high-horsepower muscle machines • Classic pony-car rivalries are reignited: Ford's retro-styled Mustang is a sales sensation, prompting Chevrolet and Dodge to respond with reborn versions of the Camaro and Challenger with similar throwback design cues • Cadillac follows up the first-generation CTS-V with an even more menacing redesigned version for 2009; under the hood is a 556-bhp supercharged 6.2-liter V-8 borrowed from the Corvette ZR1 • Muscle-car fans grieve as GM's Pontiac Division dies, a victim of low sales and General Motors' bankruptcy after the late-2008 financial collapse and subsequent "Great Recession" • Nostalgic "heritage" styling statements reign supreme; loud color options, classic body stripes and graphics, and revived names such as ZL1, R/T, and Boss 302 all pay homage to the muscle car's late 1960s—early 1970s heyday

▲ The venerable Super Bee package returned to Dodge's Charger for 2007, with Detonator Yellow paint, hard-to-miss graphics, and a 6.1-liter SRT8 Hemi V-8. Output was a thumping 425 bhp, with 420 pound-feet of torque. The cars were assembled in Ontario, Canada.

▶ In base SE form, the '08 Dodge Caliber was a humdrum grocery hauler. Get into the top SRT4, though, and you got to play with a 2.4-liter inline turbo four cranking 285 horsepower and 265 pound-feet of torque. A six-speed Getrag manual gearbox, stabilizer bars, stability control, and electronic traction control helped keep Caliber moving where it was supposed to go. The 0-to-60-mph sprint was accomplished in 6.0 seconds.

▲ Chrysler took the unusual step of debuting the hotly anticipated production 2008 Dodge Challenger in top-line SRT8 trim only. Sticker price was $37,995, but buyers also had to pay a $2100 gas-guzzler tax. Just three colors were available: Hemi Orange, Bright Silver Metallic, and Brilliant Black Crystal Pearl Coat. A power sunroof, wider rear tires, and a navigation system with Chrysler's "MyGIG" Multimedia hard drive were the only options.

◀▲ Under the skin, the Challenger SRT8 was a shortened Chrysler 300C with a tighter suspension, a 6.1-liter Hemi V-8, 425 bhp, 420 pound-feet of torque, and 0-60 times clocked at a hair over five seconds. Not just ferociously powerful, Challenger was also a pleasant and quiet highway cruiser. One big drawback for muscle enthusiasts was the mandatory five-speed automatic, but a six-speed manual was on the way for 2009.

▶ By taking design elements from its aggressive 2001 Bullitt edition, Ford produced the very capable '08 Bullitt Mustang, running with a 4.6-liter V-8 producing 315 horsepower, 325 pound-feet of torque, and zero-to-60 times of about 5.2 seconds. The Tremec five-speed manual was designed expressly for the Bullitt, and the car had uprated shocks, a black-mesh grille, and an exhaust note tuned to recall the sound of Lt. Bullitt's ride from back in 1968. A solid anniversary present indeed.

▲ The "King of the Road" 2008 Shelby GT500KR one-upped the already brutal GT500 with a 540-bhp version of its supercharged 5.4-liter V-8, plus a uniquely tuned suspension and carbon-fiber hood with scoops patterned after the original 1968 GT500KR.

▲ Although the modern and capable 2008 Pontiac G8 GT was a rebadged Holden from Australia, it was powered by a variant of Corvette's very American 6.0-liter V-8, detuned to 361 bhp and linked to an effective six-speed automatic.

▲ Top Caddy sedan for '09 was the CTS-V, which boasted a supercharged version of Corvette's 6.2-liter V-8. The engine produced an astounding 556 bhp, and propelled the 3509-pound four-door from zero to 60 in a dizzying 3.9 seconds with automatic or manual.

▲ Livonia, Michigan-based Roush Performance turned Mustang GTs into Roush 427Rs by adding a full complement of appearance and performance upgrades. The GT's 4.6 V-8 was bumped from 300 bhp to 435 with the help of a Roush-engineered supercharger.

▲ For 2009, the Pontiac G8 lineup gained a top-dog GXP model with a 415-bhp version of the 'Vette's 6.2-liter V-8. Sadly, one of the best high-performance Pontiacs ever would also be the last; all G8 production ended soon after the April 2009 announcement of the Pontiac brand's imminent cancellation. G8 GXP production totaled a mere 1824 units. Of them, 981 were fitted with the automatic transmission and 843 were built with the optional six-speed manual. With that, the marque that essentially created the muscle car as we know it was history.

▲ The Challenger line expanded for 2009, with base SE (3.5-liter V-6; 250 bhp with mandatory automatic transmission) and performance-oriented R/T (5.7-liter Hemi V-8; 372 bhp with automatic or 376 with the newly available six-speed manual) joining top-dog SRT8 (6.1-liter V-8; 425 bhp with automatic or manual). Mopar fans rejoiced. Both performance Challengers were swift, but rather hefty; the SRT8 weighed in at more than 4100 pounds.

After three years of anticipation and hand-wringing speculation, the reborn Camaro finally went on sale in the spring of 2009 as a 2010 model. A faux nose scoop situated just above the grille opening was an SS-only styling feature. The Camaro's "heritage" body styling made nostalgic stripe packages a no-brainer; GM Accessories offered the hood and deck-lid stripes shown here, along with "hockey stick" bodyside stripes.

Camaro's cockpit for 2010 was snug, handsome, and nostalgic—as witness the gauge pack sited ahead of the meaty shift lever. Large primary gauges were well-placed, and seats were supportive, but some fans thought the dash was layered with too much black plastic.

Even as GM grew increasingly estranged from rear-drive layouts, the corporation tapped its Holden "Zeta" platform for the new Camaro. Zeta was designed by GM-Australia to accommodate a variety of wheelbases and track widths; Camaro's 112.3-inch wheelbase was unique. This cutaway is by illustrator David Kimble.

Top of the Camaro line, the SS, came with an uprated FE3 suspension, stability control, four-piston Brembo brakes, and a launch-control setup for manual-trans models. Also standard were a spoiler, limited-slip differential, and 20-inch wheels.

SS Camaros ran with a version of Corvette's 6.2-liter LS3 V-8; the mill was rated at 426 bhp with the six-speed manual transmission, or 400 with the extra-cost six-speed automatic.

Chevrolet built a one-off 2010 Camaro for *Tonight Show* host Jay Leno. Its unique features included an aggressive front fascia, air extractor hood, and a twin-turbo 3.6 V-6 that made about 425 bhp.

▲▶To commemorate Challenger's 40th Anniversary, Dodge released the Furious Fuchsia Challenger for 2010, in both R/T Classic and SRT8 trim. SRT8s were limited to just 400 examples and sported kitschy Pearl White leather seats, chrome exhaust tips, 20-inch SRT forged-aluminum wheels with satin black accents, and a serialized dash plaque. Dodge's limited-edition Challenger colors effectively revived the spirit of the fondly remembered "High Impact" Mopar hues of the early 1970s.

▲ The 2010 Mopar '10 Challenger was a 500-unit limited run. Body color was restricted to Brilliant Black, with Mopar Blue, Red, or Silver as available accent colors. More accents: 20-inch forged gloss-black wheels and a dramatic black-chrome grille. Power came from the 5.7-liter Hemi V-8 that developed 379 bhp and 410 pound-feet of torque. A cold-air intake fed the motor. Automatic-transmission versions of Mopar '10 came with a T-handle shifter; manuals had a pistol grip. Suggested retail price was $38,000, and the manual added another $1000.

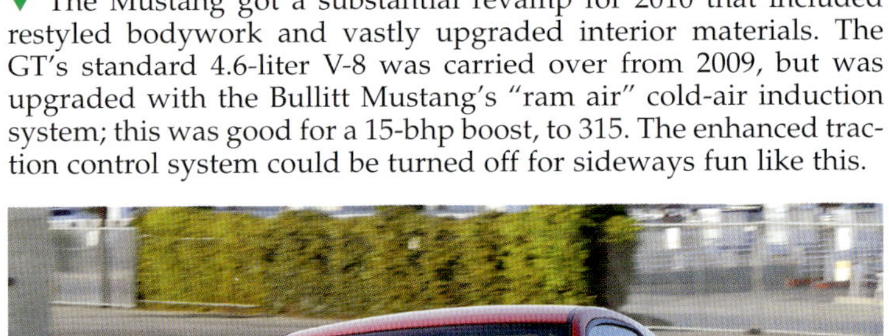

▼ The Mustang got a substantial revamp for 2010 that included restyled bodywork and vastly upgraded interior materials. The GT's standard 4.6-liter V-8 was carried over from 2009, but was upgraded with the Bullitt Mustang's "ram air" cold-air induction system; this was good for a 15-bhp boost, to 315. The enhanced traction control system could be turned off for sideways fun like this.

◀ Roush Performance continued to work its magic on 2010 Mustangs, offering a variety of "mild-to-wild" upgrades. The 427R was on the wild side of the scale, boasting flashy stripes, 20-inch chrome alloy wheels, a revamped sport suspension, short-throw shifter, and a "Roushcharged" 435-bhp 4.6 V-8. A dealer-installed Roush exhaust system delivered a positively evil-sounding exhaust note. This 427R's upgrades tacked on a substantial $21,006 to the price of the base GT, for a total price of $54,146.

▲ The Shelby GT500 was revamped for 2010 like other Mustangs. Again available in coupe and ragtop form, the 2010 GT500 got its own styling enhancements, which included such functional features as air-extractor vents on the hood and a pronounced rear spoiler for improved downforce. The supercharged 5.4-liter V-8 gained a healthy 40 bhp over its 2009 predecessor, for a whopping 540 bhp total. The Shelby-signature racing-stripe motif was even extended to the shift knob of the mandatory six-speed manual transmission. Convertibles like this one started at $51,325; coupes were $5000 cheaper.

▼ Ford revived its SHO (Super High Output) nameplate on a substantially revamped 2010 Taurus. The SHO's turbocharged "EcoBoost" 3.5 V-6 put out 365 bhp and was good for 0-60 times in the low five-second range. An optional "Performance Pack" included upgraded brakes and 20-inch summer performance tires.

▶ To no one's surprise, a drop-top variant joined the Camaro model roster for 2011. Well-engineered internal reinforcements and bracing created an impressively solid body structure, which made convertible Camaros almost as nimble as their coupe siblings. Though true muscle aficionados opted for the copious V-8 muscle of SSs like this one, even base models were surprisingly gutsy. For 2011, Camaro's 3.6-liter V-6 got an eight-horsepower boost, to 312 total.

▼ The 2011 Camaro SS convertible was chosen as the Official Pace Car of the 2011 Indianapolis 500, and Chevrolet celebrated by producing 500 replicas for sale to the public. All were well-equipped with the uplevel "2SS" equipment package and were available with a six-speed manual or automatic. The Summit White paint job with bright orange stripes and orange leather interior was a tip of the hat to the classic 1969 Camaro Indy Pace Car. Both Chevrolet and the Indianapolis 500 celebrated their 100th anniversaries in 2011.

◀▲ The R/T Classic package tacked on a substantial $3300 to the bottom line of a 2011 Challenger R/T, but delivered a host of performance and appearance upgrades. These included a Boston Acoustics stereo, leather upholstery, and heated seats, plus retro touches like Challenger-script front-fender badges, chrome 20-inch five-spoke wheels that evoked classic Cragar S/S mags, and bodyside stripes that were a spitting image of the 1971 Challenger R/T's.

▲▶ The top-dog production Challenger was renamed 392 SRT8 for 2011, in recognition of its new 6.4-liter V-8—close enough to 392 cubes for Dodge to evoke the heritage of the original 1957-58 Chrysler 392 Hemi. The 2011 mill put out a hefty 470 bhp and 470 pound-feet of torque. A special run of 1492 Inaugural Edition models like this one got unique interior trim and a choice of two paint schemes: Deep Water Blue with Stone White stripes or Bright White with Viper Blue stripes.

◀▲ Dodge Chargers were seriously revamped for 2011 with aggressive new bodywork and a redesigned interior. The new look was highlighted by a scowling front fascia, bold bodyside character lines, and a full-width taillight that hinted at the shape of the 1969 Charger's taillights. All R/Ts packed a 5.7-liter Hemi with 370 horsepower. R/Ts with the Road and Track package got a blacked-out grille with a "heritage" R/T badge, among other tweaks.

▶ The Shelby GT500 Mustang got an aluminum engine block, a boost from 540 to 550 bhp, and other minor updates for 2011. This one is equipped with the SVT Performance Package, a $3495 option that delivered a 3.73 limited-slip rear axle, staggered 19-inch front and 20-inch rear wheels, unique suspension tuning, and other enhancements. All GT500s got 14-inch Brembo brakes, with four-piston calipers up front, for "whoa" power that was almost as impressive as the "go" power.

◀▲ Mustang GTs were little changed on the outside for 2011, but the big news was under the hood, where an all-new 5.0-liter V-8 debuted. It was factory-rated at 412 bhp and 390 pound-feet of torque, which blew away the 315/325 rating of the previous 4.6 V-8. Mustang enthusiasts rejoiced at the return of the celebrated 5.0 badge, as well as the neck-snapping performance and spine-tingling exhaust note of the muscular new motor.

▲ The reborn 5.0 was a state-of-the-art 32-valve DOHC screamer that utilized all-aluminum construction and Twin Independent Variable Camshaft Timing (or Ti-VCT). Despite its outstanding power, it was EPA rated at 26 mpg on the highway with the six-speed manual.

▶ The substantial improvements Mustang interiors received for 2010 made them a much more hospitable place to be, and things were little changed for 2011. GT Premium models could get a "401A Rapid Spec Premier Trim and Color Accent Package" that added cool pony badges on the door panels and "racing-stripe" seats for a reasonable $395. Also available were upscale features such as a navigation system with Ford's Sync voice command, a rear-view camera, and, for automatic-transmission models, remote engine start capability.

◀ ▲ At the 2011 Chicago Auto Show, Chevrolet unveiled its plans to launch a new super-Camaro at the beginning of the 2012 calendar year. The 2012 Camaro ZL1 packed a supercharged "LSA" 6.2-liter V-8 with 580 horsepower and 556 pound-feet of torque, connected to a mandatory Tremec six-speed manual and a short-throw shifter. The ZL1 name had historical significance; it was the code name of an exotic 427 engine from 1969 that found its way into just 69 Camaros that year.

▲ The rear view of the ZL1 was distinguished by a rear-deck spoiler and quad exhaust tips. A dual-mode exhaust system (similar to the optional setup on contemporary Corvettes) enabled a louder, more-aggressive roar in fast acceleration.

▲ Lightweight 20-inch forged-aluminum wheels mounted specially developed Goodyear Eagle F1 Supercar G:2 tires. A sophisticated Magnetic Ride Control suspension provided precise shock-damping control and included driver-selectable Tour or Sport modes for road and track use.

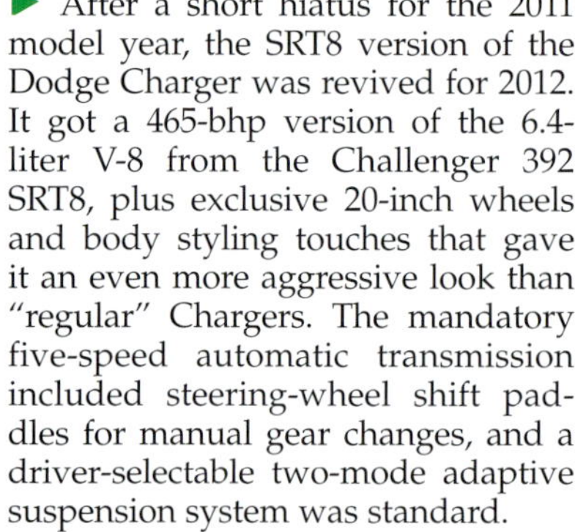

▶ After a short hiatus for the 2011 model year, the SRT8 version of the Dodge Charger was revived for 2012. It got a 465-bhp version of the 6.4-liter V-8 from the Challenger 392 SRT8, plus exclusive 20-inch wheels and body styling touches that gave it an even more aggressive look than "regular" Chargers. The mandatory five-speed automatic transmission included steering-wheel shift paddles for manual gear changes, and a driver-selectable two-mode adaptive suspension system was standard.

◀ Ford revived the hallowed Boss 302 moniker for 2012 on a car that was truly worthy of the name. Two versions were offered: a "base" Boss 302 (right) and a extra-limited Laguna Seca edition, a full-blown track car that boasted a variety of serious racing hardware such as front disc-brake cooling ducts and a not-quite-street-legal front air splitter that was sure to scrape on any speed bump or steep driveway. Ford stated that Boss 302 production would be limited to 4000, including 750 Laguna Secas.

▲ Boss 302 Laguna Seca models came standard with Recaro front seats and a chassis-stiffening X-brace instead of a rear seat. All Boss 302s got a grippy Alcantera suede-covered steering wheel, but these were no-nonsense machines that offered no luxury options.

▲ The Boss 302's 5.0-liter V-8 made 444 horsepower at a high-revving 7400 rpm, thanks to upgrades like a short-runner intake manifold, unique CNC-ported cylinder heads with larger and lighter exhaust valves, and more-aggressive camshafts.

▲ Carroll Shelby was still plugging away as Shelby American unveiled the 2012 Shelby GT350 coupe and convertible in early 2011. Unlike the Ford-produced GT500, GT350s were modified at Shelby American's own Las Vegas, Nevada, facility. Prices started at $26,995, not including the price of the Mustang GT on which the conversion was based.

2013-17

Ford raises stakes in muscle race with the 662-horsepower 2013 Shelby GT500 • Chevrolet reintroduces storied Z/28 moniker on finely honed version of 2014 Camaro aimed at serious track-day enthusiasts • All-new 2015 Ford Mustang arrives just in time for the model's 50th birthday • Dodge creates a sensation with the 2015 Challenger SRT Hellcat largely thanks to its supercharged Hemi engine rated at 707 horsepower; identically powered Charger SRT Hellcat arrives soon after • Chevy debuts smaller, lighter sixth-generation Camaro for 2016 model year; new car's base 2.0-liter turbo four good for 275 horsepower, nearly double the 145-horse rating of the '82 Z28's standard 5.0-liter V-8 • Ford brings back Shelby GT350 Mustang for 2016 as a carefully focused track weapon; even racier GT350R introduces carbon-fiber wheels • Historic colors, nameplates, and stripe designs continue to be popular, even as high-tech materials play an increasingly important part in the muscle car story

▼ Chevy added a drop-top version of the Camaro ZL1 for 2013. Performance upgrades matched the ZL1 coupe, including the supercharged LSA 6.2-liter V-8 engine rated at 580 horsepower. Buyers could choose a 6-speed manual transmission with a short-throw shifter, or a 6-speed automatic.

▼ Ford gave the Mustang another styling refresh for 2013, and added functional hood vents for GT and Boss 302 models. Boss 302 returned in "base" and limited-production Laguna Seca variants. The School Bus Yellow Laguna Seca model shown here wears the year's new stripe design that was inspired by the classic look used on the 1970 Boss 302.

▲ The 2013 Shelby GT500 didn't look much different than the 2012 edition, but Ford did a lot of work under the hood that resulted in an attention grabbing 662-horsepower rating and a claimed top speed north of 200 mph. Chevy fans surely noticed the GT500's $54,995 base price matched the slower, less-powerful 2012 Camaro ZL1's sticker.

◀ Camaro was updated for 2014, with the most visible tweaks being new front and rear fascias, along with reworked headlamps and taillights. The new-for-2013 road-race-inspired 1LE Performance Package returned for SS coupes. Mechanical upgrades included a model-specific version of the Tremec 6-speed manual transmission and a numerically higher axle ratio. The track-ready suspension incorporated many ZL1 pieces, beefier stabilizer bars, and monotube rear shocks. Visual cues included a matte-black hood, along with a front splitter and a unique rear spoiler. The black-finished 20-inch wheels wore the same Goodyear Eagle rubber found on the front of the ZL1.

◀▲ Chevy's surprise announcement at the 2013 New York Auto Show was the 2014 Camaro Z/28. An even more extreme track-focused Camaro, Z/28 featured a package of aerodynamic body enhancements including a front splitter, lift-reducing underbody panels, rear diffuser, and a larger decklid spoiler. Engineers also added extended rocker panels, along with front and rear fender flares. It was powered by a naturally aspirated 7.0-liter V-8 rated at 505 horsepower, and the sole transmission was a 6-speed manual. Other upgrades included sticky 19-inch Pirellis, carbon-ceramic brakes, and spool-valve dampers. Prices started at $75K.

◀ The 2014 Chevrolet SS was the brand's first large rear-drive 4-door muscle sedan since the 1996 Impala SS. Like the short-lived 2009 Pontiac G8 GXP, the SS was an Americanized Holden Commodore that GM built in Australia. Chevy sold the SS in one well-equipped trim level that included a black leather interior, heated and ventilated front buckets, heads-up display, push-button start, and keyless entry. The only powertrain was a 415-horsepower 6.2-liter V-8 paired with a 6-speed automatic. *Car and Driver* recorded a 0-60 mph time of 4.5 seconds and ran the quarter mile in 12.9 seconds at 111 mph. Production was limited, and prices started at $45,770 including the $1300 gas-guzzler tax.

▲ The Chrysler 300 SRT made a final appearance for 2014. The new Satin Vapor Edition added 20-inch wheels finished in Black Satin Vapor Chrome, red brake calipers, and stain-black accents. Inside, the leather interior picked up ultra-suede inserts and specific trim.

▲ New for 2012, the Jeep Grand Cherokee SRT wore some styling tweaks for 2014. The year's most significant update was a new 8-speed automatic transmission that replaced the previous 5-speed box. The 6.4-liter Hemi V-8 was still rated at 470 horsepower.

▲▶ For 2015, Chevrolet offered SS sedan buyers a choice of 6-speed manual or automatic transmissions. Stick-shift cars also came with more aggressive rear-axle gearing. This year, the standard-equipment list added GM's Magnetic Ride Control suspension and Brembo-brand rear brake calipers to match the units used up front.

◀ Dodge captured muscle-car fans' hearts with the 2015 Challenger SRT Hellcat. The headliner was a supercharged 6.2-liter Hemi V-8 rated at an astounding 707 horsepower. It could be paired with a 6-speed manual or Mopar's new heavy-duty 8-speed automatic. Chassis upgrades included a stronger driveshaft, rear axle, and half shafts. Appearance closely followed Challenger's SRT 392 model, but Hellcats wore a vented aluminum hood and a unique grille. Dodge said the car could run a NHRA-certified 11.2-second quarter mile on the stock 20-inch Pirelli tires. *Motor Trend* reported a 3.7-second 0-60 mph time with the automatic. Prices started at $59,995, and dealers could not get enough of them.

▶ The Hellcat grabbed nearly all the glory, but there was other Challenger news for 2015. Front and rear styling was touched up with details inspired by the '71 Challenger, and the interior was tweaked as well. The new Challenger R/T Scat Pack model was powered by the SRT-spec 485-horse 6.4-liter Hemi. As on other 2015 Challengers, buyers could choose the 6-speed manual or new TorqueFlite 8-speed automatic. Scat Pack pricing started at $38,495, a $7500 discount compared to the Challenger SRT 392 powered by the same engine.

◀ ▲ Dodge revised the Charger's interior and exterior styling for 2015. But as with the Challenger, the big news was the new SRT Hellcat model. Priced from $63,995, the Charger Hellcat packed the 707-horsepower supercharged Hemi, and benefitted from most of the same mechanical upgrades as the Challenger. One significant difference was that the Charger was only sold with the 8-speed automatic. Dodge talked up the car's 204-mph top speed and claimed it could run the quarter in 11 seconds flat.

▲ ▶ The redesigned 2015 Ford Mustang arrived for the model's 50th anniversary. It was a bit wider and lower than the outgoing model, and the all-new suspension ditched the live rear axle in favor of an independent rear end. The GT was powered by a 5.0-liter V-8 rated at 435 horsepower and 400 pound-feet of torque. The GT coupe (right) started at $32,925. Ford also offered 1964 copies of the 50 Year Limited Edition model (above) that started as a loaded GT and priced from $46,995.

▲ For 2016, Cadillac added muscular ATS-V variants of the brand's smallest car. ATS-V was available in two- or four-door body styles, each with rear-wheel drive and a 455-horsepower twin-turbocharged 3.6-liter V-6. Other enhancements included a strengthened body structure and GM's Magnetic Ride Control suspension. Cadillac claimed a 0-60 mph time of 3.8 seconds. Coupes priced from $63,660.

▲ The third generation of Cadillac's CTS-V arrived for 2016. Only available as a four-door sedan, the new car packed a supercharged 6.2-liter V-8 rated at 640 horsepower and an 8-speed automatic. Performance goodies included a carbon-fiber hood, Brembo-brand brakes, and forged 19-inch wheels wearing Michelin Pilot Super Sport rubber. Top speed was an even 200 mph.

◀ ▲ An all-new sixth-generation Chevrolet Camaro appeared for 2016. Slightly smaller, and about 200 pounds lighter than the car it replaced, the new Camaro used a version of GM's Alpha platform that also underpinned the Cadillac ATS-V. The 2016 Camaro was initially sold as a coupe in LT and SS models. Convertibles were added during the model run. LTs came with a 275-horsepower 2.0-liter turbocharged 4-cylinder or a 335-horse 3.6-liter V-6. The SS received a version of GM's latest LT1 smallblock V-8. The 6.2-liter mill was good for 455 ponies and could be paired with a 6-speed manual or 8-speed automatic transmission. Stick-shift models included an Active Rev Match feature that automatically blipped the throttle to help the driver optimize downshifts. *Road & Track*'s 6-speed SS test car ran 0-60 mph in 4.2 seconds and covered the quarter mile in 12.5 seconds at 113.4 mph.

▲ Dodge returned the classic Plum Crazy hue to the Challenger and Charger color charts for 2016. Here the vibrant purple is worn by the Challenger 392 Scat Pack Shaker (left) and Charger R/T Road & Track. These were the two car's top non-SRT models, but each was powered by the SRT-spec 485-horsepower 6.4-liter Hemi V-8. The Challenger included a functional engine-mounted Shaker scoop that recalled the similar piece available on the original 1970 Challenger.

▲ It wasn't a traditional muscle car, but the 2016 Ford Focus RS was an extremely serious "hot hatch." Performance was impressive thanks to the 350-horsepower 2.3-liter turbocharged 4-cylinder engine and a sophisticated all-wheel-drive system.

▲ Ford introduced an optional California Special Package for the 2016 Mustang GT Premium. It added an array of styling touches including a unique grille, hood and bodyside stripes, black-painted trim, and an upgraded interior in black with red stitch detailing.

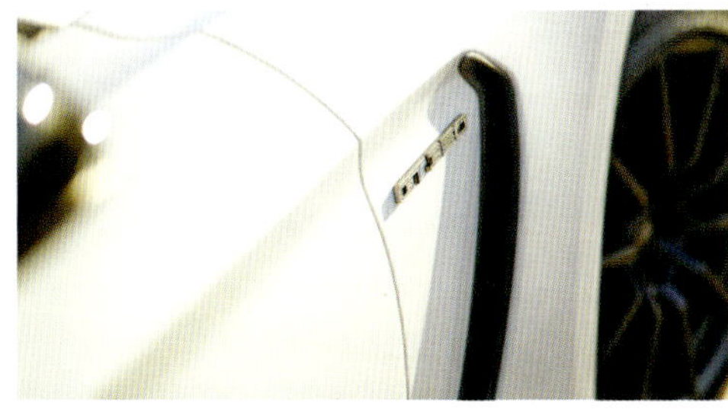

▲ ▶ Ford's plan for the 2016 Shelby GT350 Mustang was to make a street-legal racer. GT350 ran a naturally aspirated 5.2-liter V-8 that was good for 526 ponies and was not shared with other Mustangs. It was backed up with a 6-speed manual. The bodywork from the windshield forward was unique. The lowered, sloped hood helped aerodynamics, and reworked fenders made room for the wider front track. Vents in the front fenders and hood helped optimize airflow, and a decklid spoiler increased downforce. Interior changes included cloth-covered Recaro seats and a flat-bottom steering wheel.

◀ The 2016 Shelby GT350R Mustang was an even more track-focused variant of Ford's latest pony car. A revised front splitter and a carbon-fiber rear spoiler increased aerodynamic downforce, and the suspension was specially tuned for road-course handling. Engineers also removed weight by ditching the car's air conditioning and stereo systems, along with other items including the rear seats, back-up camera, and trunk carpeting. GT350R also came with lightweight carbon-fiber wheels that Ford claimed removed nearly 60 pounds of unsprung weight. Production was limited, and the GT350R priced from $62,195.

▶ For 2017, Chevrolet added new Camaro 1LE track-oriented performance packages for V-6-powered LT and V-8-powered SS coupes with manual transmission. On the SS, the 1LE option included FE4 suspension tuning, Magnetic Ride Control, an electronically controlled limited-slip differential, and upgraded front brakes with six-piston calipers. Forged 20-inch alloy wheels were shod with specially developed Goodyear Eagle F1 Supercar tires. The hood, side mirrors, and unique three-piece rear spoiler were finished in satin black, and the interior came with a flat-bottom steering wheel and Recaro seats.

◀▲ Chevrolet also announced new 2017 Camaro ZL1 coupe and convertible models. Preliminary information promised an estimated 640 horsepower from a supercharged LT4 6.2-liter V-8. Transmission choices were a 6-speed manual or an all-new 10-speed automatic.

▶ Ford issued word the 2017 Shelby GT350 Mustang (front) and Shelby GT350R Mustang (rear) would be available in three new colors: Grabber Blue (front), Lightning Blue (upper left), and Ruby Red Metallic (upper right). New standard equipment included the previously optional Track Package. It consisted of an aluminum tower-to-tower brace, a high-downforce rear spoiler, MagneRide shocks, and coolers for the engine oil, transmission, and rear differential. Customers could also order a rear seat for GT350R.